S0-BAU-042

1001 QUESTIONS AND ANSWERS

1001 QUESTIONS AND ANSWERS

HAMLYN

Published by
The Hamlyn Publishing Group Limited
Bridge House, London Road, Twickenham, Middlesex, England

Compiled and edited by Book Features Limited

Copyright © The Hamlyn Publishing Group Limited 1987
ISBN 0 600 55657 3

All rights reserved. No part of this publication
may be reproduced, stored in a retrieval system,
or transmitted, in any form or by any means,
electronic, mechanical, photocopying, recording
or otherwise, without the permission of The Hamlyn
Publishing Group Limited.

Printed in Yugoslavia

D'Artagnan, Porthos, Aramis and Athos (left to right), the heroes of *The Three Musketeers* by Alexandre Dumas

the hapless Bertie Wooster, Psmith (pronounced "Smith"), the talkative Mr Mulliner with his flow of anecdotes concerning the Mulliner family and Jeeves, the inimitable butler.

WHAT WERE THE REAL NAMES OF THE THREE MUSKETEERS?

The names that the famous swordsmen assumed when they joined the French King's bodyguard of Musketeers were Athos, Porthos and Aramis. By these names they are known throughout Alexandre Dumas' magnificent novel *The Three Musketeers*.

It is not until the swashbuckling D'Artagnan sets out twenty years later, that the true names of them all are revealed. D'Artagnan, now Captain of the Musketeers, discovers that Athos, the severe ex-musketeer, is now the Count de la Fère who is living on an estate near the town of Blois.

The giant Porthos, so gentle and trusting, the most lovable of the

Musketeers has become the proud Seigneur du Vallon de Bracieux de Pierrefonds, a country gentleman still yearning for the days of high adventure.

Aramis, always secretive, a born conspirator with an eye for the ladies, has entered the church and is now known as the Abbé D'Herblay.

It is in *Twenty Years After*, the fast-moving sequel to *The Three Musketeers* that D'Artagnan meets up with his friends once again, but the days when the four good friends rode together, all for one and one for all, are at an end. D'Artagnan and Porthos, fighting in England in the ranks of Oliver Cromwell's Roundheads, come face to face with Athos and Aramis who have joined the army of King Charles the First. All ends well for the four friends, however. Their friendship as firm as ever, they part at the end of *Twenty Years After*, not knowing whether they ever will meet again.

This, though, they do in the continuing saga of the Three Musketeers — the long novel known as *The Viscount of Bragelonne*. The Viscount, hero of this book, is the son of Athos.

WHICH SECRETARY OF THE BANK OF ENGLAND WROTE BOOKS FOR CHILDREN?

Kenneth Grahame who wrote *The Wind in the Willows*. He had just retired as Secretary of the Bank of England when in 1908 he published his world-famous book, destined to become one of the greatest of all children's classics.

To his former colleagues at the Bank, the news came as a surprise. Known as a silent, shy businessman, Grahame was thought hardly the sort of person to write about the amusing and touching adventures of a mole, a rat and a toad.

Yet there was a side of Grahame not revealed to the outside world. He was a born whimsical dreamer, an escapist appalled by the speed and bustle of the mechanized twentieth century. Part of him still lived as a small boy who refused to grow up.

"The part of my brain I used from four till about seven can never be surprised to meet myself as a little chap of five suddenly coming round a corner," he said.

Grahame was born July 20, 1859 in Edinburgh, Scotland, the son of a lawyer. His parents died when he was very young and he was brought up mainly by his grandmother, who had no time for Kenneth's dream of going to a college at Oxford.

By his own efforts, Grahame succeeded in joining the staff of the Bank of England, and there his careful, meticulous brain ensured him promotion. The poetic side of his nature, however, sought its expression and though he never felt strongly enough to become a full-time author, he spent his spare time writing essays, verse and well-observed studies of children.

Asked once about the smallness

Contents

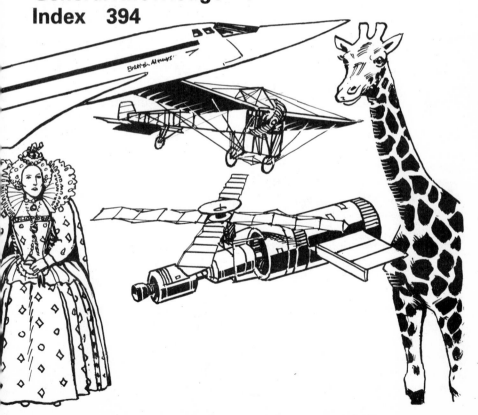

Books and Writers

WHICH FAMOUS AUTHOR'S FIRST NAMES WERE PELHAM GRENVILLE?

P G Wodehouse. Known all over the world for his hilariously funny books, Wodehouse was born October 15, 1881, at Guildford, Surrey, England. He was educated at Dulwich College in South London and after leaving school, he worked in a London bank. He left when he found he could make a living from freelance writing.

"I started writing stories," he said, "about girls who wanted to be loved for themselves alone. From there I proceeded to stories about earls and butlers and young men finding snakes in their beds."

From 1906 to 1909 he was a columnist on a London newspaper. But after selling several short stories in America, he went to live there. In 1955 he became an American citizen.

His first successful novel was *Piccadilly Jim* in 1918 and from then on he turned out a stream of novels, plays, musical comedies and humorous articles.

He was unfortunate enough to be in France when that country was overrun by German forces in 1940. Wodehouse was arrested and interned. The next year, on June 21, he was released. He was nearly sixty years old, the age when internees could be given conditional freedom but he had to remain in German-occupied France.

During the following war years, Wodehouse earned harsh criticism for having broadcast to America five humorous talks about his life as an internee. For this he was regarded as a collaborator but after the war he was cleared of this accusation.

He resumed his successful career and on New Year's Day, January 1975, now 93 years of age, he was created Knight Commander of the British Empire. Less than two months later, on February 14, he died of a heart attack in a Long Island hospital.

No other writer could equal his expertise in the creation of such immortal and loved characters as

of his literary output, he replied: "Writing is not easy. There is always a pleasure in the exercise; but also always an agony.

"If I should ever become a popular author, my privacy would be disrupted and I should no longer be able to live alone."

He kept his word on this and published nothing more up to his death on July 6, 1932. Two other books by Kenneth Grahame are worthy of mention, *The Golden Age* and *Dream Days*, in which appears *The Reluctant Dragon*.

WHY IS THERE A DODO IN *ALICE IN WONDERLAND*?

When Lewis Carroll wrote *Alice In Wonderland*, he introduced the nicknames of some of his friends. The Lory was young Lorina Liddell, the sister of Alice on whom Carroll based his book. The Eaglet was Alice's other sister Edith. As for the Dodo, this was Carroll himself.

Lewis Carroll was born January 27, 1832. In 1861, he decided to enter the church. He was ordained deacon but his hopes of preaching were dashed because he stuttered. This had the effect of provoking his listeners to laughter.

His real name was Charles Ludwidge Dodgson and when he introduced himself he would stutter: "Do-do-Dodgson." That was why he wrote a Dodo into his great book.

Lewis Carroll died January 14, 1898.

WHO WROTE THE BOOK *MOBY DICK*?

The American author Herman Melville. He was born August 1, 1819 in New York, the son of Allan Melville, a ne'er-do-well importer of the most fashionable clothes and expensive materials. When in 1812 war broke out between Britain and the United States, the business failed. In 1832 Herman Melville's father died, his mind unbalanced by the misfortunes of his business affairs.

Young Herman was then attending an academy in Albany. Two years later, at the age of fifteen, he commenced work in a bank, his uncle being the president. This job did not last long and Herman Melville then worked for his mother and his elder brother Gansevoort in a store which they owned. Once again, however, he was soon on his way, but this time to be a farmhand on another uncle's farm.

The spirit of adventure ran very strongly in Herman's veins and he was eighteen years of age when he signed on as an ordinary seaman on board the freighter *Highlander*, then bound for the English port of Liverpool.

It was a life of terrible hardship and when the ship returned to New York, Herman made off and found employment as a schoolteacher. During his schoolteaching days, he tried his hand at writing but met with no success.

Again, adventure lured him to sea and once more, as an ordinary

The white whale fights for its life

seaman, he was a member of a ship's crew when it set sail for the South Pacific, hunting for whales.

He was now twenty-two and there followed two years of harsh treatment at the hands of ruthless officers. He deserted his first ship, then joined another whaler and took part in a mutiny. Arrested later, he and other mutineers were imprisoned. Luck was with him for he escaped and after working for a time in a store in Honolulu, he joined the US Navy as an ordinary seaman. On board the frigate *United States* he then returned home.

Then began his successful career as an author and for nearly twenty years he also occupied a post in the custom house in New York. He died there on September 27, 1891.

He wrote several novels of which *Moby Dick* is considered his masterpiece. Moby Dick is a monstrous white whale, hunted with a ferocious obsession by the half-crazy Captain Ahab who has lost his right leg in a previous encounter with the great whale. After many adventures, Ahab finally catches up with Moby Dick. In the terrible battle that follows,

Ahab's ship is sunk and only one seaman survives to tell the tale.

Other famous books by Melville are *Typee, Omoo,* and *White Jacket. Typee* is a fictional version of the young Herman Melville's exciting adventures at sea and is of special interest because it was the first book written about the South Seas.

WHERE DOES PETER PAN LIVE?

On an island known as the Neverland. A tribe of redskins live there. They are members of the Piccaninny tribe. Anchored off-shore is a pirate ship called the *Jolly Roger* once captained by James Hook, ex-bo'sun of the evil buccaneer, Blackbeard.

It is also the home of the Lost Boys, Peter Pan's own band of loyal followers and Tinker Bell, the mischievous tiny fairy.

If any reader would like to go there, here are Peter Pan's own directions:"Second to the right, and straight on till morning."

The celebrated book *Peter Pan and Wendy* was written by Sir James Matthew Barrie.

WHAT IS THE NAME OF THE PRIVATE DETECTIVE WHOSE ADVENTURES WERE WRITTEN BY RAYMOND CHANDLER?

Philip Marlowe. He first appeared in *The Big Sleep*. Chandler had been writing for a popular periodical entitled *Black Mask* for some years when he wrote his first novel *The Big Sleep* in 1939. It met with great success, so much so that Chandler continued Philip Marlowe's bleak adventures in *Farewell My Lovely, The High Window, The Lady in the Lake, The Little Sister, The Long Goodbye* and *Playback*.

Raymond Chandler was born in Chicago, January 23, 1888, but from the age of seven was brought up in England where he lived for 17 years.

During this time he was educated at Dulwich College. Interested in writing, he worked as a journalist in London but returned to America when he was 24. The First World War broke out in 1914. Chandler joined the Canadian army but when demobilised he started work with an oil company in California, the background for his Philip Marlowe thrillers. In 1933 he again took up his writing activities and forsook his business career. He died March 26, 1959.

WHO WROTE, ILLUSTRATED AND THEN PUBLISHED AT HER OWN EXPENSE *THE TALE OF PETER RABBIT*?

Helen Beatrix Potter, born July 6, 1866, paid for only 250 copies of *Peter Rabbit* to be printed in December 1901. Two months later, a second edition of 250 copies were printed. Later, in 1902, Beatrix Potter (the name she wrote under) published, again at her own cost, *The Tailor of Gloucester*. 500 copies were published.

In the year 1903, the publishing firm of Frederick Warne took over publication of her books. The first was *Squirrel Nutkin* which proved to be a great success.

Beatrix's fame was assured and a long series of books all written and illustrated by her then followed, until 1918 when *Johnny Town-Mouse* appeared. Regrettably this was the last of her charming little animal books. She continued to produce books, *The Fairy Caravan* for example in 1928, but none enjoyed the success of *Squirrel Nutkin, Two Bad Mice, Mrs Tiggy Winkle, Tom Kitten, Jemima Puddle-Duck, The Flopsy Bunnies* and the others that enchanted millions of children everywhere.

Beatrix Potter was the daughter of wealthy parents and never went to school. In fact, she taught herself to draw and although some later artists tried to imitate her inimitable style, none could capture her innate style and emotion.

In 1905 she purchased Hill Top Farm at Sawrey in the English Lake District. Later she was to buy two more farms and specialised in the Herdwick breed of sheep which were particularly suitable for that area. She worked on her farms, wrote her books, married, and died April 30, 1943.

BY WHAT NAME IS LORD GREYSTOKE BETTER KNOWN?

Tarzan the Ape-man, whose fantastic adventures were written by Edgar Rice Burroughs, an American novelist who was also responsible for another long series of books about the exploits of one John Carter, on Mars.

It is to the American periodical *All-Story* that we owe the advent of John Carter in *Under the Moons of Mars*, later published as *A Princess of Mars* and in 1912 the ever-enduring *Tarzan of the Apes*.

Tarzan is the long-lost son of Lord Greystoke, an English nobleman, who, left as a baby in the African jungle, is adopted by a female ape whose young son has just died. Tarzan grows up, able to converse with the apes in their own language and, like them, able to swing powerfully through the dense jungle from tree to tree. The Tarzan series spawned many popular films and periodicals around the world.

Edgar Rice Burroughs, born on September 1, 1875, is considered to have been largely responsible for the immense popularity of the fantasy genre, now labelled as "Science Fiction."

He died March 19, 1950.

WHAT FAMOUS MYSTERY NOVEL WAS LEFT UNFINISHED BY WHICH WELL-KNOWN AUTHOR?

The Mystery of Edwin Drood was still incomplete when Charles Dickens suddenly died in 1870. Edwin Drood is a young man engaged to a lovely girl named Rosa Bud although little love exists between them. Rosa has attracted the attention of another young man, by name Neville Landless. Edwin and Neville quarrel violently one day and soon afterwards, Edwin and Rosa decide not to marry after all. That night Edwin disappears.

Foul play is suspected and Neville is arrested. He is later released but the mystery remains. What can have happened to Edwin Drood? Only Charles Dickens knew, so the rest is silence.

WHICH NOTORIOUS DUELLIST WAS ALSO AN AUTHOR AND PLAYWRIGHT?

Savinien Cyrano de Bergerac. He was a Gascon, as was D'Artagnan the hero of *The Three Musketeers*. In fact, both swordsmen lived at the same time for D'Artagnan really lived. He was a King's Musketeer who became a Marshal of France. Cyrano de Bergerac was born in Perigord in Gascony, a south-west province of France in 1619. He was educated at the College Beauvais and later joined the King's Guard. He divided his time between fighting duels and literature. He fought a great number of duels, most of them to avenge insults about his enormous nose.

His best known books are the *Comic History Of The States and Empires of the Moon,* and the *Comic History of the States and Empires of the Sun.* Hints of these two books are seen in books written two centuries later by Jules Verne. De Bergerac also wrote successful plays.

His turbulent life came to an end in 1655, when he was only 36 years of age.

WHO WROTE *THE SWISS FAMILY ROBINSON*?

A certain professor of philosophy at the Swiss University of Berne. His name was Johann Rudolph Wyss and he was the son of a pastor, born at Berne, March 13, 1781

The Swiss Family Robinson was based on a tale told to Johann Wyss by his father.

WHO WAS THE ARMY NURSE WHO WON FAME BY WRITING BOOKS FOR GIRLS?

Her name was Louisa May Alcott. She was born in Germantown, Pennsylvania, on November 29, 1832, the daughter of Amos Bronson Alcott, a struggling educationalist who could obviously have profited by a little education himself in a few financial matters.

Louisa became an army nurse during the American Civil War and in 1863 her book *Hospital Sketches*, a record of her army experiences, was published. It was this book that earned her some measure of success, although her first book *Flower Fables* had been published in 1855.

She wrote primarily to support her family and rather feckless father. In 1869, her book *Little Women* appeared and Louisa May

Alcott's name was ranked with the famous writers.

There now followed more books in the same vein, *An Old Fashioned Girl, Little Men, Good Wives* and *Jo's Boys*.

She died March 6, 1888, but her books have never lost their appeal.

WHO TAUGHT LESSONS AT THE AGE OF SEVEN?

Charlotte Mary Yonge at the tender age of seven began to teach in the local village Sunday school. Prior to this, she had been taught at home by her father.

Charlotte was born August 11, 1823, in Otterbourne, Hampshire. She was only 15 years old when she published her first novel. By this time, she was very interested in religion, and with the money she received from her most popular book *The Heir of Redcliffe*, she helped to finance a missionary ship bound for the South Seas.

She wrote many books but the only one that has survived into this century is *The Little Duke*.

Charlotte M Yonge died March 24, 1901.

WHICH QUEEN'S FAVOURITE STARTED TO WRITE *THE HISTORY OF THE WORLD* WHILE AWAITING EXECUTION?

None other than the famous courtier to Queen Elizabeth I, Sir Walter Raleigh.

After Queen Elizabeth I died, King James I ascended the throne.

James did not like Raleigh who was soon arrested on a trumped-up charge of high treason, condemned to death and imprisoned in the Bloody Tower at the Tower of London.

It was there that he wrote the first and, as it transpired, only volume of *The History of the World*.

Raleigh was reprieved on the scaffold and returned to prison. He obtained his release on condition that he should lead an expedition in search of gold, which the king badly needed, to Venezuela in South America.

He promised not to interfere with Spanish settlements but came into collision with the Spaniards when his son, Walter, was killed.

The grief-stricken man then sailed back to England where the furious Spanish ambassador was demanding punishment. Raleigh was once again arrested on the old charge of treason and was executed on October 29, 1618.

WHO WAS THE FIRST AMERICAN AUTHOR TO ACHIEVE INTERNATIONAL FAME?

Washington Irving, who had fought against the British in the War of Independence. He wrote many books, amongst them his *Legends of the Alhambra* and *The Legend of Sleepy Hollow*. But it is *Rip Van Winkle* for which he is best remembered today.

Born on April 3, 1783, he died November 28, 1859, already regarded as an author of note throughout the world.

WHY DID ARNOLD BENNETT WRITE UNDER THE NOM-DE-PLUME OF "GWENDOLYN"?

Because he first started writing on the staff of a women's periodical. He spent four years writing a gossip column under the odd pen-name of "Gwendolyn." He regarded the time thus spent as the most valuable part of his life. He later became the assistant editor and then editor of a weekly magazine called *Woman*. His later comment was: "I learnt nothing of letters in that office, but I learnt a good deal about the secret nature of women."

Arnold Bennett's best writing was invariably about ordinary working people and their lives. When he attempted to portray the life of high society, his approach

Denry Machin in Arnold Bennett's *The Card* relates a merry story to two unconvinced listeners

15

was rather clumsy and artificial. He was born May 27, 1876, the son of a solicitor. He went to London in 1888, working first as a clerk and then as a journalist. His first novel *A Man from the North* was published in 1898.'One of his most popular books was entitled *The Card*.

"Card" is a slang name for a person who loves to attract much attention. Edward Henry Machin, better known as Denry, is just such a person, albeit a very likeable one. "He is identified," says one of his friends at the close of the book "with the great cause of cheering us all up."

This, Denry does with rare flair. His merry adventures with the local aristocracy, football team and a host of councillors and city elders who are suspicious of his rapid money-making ways, have a freshness and vigour which Arnold Bennett rarely touched again.

Enoch Arnold Bennett, which was his full name, wrote many stories about the "Five Towns" that today make up Stoke-on-Trent in Staffordshire, England. The background of *The Card* is that district.

Bennett later married a French woman and lived for eight years at the town of Fontainebleau, 31 miles (50 km) south of Paris, an experience which stood him in good stead when he wrote his best book *The Old Wives Tale*.

He died March 27, 1931, still at the height of his powers.

WHO WROTE *THE SECRET GARDEN*?

Frances Eliza Hodgson Burnett, well-known as an American writer, who was born in Manchester, England, on November 24, 1849. She went with her parents to the USA in 1865 and eight years later married Dr Burnett, whom she divorced in 1898.

Frances Hodgson Burnett was equally at home describing the people of Lancashire she had known in her youth and the Americans. Her greatest success was the well-known *Little Lord Fauntleroy*. She based the young lord on her son Vivian. His velvet suit, as worn by Fauntleroy, established a popular fashion.

The Little Princess was another of her popular children's books. Both *Little Lord Fauntleroy* and *The Secret Garden* have been the subject of successful Hollywood films.

Frances Hodgson Burnett died on October 29, 1924.

WHEN WAS *THE ARABIAN NIGHTS ENTERTAINMENTS* FIRST WRITTEN?

It is difficult to pin an exact date for this very popular series of stories because they come from various sources, Indian, Persian and Arabian. Sir Richard Burton, who was responsible for the most popular translation, reckoned that some of the stories — *Sinbad*, for instance — dated back over a thousand years.

WHO WAS THE ENGLISH BARON WHO LIKED TO USE THE WORDS "THE LAST" IN THE TITLES OF HIS BOOKS?

He was Edward George Earle Bulwer-Lytton, first Baron Lytton who was born on May 25, 1803. Although his works were admired by Charles Dickens and were popular in his time, they are not often read today.

Four of his most famous books are entitled The Last Days of Pompeii, Rienzi, The Last of the Roman Tribunes, The Last of the Barons and Harold, the Last of the Saxon Kings.

Renowned as a wit and a dandy, Lytton was twice a member of Parliament and was also acclaimed as a playwright and poet of some considerable ability. He died January 18, 1873, and was buried in Westminster Abbey.

WHO WAS THE FAMOUS RIDER WHO TILTED AT A WINDMILL?

Don Quixote. The amazing adventures of this poor Spanish gentleman were recounted by Miguel de Cervantes Saavedra (to give Cervantes' full name) in his book Don Quixote de la Mancha, which is today one of the most popular classics.

Don Quixote is a poor gentleman living in the village of La Mancha. He is somewhat crazy due to reading too many books and tales of high chivalry. He fancies himself to be a knight errant and sets out on his old horse, Rosinante, to rescue gallant maidens in distress. He takes as squire a faithful peasant, named Sancho Panza.

There follows a series of exploits, both perilous and amusing. The book ends with Don Quixote forsaking the path of adventure and resigning himself to the life of a shepherd back at La Mancha. Sadly, he falls ill soon after his return and dies.

Miguel Cervantes' own life was as picturesque and dangerous as Don Quixote's. Cervantes was born (exact date is unknown) of a good but poor family — his father was a surgeon — and leaving home in search of fame and fortune, he joined' the army and fought at the Battle of Lepanto against the Turks. Badly wounded, he lost the use of his left hand. Even so, he continued his military career, fighting on both sides of the Mediterranean.

He was in Italy in 1576 and set out on a ship from Naples in September of that year.

The ship was attacked by pirates and Cervantes was captured and taken to Algiers where he was imprisoned until 1580. He suffered much at the hands of his jailers, before he was ransomed.

Returning home, he commenced to write but always seemed to be in trouble for one reason or another, largely debt. Indeed, he was in prison for the third time when he wrote his masterpiece, Don Quixote de la Mancha.

Miguel Cervantes died in Madrid, April 23, 1616, of dropsy.

WHY DID CAPTAIN FREDERICK MARRYAT RESIGN HIS COMMISSION IN THE ROYAL NAVY?

To write books about the sea. He was born July 10, 1792, and ran away to sea as a child. In 1806 he joined the Royal Navy and during the wars against Napoleon, saw active service both in European and American waters. During the Burmese war of 1824-1825 he commanded a King's ship.

His first book was *The Naval Officer: or Scenes and Adventures in the life of Frank Mildmay*. This was greeted with success and in 1830 he resigned from the Royal Navy and settled down to writing more books about the sea, namely *Peter Simple, Jacob Faithful* and *Mr Midshipman Easy*.

These adventure books attained considerable popularity, especially among boys. His later works included such well-known novels as *Masterman Ready, The Settlers in Canada* and *The Children of the New Forest*.

The best of his books rank as classics in English literature.

He died at Langham, Norfolk, August 9, 1848.

WHO WROTE 66 BEST-SELLING MYSTERY NOVELS IN 56 YEARS?

The author responsible for this phenomenal output was Mrs Agatha Mary Clarissa Christie.

She was born in Torquay and during the first World War she took a job as a hospital dispenser. While she carried out her duties, she learned much about various deadly poisons and the knowledge she gained was to stand her in good stead when, after the war ended in 1918, she commenced to write murder mysteries.

Her first novel was *The Mysterious Affair at Styles* which was published in 1920. Its success encouraged her to continue with her writing and from then until she died in 1976, she wrote 66 books.

Agatha Christie's two most famous detectives are Hercule Poirot, the Belgian private investigator and Miss Marple, who manages very quietly to solve the most intricate of mysteries.

WHAT WAS THE RED BADGE OF COURAGE?

The red badge referred to in the title of Stephen Crane's stirring novel *The Red Badge of Courage*, is the head wound sustained in battle by Henry Fleming, the young hero of the book.

The background of the book is the American Civil War and when the story begins, Henry and his comrades of the Union army are impatiently waiting to charge into action. When the time comes, Henry is scared, especially by the shocking carnage that surrounds him. He stands, bewildered, amongst a retreating line of panic-stricken men as they flee from the battle raging ahead. It is now that Henry sustains his wound, for one

In *The Red Badge of Courage* Union sharp-shooters lead the attack

of the fugitives hits him on the head with the butt of a rifle.

Henry staggers away and meets up with Wilson, a friend of his who cleanses Henry's wound and tells him to get some sleep.

Next morning, another battle is fought and Henry recovers his courage. When the colour bearer is killed, it is Henry who takes up the flag and leads the charge. He survives the battle, fights through another engagement and as the book comes to an end, he and Wilson march away with the regiment.

Henry is now a hard-bitten veteran, forever ready to do or die for his country.

Crane, born November 1, 1871, wrote other books but none so famous as *The Red Badge of Courage*. He died in Germany, June 5, 1900.

WHO WAS THE MARKET GARDENER WHO WROTE A FAMOUS ROMANCE ABOUT ENGLAND'S WEST COUNTRY?

This was the man who wrote *Lorna Doone* in 1869. His name was Richard Doddridge Blackmore, born June 7, 1825. He was educated at Blundell's School, Tiverton and at Exeter College. Oxford.

He was called to the Bar in 1852 but was left a legacy and settled down in Teddington, where he owned a market garden.

Blackmore commenced to write books and his first two novels *Clara Vaughan* and *Cradock Nowell* met with no success. Then he wrote *Lorna Doone*. It was published in 1869 and was so popular it started a revival of romantic fiction.

Blackmore died at the turn of the century, January 20, 1900.

WHAT IS THE NAME OF THE PRIEST WHO IS FAMOUS FOR SOLVING MYSTERIES?

It is Father Brown and his exciting adventures were written by Gilbert Keith Chesterton who was born in London, May 29, 1874.

Next to Sherlock Holmes, Father Brown is probably the most original and eccentric detective in English fiction. He is timid and absent-minded, and in his appearance is short and dumpy, with a round innocent face. He carries a large umbrella and has the air of someone who is unable to read a train time-table successfully, let alone solve a cunning murder.

Father Brown first appeared in the book entitled *The Innocence of Father Brown*, in 1911. Four more Father Brown volumes were to follow, namely *The Wisdom of Father Brown*, *The Incredulity of Father Brown*, *The Secret of Father Brown* and *The Scandal of Father Brown*.

G K Chesterton, who created Father Brown, was the son of a real estate agent in Kensington. He was educated at St Paul's School and later studied art at the Slade school in London. He was proficient enough to illustrate the novels of his friend, Hilaire Belloc. However, it was to journalism that he finally turned. Soon he was producing essays and articles which were published in book form.

In 1901 he married and three years later published the first of his popular fantasies *The Napoleon of Notting Hill*.

G K Chesterton died on June 14, 1936.

WHICH KING DEMANDED A HORSE IN EXCHANGE FOR HIS KINGDOM?

King Richard III in the last scene of William Shakespeare's historical play *Richard III*.

The play ends with the Battle of Bosworth Field. The invading force of Henry, Earl of Richmond, later King Henry VII, are fighting desperately against the army of Richard III. Suddenly, as the battle reaches a climax, Lord Stanley, one of Richard's supporters, betrays his king and orders his men to fight for Henry, Earl of Richmond instead. Nothing loth, they switch sides at once.

Now faced by an overwhelming enemy, King Richard's troops begin to retreat. Richard, in the very thick of the fighting, has been unhorsed. Desperately, he shouts: "A horse! A horse! My kingdom for a horse!"

Only when he is mounted, will his soldiers be able to see him and be heartened by the sight of their king. Nothing, however, can now save Richard. He is killed and the Earl of Richmond is hailed as King of England.

WHO WAS THE LAST OF THE MOHICANS?

In his world famous book, James Fenimore Cooper names Chingachgook, the Mohican friend of Natty Bumppo, better known as Hawkeye the Hunter.

The story takes place at the time of the French and Indian Wars in America.

It begins with an English officer, Major Duncan Heyward, in company with Cora and Alice, the daughters of Colonel Munro, setting out from Fort Edward to travel through the dense forest to Fort William Henry. There they are to meet with the girls' father, the commandant of Fort William Henry.

Magua, a renegade Huron Indian, offers to lead them to the fort by a short route. The Huron plans to lead Cora and Alice into a trap but the little party meet up with Chingachgook, his son Uncas, and Hawkeye the Hunter.

These three men swiftly realise what Magua is about and reveal him for what he is. They try to capture the Huron but the cunning rascal makes good his escape.

The book finally ends in tragedy with Uncas slain by Magua who is, in turn, killed by Hawkeye. Cora dies at the hands of a savage Huron, leaving Alice and Heyward the only survivors of the

**Magua attempts to escape the vengeance of Hawkeye
and Chingachgook, the last of the Mohicans**

little party that originally set out
from Fort Edward.

Hawkeye returns to his beloved
forest, there to remain forever with
his good comrade, Chingachgook,
the last of the Mohicans.

James Fenimore Cooper, the
American novelist, was born at
Burlington, New Jersey, Sept-
ember 15, 1789. Educated at Yale
for a time, he served in the
American navy.

His books about the colonial days in America and his novels about the sea, enjoyed great success but his habit of criticising the United States made him very unpopular with his fellow countrymen.

He was 61 when he died the day before his birthday in 1851.

WHICH ENGLISH WRITER OF CHILDREN'S BOOKS MARRIED THE SECRETARY OF A FAMOUS RUSSIAN REVOLUTIONARY?

Arthur Michell Ransome, who wrote *Swallows and Amazons*, the first in a series of 12 children's books, all of which, in time, were extremely successful. In fact, other authors tried to copy his style and themes.

He was born in Leeds, Yorkshire on January 18, 1884, the son of a professor of history. Arthur went to Rugby School but he was never happy there for he was hopeless at sports. This was probably because he was short-sighted. Then, too, he was subject to much bullying by some of the other boys.

He went on to Leeds University where he studied chemistry but he showed no particular promise and when he reached the age of 17 he went to London where he worked in a publisher's office.

In 1915 he was working as Russian correspondent for a London newspaper and his duties, naturally, took him to Russia. After the Revolution broke out in 1917, he met several leading Revolutionaries, among them Leon Trotsky.

Back in England in 1924, he married Evgenia Shelepin who had been Trotsky's secretary.

His first book for children was *Swallows and Amazons* which was published in 1930. It was not an immediate success but in America several thousands of copies were ordered by a book club.

He was then asked by his publishers to write a sequel. This was *Swallowdale* which appeared in 1931 but it was not until the third book, *Peter Duck*, was published that Arthur Ransome knew that he was headed for fame.

He died June 3, 1967.

WHO WROTE A BOOK ABOUT THE SON OF ALADDIN?

Noel Langley, who was born in South Africa, December 25, 1911. The title of the book is *The Land of Green Ginger*. Like the original story of Aladdin as told in *The Arabian Nights Entertainment*, it concerns the adventures of a boy amid wizardry and magicians.

So far as writing is concerned, Noel Langley was a man of many parts. He wrote books for adults — *Cage me a Peacock* is one of his best-known — and novels for children, as well as film scripts for Hollywood studios. He was one of three writers for the screen-play of *The Wizard of Oz*.

Noel Langley died November 4, 1980.

WHO WAS O HENRY?

He was an American author whose real name was William Sydney Porter. He was born September 11, 1862, in the quiet little village of Greensboro in North Carolina. He fell ill with a bad lung in 1882 and left North Carolina for a ranch in Texas where he worked as a cowboy. He recovered his health and later worked as a newspaper reporter.

In 1894 he became proprietor and editor of a humorous weekly entitled *The Rolling Stone*. He was, for a short while, a bank clerk but the bank failed and later he was falsely charged with the embezzlement of a small amount of money.

He was on his way to stand trial but boarded the wrong train and ran away to Central America. It was then that he took to the outlaw trail and for twelve months, was either at sea with smugglers or riding with bandits.

It was when he heard that his wife was seriously ill that Porter returned to Texas and surrendered to the law. He was allowed to stay with his wife until she died and he was unjustly sentenced to five years' imprisonment. He wrote the first of his famous short stories while he was in the penitentiary. It was now that he adopted the pen-name of O Henry, sending his stories through a sister living in Pittsburgh, to various magazines.

He was released in 1902 after serving a minimum term of imprisonment and he went to New York, sure of a welcome from editors who had been buying his work.

His first book of short stories, *Cabbages and Kings*, was published in 1904. This was largely based on his own adventures in Texas and Central America. Then he turned his hand to tales of New York City and in particular, to the poor people who dwelt there. His stories could be wry, thrilling and amusing in turn, with O Henry making the most of a vast canvas of fascinating characters.

Although he became the most popular short story writer of the time, he was always modestly paid and being a generous man, was constantly having to pour out material to make ends meet. It is on record that at certain times he turned out as many as fifty stories a year. He made famous the dramatic twist at the end of a story that was copied by many authors after him. O Henry died June 5, 1910.

WHO WROTE THE FAMOUS FAIRY STORY *CINDERELLA*?

This story is considered one of the greatest fairy tales. Indeed, most critics would undoubtedly accord it the accolade of being **the** greatest.

The idea of a poor young girl being ill-treated by her step-mother, and then with fairy help, receiving beautiful clothes, complete with rich shoes which lead to a Royal marriage, dates as far back as the 9th century when it appeared in China in a volume of tales of magic.

First publication in print of the famous story is credited to the French author, Charles Perrault who was born in Paris, January 12, 1628.

He was a poet who also wrote memoirs and other works but his fame rests on a series of immensely popular fairy tales, issued in volume form in 1697. It contained the tales of *Puss in Boots, Little Red Riding Hood* and *The Sleeping Beauty* as well as *Cinderella*. Charles Perrault died May 16, 1703.

THE COWARDLY LION, THE TIN WOODMAN AND THE SCARECROW APPEARED IN WHICH BOOK?

The Wonderful Wizard of Oz which was written by Lyman Frank Baum who was born May 15, 1856. It was his most famous book and the subject of an extremely celebrated film which gave the singing star Judy Garland the theme song for which she will surely always be remembered, *Somewhere Over the Rainbow*. She is seen below with Bert Lahr, Jack Haley and Ray Bolger as The Cowardly Lion, the Tin Woodman

The Cowardly Lion, the Tin Woodman, Dorothy and the Scarecrow as they appeared in the MGM film *The Wizard of Oz*

and the Scarecrow respectively.

The story concerns itself with Dorothy, an orphan, who sets out with her three friends to find the Wizard who can grant each of them his or her heart's desire.

The book was first published May 15, 1900, and during the next eight months nearly 100,000 copies were sold.

Although L Frank Baum wrote many other books, it is for *The Wonderful Wizard of Oz* and its sequels that he has earned himself a place in the hall of literary fame.

He died May 6, 1919.

WHO WAS ALLAN QUATERMAIN?

Allan was the big-game hunter who accompanies Sir Henry Curtis and Captain John Good into Darkest Africa to search for Sir Henry's younger brother who has not been heard of since he set out in search of .*King Solomon's Mines*, in the book of that title.

They all suffer great privations and struggle through many perils before their quest ends successfully. Sir Henry's brother is found and so is the great treasure of Solomon. The bulk of the trove has to be left behind though, when the adventurers make their escape.

All ends happily with Allan Quatermain, Curtis and Good more than content with the pocketful of priceless gems that Allan manages to bring away with him from King Solomon's Mines.

The adventures of Allan Quatermain continue in other books that were written by Sir Henry Haggard such as *Allan Quatermain* and *Allan's Wife*.

Haggard was born at Bradenham, Norfolk, June 22, 1856, the sixth son of W M Rider Haggard of Bradenham Hall. He was educated at Ipswich Grammar School and privately, but as a boy showed little aptitude and desire for learning. Indeed, his father, angered by an unsatisfactory school report, once declared that he was "only fit to be a greengrocer."

He was studying to join the Civil Service at the age of nineteen when he was unexpectedly offered an appointment on the secretarial staff of Sir Henry Bulwer, Governor of Natal in South Africa.

He held various offical posts in South Africa from 1875 to 1879. He then wrote his first book entitled *Cetewayo and His White Neighbours*. It was published in 1882 and South Africa figures prominently in the novels he wrote later, the success of which was due largely to the author's exceptional descriptive and story-telling power.

King Solomon's Mines was his most popular novel. During the year following its first publication in 1885, 31,000 copies were sold in Great Britain and in the United States it ran to 13 editions in the same period.

Other well-known books by Haggard are *Cleopatra*, *Nada the Lily*, *She*, *Ayesha* and *Montezuma's Daughter*.

He was knighted in 1912. After his African experiences, he returned to his native land which he dearly loved.

He became a practical farmer and a well-informed agricultural economist.

He died May 15, 1925, leaving behind him a narrative ability seldom surpassed.

WHAT WAS *THE ROARING U.P. TRAIL*?

It was the title of a novel written by the American author Zane Grey. The initials U P stand for Union Pacific and that was the name of the first railroad to cross the American continent, the construction of which is the background to the novel.

Like all Grey's novels, the book is packed with adventure and fast-moving incidents along epic lines.

Zane Grey was born in Ohio, January 31, 1875. His first novel was *Betty Zane* in 1904 and this was succeeded by a rapid outflow of books including *The Spirit of the Border, Desert Gold, Wildfire, The Man of the Forest, Forlorn River* and *Sunset Pass*. Several of his novels such as *To the Last Man, Riders of the Purple Sage* and *Robbers' Roost* have been filmed by Hollywood.

Grey became also extremely well-known for his exploits and books concerning sport and particularly big-game fishing.

He died in Altadena, California, October 23, 1939.

WHO WROTE UNDER THE NOM-DE-PLUME OF SAKI?

This was Hector Hugh Munro, born in Burma on November 12, 1870. His fame as a writer rests on his brilliant short stories which have been collected in several volumes such as *Reginald, Reginald in Russia* and *The Chronicles of Clovis*. He was only a child when his mother died and, in Devonshire, England, he was brought up by two aunts. Returning to Burma in 1893, he joined the military police but fell ill and was invalided home.

He began to write and his first book was *The Rise of the Russian Empire*. He then wrote newspaper articles and in 1904 wrote his first book of short stories *Reginald*.

Several more books of short stories followed, all showing his mastery of style, a biting wit and a superb power of describing the macabre and the supernatural.

When the war broke out in 1914 he enlisted and was killed at Beaumont Hamel, France on November 13, 1916.

BY WHICH NAME IS SIR PERCY BLAKENEY BETTER KNOWN?

The Scarlet Pimpernel. In the novels written by Baroness Orczy (Mrs Montague Barstow) he was the leader of the League of the Scarlet Pimpernel, a gallant band of Englishmen who risked their lives to save the innocent people who were being sent in droves to the guillotine by the ruthless men

The French secret agent suspects Sir Percy Blakeney of being the man he is hunting in *The Scarlet Pimpernel* by Baroness Orczy

who had brought about the French Revolution.

The pimpernel is a plant which bears white, blue or scarlet flowers and Blakeney has adopted this pseudonym to disguise his true identity. In secrecy, as Sir Percy Blakeney, he is the effete dandy and fashion-plate whose friendship even the Prince Regent is happy to claim. Behind the plaintive indolent exterior of the courtier, however, there is a man of lightning brain and immeasurable daring who, time and time again, evades the well-laid plans of the crafty Citizen Chauvelin, agent of the dreaded Committee of Public Safety who rule France.

Chauvelin begins to suspect Sir Percy when one evening at a ball attended by the Prince Regent, Sir Percy's wife intercepts a note from her husband which he has written to Sir Andrew Ffoulkes, one of the Scarlet Pimpernel's most trusted henchmen.

The note requests Sir Andrew to meet the Scarlet Pimpernel in the supper room at the ball in two hours time.

Chauvelin, his hopes raised at the prospect of learning for the first time the identity of the Scarlet Pimpernel, glides quietly into the supper room at the appointed hour but the only other person he can find in the room is that ass of an English aristocrat, Sir Percy Blakeney, who is sprawled seemingly sound asleep on a settee. Nobody else appears to keep the secret appointment with the Scar-

let Pimpernel and Chauvelin's feverish brain now has to grapple with the suspicion that the hated enemy of the French Republic is indeed none other than that posturing scion of the English nobility, Sir Percy Blakeney.

Baroness Emmuska Orczy was born at Tarnaors, Hungary in 1865, the daughter of Baron Orczy. He was an enterprising farmer who was trying to introduce more modern farming but his reactionary workers did not welcome his innovations. They burnt his crops and the disgusted Baron took his family to England where they settled in London.

The Scarlet Pimpernel was written in 1902 but failed to attract the interest of a publisher until the play of the same name, written by the Baroness and her husband Montague Barstow, the illustrator, was produced. The play was an instant success and so was the book when it was published in 1905. Several Pimpernel sequels were subsequently published.

Baroness Orczy and her husband went to live in Monte Carlo in 1918. She died at Henley-on-Thames, on November 12, 1947.

WHO WAS THE OYSTER PIRATE WHOSE BOOKS BECAME FAMOUS?

This was Jack London, the celebrated American author, who was born at San Francisco, January 12, 1876. His full name was John Griffith London (the surname of his stepfather). He was successively an oyster pirate, member of a fishing patrol and a seaman on a sailing vessel. He took part in the Klondike gold rush of 1897 and tramped through the United States and Canada.

Taking advantage of all his various experiences, he wrote a book of short stories in 1900 about the Far North, *The Son of the Wolf*. It was *The Call of the Wild*, though, that made him a best-selling novelist. The book was published in 1903. This was followed by *The Sea Wolf* in 1904 and *White Fang* in 1907, both very popular books. Meanwhile in 1905 he was a war reporter, covering the Russo-Japanese War.

He was responsible for non-fiction books such as *The War of the Classes* and other volumes of a socialist nature.

He was only 40 years of age when he died November 22, 1916.

WHO WAS CHRISTOPHER ROBIN'S FATHER?

Christopher Robin Milne was the son of Alan Alexander Milne who was born January 18, 1882.

It was A A Milne who was responsible for the world-famous books about the fabulous honey-lover Winnie-the-Pooh and Winnie's close friend, Milne's own son, Christopher Robin.

Christopher Robin first appeared in a book of verse entitled *When We Were Very Young* in 1924. Prior to this, A A Milne had worked on the staff of *Punch*, the English humorous weekly magazine and was its assistant editor from 1906 to 1914.

Although several of his contributions had appeared in books such as *Once A Week* in 1914 and *If I May* in 1922, it was *When We Were Very Young* that set him amongst the best-known writers of his day.

Winnie-the-Pooh which was published in 1926, was the first book to feature the lovable little bear. *Now We Are Six*, like *When We Were Very Young*, was a book of verse in which Winnie-the-Pooh and his friends re-appear. This was published in 1927 and the following year saw the appearance of the last book concerning Christopher Robin, Winnie-the-Pooh, Piglet, Kanga and Tigger and the rest of that merry crew. *The House at Pooh Corner* was its title.

In 1919 A A Milne wrote a children's play *Toad of Toad Hall* based on the book *The Wind in the Willows* which had been written by his friend, Kenneth Grahame.

After that he wrote another play for children, *The Ugly Duckling* which was published in 1941 and thereafter Milne wrote no more for children.

He died January 31, 1956, in Hartfield, Sussex at the age of 73. As for his son, who has enjoyed the glories and suffered the torments of being immortalised in his father's famous books, he is nowadays a book-seller in Devon.

WHICH AUTHOR WROTE THREE BOOKS, EACH CONTAINING THE WORD BEAU IN ITS TITLE?

The titles of the three books are *Beau Geste, Beau Sabreur* and *Beau Ideal* and they were written by Percival Christopher Wren who was born in 1885.

Having served in the British, French and Indian armies and having been a member of the French Foreign Legion, he was for a while assistant director of public education in the Bombay Presidency.

His dramatic and action-packed novels of life in the Foreign Legion won him immense popularity as an author. *The Wages of Virtue*, published in 1916, was the first. *Beau Geste* came along in 1924 and it is for this book that he is world-renowned. *Beau Sabreur* in 1926, *Beau Ideal* in 1928 and *Flawed Blades* in 1933 were the rest of his Foreign Legion novels.

He wrote other books but not one achieved the same success as those with a Foreign Legion background.

Beau Geste has been filmed by Hollywood on at least three occasions. It has also appeared as a television serial.

P C Wren died November 23, 1941.

WHERE IS RURITANIA AND WHO WROTE ABOUT THE KIDNAPPING OF ITS KING?

Ruritania does not exist. It was a fictional Balkan country conceived by the author Anthony Hope, as a background to his bestseller *The Prisoner of Zenda* published in 1894.

Anthony Hope Hawkins was born in London, February 9, 1863. At first he studied law and was called to the Bar in 1887. He had, however, always been keenly interested in literature to which he devoted himself entirely from 1893.

The Prisoner of Zenda, his first novel, dealt with the kidnapping of the King of Ruritania just before his coronation. On the spur of the moment his place is taken by Rudolph Rassendyll, his look-alike cousin. It is action all the way, highlighted by hair's-breadth escapes and romances. It was followed in 1898 by its sequel *Rupert of Hentzau*. Both novels were equally well received and successfully dramatised and filmed.

Anthony Hope wrote many popular novels in the years that followed as well as several plays. In 1918 he was knighted and his last work *Memories and Notes* appeared in 1929. He died July 8, 1933.

WHERE DID TOM BROWN SPEND HIS SCHOOL DAYS?

Thomas Hughes in his classical novel of school life, *Tom Brown's Schooldays*, relates the exciting adventures of Tom, the son of a country squire, at Rugby, a well-known English public school. Later Tom goes to Oxford.

Thomas Hughes, the author, was born October 22, 1822, at Uffington, in Berkshire, and himself educated at Rugby under the headmastership of the scholarly and celebrated Dr Arnold. In 1848 he became a barrister, and a Queen's Counsellor in 1869. He was a Member of Parliament from 1865 to 1874 and was made a county court judge in 1882. He died at Brighton, March 22, 1896.

Although Thomas Hughes wrote a number of books he is remembered almost solely for his masterpiece *Tom Brown's Schooldays*. Its sequel, *Tom Brown at Oxford* did not equal the popularity of its predecessor.

WHICH WRITER ROMANTICISED A WICKED HIGHWAYMAN AND IN WHICH NOVEL?

It was William Harrison Ainsworth who bathed Dick Turpin, the infamous highwayman, in the glowing colours of a romantic hero in his thrilling book *Rookwood*.

Ainsworth was born in Manchester on February 4, 1805, and he attended Manchester Grammar School. It was intended that he should follow his father's profession, that of a solicitor. He studied law in London but soon decided that the legal life was not for him. He settled down as a historical novelist and magazine editor. His first effort was soon a popular favourite. It was *Rookwood*, which was published in 1834.

Ainsworth had been reading the lives of the highwaymen and was particularly struck by the story of a whirlwind ride from London to York made by a rip-roaring malefactor, by name John (or William, accounts differ) Nevison.

Early one morning, he robbed a traveller of his purse on Gad's Hill near Rochester. For some reason, Nevison appears to have been afraid of being recognised by his victim in the future and decided to establish an alibi for himself. He set out to ride to York and by using several remounts, achieved his aim, supposedly reaching York that same evening.

He passed the time of day with the Lord Mayor who was playing bowls there. The alibi stood him in good stead at a later date when he was arrested for another crime and was identified while in custody by the man he had robbed on Gad's Hill.

It is said that King Charles II granted Nevison an interview after he had been acquitted on all charges, listened to the tale of the fabulous ride and promptly pardoned the highwayman. Nevison was irredeemable, however, and was later hanged.

It was Harrison Ainsworth who took this story and grafted it on to one of the biggest rogues who ever rode the moonlit highway, none other than Richard Turpin. Overnight, Turpin became the "Knight of the Road" for thousands of "penny-dreadfuls" and in recent years has appeared in two lengthy television series and a full-length

A coach is held up by Dick Turpin, the rascally highwayman, in W Harrison Ainsworth's novel *Rookwood*

film. Needless to say, Dick is still presented as a hero and not the heartless killer that he truly was.

Harrison Ainsworth enjoyed a long and successful career. Jack Sheppard, renowned for his astonishing escapes from prison, and Guy Fawkes, the Gunpowder Plot conspirator, were just two more rascals he glamorised.

Harrison Ainsworth died at Reigate, Surrey, January 3, 1882.

TO WHOM DOES *THE SWAN OF AVON* REFER?

To William Shakespeare, the son of John Shakespeare, a dealer in wool and leather, who lived in Stratford-upon-Avon. In this little town standing on the banks of the River Avon in Warwickshire, was born in April 1564, the boy who was to win immortal fame as the world's greatest dramatist, the good friend of nobles and the wonder of his and every age.

This gentle man of immeasurable genius has, through the hundreds of years since he died on April 23, 1616, been unmatched as a poet and playwright.

Often referred to in the words of his great friend Ben Jonson as "The Swan of Avon," William Shakespeare is England's greatest gift to the literature of the world.

WHICH POET WAS SLAIN IN A TAVERN BRAWL?

His name was Christopher Marlowe. He was the son of a shoemaker living in Canterbury, Kent. Kit, as he is often referred to, was born February 6, 1564. He went to King's School, Canterbury and from there to Benet (Corpus Christi) College, Cambridge, graduating M A in 1587.

It was at Cambridge that he first indulged himself in the freethinking theories that later incurred the anger of the authorities when he came to London. In the capital city, he was attached as playwright to the Lord Admiral's company of players. His brilliance secured him an introduction to Sir Walter Raleigh. In 1593, he and Raleigh were accused of atheism, and shortly after that a warrant was issued for his arrest on some unknown charge. Before he could be taken into custody, he was involved in May, 1593, in a tavern brawl in Deptford, daggers were drawn and a serving man by the name of Francis Archer, stabbed and killed Christopher Marlowe.

It was he who first introduced blank verse into drama, lines that were noble and inspired. He wrote the first great tragedy in English. He composed the first great English historical drama. There is no doubt that Shakespeare owed more to Marlowe than to any man.

Marlowe's first tragedy, *Tamburlaine the Great*, was produced about 1588. The *Tragical History of Doctor Faustus* containing some of the finest poetry in the language, was produced a year later. It is in this play that the famous lines occur:

> Was this the face that
> launch'd a thousand ships
> And burnt the topless
> towers of Ilium?
> Sweet Helen, make me immortal with a kiss.

The Jew of Malta and *Edward the Second* were two more plays written by Marlowe. Only a man of gigantic creative ability could have written such magnificent dramas. Once heard always remembered is his celebrated line *Who ever lov'd, that lov'd not at first sight?*

WHO WAS THE AMERICAN CONSUL RENOWNED FOR HIS NOVELS OF THE FAR WEST?

Francis Bret Harte. He was born 25 August, 1839, at Albany, New York State, the son of a school teacher. Due to ill-health and the poverty of his parents, he received only three years of regular schooling.

His first poem was published when he was only 11 years of age.

When he was 18, he went to California, where he worked as a gold miner, schoolmaster, printer and journalist. He never ceased writing poems and stories and became a sub-editor with a San Francisco journal in 1857.

From 1871, Bret Harte was the most popular American writer both at home and abroad. His books were widely translated and his lecture tours were very successful.

He fell into money difficulties, however, and was given the post of American consul in Crefeld, Germany, from 1878 to 1880 and was then moved to Glasgow, Scotland, where he lived until 1885. Thereafter he lived in England. He died May 5, 1902.

His most famous stories are *The Luck of Roaring Camp*, *The Outcasts of Poker Flat*, *Miggles* and *Tennessee's Partner*, all of which have appeared as films and on television.

WHO WROTE THE *BULLDOG DRUMMOND* NOVELS?

His pen-name was Sapper, his real name being Cyril McNeile, born 28 September, 1888. He was the son of a naval captain and entered the Royal Engineers, (whose nickname is The Sappers) in 1907. He served through the First World War, retiring from the army with the rank of lieutenant colonel in 1919.

He began his writing career with *Sergeant Michael Cassidy* and other works inspired by the war but it was in 1920, with *Bulldog Drummond*, that his reputation as the author of exciting tales was established. This book, truly a classic among adventure stories, was dramatised several times, filmed and enjoyed a great success.

The sequels to *Bulldog Drummond* were also best-sellers. They are: *The Black Gang*, *The Third Round*, *The Final Count*, *Temple Tower*, *The Female of the Species*, *The Return of Bulldog Drummond*, *Knock-Out*, *Bulldog Drummond at Bay* and *Challenge*.

Cyril McNeile died August 14, 1937.

WHAT WAS THE ONLY BOOK FOR WHICH JONATHAN SWIFT, WHO WROTE SCORES OF BOOKS, WAS PAID?

Gulliver's Travels. Its title was originally *The Travels into Several Remote Nations of the World by Lemuel Gulliver.*

The book was so well presented with an illustrated portrait of Gulliver and maps, that many credulous people believed it to be a true story. Indeed, a bishop in Ireland angrily asserted that in his opinion it was full of improbable untruths to such an extent that he scarcely believed a word of it.

The book is popularly regarded today as a children's classic but in fact it was published as an adult

Gulliver (as played by Richard Harris in the EMI/Valeness-Belvision film *Gulliver's Travels*) falls asleep in Lilliput

book, packed with bitter satire, ridiculing the society of the day.

Jonathan Swift, who was born in Dublin, November 30, 1667, was ordained a priest in 1695 but soon tired of a country parson's life.

He commenced to write poetry but his verse was harshly criticised and he turned his attention to the shortcomings of the day's politics. With wit and savagery he attacked the accepted customs of the land and made the church the particular target for his wicked humour.

Always outrageous in his attacks, he at long last, in 1741, became completely insane and died October 19, 1745. He was buried in St Patrick's Cathedral, Dublin.

WHICH FRENCH POET WAS THE HERO OF THE VERY POPULAR OPERETTA *THE VAGABOND KING?*

He was François de Montcorbier, known as Villon, born in 1431. His father died when he was quite young and he was brought up by a relative, Guillaume de Villon, whose name he adopted. He was educated at the University of Paris from where he graduated in 1449.

He soon fell into bad company and roistered through the seedy taverns of Paris with thieves and murderers. He was himself charged with murder when on June 5, 1455, he quarrelled with and mortally wounded a priest. He fled from Paris. Later he obtained a letter of remission due to the pleading of some more law-abiding friends.

He continued his wayward and dishonest life and was concerned in a serious theft of money from the College of Navarre.

Guy Taberie, who was a member of the gang of thieves, betrayed Villon who promptly ran away from Paris yet again.

He surfaced eventually in Blois in 1457 where he took part at the court of Duke Charles d'Orleans in a poetical competition. Next heard of in prison at Meung-sur-Loire, he only escaped hanging because a general amnesty was proclaimed when King Louis XI and his court passed through that town.

Back in Paris, he was accused once again of theft and thrown into prison but released. Soon, in further trouble, he was re-arrested and condemned to death. He appealed and the sentence was commuted to one of banishment for ten years. Nothing more is known of him.

It cannot be denied that Villon was certainly not the heroic figure he cuts in the musical play *The Vagabond King* but the bitter beauty of his verse — in fact his output was quite small — has been admired across the centuries. At the request of his mother, he wrote, in the form of a ballad, a prayer to the Virgin Mary which is touching and beautiful.

WHY DID SAMUEL LANGHORNE CLEMENS CALL HIMSELF MARK TWAIN?

He took his famous pen-name from the call ("by the mark twain" meaning two fathoms deep) of a leadsman on a River Mississippi steam-boat when reporting the soundings (or depths) of the river. He was born at Florida, Missouri, November 30, 1835, but when he was 12 years old his father died and he had little regular education. He started life as a printer's compositor and worked in various states, yet he was only 16 years old when he became a steam-boat pilot on the Mississippi. He remained a pilot for the next ten years and then became a reporter on a newspaper in Nevada.

He then tried mining and later went on to San Francisco where he returned to journalism.

He commenced to write fiction and his first story *The Celebrated Frog of Calaveras County* appeared in a magazine in 1867. Perhaps his two best known volumes are *The Adventures of Tom Sawyer* and *Huckleberry Finn*, both of which have appealed to young readers and are still regarded as American classics.

His books are prime examples of humour but at times Mark Twain displayed a mastery of pathos, even tragedy. He loved a practical joke but hated all forms of sham.

This much-loved author died at Redding, Connecticut, April 21, 1910.

THE AFRICAN QUEEN WAS A FAMOUS MOVIE BUT WHO WROTE THE BOOK ON WHICH IT WAS BASED?

Cecil Scott Forester. He is best known for the books he wrote concerning the exciting adventures of Horatio Hornblower, an officer in the British Royal Navy during the Napoleonic Period.

He was born in Cairo, Egypt, on August 27, 1899, the son of a British Government official. From 1910 to 1917 he was educated at the renowned Dulwich College in England which the American crime writer, Raymond Chandler, also attended.

He first studied medicine but gave this up to write. *The Happy Return*, his first novel about Hornblower, appeared in 1937. For a short while he sailed with the Royal Navy during the Second World War to afford him material for *The Ship* which was published in 1943.

C S Forester died February 4, 1966, before he could complete his last book *Hornblower and the Crises*.

WHO — WHEN ASKED BY A CUSTOMS OFFICER "WHAT HAVE YOU TO DECLARE?" — REPLIED "ONLY MY GENIUS."?

Oscar Wilde, the Irish poet and playwright. He was born in Dublin October 15, 1856, the younger son of Sir William Wilde, a surgeon.

A master of deadly witticisms, Oscar Wilde wrote many famous plays such as *An Ideal Husband* and *Lady Windermere's Fan*. He also wrote children's fairy tales.

He died November 30, 1900.

WHO WAS BANJO PATERSON?

He was Andrew Barton Paterson, an Australian author and poet, who was born in New South Wales. Educated in Sydney, he was a solicitor but when the Boer War broke out in South Africa, he went there as a war correspondent. Returning home, he became the editor of a newspaper, until the First World War began in 1914, when he gave up journalism to serve his country. After the war, he made his home in Sydney. He died in 1941.

Although he wrote some novels, it is as a poet that he is famous. He penned several ballads for a paper called *The Bulletin* and a number of these were collected together and published as a book entitled *The Man From Snowy River*. The background of the poems is the Australian Bush, and bushrangers and their matchless mounts play a big part. He gathered also many traditional songs of which *Waltzing Matilda* must be deemed the most popular. It is Australia's national song. Today he is known far and wide as Banjo Paterson, his pen-name when he wrote for *The Bulletin*.

WHICH FAMOUS ENGLISH DIARIST WAS ARRESTED FOR BETRAYING NAVAL SECRETS TO THE FRENCH?

Samuel Pepys who was born in London, February 23, 1633. He was secretary to the Royal Navy when he was arrested on May 21, 1679. Two months later he was bailed out and the charge against him was dropped.

This was not the only time that Samuel was in trouble. After William of Orange was crowned King of Britain, Pepys was twice imprisoned on suspicion of being an active supporter of the previous king, James II, who, although he had been driven from England, still laid claim to the throne.

Samuel Pepys was eventually freed. His public career which began in 1659 when he became a clerk in the Exchequer was full of variety. He became the member of Parliament for Harwich in 1679 and held sundry very important posts but it is for his splendid diary that he is justly famous. It affords us a remarkable insight of English life and society.

He died May 26, 1703.

THREE MEN IN A BOAT IS ONE OF VERY FEW HUMOROUS CLASSICS BUT WHO WROTE IT?

It was written by an actor, ex-schoolmaster and clerk in the City of London. His name was Jerome Klapka Jerome, born at Walsall, near Wolverhampton, May 2, 1859.

Turning to literature, his first book was *On the Stage and Off*, published 1885, an account of his theatrical adventures. Four years later his masterpiece *Three Men in a Boat* appeared. It received immediate wide and prolonged popularity. Jerome later wrote some plays of which *The Passing of the Third Floor Back* is the best known.

He died June 14, 1927.

WHO WROTE THE TWO BAFFLING MYSTERY NOVELS, *THE WOMAN IN WHITE* AND *THE MOONSTONE*?

William Wilkie Collins who was the son of William Collins, the painter. Born in London, January 8, 1824, he studied law and was called to the Bar in 1851. He was already writing and in 1850 his novel *Antonina* had appeared but his high rank in literature stands on his two well-known mystery novels.

Wilkie Collins was a close friend of Charles Dickens who admired his writing and helped him to strengthen his characterisation.

Collins died in London on September 23, 1889.

WHEN SIR WALTER SCOTT WAS MADE BANKRUPT, HOW DID HE PAY OFF HIS DEBTS?

In his own words "This right hand shall work it all off."

In 1809 he had supplied half the capital of the publishers, Ballantyne & Co. Although he made a lot of money from his poems and books, he spent much of it on building his home, Abbotsford. In 1826 Ballantyne were in very serious financial difficulties and Scott had not enough cash left to save the company from bankruptcy.

At the age of 55, with outstanding debts of £250,000, an enormous sum in those days, Sir Walter bravely wrote as much and as fast as he could to pay off the creditors.

The strain at last began to tell. In February 1830, he had an attack of apoplexy. In spite of this, he continued to write and completed his last two novels, *Castle Dangerous* and *Count Robert of Paris* in 1831.

The following year, having suffered another severe attack of apoplexy, he died at Abbotsford, on September 21, 1832.

Ivanhoe, having been the subject of more than one successful film, is probably his most famous book.

FIRST IMPRESSIONS WAS THE TITLE JANE AUSTEN GAVE TO HER FIRST BOOK BUT UNDER WHAT TITLE WAS IT PUBLISHED?

Jane Austen completed her first novel in 1797 when she was 22 years old. It was published 16 years later when it appeared as *Pride and Prejudice*. *First Impressions* was not her first book to be published for that was *Sense and Sensibility*, published in 1811.

Jane Austen was born December 15, 1775, at Steventon rectory in Hampshire, the seventh and youngest child of the Rev George Austen. His salary was not sufficient to raise so large a family so he accepted pupils to learn music, dancing, French and a little Italian. Jane took her place with the other pupils.

From 1801 to 1805 her home was in Bath. Then the family moved to Southampton and later to Chawton in Hampshire. Devoted to her family, she lived her whole life with them, apart from occasional visits to London and during her last illness in the town of Winchester where she died July 18, 1817.

She never married although it is said she was once in love with a man who died young.

**Elizabeth Bennett, the heroine of *Pride and Prejudice*
takes an instant dislike to the proud Mr Darcy**

All her writing was carried out in the family's sitting room, subject to casual interruptions.

Her other novels apart from *Sense and Sensibility* and *Pride and Prejudice* were *Mansfield Park, Emma, Northanger Abbey* and *Persuasion,* the last two being published after her death. She left an unfinished book entitled *Sanditon.*

WHO WROTE THE BOOK ON WHICH THE WORLD'S MOST POPULAR OPERA WAS BASED?

Prosper Merimée wrote *Carmen,* the novel that attracted the attention of Georges Bizet, the composer.

Merimée was born September 28, 1803, in Paris. He grew up a melancholy man of sensitive temper and a great writer of imaginative prose.

He died September 23, 1870.

THE VIRGINIAN HAS BEEN OFTEN FILMED BUT WHO WROTE THE BOOK?

Owen Wister, who, like several other writers, first studied the law.

Born at Philadelphia, July 14, 1860, he became a barrister in 1889 but he abandoned the law to write books. He excelled in stories of the West and is regarded as the writer who laid the foundations of the later form of cowboy stories.

The Virginian has been filmed for the cinema screen and a long television series was based on it.

THE CONTEMPORARY ACCOUNTS OF JULIUS CAESAR'S WARS IN GAUL AND BRITAIN WERE WRITTEN BY WHOM?

By Julius Caesar himself. As a man of letters, Caesar stands in the highest rank. Regrettably the only works of his that have come down to us are his famous commentaries on the Gallic war and Civil war.

His accounts of his campaigns reveal the brilliant genius that certainly made him one of the greatest warriors of all time.

WHY DID LEW WALLACE WHO WROTE *BEN HUR* MEET AND HAVE A LONG TALK WITH THE OUTLAW BILLY THE KID?

In 1878 Lew Wallace, who had been a major-general in the Civil War, was appointed the Governor of New Mexico by President Rutherford. At that time much bloodshed was taking place in New Mexico, and prominent amongst the ringleaders was none other than young Billy the Kid.

A meeting was arranged between Billy and Governor Wallace. It was agreed that if Billy would lay down his guns and surrender, he would receive a pardon.

Billy **did** surrender but later broke out of prison before his pardon could be arranged. He sped away only to meet his end when he was shot by Sheriff Pat Garrett, who had been ordered to track him down.

Lew Wallace was born at Brookville, Indiana, April 10, 1827. He joined the army and served in the Mexican War, later achieving the rank of major-general during the Civil War. He was Governor of New Mexico from 1878 to 1881 and thereafter the U S Minister to Turkey from 1881 to 1885.

As a novelist he is best known for Ben Hur, a story of Palestine and Rome when Jesus was alive. It achieved great success not only as a novel but also as a play and a film. Two other novels which proved successful were The Fair God and The Prince of India.

Lew Wallace died February 17, 1905.

WHO IS IAN FLEMING'S FAMOUS HERO, FEATURED IN MANY FILMS?

James Bond. Ian Fleming introduced Bond in his novel Casino Royale which was first published in 1953.

Ian Fleming was born May 28, 1908, and educated at Eton College and then the military academy, Sandhurst.

He worked with the well-known news agency Reuters and later as the foreign manager of a newspaper combine. Among his other Bond novels are Live and Let Die, Diamonds are Forever and On Her Majesty's Secret Service. Successful James Bond films, often seen on television today, are Dr No, From Russia with Love, Goldfin-

ger, and Thunderball.

Young readers know Ian Fleming best as the author of Chitty-Chitty-Bang-Bang, the amazing automobile which can fly and turn itself into a hovercraft. It is the brain-child of a brilliant inventor, Commander Caractacus Potts. One of his other clever ideas is sweets that whistle.

Fleming died August 12, 1964.

WHICH POET LAUREATE WAS SAID TO HAVE WORKED HIMSELF TO DEATH?

Robert Southey was born at Bristol, August 12, 1774. When he was 20 years old, the French Revolution was in full swing and Southey was so inspired by this that he stupidly conceived the idea of founding a communal republic in the United States. He was ably abetted in this notion by Samuel Coleridge, also a poet. The two young men (Coleridge was 22) worked together and Southey began to publish his early verse and prose in an attempt to raise the funds for this useless enterprise. Eventually, the young poets realised the futility of the project and abandoned it.

Thereafter, Southey devoted himself continually to hard work and he turned out immense amounts of books and poems. Finally the years of continuous overwork took their toll. His health was seriously affected and he became insane. He died March 21, 1843.

Today, in spite of all his hard work, he is remembered only for his *Life of Nelson* and a few ballads such as *The Battle of Blenheim* and *The Inchcape Rock*.

In later years he cast aside his earlier republicanism, became a Tory and was appointed Poet Laureate in 1813.

WHO WAS THE FRENCH FOREST RANGER FAMOUS FOR HIS FABLES?

His name was Jean de la Fontaine. His father was the ranger of the forest of the duchy of Château-Thierry in Champagne. Jean was born there July 8, 1621, and educated at first for the Church. He turned, however, to the law but abandoned this on succeeding to his father's rangership in 1647.

He married the same year but soon separated from his wife and he must have decided that forest ranging was not for him for it is known that from 1660 he lived in Paris. He began to write verses and translated some of the minor classics.

In 1668 his first six books of animal fables were published. In wonderfully easy verse, they rate high among the glories of French literature. In them Fontaine demonstrated a deep knowledge of nature, gained probably from the days when he roamed the forest of Château-Thierry as a ranger.

A second series of fables appeared in 1679 and a third in 1693.

They are today still read extensively throughout the world.

Jean de la Fontaine died in Paris April 13, 1695.

DID ROB ROY REALLY LIVE?

Yes. He was Robert MacGregor, the leader of a band of Scottish outlaws. Sir Walter Scott featured him in a heroic role in his popular novel *Rob Roy*. MacGregor called himself Rob Roy, *roy* meaning red. Rob Roy had red hair. He was born 1671, in Buchanan parish, Stirlingshire. As a cattle farmer at Balquhidder, he raised a band of armed men, who also guarded the herds of neighbouring farmers on payment of a tax.

Unable to repay a loan made to him by the Duke of Montrose, he was in 1712 evicted by the duke from his estates and outlawed. At the head of a band of followers, he raided the estates of the duke and his tenants, defying all attempts to capture him.

He at last made friends with Montrose but he was still an outlaw. In 1722 he surrendered to the English and was taken to London to Newgate Prison.

He was sentenced to be transported but in 1727 was pardoned. Rob Roy MacGregor, regarded by many as the "Robin Hood of Scotland," died December 28, 1734.

Rob Roy is not only a well-known novel. A very successful film was made about the notorious outlaw by Walt Disney Productions.

Rob Roy McGregor, who appears in Sir Walter Scott's book
Rob Roy, leads his band of outlaws on another daring raid

WHAT WAS MR MICAWBER ALWAYS WAITING FOR?

Something to turn up. Micawber is a most engaging fellow who appears in *David Copperfield* which was written by Charles Dickens. Without doubt, Wilkins Micawber is one of Dickens' greatest characters.

When young David Copperfield is placed by his cruel stepfather Murdstone with the firm of Murd-stone and Grinby, suppliers of wine and spirits to certain packet ships, arrangements are made for David to lodge with Micawber and his family.

Micawber is always in debt but hopes that in time "something will turn up" to help him out of his difficulties. Unfortunately nothing ever does.

Still, Micawber retains his good humour and is finally the man who unmasks the criminal activities of rascally Uriah Heep who has been swindling the father of the girl David Copperfield marries. As a reward David's aunt, Miss Betsy Trotwood, proposes to Micawber that perhaps he would meet with better fortune if he emigrated to Australia and offers to assist him if he agrees.

Once again, Micawber's unfailing optimism comes to his rescue.

"I entertain the conviction," says he, "that it is, under existing circumstances the only land for myself and family; and that something of an extraordinary nature will turn up on that shore."

And with that, Wilkins Micawber, still hoping for the best at all times, prepares to take his long-suffering wife and family to Australia, in those days a very different place from the thriving country that it is today.

Mr Micawber, one of Charles Dickens' most engaging characters

WHOSE NOVEL ABOUT ENGLISH COUNTRY LIFE WAS PRAISED BY A BRITISH PRIME MINISTER?

Mary Webb was born at Leighton, Shropshire on March 25, 1881. Her family name was Meredith and in 1912 she married a schoolmaster, Henry Bertram Webb.

In 1914 Mr and Mrs Webb began work as market gardeners and sold their fruit and vegetables on a stall in the market place of Shrewsbury Town.

Mary Webb started journalistic work at an early age while living in Shropshire. Her first novel The Golden Arrow was published in 1916. After that came The Spring of Joy, Gone to Earth, The House in Dormer Forest and Seven for a Secret.

It was not, however, until 1924 when her best-selling Precious Bane appeared that she first attracted attention. It was awarded an important prize specially given annually for the best novels or verse descriptive of life in England, written by an author who had not yet acquired any outstanding success.

Stanley Baldwin, at that time Prime Minister of Britain, wrote an introduction to the book, and addressed it from No 10 Downing Street, London, the residence of Britain's premier. The praise he deservedly lavished on the book in his introduction ensured its continuing popularity.

Sadly, Mary Webb did not live long to enjoy her well-won success. Her last book *Armour Wherein He Trusted* was published in 1926 and she died at the height of her fame October 8, 1927.

Her books excel in the vivid descriptions of the dour countryside of Shropshire and the Welsh Marches, threaded throughout by a certain wildness and fateful mystery.

Precious Bane has been featured as a television serial and *Gone to Earth* was filmed in 1948.

BY WHICH NAME DO WE KNOW THEODOR JOZEF KONRAD KORZENIOWSKI?

The name under which he wrote his many sea-faring novels was Joseph Conrad. He was born in the Ukraine in Russia on December 6, 1857. His boyhood was passed in Cracow in Poland. There he learned to speak and write French fluently and first began to take a great interest in the sea.

At the age of 17 he served for two years in French ships in the Mediterranean Sea and on South American coasts. Four years later he forsook his interest in France and instead turned to England and took passage to Lowestoft on the east coast of England. He landed there in 1878 and later qualified as an able seaman.

He served on a coasting vessel. He sailed as third mate to Sydney, Australia, on a sailing ship in 1880. Four years later, he became a master in the British merchant service and took British citizenship.

Conrad left the sea in 1894 and after his marriage in 1896 settled in Kent.

He fell ill of Congo fever and, during his convalescence, started work on his first novel, entitled *Almayer's Folly*. He worked on this book for nearly five years.

He wrote many books about the sea, prominent among which are *Victory, An Outcast of the Islands* and *Lord Jim*, all of which have been filmed.

Joseph Conrad died August 3, 1924.

WHAT ARE THE FIRST AND LAST SENTENCES IN THE BIBLE?

The first book of the Bible is Genesis and the first words are "In the beginning God created the heaven and the earth." The last book in the Bible is Revelations and the last words read "The grace of our Lord Jesus Christ be with you all. Amen."

WHO GAVE FOUR WHITE FEATHERS TO HARRY FAVERSHAM?

Harry Faversham is the hero of the novel *The Four Feathers* which was written by Alfred Edward Woodley Mason and first published with great success in 1902.

When the story starts Harry Faversham is a young officer in the British army. He is tired of army life and wishes to settle down and marry his fiancée, Ethne Burroughs. Harry is forced to consider his future as an army officer when his regiment is posted to the African country of the Sudan to take part in the campaign that is being fought there.

On the very eve of the regiment's departure, Harry resigns his commission, much to the disgust of his fiancée and his three fellow officers, Captain John Durrance, Lieutenant Thomas Willoughby and Lieutenant Peter Burroughs, Ethne's brother. Later Harry is given four white feathers (a white feather being the symbol of cowardice) by Ethne and the three officers.

How Harry sails for Egypt to rescue his three officer friends from great danger and redeems himself in the eyes of his fiancée makes for a most exciting novel. He returns the four feathers to Ethne and his three friends and all ends happily in the tradition of adventure books of this type.

A E W Mason, who wrote the book was born May 7, 1865 and scored his first publishing triumph with *The Courtship of Morrice Buckler* in 1896.

Books of his, such as The House of the Arrow, At the Villa Rosa, and The Four Feathers, were filmed, the last, the most popular, at least three times.

Perhaps it is worth mentioning that "Alf Mason" is one of Captain Hook's pirates in *Peter Pan* which was written by Mason's good friend, J M Barrie.

A E W Mason died November 11, 1948.

IS THERE ANY CONNECTION BETWEEN CAPTAIN BLOOD AND COLONEL BLOOD?

No. Captain Blood is a fictional character, the hero of Rafael Sabatini's novel of piracy on the high seas *Captain Blood* while Colonel Blood was the real-life rascal who stole the crown jewels from the Tower of London May 9, 1671. He was captured but later pardoned by King Charles II.

Rafael Sabatini was born of Italian and English parentage at Jesi, Italy in 1875 and first made his name as a writer of historical fiction with *The Tavern Knight*, in 1904. This was followed by a long series of similar tales that enjoyed great popularity for their historical accuracy and the author's charm of style.

His books, *The Sea Hawk, Captain Blood, Scaramouche* and *Bardelys the Magnificent*, have all been rendered into outstandingly successful films.

A scene from the Warner Bros film of *Captain Blood* with J Carrol Naish, Errol Flynn and Basil Rathbone

Rafael Sabatini also wrote the biographical works, *Life of Cesare Borgia* and *Torquemada and the Spanish Inquisition*.

He died February 13, 1950.

WHO WAS QUASIMODO?

The pathetic deformed bellringer of Notre Dame Cathedral. He is described as having a square nose, a horseshoe-shaped mouth, one eye, overhung by a bushy red eyebrow, and a strange expression of amazement, malice and melancholy; a giant broken in pieces and badly mended.

Victor Hugo, the renowned French author, wrote *Notre Dame de Paris*, the book in which the tragic bellringer appears. Claude Frollo, archdeacon of Paris has always taken care of Quasimodo and the bellringer is devoted to him.

Then one day Quasimodo is arrested for causing a disturbance and is condemned to a flogging at the hands of the public executioner. Bound hand and foot and completely helpless, the bellringer is beaten and tormented by the cruel Parisian mob. He is dying of thirst when a gypsy girl named Esmeralda runs forward with a flask of water.

Later Quasimodo is released but from then on he worships the gypsy girl. Claude Frollo secretly loves Esmeralda but is also jealous of Quasimodo's adoration of her.

The end of this book is tragic indeed for Frollo attacks a Captain Phoebus who is understood to be mortally wounded. Esmeralda is accused of the crime and sentenced to death. The gypsy is hanged but Quasimodo is determined to avenge her death and he slays Frollo. Quasimodo disappears and is never seen alive again.

Notre Dame de Paris was the third of Victor Hugo's novels to be published and is probably the best known of all his books. Another, Les Miserables, is well-known today if only for the successful award winning musical play which has been based on it.

Victor Marie Hugo was born February 26, 1802. His father was one of Napoleon's generals.

It was Notre Dame de Paris that made him famous. He went on to write many other successful books and plays but met with disaster when he ventured into politics. A result was an 18 years' exile in the Channel Islands.

He returned to France in due course and died May 22, 1885 of pneumonia, an honoured contributor to French literature.

WHO WROTE THE ONE HUNDRED AND ONE DALMATIANS?

Dorothy Gladys Smith, better known as Dodie Smith and in theatrical circles by her pen-name C L Anthony. She was born May 3, 1896 at Whitefield, Lancashire and educated at Manchester and at St Paul's Girls' School in London.

After studying at the Royal Academy of Dramatic Art, she first appeared on stage in musical comedy in 1915. After several years touring with various companies, she left the stage to go into business. Her first play, Autumn Crocus, was produced at the Lyric Theatre, London, in 1931 and was an immediate success. In 1932 her second play Service was produced at Wyndham's Theatre. Both these plays have been filmed.

The One Hundred and One Dalmatians was also filmed but as an animated cartoon feature in 1961 by Walt Disney Productions. She wrote this in 1956 and then in 1967 another children's book, The Starlight Barking was published to be followed by yet another, The Midnight Kittens in 1978.

WHO SANG FIFTEEN MEN ON THE DEAD MAN'S CHEST?

Billy Bones in Robert Louis Stevenson's romance of the Spanish Main, Treasure Island.

Billy Bones is the buccaneer who, one day, appears at the Admiral Benbow Inn seeking somewhere to hide from a pursuing gang of pirates. Billy Bones has a treasure map drawn up by his now-dead captain, by name Flint. The pirates are determined to have that map.

Adventures come thick and fast for young Jim Hawkins, son of the Benbow's landlord, when Blind Pew, a villainous pirate, calls at the inn, asking for Billy Bones.

As events turn out, Jim finds himself on the high seas aboard the good ship Hispaniola. Captain Smollett is the captain and Squire

Trelawney and Dr Livesey are there, too, all bent on locating the lost treasure. Aboard too, though, is a sea-cook, a treacherous fellow by name Long John Silver. Lacking a leg, Silver hobbles along on a crutch but when mutiny breaks out, Silver is actively the ringleader.

The story ends with the treasure discovered, Long John Silver making good his escape and Jim, now a rich boy, returning to the loving arms of his mother.

Robert Lewis Balfour Stevenson was born November 30, 1850 in Edinburgh.

When he began to write, he altered the spelling of his second name Lewis to Louis and dropped the name Balfour.

Stevenson wrote several other well-known books, *Kidnapped*, *The Black Arrow* and *The Strange Case of Dr Jekyll and Mr Hyde*, together with *Treasure Island*, being the most popular of his novels while *A Child's Garden of Verse*, beloved of children, is full of delicate and beautiful poems.

On December 4, 1894 Stevenson died suddenly amidst the fairy-like beauty of Opolu, one of the Samoan Islands. He went to Samoa because he had been commissioned to write about the islands and strangely, before sailing, he had expressed doubts about going.

Billy Bones, in *Treasure Island* leads a chorus of *Fifteen Men on the Dead Man's Chest*

LORD BYRON ENLISTED IN A FOREIGN ARMY AND DIED LATER IN THE ARMY'S COUNTRY. WHAT COUNTRY?
Greece.

WHAT ARE THE NAMES OF THE FAIRY KING AND QUEEN IN SHAKESPEARE'S PLAY *A MIDSUMMER NIGHT'S DREAM?*
Oberon and Titania.

WHAT WAS THOMAS HARDY'S FIRST PROFESSION?
At the age of 16 he was apprenticed to an architect and later worked for an architect in London.

WHAT DID WYNKYN DE WORDE DO?
He printed books. His real name was Jan van Wynkyn. He assisted William Caxton and in 1491 succeeded him.

WHO WERE THE TWO MEN WHO WENT ROUND THE WORLD IN EIGHTY DAYS IN JULES VERNE'S GREAT BOOK?
Phileas Fogg and his manservant, Passepartout.

WHO WROTE THE BOOK ON WHICH WALT DISNEY'S FILM *THE SWORD AND THE STONE* IS BASED?
Terence Hanbury White (1906-1964).

THE ENGLISH POET WHO WROTE *LA BELLE DAME SANS MERCI* DIED WHEN HE WAS ONLY 26. WHO WAS HE?
John Keats (1795-1821). He died in Rome and is buried there.

WHO WAS SHERE KHAN?
In Rudyard Kipling's *Jungle Book*, Shere Khan is a tiger, the deadly enemy of Mowgli, the story's hero.

IN WHICH TWO BOOKS BY ROBERT LOUIS STEVENSON IS DAVID BALFOUR THE HERO?
Kidnapped and *Catriona*.

WHAT WERE THE CHRISTIAN NAMES OF THE THREE BRONTE SISTERS?
Charlotte, Emily and Anne.

WHO WROTE THE FAMOUS BIOGRAPHY OF DR SAMUEL JOHNSON?
James Boswell, friend and·travelling companion of Johnson.

TO WHOM IN THE BIBLE DID JESUS SAY: "FEAR NOT, HENCEFORTH THOU SHALT CATCH MEN"?
Peter, the disciple.

WHO CREATED MARY POPPINS?
Pamela Lyndon Travers, born in Australia in 1906. She was conval-

escent after an illness when she wrote the first Mary Poppins stories.

WHO WROTE WYNKEN, BLYNKEN AND NOD?

Eugene Field (1850-1895), an American journalist and poet.

WHO LIVED AT DOVE COTTAGE IN THE ENGLISH LAKE DISTRICT?

William Wordsworth (1770-1850), famous for his poems on nature.

WHAT WAS THE YEARLING?

The yearling is a tame fawn, the pet of young Jody Baxter in the book *The Yearling* by American author Marjorie Kinnan Rawlings (1896-1953).

WHO WROTE THE BRER RABBIT STORIES?

Joel Chandler Harris (1848-1908) who was born in Georgia, U S A. He was a printer's devil before working as a journalist on various newspapers.

IN WHOSE BOOK DOES A FEMALE VAMPIRE APPEAR?

Joseph Sheridan Le Fanu (1814-1873) wrote *In A Glass Darkly* in which appears the short story *Carmilla*, who is the vampire. It appeared 25 years before *Dracula* was published.

WHAT WAS BRAM STOKER'S MOST FAMOUS BOOK?

Dracula. Born Abraham Stoker in 1847, he wrote many novels and short stories now largely forgotten. He died in 1912.

WHICH AUTHOR WAS ONCE APPOINTED CHIEF SCOUT OF AMERICA?

Ernest Thompson (1860-1946), who wrote under the pen-name of Ernest Thompson Seton. He wrote animal stories.

GINGER AND MERRYLEGS APPEAR IN WHICH BOOK BY ANNA SEWELL?

Black Beauty. They are two horses, friends of Black Beauty.

WHO WAS THE GREAT HERO OF *THE SCOTTISH CHIEFS*?

William Wallace (1272-1305), known as "The Scourge of England". The book is by Jane Porter (1776-1850).

WHO WAS THE NOVELIST WHO INVENTED THE PILLAR BOX FOR POSTING LETTERS?

It was Anthony Trollope (1815-1882), who apart from his writing activities was a post-office surveyor. It was while he was travelling around the country on his post-office duties that he wrote in pencil his novel *Barchester Towers*, published in 1837.

JANE LANE BRAVELY HELPED KING CHARLES II TO ESCAPE AFTER THE BATTLE OF WORCESTER IN 1651 BUT WHY IS HER NAME FAMOUS TODAY?
Jane Lane is a modern-day author who has written many splendid novels for children and adults as well as historical biographies. The majority of her books concern the Stuart period of British history.

WHAT FILM-OF-THE-BOOK WON NINE AWARDS BY THE ACADEMY OF MOTION PICTURE ARTS AND SCIENCES IN 1939?
This was Gone With The Wind by Margaret Mitchell. The awards it received were as follows: Best production, Clark Gable for best actor, Vivien Leigh for best actress, Hattie McDaniel for best supporting actress, direction, best-written screenplay, cinematography (colour), art direction, and film editing.

WHAT ARE THE NAMES OF THE THREE BOYS IN THE NOVEL THE CORAL ISLAND AND WHO WROTE IT?
The boys' names are Ralph, Jack and Peterkin and the book was written by Robert Michael Ballantyne (1825-1894).

IN THE BIBLE WHAT ARE THE NAMES OF THE THREE WISE MEN?
Balthazar, Caspar and Melchior.

WHAT WAS RICHARD HENRY DANA'S MOST FAMOUS BOOK?
R H Dana (1815-1882), was an American author and lawyer. His best-known book is Two Years Before the Mast.

WHO WROTE THE WORDS OF RULE BRITANNIA?
James Thomson (1700-1748), who was a famous British dramatist and poet. Thomas Arne (1700-1778), was responsible for the stirring music.

WHAT FAMOUS BATTLE IS DESCRIBED IN WILLIAM MAKEPEACE THACKERAY'S NOVEL VANITY FAIR?
Waterloo.

WHO WROTE THE CANTERBURY TALES?
Geoffrey Chaucer (1340?-1400), spent most of his life working for the monarchy. He served under Edward III, Richard II and Henry IV.

WHICH KING OF GREAT BRITAIN WROTE A BOOK ABOUT TOBACCO?
King James the First.

WHICH WAS THE BOOK HAILED AS "THE BEST BOOK ABOUT WALES" EVER PUBLISHED?
This was George Borrow's Wild Wales, its People, Language and

Scenery which was published in 1862. It was the popular journal *The Spectator* which printed this well-earned praise.

WHICH OF RICHARD BRINSLEY SHERIDAN'S POPULAR PLAYS WAS HIS FIRST PRODUCED IN LONDON?

The Rivals at Covent Garden in 1775. Sheridan, dramatist and poet, wrote several other witty plays, perhaps the best-known being *The School for Scandal, The Duenna* and *The Critic*.

Richard Brinsley Sheridan

WHICH POET WAS OLIVER CROMWELL'S SECRETARY FOR FOREIGN TONGUES?

John Milton.

WHO WAS BOZ AND WHY DID HE CHOOSE THIS PEN-NAME?

Charles Dickens adopted this pen-name during his early days as an author because it was the nickname of his brother Augustus.

In 1835 Charles began to contribute sketches to an evening edition of the newspaper *The Morning Chronicle*. The following year he collected the series into two volumes under the title *Sketches by Boz*.

His next work, *The Posthumous Papers of the Pickwick Club*, first issued in shilling parts was credited as "Edited by Boz".

WHO WAS NED BUNTLINE?

His real name was Edward Zane Carroll Judson (1823-1886) and he acquired fame as the author of many stories about Buffalo Bill in "dime" novels.

WHAT WERE "DIME" NOVELS?

They were popular stories that were published for a dime (ten cents). They were written in a very sensational style. Irwin Beadle & Co of New York were the first dime novel publishers in 1860.

A TINKER'S SON WROTE ABOUT THE TRAVELS OF A MAN NAMED CHRISTIAN. WHO WAS HE?

John Bunyan (1628-1688). Christian appears in *The Pilgrim's Progress*.

Plants and Animals

WERE GREYHOUNDS EVER FORBIDDEN?

Today, if you want to keep a dog you only need a dog licence. But back in the Middle Ages things were very different, especially if your dog was a greyhound.

It was in the time of Canute, the Danish king who reigned in England from 1016 until 1035, that the greyhound first became the subject of special laws. It was then that stern rules were made to protect the Royal Forests, or hunting grounds, from poaching by the ordinary people who used greyhounds to help them.

The fleet-footed greyhound was especially trained, and valued, as a hunting dog. Under Canute's laws, neither the peasants nor the serfs, who were little better than slaves, were allowed to keep these dogs. Even freemen, not of noble birth, if they dwelt within ten miles of a Royal Forest, could only keep a greyhound if it was deliberately lamed to prevent it from pursuing game.

The Royal Forests came to occupy so much of the land that there were few areas left where it **was** permitted to keep an active greyhound!

These harsh laws continued in force for much of the Middle Ages. A peasant lad who had a greyhound pup must have dreaded the coming of the king's officers whose duty it was to enforce the forest laws. Discovery would surely have led to the confiscation of the dog, and probably stern punishment for its owner.

WHERE DID GOLDFISH COME FROM?

Goldfish appear to have had their origin in China many, many centuries ago. First there were the natural goldfish (members of the carp family) which were greeny-bronze in colour. In an effort to obtain new varieties, cross-breeding began during the 4th century AD and in due course, goldfish of various shapes, colours and sizes were produced. Eventually, specimens reached other

The two-horned rhinoceros is in danger of extinction

lands, but it was late in the 17th century that goldfish were brought to Europe.

WHICH RHINOCEROS HAS TWO HORNS?

Unlike the single-horned Great Indian Rhinoceros which is most commonly seen in zoos, the two types of rhinoceros that live in Africa carry two horns. The black rhinoceros is the smaller of the two and feeds exclusively on leaves and the branches of bushes. The other is the white, or Burchell's Rhinoceros, which lives entirely on grass, and spends its time in open country. This is the largest land mammal apart from the elephant. It is not very aggressive, but it is not harmless. The rhinoceros is a dangerous and unpredictable animal. Being extremely short-sighted, the rhinoceros when it attacks, is guided by its keen sense of smell.

There are now only five varieties world-wide in existence — and even these are in some danger of extinction as a result of being hunted for their skins and their horns, which among superstitious tribes are supposed to have special medicinal qualities.

WHAT IS AN EARTH PIG?

The aardvark. This name is an Afrikaans word meaning earth pig.

This strange looking animal has a pig-like muzzle, donkey-like ears and powerful claws which it uses to rip down the walls of termites' nests. Termites are the aardvark's principal food and it extracts them from the nests with its long tongue. It will also seek them out in rotting wood, or descend upon them while they are on the march. It also eats soft-bodied insects and some fruit.

For a long time the anteaters, armadillos, sloths, pangolins and the aardvarks were all grouped together in an order of animals known as the Edentata, or toothless ones. Although they all differ widely in their habits and appearances, they all have in common the fact that they are without incisor or canine teeth in the front of the mouth. The aardvark has now been placed in the order of tubulidentata.

WHAT BIRD TAKES OFF LIKE A SEAPLANE?

The take-off of an albatross from the water is not unlike that of a seaplane. Stretching out its wings and extending its neck it paddles at full speed into the wind until its breast is out of the water, with its webbed feet frantically beating the surface. The moment it is airborne the albatross resumes its normal shape with its neck retracted and its feet drawn up.

The albatross, which is the largest of all sea birds, has the biggest wing span of any bird, and will often accompany a ship for days without ever being observed to settle on the water, continuing its flight, apparently unaffected even by stormy weather.

Its effortless flight has been the subject of much speculation. The general opinion is that it actually flies no higher than 46ft (14m), using the slight increase in wind speed at this height to remain airborne, as it glides and swoops in the wake of a ship.

Called the Cape sheep by sailors from its habit of frequenting the Cape of Good Hope, it was said to sleep in the air without any apparent motion of its wings. Sailors say that to shoot one is to bring bad luck on oneself. This legend was perpetuated in Samuel Taylor Coleridge's narrative poem, *Rime of the Ancient Mariner*. This tells the story of a sailor who, having shot an albatross, has been subjected to fearful penalties, before eventually being forgiven. But still tormented in his mind, the mariner continues to wander from land to land with his tale of woe, while at the same time pleading for all men to love God's creatures.

WHAT IS A QUINCE?

It is a small tree which bears a fruit that looks rather like a pear. It has an acid taste. For this reason it is not eaten raw although it is made into jellies and jams.

WHICH FROG IS OFTEN KEPT AS A PET AND CAN BE TRAINED TO EAT OUT OF ITS OWNER'S HAND?

The green tree frog of Australia.

OF WHAT COUNTRY IS THE MAPLE LEAF A NATIONAL EMBLEM?

Canada.

THE RED PANDA IS ALSO KNOWN BY WHAT OTHER NAME?

The cat-bear.

HOW DO FISH BREATHE IN THE WATER?

Every living creature must breathe. We live by breathing air into the lungs, which control the supply of oxygen to the blood. Fish live by sucking water into the gills, which extract the oxygen needed by the blood. The water is then discharged through the gill-clefts, or slits, behind the head. Our lungs cannot extract oxygen from water and so we drown, or suffocate, if kept under water too long. Gills cannot extract oxygen from the air, and so fish suffocate if kept out of water.

There are certain fish, however, like the mudfish, which have lungs as well as gills and therefore are able to live in or out of water. An even more notable example is the South American lungfish which lives in the Parana and Amazon river systems, for there it inhabits shallow swamplands and the stagnant backwaters where oxygen is sparse. The region is, moreover, liable to seasonal droughts and the lungfish is then forced to survive in the mud, where it breathes air until the rain returns.

The Australian lungfish, found in the Burnett River and its tributaries of South-east Queensland, lives in waters which do not dry up but often become stagnant with little oxygen in them. When this happens, the lungfish breathes air at the surface, filling its lungs by using its nostrils.

DOES THE ABOMINABLE SNOWMAN EXIST?

The existence or otherwise of the Abominable Snowman has long been a cause for speculation, going right back to the end of the 19th century, when rumours of it having been seen began to filter through to the West.

The alleged sightings of a hairy creature that was half man and half beast were not taken too seriously until a number of scientific expeditions returned with stories of having seen the footprints of a large creature in the snow. Faced with this "evidence", zoologists began to think that just perhaps the creature might exist in the Himalayan Mountains.

Interest in the Abominable Snowman or the Yeti, as it was called by the natives, increased still further in 1951 when photographs of tracks taken by a famous mountaineer named Eric Shipton, were published. These showed enormous footprints in the snow, which might or might not have belonged to the Abominable Snowman. Over the next few years a number of expeditions were mounted solely with the object of finding the creature, but none of them succeeded in definitely proving it existed.

In 1960, Sir Edmund Hillary returned with a skin lent to him by some villagers which they claimed to be a skin of a Snowman, which had been in their possession for 240 years. But on examining it, the scientists mutually agreed that it could not have belonged to a Snowman.

The existence or otherwise of the Abominable Snowman therefore remains unanswered to this day.

WHICH CREATURE CAN IMITATE A FLOWER?

This is an insect called the empusa. Known as the "Little Devil" in the Mediterranean countries where it lives, the empusa is related to the grasshopper and the praying mantis and can be distinguished from them by what looks like a bishop's mitre growing out of the top of its head. It has a light green body with touches of rose pink at the edges, with green and white stripes on the underside. With such brilliant colouring this insect has little difficulty in deceiving its prey.

When it is hungry, the empusa adopts its characteristic stance on the leaves of a bush or plant to take on the shape of an anemone. This pose is not to protect itself from its enemies as is the case with leaf insects, but to mislead insects into believing that it is a flower so that it can entice them within reach of its vicious looking legs. This means that instead of going in search of its prey, as most other creatures have to, the empusa can lie in wait for its food to come along.

An unsuspecting insect passing by is instantly attracted by the colour and shape of the "flower," and as soon as it draws near, receives a sharp blow from the "mitre" on the insect's head. Before its prey can recover from the shock, the empusa lashes forward its fearsome forelegs, and the victim is trapped. Once caught in the empusa's deadly, unshakeable hold, the insect is helpless, and is promptly devoured.

DOES A FISH HAVE A VOICE?

All animals and birds have ways of making sounds which are understood by their own kind; fish, therefore, make sounds. For example, the conger eel has a bark.

Tests on deep sea fish produced many strange sounds, among them a noise rather like that of an aeroplane engine and made by the

A pangolin feeds on ants and termites

which enables the fish to adjust itself to varying levels. The swimbladder is really the equivalent of the lung in land creatures, but in many fish is an organ for the making of sounds.

WHAT HAVE BEEN CALLED ANIMATED PINE-CONES?

Pangolins have sometimes been called this because the hair on their backs has been converted into large overlapping brown scales, and with the exception of their undersides these scales cover the whole of their body. This gives them very much the appearance of a pine cone.

These strange-looking scaly beasts, which are to be found in Africa and Asia, are nocturnal. They feed on ants and termites, and like other anteaters, rip open ant and termite nests with their strong claws and then lick up the insects with their long sticky tongues.

Although pangolins live mostly on the ground they can swim and climb trees but this they do slowly and laboriously by hitching themselves up, first with their front and then with their back legs. While doing this, their tails are pressed against the tree trunk for extra support.

Pangolins are in an order of their own, Pholidota, and their name comes from the Malay word meaning "roller" which refers to their habit of curling up into a ball for protection.

North American toad fish. Honks, hisses, mooing, grinding of teeth, these are all sounds made by deep water fish.

The sounds are caused through the vibrations of the swimbladder, which is beneath the backbone and contains air or gas

THE GREATER CELANDINE IS A MEMBER OF THE POPPY FAMILY. TO WHICH FAMILY DOES THE LESSER CELANDINE BELONG?
The buttercup family.

IS IT TRUE THAT A RACCOON WASHES ITS FOOD BEFORE EATING IT?
The raccoon of the American continent is a furry land animal about the size of a badger which spends much of its time in the water in search of fish, crayfish and oysters and mussels which it crushes with its strong teeth. It has the curious habit of seeming to wash its food before eating, but this has only been seen when it is in captivity. Recent studies of the raccoon have shown that on entering the water it paddles its fore paws, even when it does not hold food, so there is no good reason to suppose it is washing its food when it holds something edible.

HOW LONG CAN A SEAL REMAIN UNDER WATER?
Ten minutes.

WHAT IS A BABY GOOSE CALLED?
A gosling.

IS A FROG AN AMPHIBIAN OR A REPTILE?
An amphibian.

WHEN DID THE WOOLLY RHINOCEROS BECOME EXTINCT?
In the First Ice Age, about 500,000 years ago.

WHICH NIGHT HUNTER HAS AN EERIE SPINE-CHILLING LAUGH?
The hyena.

IS A SPIDER AN INSECT?
No. It is an arachnid.

WHAT IS A GRIFFON VULTURE?
A Griffon vulture is a carrion bird that can go without food for days on end without any inconvenience, while at the same time gorging itself to the utmost when it does break its fast. This enormous capacity for eating, while also being capable of long periods of fasting is more than a little useful to a creature which is never sure where its next meal is coming from. The Griffon is born ravenous. In one day a very young bird has been known to devour a carp, a kite and the entrails of several birds before tucking into an additional meal of wood and soil.

The Griffon vulture can be found in various regions right across Central Asia as well as in North and South Africa.

WHICH IS THE LARGEST BIRD OF PREY?
The Andean Condor.

WHAT TYPE OF FOOD DO FROGS AND TOADS EAT?

Insects, worms and snails.

DOES THE IRISH ELK LIVE IN IRELAND?

No. The Irish Elk no longer exists. It was a large species of elk, so-named because remains of this extinct animal have been found in Ireland.

WHAT IS A FEMALE RABBIT CALLED?

A doe.

WHICH ANTS TAKE CAPTIVES?

Both the warrior ants and the Amazon ants raid the nests of other ants and take captives, carrying off the pupae to their own homes, where they are hatched, reared and brought up to work and fight for their captors.

The warrior ants are larger than the Amazon ants and are said to exhibit more intelligence when going out on one of their slave hunting expeditions. Unlike the Amazon ants which made a headlong rush upon their victims, the warrior ants lay siege to and surround the next they intend to rob. It sometimes happens that a colony of warrior ants meets a rival party of Amazons, with the result that a pitched battle often follows, with heads and legs being nipped off by the powerful jaws of the combatants.

THE JERBOA IS A NATIVE OF WHICH PART OF THE WORLD?

Central and Southern Asia and North Africa.

WHAT DOES THE WORD JAPONICA MEAN IN THE NAME OF A PLANT?

It means that the plant originally came from Japan.

WHAT IS AN UNGULATE?

A hoofed animal

THE NAME GILT IS GIVEN TO WHICH TYPE OF PIG?

A young sow.

TO WHICH INSECT FAMILY DO FIREFLIES AND GLOW-WORMS BELONG?

The beetle family.

A GUANACO IS THE WILD FORM OF WHICH WELL-KNOWN ANIMAL?

The llama.

TO WHICH WILD ANIMAL DOES THE LATIN NAME OF FELIS LEO APPLY?

The lion.

WHAT SORT OF FLOWER IS A HEARTSEASE?

A pansy.

The name of panda means "bamboo eater"

WHO DISCOVERED THE PANDA?

The panda was discovered by a famous 19th century French explorer, a missionary named Père David, who had made a reputation for himself while in China, where he had found a large number of plants and insects, many of which bear his name.

His discovery of the panda came about quite by accident. In 1869, while in Szechawen, he was invited to the home of a local landowner where he saw the pelt of an animal which resembled that of a furry creature he had seen on a number of Chinese vases. Until then, he had thought the creature did not really exist.

Excited by seeing the fur, Père David asked if any of the creatures could be captured for him. A few days later, two specimens, one dead and one living, were brought to him. Later, others were found and in the same year the first panda, so called from a native word meaning bamboo eater, arrived at the London Zoo. It later disappeared from the zoo and was never found.

Expeditions were hastily mounted to find another panda, but no trace of one could be found.

The panda did not reappear again until President Theodore Roosevelt's two sons came across one on a hunting expedition — and promptly shot it. Other pandas were found later and wantonly shot by other "sportsmen." In 1937, a Mrs Ruth Harkness managed to find one and succeeded in getting it unharmed to a zoo in Chicago, where it killed itself by overeating.

From that point on, the situation with regard to the panda began to improve, first with Mrs Harkness finding another which was followed by the discovery of four more, one of them becoming a great attraction at the New York World's Fair of 1939-1940.

By now the Chinese Government had become concerned at the widespread hunting of the panda that was taking place, which it feared might lead to the animal's extinction. From then on, casual hunting of the panda was forbidden.

Père David died in 1900. He is remembered today not only for his discovery of the panda, but also for the discovery of a species of deer, which were called Père David's deer in his honour.

WHAT IS A CROWN-OF-THORNS?

It is a starfish that lives off the coral of Australia's Great Barrier Reef, leaving in its wake vast areas of lifeless limestone skeletons as it works its way southward. Already much of the reef has been stripped bare by starfish which may have up to 23 arms. Its spines, which give this starfish its name, contain a venomous toxin that can cause severe vomiting in humans.

In the past one of its few natural enemies has been the triton shellfish. The triton shellfish is now much sought after for its shell and this in turn has led to it becoming relatively scarce enabling the "crown of thorns" to continue destroying the Great Barrier Reef.

WHICH ANIMALS HAVE TAILS WITH SPECIAL NAMES?

Several animals have tails with particular names. For instance, the rabbit's tail is a *scut*, the tail of a fox is a *brush* while that of the boar is called a *wreath*. The wolf's tail is a *stern* and so is the hound's. Not surprisingly, the tail of the otter is a *rudder* and the deer's tail is a *single*.

In all vertebrate animals (that means animals with a backbone), the tail is an extension of the backbone. It contains no vital organs but consists entirely of bone and muscle. Fishes use their tails mostly as a means of moving, but some monkeys use their tail as a fifth "hand," or for grasping branches of trees or their perches in zoos. The prickly porcupine uses its tail for defensive purposes, and all leaping animals, such as kangaroos, use them as "balancers," or "sit-downs."

Horses and cattle must be grateful for their tails for they can use them to ward off flies in the summer time. Dogs wag their tails when they are pleased and cats when they are displeased, so really, every tail has a "tale" to tell.

Chameleons wrap their prehensile tails around a branch to steady themselves when they aim

their long tongues to snap up insects, while the beaver uses its tail as a paddle or oar when swimming. One of the strangest tails is the rattlesnake's. The tip consists of a number of loosely connected horny segments which are vibrated to make a warning rattling noise. A species of porcupine native to South America also has a rattle which it uses for its defence as well as giving a warning to others.

Some creatures start with a tail but lose it as they develop. An example of this is the frog. In its tadpole stage it has a long tail, but as it changes into a frog the tail disappears.

OF WHAT USE TO A LEOPARD IS ITS SPOTTED COAT?

The leopard is an animal that lives in the forests of Africa and Asia, where the sun filtering through the trees gives a spotted effect to the ground where the leopard stalks. The leopard's spotted coat, therefore, blends perfectly into this background, helping to hide the animal from its prey and its enemies.

Many hunters believe that the leopard is the most frightening of all the wild cats. Anecdotes abound from hunters of pursuit and combat, usually resulting in a fight to the finish with this fierce creature which will sometimes attack a man without the slightest provocation. It hunts ceaselessly and will prey on anything from small birds to antelopes and cattle. Some of them have taken to hunting for man, even going into their homes to seek out their prey. The fact that they can run, jump, climb trees and swim makes them really formidable enemies.

They can be tamed when young, but as their wild nature is liable to reassert itself when they grow older, no tamer could really trust them. Yielding to no other animal in its ferocity, it often kills more victims than it can devour at once, merely to satisfy its blood lust.

WHICH DEER HAS BEEN DOMESTICATED?

The only deer that has been domesticated is the reindeer, an animal that the Laplanders, living in the Arctic Circle, have trained to carry out most of the work which in other countries is done by cattle.

As well as providing the Lapps with milk, cheese and meat, the reindeer has become a reliable pack animal, and can carry heavy loads over the snow where horses would flounder. Each foot of the reindeer has a pair of hoofs in front and a second pair at the back and sides. Between these hoofs is a patch of dense coarse hair and it is this which stops the reindeer slipping on the icy ground.

The Lapps waste nothing when they kill a reindeer. Its hide is used for clothing, its sinews are for making into thread and its bones as needles.

DO ANY BIRDS HIBERNATE?

The North American poorwill is a bird that hibernates by falling asleep during much of the winter. During this period its oxygen consumption is almost nil. As a result its body mechanism slows down so much that it is able to survive throughout the most severe winter without any harmful effects, living only on a minute portion of its body fat. One bird was known to have slept without interruption for 88 days.

This bird, which is known to the Hopi Indians as "the sleeper", catches its food in flight by flying with its beak wide open to take in flying insects.

WHAT BEETLE WAS IMPORTANT IN THE LIVES OF THE ANCIENT EGYPTIANS?

The scarab beetle. This insect was considered to be sacred by the Ancient Egyptians for whom it was a symbol of their Sun God.

The scarab is a form of dung beetle which is to be found in many warm parts of the world. It is very useful in fertilising the earth because it gathers together the manure left by larger animals. The scarab beetle lays its eggs in the manure and then rolls it up into a ball about the size of a crab apple and buries it — a Herculean task for so small a creature.

The Ancient Egyptians believed that the beetles rolled these balls from sunrise to sunset — the ball representing the Earth and the beetle representing the Sun. They thought the beetles buried the ball for twenty nine days and then on the thirtieth unearthed it and cast it into the Nile, where a new beetle emerged from it, fully formed.

WHY IS THE CUCKOO A BAD MOTHER?

The cuckoo has a reputation for being a bad mother which is certainly well deserved. She does not build a nest and to bring up her young the cuckoo victimises a small bird such as a reed warbler, a hedge sparrow or a robin, by removing one egg from a nest, where three or four have been laid, and replacing it with one of her own. When the egg hatches, the young cuckoo is very sensitive to touch and will kick and jerk if the other fledglings in the nest touch it. One by one, the young "rightful" occupants are kicked out of their home until only the cuckoo is left. In this way the gluttonous baby receives all the food that would have been given to the other birds. This makes it grow at an alarming rate, but it still clamours for food from its unfortunate foster parents, even after it has left the nest.

The cuckoo is unique among British birds in another way because the adults start the migration journey back to their winter quarters in Africa, in late July or early August, some weeks before their youngsters are ready to fly.

It remains a mystery how these young birds, completely neglected by their real parents, are able to make the long and difficult journey to Africa over sea and land entirely unaided.

WHAT HAS A TRUNK LIKE AN ELEPHANT?

The tapir, which is among the most ancient of living mammals, has a pig-like body and a head which tapers into a snout so elongated it could almost be a trunk.

Tapirs are hoofed mammals, but unlike all other members of their family they have four toes on the front feet. Their hind feet have three toes, like the rhinoceros, whose ancestors they are thought to be.

The tapir is also unique among mammals in that it has hardly changed for 55 million years. Fossilised skeletons which have been found are nearly identical in their formation to the bodies of the tapirs that exist today.

Normally, tapirs are docile and very timid, and will rush off into the undergrowth when disturbed. But if they are cornered with their young by a wild and dangerous creature like a jaguar or alligator, they will attack with a savagery that is surprising in such a normally gentle creature.

Tapirs are found in two main regions. One species known as the Malayan tapir lives in the jungles of Malaya, Burma and Thailand and the island of Sumatra. Three

A mother wolf prepares to defend her family

other species live in Central and South America.

DO WOLVES HUNT MAN?

It is not a characteristic trait of wolves to hunt man. In fact, all those stories we have read of packs of wolves silently padding through the snows in pursuit of a fleeing sledge or Russian troika are nothing more than pure fiction.

Wolves do hunt in packs, and they often attack animals larger than themselves, or follow herds of caribou, until they are able to "cut" one of them out from the herd, often using great cunning and well thought-out team work to separate the animal from the rest.

Each pack, generally made up of several families, ranges over established trails which can cover an area of more than a thousand square kilometres. They move fast and far when hunting, often covering fifty to sixty kilometres in a single night.

A wolf's diet varies according to what is available. Elk, reindeer, cattle and deer are its favourite fare, but it will make do quite happily on a diet of hares, birds and even the occasional reptile when times are hard. When it does make a kill it gorges itself, eating up to one fifth of its own weight at a time, always bolting down its food at a fast rate — hence the phrase to "wolf one's food." When a pack does bring down a quarry, they share it without quarrelling.

ARE LIZARDS POISONOUS?

There are only two living poisonous lizards and these are to be found in the deserts of Arizona and Mexico. One of them is the gila monster, which is recognisable by its brightly contrasting colouration of black and orange or pink. It grows to a maximum of 60 cm (2 ft) and is smaller than the other poisonous lizard, the beaded lizard of Mexico. Unlike most snakes they do not inject their venom, but chew on their victim, while gradually discharging their venom, which is rarely fatal to humans.

WHO IS MAN'S DEEP SEA FRIEND?

Dolphins have been the friends of man for many centuries, following ships and playing around them with obvious enjoyment, often for hours on end. Sailors have always considered their presence a good omen for a voyage.

Stories abound about how they have tried to help humans in trouble, mostly from sailors who had firmly believed that a dolphin had tried to save them from drowning or had driven a shark away when they had been shipwrecked. Some of these stories can be possibly attributed to the fact that dolphins are the natural enemy of sharks. As for helping sailors from drowning, this may have been merely a display of a dolphin's playful friendliness. But against all this one has to place the countless eye-witness accounts of dolphins going to the aid of another dolphin in distress. It seems reasonable, therefore, to believe that they have tried to do the same for humans with whom they have an undoubted empathy as one can see merely by visiting an oceanarium, where the dolphins show quite clearly that they enjoy the presence of humans. It is known that they have chased sharks away from life-rafts.

The Roman writer, Pliny the Elder, wrote of a dolphin which carried a boy regularly on its back across a bay to a school until the day the boy died. The dolphin then came each day to where they had met until it realised that the boy would never come again, whereupon it died of a broken heart. Fanciful though this story may be, it shows how highly the dolphin was regarded.

In recent years a great deal of additional data has been gathered about the dolphin — even that it has an ear for music and may well have a recognisable language of its own — all of it proving that dolphins are the most intelligent of all the mammals of the sea.

WHAT IS A GERENUK?

A gerenuk is a form of gazelle from East Africa which has the habit of standing erect on its hind legs to browse on the foliage of trees. This is made possible because it is quite unlike any other gazelle in that it has long, spindly legs and an extremely long neck.

Also known as the giraffe-necked gazelle, it was first seen by a European in 1878, when a missionary named Horace Waller found it on the coast of East Africa. The local Africans called the animal a gerenuk. Puzzled by its appearance, Waller sent it to a zoologist named Henry Brooke who gave it the name of *Gazella Walleri* in honour of the man who had discovered it.

The gerenuk is a confirmed nibbler of food from the trees, choosing to munch from its leaves rather than eat grass even when it is available. Gerenuks kept in zoos behave in exactly the same manner, ignoring grass and other food that can be picked from the ground.

WHAT ANIMAL HAS WEBBED FEET, A DUCK'S BILL AND LAYS EGGS?

The creature which has all these characteristics is the duckbilled platypus, an Australian animal that was eventually classified under a new order of mammals, the Monotreme. Only one other creature shares this order with it — the spiny anteater, another Australian animal.

The first platypus was discovered in 1797. This extraordinary animal which seemed to have a duck's beak attached to the head of a quadruped was greeted with such disbelief when it was first seen in England that an eminent scientist declared it to be a fake animal. Today, it is one of Australia's best known animals, even though it is a shy creature. It is seldom seen as it inhabits the lakes and streams of Eastern Australia and Tasmania, regions which are sparsely populated by man.

The platypus is a strong swimmer which makes its way through the water propelled by its webbed front feet, while it steers itself by its rear feet. The beaver-like tail controls its up and down movement as it dives to the bottom for food before coming up to breathe. Its broad, flat beak is ideal for grubbing in the sandy or muddy river bottoms.

Although it is a very strong swimmer, the platypus spends only a few hours a day in the water. The rest of the time it stays in the burrow it has made for itself in a river bank. It is here that the female lays her eggs, mostly only two of them at a time.

HOW DID THE MANX CAT LOSE ITS TAIL?

According to legend the Manx lost its tail because it arrived late at the entrance to Noah's Ark. Impatient to be off, Noah slammed the great door shut on its tail.

Manx cats, which come from the Isle of Man, are called rumpies or stumpies, according to whether they possess absolutely no tails at all, or just rudimentary tails. The genuine native products are the totally tail-less rumpies, always considered more valuable both as national assets and as household pets than cross-bred stumpies.

Tail-less cats have in fact existed in other parts of the world, and no-one is quite sure just how they ever reached the Isle of Man.

HOW DOES THE SNAKE'S VENOM FORM?

All snakes have salivary glands and the secretions from these glands help them to swallow any big objects they might otherwise have trouble in taking down. In venomous snakes some of these salivary glands have been adapted into poison producers.

Snake venom is made up from a variety of substances, mostly proteins and enzymes that can have a fatal effect when pumped into the body of the snake's victim. Some of the substances act on the circulatory system, clotting blood cells while at the same time destroying capillary walls. Others act on the nervous system, paralysing the muscles of the heart, or the breathing system, or both.

WHY DO LEAVES CHANGE COLOUR IN THE AUTUMN?

The green colouring of leaves comes from a chemical matter called chlorophyll. It is in grass and all other plants that are green and it is vital to them, for it absorbs light and air and in a wonderful and mysterious way turns them into food which helps to make plants grow. The trees and shrubs we call evergreens shed their leaves gradually and at all seasons of the year. Other trees take a rest in winter and get rid of all their leaves; but they first take from the leaves everything that will be useful. While this is happening the leaves turn to gold and yellow and purple colours that make trees so beautiful in the autumn.

WHICH ANIMAL'S HEAD IS CONSIDERED A GREAT DELICACY?

The wild boar's head which has long been considered a great delicacy was once served with a great deal of ceremony. At one time at Queen's College, Oxford, it was brought to the table on Christmas Day accompanied by a stately procession and the singing of a Christmas carol. Even today, it still remains something of a delicacy.

The wild boar stands three feet high and four feet in length.

From the earliest times the boar has been one of the favourite beasts of the chase and honoured for its great speed, strength and ferocity when at bay. Under the old forest laws, it was classified as one of the "beasts of the forest," and under the Normans its killing by an unauthorised person was punishable by death or the loss of

The wild boar enjoys wallowing in mud

a vital limb — an arm or a leg.

Despite their reputation for ferocity, wild boars are not, by nature, killers. They are quiet, sociable animals when with their own kind. They are very partial to beetroot, potatoes and artichokes, but they will also feed on chestnuts, acorns, insects and any form of fallen fruit.

Their dormant aggressive nature only shows itself during the mating season when savage duels take place between the males often causing terrible injuries to each other. Otherwise, the wild boars lead a quiet, amiable existence, unless they are attacked or think they are about to be attacked by a human.

The okapi can run very fast through the Congo rain forest

WHERE ARE CANARIES FLYING IN THE WILD FOUND?
In the Canary and Azores Islands.

WHICH ANIMAL HAS LEGS LIKE A ZEBRA?
The okapi, a member of the Giraffe family, that has legs resembling those of a zebra with their black and white stripes.

The okapi was discovered in 1878 by an African explorer from Germany named Wilheim Junker, who thought it might be a zebra-antelope.

This very timid and elusive animal is mainly nocturnal in its habits and lives alone or in pairs in the densest parts of the forest where it feeds on plants, fruit and leaves.

WHAT IS A GROUP OF FOXES CALLED?
A skulk.

WHAT WAS THE HEAVIEST OF ALL PREHISTORIC ANIMALS?
The brachiosaurus.

WHAT IS A SKEWBALD?
It is a horse that is white and any other colour except black.

WHO WHERE THE FIRST ZOOLOGISTS?
Aristotle, the Greek philosopher was the first man to be seriously interested in zoology when he decided he would classify animals and study their relationship to each other. This he was able to do because a relative and pupil of his named Callisthenes, supplied him regularly with wild animals. The project ended suddenly when Callisthenes incurred the displeasure of the king and was thrown in jail where he died.

Three hundred years later, a Greek historian named Diodorus wrote a 40 volume work, *The Library of History*, but his so-called nature facts were so fanciful they could not be taken seriously.

In AD 77, the Roman writer Pliny the Elder published his 37 volumes on natural history, but much of this was a rehash of other writers' work, and once again very little of it was reliable.

It was not until the end of the 14th century when the great age of discovery began, that reliable work was done in the field of natural history. The returning voyagers who had sailed to all corners of the world brought back with them all manner of exotic animals, and for the first time scientists were able to study them at first hand, instead of relying on travellers' stories for their facts.

WHICH BIRD WAS CONSIDERED AN EVIL OMEN?
This was the nightjar, a creature thought to be surrounded by mystery and myth, probably because of its shadowy appearance, and its almost reptilian cunning with camouflage. Of the family of birds known as goatsuckers, the nightjar is the largest. At one time countryfolk called the bird a goatsucker because they believed its huge gape enabled it to steal milk from their animals and turn them blind as a result.

An explanation of the origin of this ancient belief is provided by naturalists. It has arisen, they say, because of the bird's habit of hawking around the udders of animals in search of flies.

The strong chirping sound it makes has been feared as an omen of death. Nightjars were said to embody the souls of unbaptised infants doomed to wander forever in the air. Even today, the nightjars of the Amazon are not killed by local hunters because they believe them to be the souls of the departed.

Fables apart, the nightjar is no more offensive or threatening than a butterfly. They arrive from Africa in May. Their soft, grey-brown plumage is perfect camouflage, enabling them to blend into the background, where they may look like lichen-covered twigs or chunks of bark during the day. The nightjar will also rest on the ground among fallen leaves and it usually rests with its eyes closed. This is probably the only time the nightjar spends much time on the ground. Its feet and legs are so small that it can only shuffle along and, therefore, it flies from one spot to another.

It is at dusk when the nightjar begins its nocturnal hunt for a diet of insects. This is why nightjars are found in countries where there are large numbers of nocturnal insects and these the bird catches while in flight.

As their name suggests, nightjars are noisy during the night and their loud continuous calls do jar the night.

An unusual feature of the nightjar is its curious ability to create a whip-crack sound with its wings, usually during display in the mating season. Some naturalists believe it actually claps its wings together; others that the sheer force of the swift downbeat creates the strange sound.

WHAT ARE MARSUPIALS?

The "pouched ones", or marsupials, are a group of animals which have a pouch or protective skin around the female's teats, but some have two flaps of skin instead.

The pouch is a first home for baby marsupials, which are all born at a very early stage of development. They find their way to the pouch and there they feed and grow until fully developed.

Although marsupials were once found all over the world, most of them now live in Australia and nearby islands. The opossum is still found in North and South America.

The kangaroo is the best known marsupial, and lives only in Australia, Tasmania, New Guinea and other nearby islands. We usually associate it with Australia, and it is found on the Australian coat of arms.

There are over 120 kinds of kangaroo, ranging in size from the rat kangaroo, which is the size of a rabbit, to true kangaroos which are over nine feet from nose to tail.

Another famous Australian marsupial is the koala. The koala, which is often called the native bear of Australia, is not a true bear at all.

It is a tree-living marsupial. Its name means "no drink" because the koala never drinks, and it also has a very specialised diet. It feeds only on the leaves of particular species of eucalyptus trees of a certain age.

WHAT FISH HAS AN ARMOUR PLATING?

The trunkfish, also known as the boxfish or coffer fish, have their whole bodies enclosed with bony plates which leave only their fins and tails unprotected. The head is blended into the trunk, with the mouth being nothing more than a tiny round hole armed with powerful crushing teeth. The plating which encloses the fish is so rigid that only the tail, fins and mouth are capable of independent movement. Because the body has no flexibility the trunkfish has to rely on its tail to propel it.

This strange fish, which inhabits tropical waters in all parts of the world is doubly protected by its ability to change colour almost at will. One species found off the coast of America is green with blue spots and lines which it can change to a yellow background with blue spots. It has even been known to become completely white.

In order to gain additional protection some species of trunkfish are capable of releasing into the water a poison, toxic to other fish. Only strong and powerful fish like the moray eel are immune to the poison.

WHAT WAS THE SONG OF THE PRAIRIE?

When the Western States of America were less inhabited than they are today, anyone crossing them was almost certain to have heard what became known as "the song of the prairie." This was the song of the coyote, a hideous serenade of barks and howls. Despite the urbanization of the West, it can still be heard today in the more isolated areas.

That the coyote is still there is something of a miracle as its wholesale slaughter of wildstock led the U S Government to hire professional trappers to try and exterminate it. The trappers were so successful that they killed 1,800,000 coyotes between the years of 1915 and 1946. Despite this the almost uncanny intelligence of the coyote has made it possible for it to survive in the West and, moreover, manage to extend its territory from the Western Plains to as far east as New England.

Normally a lone individual looking very much like the gray wolf in appearance, the coyote lives today mostly on a diet of rabbits, carrion and small domestic animals.

DOES THE CROCODILE USE A TOOTH BRUSH?

In a sense it does. A small bird called the Egyptian plover, which is also known as the spur-winged plover, is the very successful tooth cleaner for the crocodile. This bird obtains its food by extracting parasites living inside the crocodile's mouth. The Egyptian plover is in no danger from the crocodile which will open its

The African and Indian elephants are becoming more rare in the wild

mouth in order that the bird can enter and peck out the scraps of food from between its teeth and to remove leeches from the crocodile's tongue.

This remarkable creature is, in fact, a tremendous help to the crocodile. Apart from acting as a highly efficient tooth-brush, it provides another valuable service for the crocodile. When any danger threatens, the bird will take sudden flight, its hurried escape thereby giving the alarm. Sometimes, the crocodile may not

heed this warning, and when this happens the intelligent Egyptian plover is said to peck continually at its head until the crocodile moves away to safety.

HOW DOES AN ELEPHANT USE ITS TRUNK?

Elephants use their trunks in many ways, apart from the more obvious one of taking in water to squirt into its mouth and for feeding itself.

In times of danger when an

elephant wants to frighten a potential enemy, the trunk is curled up and held over the back of its head. The next aggressive stage is for the trunk to be swung out rigidly, like a slightly upturned spear. This is a signal that at any moment it is going to make a frontal attack.

When standing around in family herds, elephants use their trunks constantly to feel, caress, reassure and communicate with each other. Their trunk movements have many complicated meanings, not the least of them being a way to express its social status in the herd. The strongest animal in the herd will always extend a stiffened trunk towards a weaker one's mouth as a sign of its dominance.

But the most complex and beautiful trunk movements are reserved for a smooth and graceful sort of "love dance" that elephants perform to show affection before they mate.

In India where the elephant is still a working animal, the trunk is used for carrying and moving heavy loads. And anyone wanting to ride on an elephant will have to step on the elephant's trunk which it will then raise to lift the rider on to its back.

HOW MANY KINDS OF THE CACTUS PLANT ARE THERE?

There are about 2,000 different species of these fascinating plants. Most of them are prickly and have very long names. Some, like the Trichocereus, grow six feet high or more in their native deserts; others are tiny. As a rule, cacti do not have leaves, but have thick, strangely shaped forms in which they store up moisture, for they grow in hot, dry countries. They also have barbed hairs or sharp spines which protect them from animals.

Some of the most popular kinds are the Opuntias, with their flat round pads; the Rebutias (rather like prickly globes); and the finger-shaped Mamillaria. One unusual cactus is the Christmas Cactus, or Zygo-cactus. It grows in the tropical forests of South America, clinging to the branches of trees.

DOES AN OSTRICH REALLY BURY ITS HEAD IN THE SAND?

No. When an ostrich is being pursued, it may drop down in a heap so that from a distance it looks like a pile of stones or a hillock in the desert. On doing this it puts its long neck forward, flat on the ground, so that its head cannot be seen. Early travellers thought that the head was buried in the sand and this gave rise to the legend that these birds are under the impression that if they cannot see anything, then they themselves cannot be seen; so when people say that somebody is acting like an ostrich, they mean that that person chooses to ignore unpleasant facts rather than face them.

WHICH INSECT USES A "BOLAS" TO CATCH ITS PREY?

When a gaucho, as the South American cowboy is called, has to capture a steer he uses a bolas which consists of two round stones attached to each end of a hide rope. Connected to the centre of this rope is another much longer rope. To bring down a steer, the gaucho fastens the free end of the rope to his saddle and whirls the stones round his head. Riding beside the animal to be captured, he lets go of the rope and the stones hurtle away and tangle the rope around the legs of the steer.

Long before the first gaucho caught a steer, the mastaphora spider had been capturing its prey with a form of bolas.

Most spiders weave silk nets or webs in which to ensnare their prey. The mastaphora, found throughout the American continent, is one of the few spiders that does not make a web. Instead it weaves silk ropes to make a bolas. The bolas itself is made from a viscous liquid which is pushed along the line to form at its end a shining globule which dries into a solid ball. Once this has been done, the spider suspends itself on a loopline like an acrobat, while holding the weighted line with one of its front legs. When a victim comes within range, the spider throws the line forward in the direction of the flying insect. The weight on the end of the line causes the thread to wrap itself round the insect. The spider then injects the insect with a venom which paralyses it. The victim is then quickly bound up with silk thread and stored away.

WHAT IS THE COMMON NAME FOR THE INDOOR PLANT NAMED IMPATIENTS?

Busy Lizzie.

WHAT IS DRESSAGE?

It is the training of a horse in obedience and deportment.

DOES A GIRAFFE HAVE MORE JOINTS IN ITS NECK THAN A MAN?

No. Both have the same number of neck joints.

HOW DO ANTS COMMUNICATE WITH EACH OTHER?

By means of the antennae or feelers projecting from their heads.

DO CENTIPEDES HAVE 100 PAIRS OF LEGS?

Centipedes do not always have 100 pairs of legs as their name implies. Some have more than that, while others only have 28.

The flat bodies are made up of many segments joined together and each segment has a pair of legs growing out of it.

The two types of centipede most often seen in English gardens are the *lithobius* and the *geophilus* (unfortunately there are no simple, common names for them). Centipedes can grip a slug in their two poisonous claws which are like little legs on the first segment of their body near the head. Once the victim is caught, the poisonous liquid flows from the curved, hollow organs of the claws and is injected into the prey's body, instantly paralysing it.

This poison is harmless to man but there are some tropical centipedes capable of inflicting a painful bite which can cause a fever in human beings.

WHAT SEA-CREATURE LOOKS LIKE A PIECE FROM A CHESS SET?

This is the seahorse which looks like the knight from a chess set. This oddity of nature spends much of its time with its tail wrapped around seaweed from where it snaps up any creature small enough to enter its mouth. Its eyes are on turrets and move independently. It swims in a vertical position, while propelling itself along by rapid movements of the dorsal fin which may oscillate up to thirty five times a second, giving it the impression of a revolving propeller. The male carries the babies in a pouch deposited there by the female.

There are twenty known species of seahorse, half of them living in the Indo-Australasian region. The others live off the Atlantic coasts of Europe and North America.

HOW IS SOIL FORMED?

By the action of weather on rock, also by the presence of vegetation and movement of animals. Frost, ice and wind, and running water break the rock into smaller pieces and dying vegetation releases a substance called carbon dioxide which, when dissolved in water, attacks many hardening minerals and adds organic matter to the soil. This process of soil making does not happen overnight. It has taken thousands of years to make the rich soil of our lands, and we must not forget the valuable part the earthworm takes in the forming and refining of the soil. There are various kinds of soil: loam, sand and marls. Humus soils are peaty and very rich, but some soils are poor and have to be chemically enriched.

WHAT HAPPENED TO THE GREAT AUK?

The Great Auk was a species of wild fowl that was gradually exterminated by man, the last of them being killed in 1844 on a group of islands off the southwest coast of Iceland. In the 18th century these birds were common to the Faroes and the Iceland seas, from where they were gradually driven from one settlement to another until their final extermination. In 1813 alone vast numbers of them were destroyed by sailors from a Faroes craft. As if nature was conspiring with man to destroy them, one of their haunts was engulfed by the sea, following a submarine eruption.

Even in earlier times, they were ruthlessly hunted for food. In 1536 French and English vessels forced them ashore in droves before killing and then salting them down for provisions.

Although man did much towards the extermination of the Great Auk, its habit of laying only one egg did nothing to help maintain the species.

WHICH BIRD EATS ITS FEATHERS?

It is the crested grebes that have the strange habit of regularly eating their own feathers, and it is thought that this makes it easier for them to regurgitate sharp fish bones in the form of pellets. But it is their spectacular and complicated courtship dance for which they are famous. A pair will approach one another with necks stretched along the water and then rear up chest to chest with heads high in the air, and engage in a gentle fencing match with their beaks, followed by vigorous head shaking. They then dive and come up above the surface of the water with beaks full of weed and again face each other for more head shaking and swaying from side to side before taking a rest.

WHAT ARE LEPIDOPTERA?

Lepidoptera is the name given to butterflies and moths. It means "scaly-winged," and refers to the tiny scales which cover the wings of these fascinating insects.

As they belong to the same order of insects, it is not always easy to tell moths and butterflies apart. One of the best ways to distinguish between them, apart from any difference in colour and shape, is by watching them at rest. Butterflies close their wings together so that they stick up from the back, and sometimes fan themselves with them in the heat of the sun. Moths, on the other hand, spread their wings out flat on the surface where they are resting. They may sometimes fold them over their backs either in the shape of scissor blades, or in an arch.

Both butterflies and moths use the same methods to escape from their enemies. Apart from simply hiding, they use camouflage, mimicry and protective colouring. Those which rely on camouflage look exactly like the surface on which they rest, or have colours and patterns which blend with their surroundings.

WHAT WAS THE GREAT BUFFALO MASSACRE?

Two things led to the near extinction of the American buffalo or bison. The first threat to them came when the Indians began hunting on horseback, instead of following the migratory hordes and killing them on foot. But this was still of small account compa-

Hunters set out to exterminate the buffalo

red to the wholesale slaughter that went on when American colonists set out   exterminate the buffalo in order to deprive the hostile Indians of their primary source of food. This began in the 1870s and became known as the Great Buffalo Massacre. Sadly, this was so successful that by 1889, a population of some 75 million buffaloes was reduced to a mere 540, a horrendous situation that led to the prairies being littered with the bones of the slaughtered buffalo. By the turn of the century, these few pitiful survivors were reduced to a mere few dozen.

Almost before it was too late, Congress realised the enormity of the crime that had been committed in the name of progress. In 1902, 50,000 dollars were set aside for the protection of the country's last herd in the Yellowstone National Park. Since then the buffalo have thrived.

CAN ANIMALS FORECAST THE WEATHER?

It has been known for a long time that swifts can detect the approach of an electric storm which they respond to by flying at right angles to the storm, or by simply migrating to an area well out of its path, returning only when the storm has passed.

Shepherds have long claimed that they can forecast the weather by the behaviour of their flocks, and a farmer in Texas even claimed that he could forecast the weather by the behaviour of his pigs. He proved the point under tests when his pigs correctly forecast eight rainstorms out of ten, while the local meteorologists forecast only one of them.

In New Zealand, scientists have established that the movements of moths give indications of the weather to come by their reaction to particles in the atmosphere.

HOW DID THE TURKEY GET ITS NAME?

A turkey for Christmas dinner is a tradition, although this bird of the pheasant family did not become very popular until towards the end of the eighteenth century. Its name has nothing to do with the European country of Turkey; in fact, the bird originally came from Mexico and was introduced into Europe by Spanish explorers of Central and South America in the sixteenth century.

The most likely theory is that the turkey got its name from the bird's call-note — turk, turk, turk.

WHICH ARE THE NOISIEST MONKEYS IN THE WORLD?

This doubtful honour belongs to the South American howler monkeys. They indulge in their vocal performances at intervals throughout the night, and will make the forest resound with their cries for several hours on end. The reason they are able to produce this large volume of noise for which they are so famous, is because they have a series of air sacs, or resounding chambers that extend along the front and sides of the neck, which intensifies every sound they emit. It is thought that the terrible din they make is to advertise their ownership of the territory they are occupying.

Howler monkeys are the largest of the New World monkeys, the male being the larger of the two. They are bearded and have prehensile tails.

WHAT IS A DAMSEL-FLY?

A smaller relation of the dragon-fly.

THE FLOWERS MARIGOLDS, LOBELIA AND MIGNONETTE ARE ALL ANNUALS. WHAT DOES THIS MEAN?

They flower and die in the same year as they are raised from seed.

WHAT IS AN EAGLE'S NEST CALLED?

An eyrie.

WHAT OTHER NAME FOR A STOAT IS USED ESPECIALLY TO DENOTE ITS WINTER COAT?

The ermine.

The flying fish will escape danger by darting out of the water

IS THERE A FISH THAT CAN REALLY FLY?

Approximately 60 species of so-called flying fish are known. However, they do not fly as birds do. All except one simply glide through the air. The single exception is the flying hatchet fish which can propel itself through the air by beating its fins as birds beat their wings.

The hatchet fish has very strong pectoral fins with large pectoral muscles and it is these fins that enable it to "fly". There are reports that the hatchet fish can "fly" for some 20 feet (about six metres). It is a native of South American waters. It feeds on flying insects which it gobbles up as it soars through the air. For this reason it is very beneficial for the people who live there because it keeps down the mosquito population in many streams.

WHAT IS A KNOT IN A PIECE OF WOOD?

The small brown rings in wood which we call knots are the places from which branches once grew out of the tree trunk. First, from the stem of the tree there would come a bud, which developed wood-cells as it grew. Outside these, further cells grew to form the bark, and in time the bud would have grown into a branch. When the branch was broken from the tree, the stump remained firmly in the trunk. So when a branch or tree trunk has been cut into timber, the stumps of other branches are also sawn through, to appear as the rings called knots.

The gorilla was first called a pongo

HOW DID THE GORILLA GET ITS NAME?

The name of this African animal has an interesting history. It was an African word for a wild, hairy man, and was first known in Europe about 500 P ⁆., when a Greek traveller na ed Hanna wrote an account of his voyage along the west coast of Africa. About 2,000 years later an English sailor named Andrew Battell brought home news of a big and hairy creature which the natives of West Africa called a Pongo.

From time to time after this, other travellers spoke of this big ape, but it was not until 1847 that more precise information about it reached the civilized world. In that year an English missionary sent skulls of the mysterious animal to scientists in London and Boston, together with sketches and a description which stated that it was much bigger than a chimpanzee and was much feared by the natives. An American scientific paper then published the description of the ape and called it a gorilla, taken from a Greek work *Gorillai*, used for an African tribe renowned for their hairy appearance.

The gorilla is the biggest and strongest of all the primates. It has few natural enemies except man, and is in no way aggressive unless provoked. Nomadic by necessity because of the large quantities of fruit it needs, it comes to a halt only at night. The gorilla often travels with other families.

WHAT IS A KOODOO?

A graceful antelope found in South and East Africa.

TO WHAT COUNTRY DOES THE KOLINSKY BELONG?

It is a polecat or mink which inhabits Siberia, in Russia.

WHICH ANIMALS WHEN ATTACKED APPEAR TO BE DEAD?

The opossums.

BLACKBERRIES ARE THE FRUIT OF WHICH PLANT?

The bramble.

WHAT ARE RAINBOW LORIKEETS?

They are members of a group of Australian multi coloured birds known as brush-tongued parrots. Their tongues are provided with a brush of tiny papillae for dealing with the very fine pollen of gum blossom which forms a very important part of their diet.

When Captain Cook's ship, *Endeavour*, was anchored in Botany Bay in 1770, one of the ship's crew took a Rainbow Lorikeet aboard as a pet. The captive survived its trip back to England where it was made famous when a coloured picture of it appeared in *New Illustrations of Zoology*, which appeared in 1774. It was the first picture ever in colour of an Australian parrot.

More than two centuries later, towns and cities have replaced much of the Lorikeet's bush habitat. but the Lorikeets are sociable birds and they have adapted easily to the change. They have become welcome visitors to gardens where food is put out for them. On a hot day the birds are happy to linger in the gardens, as there is always the hope that the owner will turn on his sprinkler and give them a shower bath which they love.

WHEN DID THE IDEA OF NATURE CONSERVATION BEGIN?

Not in modern times, as one might expect. King Henry VIII of England was one of the latter-day conservationists when he banned the hunting of wild fowl and the taking of their eggs during the months of June, July and August. At the same time he ordered that landowners should pay a bounty to anyone killing a crow, a bird notorious for its raid on birds' nests.

King James I, in turn, made a small contribution to the preservation of wild life when he encouraged the breeding stocks of game on private estates. Although the birds were killed afterwards as sport, it did lead to the establishment of natural habitats where the birds could breed in peace. The Victorian gentry were later to do this on a grand scale.

King Canute was actually the first man officially to set aside areas where animals and birds were allowed to breed before being hunted for sport. William the Conqueror later greatly extended those areas protecting them with harsh laws in places like Sherwood Forest where Robin Hood and his Merry Men were supposed to have roamed, killing deer for the pot, in defiance of laws forbidding the practice.

Unfortunately the good that was done in preserving game birds was undone to a large degree by a law which classified certain animals as vermin to be destroyed on sight. These included the polecat, badger, fox, stoat and the wild boar, which disappeared from Britain in the sixteenth century and the wolf, which was made extinct in England by the seventeenth century and in Scotland by the eighteenth.

WHICH FISH ARE NOTED FOR THEIR FEROCITY?

Size for size the Siamese Fighting Fish are the most ferocious fish in the sea. When two males are put in an aquarium their colours brighten and they take up fighting positions. Their fins become erect and with lightning speed they attack. They aim for each other's fins and at the end of the battle one may have some of its fins bitten down to only bloody stumps. Sometimes they meet in a head-on collision and then interlock their jaws. They are so aggressive that a male will launch an attack on its own image in a mirror.

Contests between male fighting fish was once a popular sport with the people of Siam (now Thailand) who, for centuries, put male fighters together in a tank and then staked enormous sums of money on the result of the fight.

WHY DOES A CAT HAVE WHISKERS?

A cat's whiskers are more important to it than most people realise. They are, in fact, vital to its existence in the dark. Contrary to popular opinion a cat cannot see in complete darkness and has to find its way around by sound and smell and by using its amazing whiskers. As it moves through the darkness each object it approaches causes minute disturbances in the currents of air, movement which the cat's whiskers detect, causing it to change course whenever it approaches a solid object.

Its whiskers are also vitally important to it when it hunts in the darkness, when its whiskers act as a guide system which makes it possible for the cat to home in on its prey. Here again, its whiskers "read off" the outline of its prey in a split second. But instead of avoiding the solid object in its path, it pounces on it. A cat which has had the misfortune to have damaged its whiskers is therefore at a great disadvantage when it

hunts in the dark as its whiskers do not give it a true "reading"

On an average a cat has twenty four whiskers, twelve on each side of the nose which are all situated in the cat's upper lip and arranged in horizontal rows. The whiskers are called vibrissae.

When it is moving about in semi-darkness, a cat uses a different aid. This is a device at the rear of its eyes which is an image enlarging mechanism which helps it to use every scrap of light that enters its eyes. It is this device which causes a cat's eyes to glow in the dark.

IS THE SEA CUCUMBER EDIBLE?

Although a European would not consider that the sea cucumber was edible, it is in the Far East, where it is boiled and then dried in the sun before being used as soup.

The sea cucumber belongs to a species known as echinoderms, a varied collection of marine animals, some of them beautiful, others downright ugly. The sea cucumber, while not being actually ugly is no beauty, being an unappetising looking creature not unlike a black pudding in appearance. There are five orders of sea cucumbers, the most well known of them being the black sea cucumber which has the unpleasant habit of emitting a mass of long, sticky white threads which entangles its enemies. Like some fish it can change colour, being black when in shallow water then turning to a light greenish yellow when it descends to the depths.

WHY DO DEER HAVE ANTLERS?

The most remarkable feature of the deer family is their antlers, a pair of solid horns which are shed every year. Even so, the experts are still undecided about their primary function, although we know they are used in trials of strength between the males.

In most kinds of deer only the stags have antlers. In their first year, the fawns, or young deer grow pedicels, the base from which the antlers stem. By the following year a simple spiked horn appears, and in the following years, it becomes more intricate in shape until the stag is finally in its prime.

When the antlers first begin to grow they are covered in a fine hairy skin called the velvet which makes the antlers very sensitive. The velvet begins to come away

The deer sheds and renews its horns every year

when the antlers are fully grown, and is rubbed off by the stag against tree stems and other rough objects.

WHEN DID PIGEONS BECOME MAN'S MESSENGERS?

The Romans, Assyrians, Egyptians and Phoenicians all used the pigeon to carry military intelligence. They were used by the Persians and Saracens, and even by the Emperor Napoleon.

One famous use of the pigeon as message carrier was during the siege of Paris in 1870-71. The citizens of the city used hot air balloons to carry men and messages over the surrounding German armies. Many pigeons went with them. From places as distant as London, these birds carried communications back to the beleaguered French.

At first, the paper messages were tightly rolled, waxed and attached to a tail feather, but these were often lost. Later they were inserted into a goose quill and tied to the bird with strong thread.

There were so many urgent messages that the danger of running out of pigeons threatened. Some new technique had to be mastered, and the French developed the micro dot, a method of shrinking a photograph down to the size of a small dot which could later be projected on to a screen to be read. This enabled each bird to carry as many as 30,000 messages at once.

The British and Americans used carriers throughout World War I and II. They carried messages from "ditched" aeroplanes, from minesweepers, and even flew at night along the front lines. During the Second World War a new award, the Dickin Medal, the equivalent for animals of the Victoria Cross, was introduced. This was awarded to 32 pigeons in recognition of their services.

IS IT POSSIBLE TO TELL THE AGE OF A FISH?

Experts can tell the age of many kinds of fish by examining their scales. These scales have tiny rings which roughly represent a year's growth, rather in the same way as the rings seen in the trunk of a tree. Most fish have short lives, for they have many enemies; but it is believed that salmon average 13 years and that carp live for 40 years.

HOW LONG CAN A CAMEL TRAVEL WITHOUT WATER?

A camel can go for about 17 days without water in the desert, eating only rough, thorny cactus. The fat in its hump provides it with energy. If the camel is starving and dry, the hump shrinks in size and can slip off the animal's back, to hang down on its side.

A camel can lose up to one quarter of its total body weight with little ill-effect. When thirsty it can drink up to 29.7 gallons (135 litres) of water in ten minutes. Its body visibly grows whilst it recovers its lost weight in this short space of time.

Caravans of camels can travel about 24.8miles (40 km) a day, with each animal carrying a load as much as 1,102 lbs (500 kg). Sandstorms which are too severe for a man to bear do not deter these beasts. They simply close their nostrils and squint through their three eyelids and thick eyelashes, and plod on. One camel train travelled 537 miles (864 km) through Northern Australia for 34 days without water. Most of the camels died, but a few survived.

The animal has a deserved reputation for not being completely trustworthy. A camel dislikes everything. It will bite both men and animals (even other camels). It is easily annoyed, and will either kick out suddenly and viciously with its hind legs, or spit exactly on target. A camel often has to be fitted with a muzzle on its mouth to prevent it from giving its owner a dangerous bite.

HOW DOES A PLANT DRINK?

Plants are always thirsty, and are constantly giving out water through their leaves, and taking in more through their roots, to replace the loss.

A plant takes in water by means of root hairs. These are fine hairs which spring from the part of the root just behind the growing tip. A root hair is an extension of a cell on the outside of the root. It has a thin wall, lined by living protoplasm inside which is a large space filled with fluid called cell sap.

The cell sap is a solution of sugars, mineral salts, and other things. The water in the soil is also a solution of mineral salts, but it is very dilute. Because the cell sap is more concentrated than the soil water, it is able, by a process called osmosis, to draw in water from the soil. This water travels up the stem, and is given off as vapour by the leaves.

The root hairs make intimate contact with the soil particles, which makes their work easier.

CAN LIONS CLIMB TREES?

A lion is able to climb trees, but it is by no means as skilful at it as, for example a leopard, which is a natural climber and is as much at home in a tree as it is on the ground. A lion is capable of climbing fairly high, going upwards until it reaches those branches which would not be able to bear its weight.

In the tropical regions of Africa and South West Asia, where the lion is found, the ground becomes at times unbearably hot by midday. To avoid the scorching rays of the sun, lions will often climb high into a tree to reach the coolness of leafy branches. A lion will also drag its kill into the lower branches of a tree to prevent other animals stealing it when it is not there to guard it.

Although lions have a reputation for being ferocious creatures, they have an easy-going social nature among themselves and often unite with another family when hunting. It is the females which do the hunting and killing but, the males always eat first.

Like so many other creatures of the wild, the lion has been forced to retreat steadily from the advance of man, leading to the extinction of the Barbary lions in Algeria, Tunisia and Morocco, which disappeared in the last century.

Lions have the distinction of being the only sociable members of the cat family. They live in what are called "prides", which are made up of a few females and their cubs, and one or two males.

WHICH ANIMAL IS NOTED FOR ITS CUNNING?

The cunning of the fox has been proverbial throughout the ages, and it has been a central character in fables from the time of Aesop down to the Uncle Remus stories written by an American named Joel Chandler Harris which feature Brer Rabbit and Brer Fox. Foxes have been credited with resorting to what is known as "charming" to trap a victim. One of its most popular tricks is when it comes across a party of feeding rabbits. Knowing that they will bolt into their burrows if it makes for them, the fox puts on a little performance of chasing its tail while the rabbits look on spellbound. The fox continues chasing its tail, while at the same time managing to get nearer and nearer to the rabbits until it is near enough to pounce and hopefully catch one of the rabbits.

By nature a solitary creature, the fox makes its home usually in a burrow which, more often than not it it has taken over from a rabbit or a badger. It lives mainly off rabbits, poultry and rats and mice.

HOW DID A TREE BECOME A CHRISTMAS SYMBOL?

How Christmas trees first became associated with the Christian festival marking the birth of Jesus is not very clear, as there is a great deal of confusion surrounding the weeks at the end of December and the beginning of January when both Pagan and Christian celebrations used to be held centuries ago.

In the ancient Roman world the Saturnalia festival was held on December 17, and was a time for merrymaking and the exchange of presents. At the Roman New Year on January 1 the people used to decorate their houses with greenery and lighted candles or oil lamps. Gifts were also distributed to children and poor people.

The Christmas tree with its decorations, lights and shining star at the top, first appeared as a regular feature of the season in the

16th century in Germany. The custom spread to the rest of Europe and Britain. During this period the people used to visit one another's houses for food and good fellowship. Yule (the early Saxon name for Christmas) was celebrated by the eating of special cakes, the ceremonial burning of the yule log, and greenery and fir trees all figured in different parts of the festivities.

It is thought that this use of evergreens symbolised survival, and they have been associated with Christmas ever since the Middle Ages.

In more modern times, it became the custom in Germany for the family to hold hands round the Christmas tree and sing together.

Christmas trees became very popular in Britain after Prince Albert — Consort of Queen Victoria — provided one for a children's party at Windsor Castle in 1841. Prince Albert was, of course, German by birth.

WHAT WAS THE PHOENIX?

This was an Arabian legendary bird that was said to set fire to itself and then rise from the ashes every 500 years. It was supposed to be a bird of enormous size whose tears were of incense and its blood of balsam.

The legends of how it died actually vary. Some said that when it grew old it constructed a nest composed of cinnamon and thyme upon which it then rested and promptly expired. In time a creature rose from its bones and marrow that was not unlike a worm, which became a fowl which flew off with its nest to the city of the sun, where it placed the nest on an altar. Another ancient narrator tells us that when the bird felt that its span of life was drawing to a close it flew up into the air to such a great height that the heat of the sun burnt its body to ashes.

WHAT WERE SMILODON?

In Los Angeles in California there is a small lake surrounded by railings. The lake looks quite like any other but is, in fact, a pool of tar. There are other such lakes in the locality, which is known as Ranco-La-Brea.

These pools lay in the middle of a vast desolate plain 140,000 years ago. Dust naturally collected on the tarry surface and when rain fell the tar lakes became natural but treacherous reservoirs. From miles around the animals smelled the water and hurried to slake their thirst. The sticky tar trapped these poor creatures. Their cries of distress soon attracted the attention of the flesh-eating animals, which in turn became bogged down in the tar whilst attempting to make an easy kill.

Through the course of time the tar has protected the bones of these unfortunate creatures, preserving them so well that scientists can even find on them evidence of the various diseases

The smilodon is better known as the sabre-toothed tiger

from which they suffered.

One of the animal remains found in this way was that of the sabre-toothed carnivore known as Smilodon, more popularly known as the Sabre-toothed Tiger. Practically all the Smilodon skeletons found in the tar pools were those of young and inexperienced Smilodons, the more experienced being too intelligent to hunt their prey in this way.

The most striking feature of the Smilodon was its pair of sabre-shaped canines, which were sharpened along the rear edge and grew to a length of about 150 mm. When the mouth was closed these fearsome weapons projected far down on either side of the lower jaw. To make full use of them the beast had to open its mouth very wide and to do this it was aided by the special way in which its lower jaw was attached to its skull.

No-one could doubt that Smilodon caused much alarm and fear wherever it travelled, hunting the early forms of horse, gazelles and antelopes and even the enormous Mastodon. Its large-scale destruction of the herbivorous animals might well have aided their extinction. Their extinction in turn might well have brought about the Smilodon's own extinction.

WHAT IS THE LARGEST LIVING RODENT?

In terms of intelligence a number of animals rate very highly. After man and the ape comes the pig. Close behind the pig comes the capybara — the largest living rodent, which can reach a metre in length. Looking rather like a giant guinea pig, the capybara nevertheless spends most of its life in water, living by the rivers and lakes of tropical America. They are also known as carpinchos.

The capybara's intelligence displays itself in several ways, partly by the way it adapts itself to being domesticated, and also by the way it protects itself from its enemies by posting sentries which bark an alarm-call when they see an enemy like a puma or jaguar approaching. A single bark from the sentry is enough to send the capybara plunging at headlong speed into the nearest available water.

DO BIRDS HAVE TEETH?

The birds of today don't have teeth, but traces of teeth have been found in fossilized remains of prehistoric birds. Such remains have been found in Germany. The bird, the earliest known to man, was about the size of a crow. It had a long tail like a lizard and sixteen teeth, most of which were in the upper jaw. Some of our present-day birds have strong crushing "gums" which could be likened to a file; others have tough jagged edges to their bills.

WHAT SPECIES OF TERRIER IS NAMED AFTER A CHARACTER IN SIR WALTER SCOTT'S NOVEL *GUY MANNERING*?

The Dandy Dinmont.

SAILORS INTRODUCED GUINEA PIGS INTO EUROPE IN THE 18TH CENTURY. FROM WHERE?

South America.

WHAT NAME IS GIVEN TO THE ART OF CLIPPING TREES AND SHRUBS INTO ORNAMENTAL SHAPES?

Topiary.

WHERE DO HAWKS NEST?

On cliffs and in trees but a few kestrels, of the hawk family, live near towns in church steeples.

WHICH SPECIES OF FISH KISS EACH OTHER?

The kissing gourami is an aquarium fish which has become

famous for the way it imitates the human habit of kissing. No one knows for sure why they do this, but it is almost certain that it is part of their courtship, which is not unlike the way some fish butt each other when courting. Instead of butting each other, the gourami come face to face and then after giving each other a long, lingering kiss, they separate and circle around each other before coming together again, lip to lip. This pattern of behaviour is quite unlike that of any other species of fish which use their mouths against each other as a test of strength.

Little is known about the breeding habits of the various species of the gourami which deposit their eggs on the surface of the waters where they hatch. All of them come from Southeast Asia where they are caught for food. Their own diet consists mainly of plant matter, but in an aquarium they will eat dried shrimps, water fleas and even dried oatmeal.

WHICH IS THE WORLD'S LONGEST BEETLE?

The most widely distributed members of the animal world are the beetles. There are more than 250,000 species, flourishing in every climate from the icy regions of the Arctic to the arid wastes of the Sahara Desert.

The biggest members of this enormous family are the fearsome-looking Herculus beetles, *Dynastes hercules*. Only one

beetle — the goliath beetle of South Africa — is larger in terms of total body size, none is longer. Named after Hercules, the mythical strongman of the Ancient Greeks, these creatures are found in the hot, steamy jungles of South America, where they can grow 6.7 inches (17 cm) long — almost as long as a man's hand. Up to one half of the male Hercules beetle's length is taken by its murderous horns. The reason for this is still a mystery to scientists. It was thought that beetles with the largest horns attracted the most females ensuring the survival of the species, but since beetles with shorter horns are now known to attract an equal number of females, this theory is not valid.

In fact, the horns are only used during courtship, when two males will lock horns in a trial of strength to determine which shall win the affections of the female. These battles can appear quite savage, with one beetle catching the other in a pincer-like grip and hurling it bodily aside. Thanks to their impressive body armour little or no real damage is done.

Like the "horns" on a stag beetle (which are in reality over-developed jaws), the Hercules beetle's spectacular armament can often be a hindrance. Not only are the horns incapable of securing a really tight grip, they are also cumbersome. With a burden like that, these creatures really do need the strength of Hercules just to move about.

IS THE HORSE CHESTNUT SO CALLED BECAUSE HORSES LIKE TO EAT THE NUTS?

No. Horses will not eat chestnuts, though cattle, sheep and deer will.

WHAT ARE BABY MACKEREL CALLED?

Shiners.

ARE VOLES RELATED TO RATS AND MICE?

Yes. Like rats and mice, they are classed as rodents.

WHY DOES A SNAKE FLICK ITS TONGUE IN AND OUT?

The tongue is used to pick up the slightest trace of odours.

WHY IS IT DIFFICULT TO KEEP SQUIDS IN CAPTIVITY?

Because they often commit suicide by eating their own ten-es.

WHAT IS A GROUP OF SEALS CALLED?

A pod.

HOW MANY EYES HAS A GRASSHOPPER?

A grasshopper has five eyes. One pair of large compound eyes, one pair of small simple eyes, and one eye in the centre of the forehead.

Its "ears" or hearing organs are situated on each side of the abdomen.

There are in all about 14 species of grasshopper and the most common to be found in the British Isles is the meadow grasshopper. Grasshoppers in Great Britain range in size from .63 inches (16 mm) to one inch (25 mm).

The big locusts, which swarm in such enormous numbers and do such damage to farmers' crops belong to this group. Fortunately for English farmers, they live only in hot, dry places and cannot survive in Great Britain.

WHAT IS THE CORRECT NAME FOR THE PLANT CALLED BLEEDING HEART OR LUCY LOCKET?

Dicentra.

HOW MANY LEGS HAS A SPIDER?
Eight

HOW DOES A ZEBRA'S STRIPES PROTECT IT?
A zebra's stripes are a form of protective colouring, or camouflage. The dazzle effect of the stripes helps to break up the animal's outline and make it indistinct. At a distance and in certain lights, a zebra can become almost invisible.

Although many attempts have been made to break in and train zebras for riding and driving, without a great deal of success, the Romans used them in circuses and called them horse tigers. In many ways they are closer to asses than horses, with their long ears, stiff manes and tufted tails. All of them rely on their keen eyesight and sense of smell to avoid danger. Their chief enemy is the lion.

WHICH ANIMAL KILLS AND EATS ADDERS?
The hedgehog.

WHAT IS A NATTERJACK?
A small species of toad with a yellow stripe.

WHAT ARE THE NAMES GIVEN TO A MALE AND FEMALE FERRET?
Hob and jill.

WHY IS THE ROWAN TREE SO-CALLED?
The word rowan means red. The berries of the rowan tree are red. The old Norse word for red was ron and the Gaelic word ruadan.

WHAT IS A KOOLOKAMBA?
Koolokamba is an African name for the bald-headed chimpanzee.

IS THE WALLABY A KANGAROO?
Yes. It is a small species of kangaroo.

DO POLAR BEARS HUNT PENGUINS?
No. Polar bears live only in the Arctic while penguins belong to the Antarctic.

WHAT HAVE THE ENGLISH SUNDEW AND THE PITCHER PLANT IN COMMON?
Both are plants that feed themselves by eating insects.

WHICH CREATURE IS ALWAYS HUNGRY?
The shrew is always hungry. It has a high metabolism amd must eat its own weight in food every day to survive. Even a short period of fasting could be fatal.

There are at least 170 species, spread over Europe, Asia, Africa and North America.

DID THE ROC EVER EXIST?

In Madagascar there was said to have lived up to 200 years ago, a huge flightless bird now called the Aepyornis, which is thought to be the origin of the fabled roc which played an important part in the stories of Sinbad the Sailor.

The roc was supposed to be able to lift elephants in its talons and darken the skies when it spread its wings. Its size was so exaggerated by so-called travellers' tales like these that scientists were convinced the bird never existed. They were almost certainly proved wrong when some huge eggs were discovered in 1851 which were six times larger than an ostrich egg. From the evidence of bones that were found with the eggs, it was estimated that the bird had been sixteen feet tall. It was then given the name of Aepyornis Maximus, meaning "tallest of the tall birds".

Another find in the way of bones came in 1866, when an explorer found some in a perfect state of preservation. A complete skeleton was made and exhibited in the Paris Museum.

WHAT ARE HORSETAILS?

Horsetails are plants of such ancient ancestry that they belong to a botanical class of their own. They have been used as cleansers from the earliest times as they contain large quantities of silica from the soil which is redeposited in their stems as fine crystals and makes an ideal cleansing agent. Although invisible to the human eye, the crystals are substantial enough to make a horsetail feel like fine sandpaper if one of them is run through the hand. Throughout the ages they have been used for a variety of purposes. Dairymaids used to scour their milk pails with them and the North American Indians used them to smooth the shafts of their arrows. Knights used them for polishing their armour, and some watchmakers even used them to give an extra smoothness to the works and casing of their watches.

Horsetails were eventually given the common name of pewterwork when they began to be used regularly for scouring household pots and pans as a precursor to wire wool.

Common horsetails can be found on poorly drained land between May and October and are recognisable by their jointed stems and bristly fonds.

WHICH IS THE SMALLEST BIRD IN THE WORLD?

The colourful hummingbirds are the smallest of all birds. The species gets its name from the humming sound made by the rapid beating of the wings. The birds can hover, fly straight up or down, and even backwards. Some are very small indeed. The bee hummingbird of Cuba is not much bigger in body than a queen bumble bee.

Although most hummingbirds

live in tropical regions, some are found in the mighty Atlas Mountains, where it gets so cold at night that the tiny birds are almost frozen to death.

There are more than 300 species of these remarkable birds whose tiny size allows them to beat their wings faster than any other bird. In normal flight they can beat their wings seventy times per second, so fast as to be just a blur to the human eye. When trying to attract the female some species zoom up and down in front of a proposed mate and their wings beat at 200 times a second.

By nature they are all aggressive and often succeed in driving away much larger birds than themselves. Despite their beautiful plumage none of them has a pleasing song.

WHAT IS THE TERROR OF THE WATERWAYS?

The most fearsome of all the predators of the rivers of Europe or America is the pike. Not only does it hunt and destroy weaker fish, it also catches and eats frogs, rats and young water birds, and is known to have eaten foxes. The European pike is larger than the American pike and is the most voracious of all the fresh-water fish. It probably exceeds even the shark in the relative quantity of food it eats.

Fishermen detest pike because they destroy large quantities of salmon, trout and other fish.

Although on the whole the American pike is smaller, America has two giant pike which reign supreme as the ultimate killers of their species. One of these is the muskellunge, the giant pike of North America, which spends its days hunting and killing other fish in the Great Lakes and deep northern rivers. The other is the gar-pike, which is not, strictly speaking, a pike. In its appearance and hunting habits, however, it resembles the pike in the way it lies still among the reeds and dashes out with a sudden swift rush onto its prey.

A solitary river fish, the pike prefers to live and hunt alone, and will chase away any other pike that ventures near its feeding ground.

WHAT WERE KNOWN AS "HORSE STINGERS"?

An old country name for dragonflies used to be horse stingers. It was an inaccurate name — dragonflies never attack any creature which they cannot catch in flight.

One of the largest insects in Britain today, the dragonfly starts its life in water where it hatches from an egg, generally laid on a water plant. When it reaches maturity it is a fierce hunter and eats any tiny animal or insect that it can catch. It catches its prey as it flies.

Curiously, although dragonflies have four wings, each wing can be used independently of the others.

Wars and Warriors

A THOUSAND YEARS AGO, WHO WERE THE MOST FEARED WARRIORS IN EUROPE?

Throughout the 9th and 10th centuries Europe was ravaged by the Vikings. These ferocious warriors came from Scandinavia and raided other people's lands for gold, loot and slaves. Vikings were trained for battle from childhood and had superb weapons with which they defeated most armies who opposed them.

But there were some Vikings whom even other Vikings treated with caution. These were the berserkers and they were the most feared warriors in Europe. The build-up to a Viking battle was very tense and exciting. Both sides would slowly approach each other shouting their war cries and brandishing their weapons. This was when the berserkers bit on their shields in fury, and chanted and howled like wild animals. Finally the frenzy would become uncontrollable and the berserkers would seem to go mad.

Refusing to wear armour, the berserkers, clad only in animal skins, would rush at the enemy, lashing out at anybody within reach. When in a frenzy, the berserkers seemed to have super-human strength and ignored the wounds they suffered. They were truly the most dangerous Vikings on a battlefield, and were so unpredictable that even the other Vikings were afraid of them.

WHICH GENERAL WORE IVORY-HANDLED PISTOLS?

The Second World War raged for several years and produced many fine soldiers. One of these, however, stands out from all the rest. General George C Patton was not only a talented soldier, he was one of the most charismatic men involved in the war.

In 1943 the American II Corps was stationed in North Africa. It had just suffered a defeat by the veterans of the German Afrika Korps and was demoralised. It was at this time that Patton was given command of II Corps. He drove

The General wore two
ivory-handled pistols
slung from his belt

into the headquarters of the Corps
at the head of a heavily armoured
column. He was dressed in full
battle kit and had two ivory-
handled pistols slung from his
belt. Patton was certainly a commanding figure. Within a very
short time, Patton had restored
morale. He issued a stream of orders to instil discipline and a
battle spirit into his corps. Every
man knew that Patton was in command. Soon the Americans were
pushing the Germans back and
they won a devastating tank victory at El Guettar. Later in the war,
Patton achieved equally outstanding victories elsewhere.

WHAT WAS THE SOPWITH F.1 CAMEL?

It was a famous fighter aircraft of
the First World War. Fitted directly in front of the pilot were two
synchronised forward-firing 0.303

inch Vickers machine guns. Over the breeches of these guns was fitted a humped fairing and it was because of this that the Sopwith Camel was so oddly nicknamed

From the moment it went into commission on the Western Front in July 1917 until the war ended on November 11, 1918, the Sopwith Camel accounted for the destruction of more than 2,900 enemy aircraft. There were several single-seater 'planes flown by the Royal Air Force but of them all, the Sopwith was the top-scorer.

WHO WERE THE IMMORTALS?

Of course, no soldier is immortal. If he is not killed in battle, he will eventually die of illness or old age. But there was once a military formation seemingly immortal. No matter how many were killed in battle, there appeared to be as many men left as when the battle began.

These remarkable soldiers were the Immortals, the crack troops of the Persian army. The Persian Empire came into being in about 560 BC and its army was truly impressive. Hundreds of thousands of troops could be summoned by the Emperor, but the 10,000 Immortals were the finest. They were dressed in the best armour available and carried magnificent weapons. Their peculiar name came from the fact that whenever an Immortal died, another man was at once promoted from the normal ranks of the army. In this way the Emperor ensured that he always had 10,000 first class troops to send into battle. It also created the illusion that the Immortals were truly immortal.

WHICH WAR NEVER OFFICIALLY BEGAN OR ENDED?

After the Second World War, the Far Eastern country of Korea was divided into two. The north was held by Communists and the South by a Democratic government. On June 25, 1950, the Communist troops invaded South Korea without warning and without declaring war.

The South Koreans were pushed quickly back to the far south of their country. Several countries, including Britain and the U S, sent troops to help South Korea and the Communist troops were pushed back. Then China sent troops to help the North Koreans and the South Koreans were pushed back again. Much fierce fighting followed and hundreds of thousands of troops were involved. Finally a cease fire was agreed in July 1953, but no peace-treaty has ever been signed. The Korean War, therefore, has the distinction of never having officially begun or ended.

WHICH RACE IS NAMED AFTER A BATTLE?

Many large sporting events include a race known as the Marathon. This race is run over a course of more than 26 miles and is one of the most gruelling events in athletics. The origins of the Marathon date back more than 2,000 years to a mighty battle fought in Greece.

In 490 BC the Persian army of the Emperor Darius I invaded Greece. About 50,000 Persian troops landed from their ships on to the Plain of Marathon, close to Athens. For many days the large Persian army stayed on the plain, watched by a much smaller Athenian army. Then, while the Persian cavalry were off raiding, the Athenians attacked. The Greeks charged so suddenly and with such fury that the Persians were crushed. The Persians fled back to their ships and sailed away. The invasion of Greece was over.

The Athenian leaders were not sure that the Persians were really sailing away. Perhaps they might land at Athens and try to persuade the city to surrender by pretending to have defeated the Athenian army. It was decided to send a messenger called Pheidippedes to Athens with the news of victory. Pheidippedes had fought all day and was already exhausted, but he agreed to go. It was 26 miles to Athens and Pheidippedes ran all the way. After a gruelling journey, he at last staggered up to the gates of Athens. The citizens hurried to hear the news. No sooner had Pheidippedes gasped out the news of victory than he dropped dead with exhaustion.

Modern marathon runners cover the same distance as Pheidippedes, in honour of the superb achievement of that warrior of long ago.

WHO RODE BALD-HEADED AT THE ENEMY?

In the middle of the 18th century Europe was plunged into war as Britain and Prussia fought against France and Austria. Among many commanders involved in the war was the Marquis of Granby, who led the British cavalry.

On July 31, 1760, a British army faced a French force at Warburg on the River Diemel in Germany. The British infantry ran into trouble attacking the French so Granby and his cavalry were ordered to charge. With sabres flashing and trumpets blaring, the horsemen galloped forward towards the enemy. Granby tore ahead of his men, encouraging them on. Suddenly a gust of wind blew Granby's hat off. Not only that, but Granby lost his wig as well. As the horses pounded on, 22 squadrons of British cavalry could see that their bold commander was almost bald.

Granby did not hesitate for a single moment. Urging his men on, the Marquis charged, bald-headed, at the French. His men swiftly followed him and within a few minutes the French army disintegrated into a fleeing mob. Granby, with his bald-headed charge, had won a magnificent victory.

WHAT HAPPENED IN THE STRAITS OF TSUSHIMA IN 1905?

In 1904 Russia and Japan went to war. Both nations had long been rivals in a power struggle in the Far East, so the war came as no surprise. What was a surprise was the fact that the Japanese were very soon defeating the Russian forces.

The Tsar decided to send massive reinforcements to the east. A fleet of five battleships and 38 other warships steamed out of the Baltic on a voyage of 18,000 miles (29,000 kms) to fight the Japanese. The Russian fleet contained some of the finest ships in the world. Their admiral, Rozhdestvensky, knew he could defeat the Japanese fleet if he reached the Russian forces in the Far East before they surrendered.

Rozhdestvensky hoped to lead his ships through the Straits of Tsushima without being seen by the Japanese. On May 27, 1905, the Russians entered the straits only to find the entire Japanese battle fleet waiting for them. Confident of victory, the Russians opened fire. Within seconds the Japanese replied and soon their superior gunnery and brilliant man-oeuvring became evident. Shell after shell slammed into the proud Russian fleet. The flagship was one of the first to sink, followed by all but one of the battleships. Night fell on a scene of carnage with Russian ships battered and sinking. Next morning the Russians surrendered. Only three

Russian ships reached home. All the rest had been sunk or captured. It was a devastating defeat. In the course of a day and a night, the seemingly invincible fleet of a huge European empire had been smashed. Perhaps more important, what happened in the Straits of Tsushima established Japan as a major power.

WHO FOUND THE LEGIONS OF VARUS?

In AD 15 Germanicus, the Roman general, was leading his troops through the Teutoburger Forest on a campaign against the Germans. Suddenly, the Roman troops stopped in shock and surprise.

Lying on the ground was a group of skeletons dressed in rusting Roman armour. As Germanicus and his men gazed around in horror, they saw more skeletons amongst the trees. Everywhere there were piles of skeletons dressed in Roman armour. Germanicus knew that he had found the lost legions of Varus.

Six years earlier Governor Varus had led 15,000 Roman legionaries into Germany to quell a rebellion. At first, all went well as the Roman troops were guided through the dense forest by Arminius, the chief of the Cherusci tribe. Suddenly, disaster struck. Arminius had led Varus into a trap. Screaming German warriors leapt from cover and fell upon the unsuspecting Romans. Varus and his men were slaughtered almost to a

As the moon rose, the ships opened fire on each other

man. Only a few stunned survivors staggered back to Roman territory to tell what had happened.

The terrifying defeat of Varus meant that Rome never again tried to invade Germany. Raiding parties, such as that led by Germanicus, sometimes ventured across the Rhine but the skeletons found by Germanicus marked a boundary beyond which the Roman Empire never extended.

WHICH AMERICAN HERO WAS A SCOTSMAN?

When the 13 American colonies declared their independence in 1776, one of the first men to volunteer to fight was John Paul Jones. Jones was born in 1747 at Kirkbean, in Scotland. Since then he had spent an adventurous life as a sailor and trader. When American colonies declared war against Britain, Jones joined them because of his unshakeable belief in liberty. He was willing to fight for the principle of freedom, even if it meant his own countrymen were attacked.

Jones was a brave and clever fighter. Within two years, he had been given his own ship and sent off to harass the British. One of his more spectacular raids was an attack on his old home town. Landing with a picked force of 31 volunteers, Jones captured the forts of Whitehaven. He spiked their guns and then calmly sailed away again.

On September 23, 1779, John Paul Jones was sailing to Flamborough Head. He knew that a convoy of vital merchant ships was heading his way, and he was determined to capture it. As evening drew in, the convoy came into sight. Jones hoisted all the sail his ship would carry and dashed forward. The convoy was guarded by two ships of the Royal Navy and one of these turned to face Jones.

As the moon rose, the ships opened fire on each other. The first broadside from the British ship smashed two of Jones' guns and killed many men. Within a matter of minutes, the American ship was a shot-riddled wreck but Jones had plenty of fight left in him. He skilfully manoeuvred his ship alongside the British ship and ordered his men to lash the two together. The Americans swarmed aboard the enemy ship and soon the British had to surrender. Luck was not with John Paul Jones, however. His own ship had been badly damaged and quickly sank. With other British ships in the area, Jones had to surrender to the same men who had just capitulated to him.

It was Jones' last battle for the liberty he believed in so strongly.

WHEN DID AN EAR START A WAR?

In 1738 Captain Robert Jenkins stood before the British Parliament and explained that while he had been sailing his merchant ship Rebecca he had been stopped by Spanish coast-guards. The Spaniards had then plundered his ship of its cargo. When Captain Jenkins protested, one of the Spaniards chopped off his ear. To prove his story, Jenkins turned his head to one side. He had no ear.

Relations with Spain were already strained. Arguments, about who was allowed to trade where, had flared up several times between Britain and Spain. Both nations had been known to confiscate the other's ships, but now everyone agreed the Spanish had gone too far. In anger and indignation, Britain declared war on Spain. The war raged for nine years and became part of the wider War of the Austrian Succession, which involved France, Prussia and Austria. When peace was finally agreed in 1748, the question of trading rights had still not been agreed.

WHO WERE "THE FEW"?

In a famous speech Winston Churchill once said: "Never in the field of human conflict has so much been owed by so many to so few." He was talking about the brave fighter pilots of the Royal Air Force.

In the summer of 1940, Hitler's German forces swept across Europe and were poised for an invasion of Britain. Before they could cross the Channel, however, the Germans had to put the RAF out of action. If the RAF remained intact it could have attacked the invasion fleet with devastating effect. The Germans had 2,550 aircraft ready to attack Britain, which had just 750 fighters.

On 13 August, Hitler unleashed his forces. Massive formations of German bombers and fighters thundered over the Channel to attack RAF bases and aircraft factories. Climbing to meet them were the Spitfire and Hurricane fighters flown by pilots of the RAF. Savage battles were fought in the skies over southern England as the heavily out-numbered British pilots desperately sought to claw the enemy from the skies. Day after day Britain suffered endless air raids while her gallant pilots flew to battle. The climax came on 15 September when the Germans launched a massive attack, and lost 50 aircraft in a single day's battle. Hitler was forced to abandon his plans to invade. Britain had been saved, thanks to a few pilots who had faced the might of Germany.

WHEN DID GEESE SAVE A CITY?

In 390 BC an army of fierce Celts led by a chief called Brennus invaded Italy. They quickly defeated a Roman army at Allia and then laid siege to Rome. Abandoning the major part of their city, the Romans retreated to the Capitoline hill.

For several weeks the Celts camped around the base of the strongly defended hill, trying to find a way in. Then they spotted a Roman scrambling up the rocks. There was a route up the hill! That night a strong force of Celts quietly climbed the hill. Sure enough, they found a narrow path leading to the summit. If they could get within the walls, the Celts would have the Romans at their mercy. So silently did the warriors move that not one of the Roman sentries heard them. Unfortunately for the Celts, the path they were following ran beside the Temple of Juno. In the temple sacred geese were kept. As soon as the first Celtic warrior set foot on top of the Capitoline hill, the geese started honking and hissing.

On hearing the commotion Marcus Manlius, a Roman soldier, grabbed his sword and ran forward, yelling to his friends to follow. After hard fighting, the Celts were pushed back down the hill. With his plan foiled, Brennus realised he could not capture Rome, so he persuaded the Romans to pay him to go away. If it had not been for the geese, Rome would have been destroyed.

WHO ANSWERED A DEMAND TO SURRENDER BY REPLYING: "NUTS!"?

On December 16, 1944, enormous forces of German tanks and infantry smashed through the American lines in the Ardennes. The move caught everyone on the Allied side by surprise. The Allied Generals had thought the Germans were very low on equipment and supplies and were virtually beaten. The advance of December 1944 was a staggering blow.

Within a few days, the American front lines had been over-run and German troops were racing forward across Belgium. On December 22, two American divisions were surrounded in the town of Bastogne. All around them German formations were pouring forward. All that was known of other American troops was that they were retreating. The German General Von Luttwitz wrote to Brigadier General McAuliffe, who was in command at Bastogne. Von Luttwitz pointed out the hopeless position of the Americans and asked them to surrender. McAuliffe sent back a one-word reply: "Nuts."

Though Von Luttwitz did not really understand the message, he realised the Americans would not surrender, so he attacked. For four long days the American troops in Bastogne held out against determined German assaults. As dusk settled on Boxing Day, troops in Bastogne saw American tanks advancing from the south. The ordeal was over. Bastogne had held. The German advance was ended.

WHAT IS A PYRRHIC VICTORY?

Pyrrhus was the King of Epirus, in Greece. He was a brave and clever soldier who dreamt of glory and conquest. In 281 BC the city of Tarentum in Italy declared war on Rome. Tarentum was a Greek colony and so it turned to Greece for help. Pyrrhus was only too happy to oblige and he led his army to Italy. Pyrrhus met the Romans at Heraclea and defeated them. But in the battle, Pyrrhus lost so many men that he declared: "One more such victory and we shall be utterly ruined." Since then, the term "a Pyrrhic victory" has meant a victory won at such a cost that it is useless.

WHO SLIPPED AND SEIZED A KINGDOM?

As dawn broke on September 28, 1066, Duke William of Normandy's fleet was strewn across the English Channel. There were about 700 ships, packed with thousands of men and horses. The Duke was invading England.

William believed that he was the rightful heir to the English throne and that King Harold, then reigning in England, was a usurper. The Normans considered they were simply helping their Duke claim what was his. This was the reason why such a great fleet, full of armed men, had sailed across the English Channel.

It took several hours for all the ships to gather together and head for England. The fleet made landfall at Pevensey in Sussex. William ordered his troops to land but he was the first ashore. As he

The Duke slipped and fell to the ground

leapt from his ship on to the beach, William slipped and fell flat on his face. The Normans gasped in horror. It was a bad omen.

William was well aware of what his men would think. Quick as a flash he turned to look at them. "By the splendour of God," he shouted, "I have seized my kingdom. The earth of England is in my two hands!" Encouraged by what was now a good omen, the Normans stormed ashore. Two weeks later they were to win the Battle of Hastings and place William on the throne of England.

WHEN DID ROME FALL?

In AD 410, Alaric, king of the Goths, had an opportunity no barbarian could refuse. He marched southwards through Italy to learn that the Roman Emperor had fled to Ravenna. Rome was undefended. For eight centuries no enemy had captured Rome. The wealth of the Empire was stored there. Greedily the Goths advanced.

They entered Rome by the Salarian Gate and at once set about plundering. When Alaric and his Goths left Rome a few months later, the city had been stripped of its treasures. Though a Roman Emperor still ruled in Ravenna, the Empire was dealt a blow from which it never recovered.

WHAT WAS A FIRST RATE?

When ships were powered by sail, a system of classifying the dif-

ferent types of warship was devised. Naval ships varied from massive constructions nearly 200 feet long (182 m) and mounting 120 guns down to tiny, fast ships with a handful of guns. Each was designed for a specific task, but the pride of the fleet was the battleships. These were divided into six types or rates. The largest were know as the first rates. They were the largest ships then afloat, had three decks and carried over a hundred cannon. They were the most powerful of all warships and had a devastating effect in battle. The *Victory*, now kept at Portsmouth, is a first rate ship.

WHO WAS THE SCOURGE OF GOD?

In the 5th century, the Roman Empire was weak and surrounded by enemies. The most terrible of all these enemies were the Huns.

The Huns were horse warriors from the East and had first appeared in AD376 when they galloped into Europe and smashed two powerful barbarian kingdoms. They fought on horseback with bow and with sword. Huns were superb horsemen and could pour deadly showers of arrows at an enemy while passing at a gallop. More frightful still was the cruelty of the Huns. They killed for no reason and had no pity.

In AD 443 the Huns were led by their king Attila against the eastern Roman Empire. The Huns galloped south from the Danube, pillaging and killing as they went. Outside the gates of Constantinople, Attila defeated the Roman army. The Emperor was forced to pay the Huns 2,100 pounds of gold to leave. Four years later Attila attacked again. This time the Huns truly lived up to their reputation. Whole cities were destroyed and the people massacred. Again the Roman army was smashed and gold handed over.

Next Attila turned westwards and led his men into what is now France. Attila and his Huns plundered and massacred far and wide, but he was eventually forced to retreat after a battle in northern France. Next the Huns crossed the Alps and raged through the whole of northern Italy. Nothing could withstand Attila. His success was astounding and the terrible suffering his men inflicted on Europe became legendary. Because he destroyed anything civilised or Christian, Attila was called the Scourge of God. Just when it seemed that Europe was doomed, Attila died. The Huns turned on each other in a bitter civil war, and their threat to the rest of the world vanished.

WHO WAS KILLED BY HIS OWN CURIOSITY?

In the 3rd century, China was divided between the lands of the Chi and the Wei, and the two countries were at war. The troops of the Chi were in retreat and came to a narrow pass at dusk. The Chi general stopped and carved on a tree "Pang Chuan shall die beneath this tree".

Pang Chuan was the commander of the pursuing Wei army. A group of Chi archers were then ordered to wait in ambush. Some hours later Pang Chuan and his men arrived at the pass in darkness. Seeing something written on the tree, Pang Chuan called for a light to read the message. Instantly the Chi archers shot him through with arrows. Pang Chuan fell dead in front of the inscription which had foretold his death. He had been killed by his own curiosity.

WHAT WERE THE KAMIKAZE?

Towards the end of 1944, the War in the Pacific was drawing to a close. American military might was closing in on Japan. With surrender as far from their minds as ever, the Japanese were becoming desperate. Out of this desperation was born an amazing feature of modern warfare.

The most pressing problem which faced the Japanese was how to sink American ships. Most of the Japanese bombers had been blasted from the skies together with the experienced pilots. The solution the Japanese came up with was to put untrained pilots into small planes packed with deadly explosives and order them deliberately to crash into American ships. There was no shortage of volunteers. The

Japanese had a fanatical devotion to their Emperor and considered it their duty to die for him.

The first kamikaze attack was launched on October 25 against an American force, code-named Taffy 1. Expecting a normal air attack, the Americans could not believe what was happening. Kamikaze after kamikaze dived into the American ships.

Once the Americans had got over their shock, however, they developed tactics for dealing with kamikazes. The self-sacrificing heroism of the young Japanese pilots was in vain.

WHAT CAUSED THE FETTERMAN MASSACRE?

When Captain W J Fetterman led his 82 men out of Fort Phil Kearny in December 1866, he and his men were riding to their death.

Fort Phil Kearny was built in Wyoming to guard the Bozeman Trail. Unfortunately the Bozeman, which supplied miners in the west, ran across a section of land which the U S Government had given to the Sioux Indians as hunting grounds. Not surprisingly, the Sioux did not accept the trail and they frequently attacked isolated parties. When one such party was assaulted by Sioux, Captain Fetterman led his troops to the rescue — and into a trap. Hiding nearby were more than 1,000 Sioux warriors. Fetterman and all his troops were killed and the Bozeman Trail was temporarily closed.

WHO WERE THE RED "EYEBROWS"?

In AD 17 heavy rains fell all over China. Because the dykes were not maintained by Imperial authorities, the Yellow River flooded. Enormous damage was caused and thousands of peasants made homeless. The peasants of Shantung Province angrily turned upon the Imperial officers who had neglected their duty and rebellion broke out. In order to make themselves appear more frightening, the rebels painted their eyebrows red. Landowners joined the peasants and the revolt of the "Red Eyebrows" spread across China. The Emperor Wang Mang was killed and a new Emperor set up in his place.

WHO WAS CARACTACUS?

When the Romans invaded Britain in AD 43, their most implacable enemy was Caractacus, the chief of the Catuvellauni tribe.

Caractacus was the overlord of all the tribes of south eastern Britain. When the Roman army landed, led by Plautius, Caractacus gathered his warriors and headed south to meet them. The two armies met on the banks of the River Medway. After two days of ferocious fighting, the Britons were forced to retreat. Caractacus turned to fight at the Thames, but was again beaten. His kingdom was conquered by Rome, but Caractacus was not.

He moved westwards with a

Caractacus in chains before the Emperor

warband of picked Catuvellauni warriors. For the next four years Caractacus launched numerous raids on Roman Britain. By AD 47 Caractacus had gathered a sizeable force and had gained the loyalty of the western tribes. He launched them in a major attack on the Romans. The new Governor, Ostorius, only managed to push Caractacus back with difficulty. Next year, Ostorius launched a Roman attack, only to fail when faced by a fresh attack by Caractacus' Britons.

The strong charismatic leadership of Caractacus held the free tribes of Britons together while his careful planning launched them on a series of successful attacks which the Romans could only withstand with difficulty. In AD 51, Caractacus was betrayed to the Romans by the queen of the Brigantes tribe. He was taken to Rome in chains and paraded through the streets by the Emperor Claudius. His capture was a great victory and the Romans were determined to make the most of it. The last word though belonged to Caractacus. Gazing at the mighty temples and palaces of Rome he asked the Emperor: "Why, when you have all this, did you want my poor hut?"

WHICH WAR LASTED ONLY SIX DAYS?

The Arab states of the Middle East have never accepted the existence of Israel. They believe that the territory of Israel belongs to the Arabs. The Israelis believe that it is theirs. Tension has always been high in the area and in the summer of 1967, Israel, Syria and Egypt had all mobilised their forces in case trouble flared. Suddenly, without warning, Israeli planes roared across their borders on June 5. They swept into Jordan, Egypt and Syria and bombed the Arab air forces. Troops followed the planes and Israel seized large areas of territory. On June 10 a cease fire was organised by the United Nations. The war had lasted just six days.

WHEN DID TAXIS WIN A BATTLE?

Action on the Western Front during the First World War opened with a swift German advance. The German attack began in the middle of August, 1914, and despite a French counter-attack it continued for several weeks. By September 5, German troops were almost within sight of Paris. France was nearly defeated.

The front line ran across the Marne River. Here General Joffre, the French commander, planned a last ditch defence. In the morning, French and British troops attacked the Germans but nobody was sure whether the Allies had enough troops to turn the Germans back.

It was at this point that General Gallieni, who commanded the French 6th Army, had an idea. His troops were in Paris but they were needed on the Marne. Gallieni promptly commandeered all the taxis he could find and loaded his troops into them. He then ordered the taxi drivers to head towards the Germans. The fate of France hung in the balance as the taxis rumbled off, each one packed to overflowing with men and equipment. The extra troops tipped the balance and the Germans were pushed back, away from Paris.

France had been saved.

WHICH WAS THE MOST FAMOUS HORSE IN HISTORY?

Alexander the Great was undoubtedly one of the greatest men ever to have lived. At the age of 20 he became king of Macedonia in 336 BC. He then led a small army of Macedonians and Greeks against the Persian Empire. In a series of brilliant campaigns, Alexander not only conquered Persia, but many lands beyond. Through all this fighting, his faithful companion was a horse called Bucephalus.

Alexander saw Bucephalus when the horse was brought to Alexander's father, Philip, for sale. None of Philip's horsemen could control the beast and Philip was about to reject it when Alexander asked permission to try to ride it. He had noticed that the

The Vikings began rowing downstream with all their might

horse seemed frightened of its own shadow. Alexander turned the horse to face into the sun. As soon as the horse was unable to see its shadow, it became docile and easy to ride.

Bucephalus was trained to become a magnificent war horse. Not only was Bucephalus strong and tireless, it was also skilled in very subtle manoeuvres. At the lightest touch from Alexander, the clever horse would jump sideways, leap forward or step backward. Such sudden movements often helped Alexander to avoid sword or spear thrusts in the heat of battle. Bucephalus helped save Alexander's life many times. Alexander, in turn, loved Bucephalus so much that he named a city in honour of the horse.

WHO PULLED DOWN LONDON BRIDGE?

King Ethelred the Unready ruled England from 978 until 1016 and was constantly fighting the Vikings. The Vikings were not a united force and this Ethelred used to advantage.

According to the sagas, a force of Danish Vikings captured London while Ethelred was elsewhere in England, and fortified London Bridge to stop ships passing along the Thames. Ethelred had to recapture London.

He employed the Norwegian Viking, Olaf the Thick, an enemy of the Danes, to help him. Arriving at London, Olaf at once formed a plan. He gathered his ships together and rowed upstream to the bridge. While arrows and spears rained down the Norwegian Vikings tied great ropes to the bridge's wooden supports. These were then tied to the ships, and when Olaf gave the word, the Vikings began rowing downstream with all their might. As the ropes tightened, the bridge supports gave way. London Bridge collapsed. Soon afterwards the Danes surrendered.

WHO WAS THE LAST EMPEROR OF ROME?

Towards the end of the 5th century, the Roman Empire was in chaos. Bands of barbarian warriors roamed through Europe pillaging and looting. Central authority was weak and local men took power into their own hands. One of the most successful soldiers of Rome was Orestes. This man grew so powerful that he was able to make his young son, Romulus Augustulus, Emperor of Rome. Ten months later a band of German warriors killed Orestes and seized large tracts of land in Italy. They also grabbed Romulus Augustulus, but they forebore to kill a little child. They gave him a castle to live in, but made sure that everyone knew he was no longer Emperor. The year was 476 and Rome was in the hands of the barbarians.

WHAT IS A PARTHIAN SHOT?

The Parthians lived in what is now northern Iran. They were, for about two centuries until AD 200, troublesome neighbours of the Roman Empire.

When the Parthians went into battle they had one tactic which the Romans found particularly dangerous. The Parthians were famous for their mounted archers. They specialised in sweeping manoeuvres at full gallop. When the Romans proved too powerful, the Parthians would retreat. Just as they reached extreme range, the Parthians would turn in their saddles and shoot a final arrow while their horses still galloped away. This tactic enabled the Parthians to get the last shot in any battle and became known as a Parthian shot.

WHEN DID A FOOTBALL MATCH START A WAR?

This remarkable war was fought between the two Central American countries — El Salvador and Honduras. Trouble had begun some years earlier when peasants from El Salvador moved to Honduras.

In 1969, the Honduras government declared the peasants to be squatters and threw many of them off their farms as harvest time approached.

Tension mounted between the two countries. The anger boiled over when El Salvador defeated Honduras in a football match. Rioting aimed at the remaining migrants then broke out in Honduras.

El Salvador launched air

attacks. Honduras retaliated, but a truce was hastily patched up after four days.

WHEN DID THE MONGOLS FIGHT ON FOOT?

The Mongols were ferocious horse warriors from Eastern Asia. Their galloping manoeuvres, lightning charges and swift retreats won them numerous battles. In a few years they conquered China and surrounding lands.

In 1277, Narathihapate, the King of Burma, attacked the Mongol Empire. The two armies met in a narrow valley at Ngasaunggyan. As usual the Mongols drew themselves up in dense formations of horsemen and expected an easy victory. They were in for a shock.

As the Burmese army advanced, Narathihapate sent his war elephants forward. The Mongol horses had never seen elephants before and they panicked. No matter what the Mongols tried to do, their horses were uncontrollable. Many of them bolted off with their helpless riders clinging on for dear life.

The Mongol leader was faced with a disintegrating army, before the battle had even begun. He promptly ordered his men to dismount. Leaving their panic-striken horses, the Mongols picked up their heavy war bows. Though unused to fighting on foot, the Mongols shot clouds of arrows at the elephants. The heavy arrows bit deep into the elephants' hides. The pain-enraged beasts promptly turned round and trampled through the Burmese army.

With the elephants gone, the Mongols leapt on to their horses and charged, routing the Burmese army.

WHERE DID THE VIKINGS RAID?

For two centuries after the year 800, Viking warriors spread terror and fear throughout Europe. They would arrive off a coast in their fast ships, and leap ashore armed to the teeth with swords and axes. After stealing everything they could and killing any opposition, the Vikings would sail away before local soldiers could oppose them.

These frightful raids occurred virtually anywhere the Vikings could sail their ships. They raided deep into the Mediterranean, along the Atlantic and North Sea coasts. They even sailed up the rivers of Russia to plunder deep inland. Nowhere in Europe was safe from the Vikings.

WHO DIED ON THE HEIGHTS OF ABRAHAM?

For three months of summer in 1759, the British army had been encamped outside Quebec in Canada. The British commander, General Wolfe, had been ordered to capture Quebec from the French. He had tried everything he could think of, from outright

The British troops climbed
the cliff without being seen

attack to subtle tricks. The French commander, the Marquis de Montcalm, always found an answer and drove the British back.

At last, on September 10, Wolfe strode into a meeting of his officers and announced a plan. It was so outrageous that all the officers objected at once. Wolfe was not to be put off. His idea was to load his army into boats and row them to the base of a cliff. He would then lead the army up a precipitous slope to attack Quebec from behind. It seemed unbelievable.

Montcalm, not even considering that Wolfe could lead an army up such steep terrain, posted only a few sentries on the cliff.

On the night of September 12, Wolfe led 5,000 British troops to the foot of the cliff. Against all the odds, they climbed the cliff without being seen and deployed for battle. When Montcalm saw that Quebec was threatened from behind, he came out to fight.

A terrific battle raged at the cliff tops on land known as the Heights of Abraham. As the gunfire grew fiercer, Wolfe was struck down. Minutes later, Montcalm was also hit. The French army collapsed and Quebec fell, but the British had paid a heavy price. Wolfe lay dead on the Heights of Abraham.

WHICH WAS THE FIRST NATION ORGANISED FOR WAR?

About 1,250 BC, the Assyrians became independent and, immediately set up their state as a formidable fighting machine.

The Assyrian kings built up a formidable army which attacked and enslaved many other peoples. The bulk of the army was made up of some 20,000 infantrymen, but there were more than 1,000 chariots and over 10,000 cavalry. With this magnificent army, the Assyrians conquered vast areas.

The whole nation was organised to support the army and to live off the plunder which it brought back from its conquests. The Assyrian Empire reached its greatest size in the late 8th century BC and nobody seemed able to defeat it.'

The end came quickly. In 610 BC, the enemies of the Assyrians joined together and defeated them. The Assyrian army had to surrender. With the reason for its existence gone, Assyria vanished from history.

WHERE WAS THE FIRST ATOMIC BOMB USED?

In July 1945, it was becoming clear that Japan was beaten, but to invade Japan, America and Britain would suffer a heavy loss of troops and material. The terrible decision was, therefore, taken to drop an atomic bomb on Japan. On August 6, an American B-29 bomber dropped the weapon on the city of Hiroshima. The devastating explosion flattened 4 square miles of the city and killed 80,000 people. Later another bomb was dropped on the city of Nagasaki, with equally awful results.

The Japanese Emperor Hirohito, knew his country had no defence against such weapons. Japan surrendered on August 14. World War II was over.

WHAT WAS THE BATTLE OF THE SPURS?

In 1513 England was at war with France. King Henry VIII landed with the English Army at Calais and laid siege to the city of Therouanne.

The French king, Louis XII, sent an army to defeat Henry and save Therouanne. The French army, with glittering armour and streaming banners, met the English at Guinegate. After a battle with few casualties, the French turned and fled. Because the French had used their spurs to make their horses retreat faster, more than they had used their weapons, the English called this the Battle of the Spurs.

WHAT HAPPENED ON MAY 31, 1918, AT CHÂTEAU-THIERRY?

On the morning of May 27, 1918, the Germans launched a massive attack on the Western Front. It was totally unexpected. The Allies thought that Germany had neither the men nor material for another big offensive.

The attack had the advantage of surprise. Soon the French were retreating as fast as they could, leaving behind guns and prisoners. In desperation, General Pétain asked General Pershing if any Americans could take over Château-Thierry from the French, hoping that fresh troops might slow the German advance.

On the afternoon of May 31, the 7th Machine Gun Battalion of Americans found themselves alone in Château-Thierry. They were the centre of the main German attack. The first troops the Americans saw were hundreds of fleeing Frenchmen. Then came the Germans. Despite strong attacks, the single battalion held Château-Thierry all day. Not only had the Americans slowed the German advance, they had stopped it dead.

Next morning the battalion was reinforced and the crisis passed. The fight at Château-Thierry was the first large scale engagement, in World War I, in which American troops were involved. From the beginning they showed they were good fighters.

WHICH CONQUEROR DIED BECAUSE OF A HOT EMBER?

William the Conqueror earned his name following his conquest of England in 1066. It was not his only conquest. William was at war almost constantly throughout his life.

Before his conquest of England, William had been engaged in warfare with the king of France. Twenty years after the Battle of Hastings, this warfare flared up again. William was 60, but he was just as ruthless and brutal.

In the summer of 1087, William

captured the town of Mantes. He ordered his troops to destroy the town. They set it on fire and as the flames spread hungrily, William rode through the destruction.

Suddenly his horse trod on a hot ember. It stumbled and threw William against the pommel of his saddle. The great conqueror suffered massive internal injuries and collapsed in agony. William's followers carried him to the Priory of St Gervais in Rouen where he died some days later. Swords and spears of thousands of warriors had failed but a simple hot ember had succeeded in ending the life of William the Conqueror.

WHAT WAS THE GREATEST NAVAL BATTLE EVER?

In October 1944, American forces landed on the Philippine island of Leyte. If they captured the island, Japanese war supplies would be threatened. Admiral Toyoda of the Imperial Japanese Navy, gathered every ship available and steamed towards Leyte.

If the Japanese ships came within range of Leyte, the Americans knew their land forces would be wiped out. They had to stop the Japanese. More than 220 powerful modern warships and 2,000 aircraft gathered for what would prove to be the greatest sea battle of all time.

A detachment of the Japanese fleet was easily halted but the main fleet steamed on. On the morning of October 25, Japanese battleships and cruisers ran into the American Seventh Fleet, east of Leyte Gulf. The guns of the Japanese opened up and pounded the Americans. Kamikaze planes rained down on the American ships. It became clear that they could not stop the Japanese.

The Americans launched air strikes from their carriers. These inflicted some damage, but when they returned the pilots found their carriers sunk or out of action. The planes had to ditch in the sea. Still the Japanese battleships ploughed towards Leyte. The guns continued to thunder and shells screamed through the air. More American ships sank.

Suddenly, the Japanese stopped and turned around. They thought they faced more American ships than were actually there. By a combination of hard fighting and luck, the Americans had won.

WHO FOUGHT IN THE SHADE?

In 480 BC, Xerxes, Emperor of Persia, led an army of at least 100,000 men into Greece.

In a desperate attempt to slow down the Persians, a few hundred Greeks waited in the Pass of Thermopylae. If the Persians wanted to cross the mountains into Greece, they would have to use this pass.

The Greeks were led by Leonidas, King of Sparta. Spartans — the best soldiers in Greece — were trained for war from boyhood and they won many spectacular victories. At Thermopylae, Leonidas had only 300 Spartans, his picked bodyguard.

When the massive Persian army arrived at Thermopylae, Xerxes sent messengers forward demanding a surrender. In an attempt to frighten the Greeks, one man told them that the Persians had so many archers that their arrows blocked out the light of the sun.

"This is pleasant news," replied one Spartan. "If the Persians hide the sun, we can fight in the shade."

For three days the Greeks beat off the Persians. Then the Persians found a narrow track through the mountains. Leonidas was surrounded, but he did not surrender. He fought on, determined to delay the Persians as long as possible. In a desperate battle Leonidas and his Spartans were wiped out.

Today a magnificent memorial stands in the Pass of Thermopylae. Atop a plinth of stone a massive statue of Leonidas stands with his spear pointing towards the enemy.

WHO WERE THE TEMPLARS?

In the early 12th century hundreds of pilgrims were travelling from Europe to Jerusalem to pray at the holy Christian places. The most dangerous part of this journey was the road from Jaffa to Jerusalem, where many people were killed by bandits and Moslems.

In 1119 a strong and powerful knight called Hugues de Payen was in Jerusalem. Appalled at the death of pilgrims, Hugues and eight other knights offered to protect them.

The King of Jerusalem gave these nine knights quarters in his own palace, near the Temple of Solomon. From this fact, Hugues and his friends called themselves the Knights of the Temple and they were known as the Templars.

Within a very short time the Templars had cleared the road of Moslems. They then turned on Moslems in general and became part of the general Crusading movement.

For two centuries the Templars were in the forefront of the holy war against the Moslems. The numbers of Templars swelled into the hundreds. They distinguished themselves in battle after battle and became the most famous warriors in Christendom.

WHAT WAS THE SPANISH ARMADA?

In the late 16th century Europe was divided by religion. The leading Catholic nation was Spain, while England was Protestant. To this religious animosity was added the conflict of national interests.

In 1588 the quarrels between England and Spain erupted into open warfare.

Philip, King of Spain, assembled a massive fleet or armada, of over 130 ships. He was determined to smash England and reduce it to a nation subject to Spain. The Spanish Armada was

In the jungle war the troops were always on the lookout for ambush

sighted by the English off Cornwall on July 19. For the next week the Armada sailed up the Channel with the outnumbered English warships keeping up a running fight.

On the night of July 27, the Armada was anchored off Calais. The English sent in fireships to panic the Spaniards. Next morning, the English descended upon the Spanish Armada. Fierce fighting shattered the Spanish fleet. It then headed north to round Scotland and return to Spain. Of the 130 that had set out, only 53 ships returned to Spain.

WHAT WAS THE TET OFFENSIVE?

In 1956 the Asian country of Vietnam was plunged into civil war between the communist north and the democratic south. The war rapidly escalated and American troops became involved after communist forces fired on American ships.

It was a vicious jungle war in which troops had to creep through thick undergrowth, always on the lookout for ambush. The military might of America and South Vietnam was matched against the skill and cunning of the enemy troops coming from the north.

In January 1968, the communists launched their Tet Offensive. Instead of concentrating on guerilla tactics, the communists came out into the open. They attacked 36 cities with all the troops they could muster.

Though the communists were beaten back and suffered heavy losses, their fighting powers had impressed their enemies. The Americans began to pull out of Vietnam and in 1975 South Vietnam finally fell to the communists.

WHICH REGIMENT DURING THE FIRST WORLD WAR KICKED A FOOTBALL INTO BATTLE?

During the carnage of the Battle of Amiens in the First World War, the East Surrey Regiment was ordered to attack the German trenches confronting them.

The men followed their officers out of the trenches with bayonets fixed, expecting heavy gunfire. Instead they claim to have seen a footballer awaiting them. This soccer player began to dribble the ball encouraging the regiment forward. As the men broke into a run, the ball was kicked backwards and forwards between the ranks. Not until the East Surreys were halfway to the enemy did the Germans open fire. On reaching the German trenches, the mysterious sportsman vanished.

Who he was, no one has been able to explain.

Not surprisingly, many people doubt the event ever took place. But after the Battle of Amiens, whenever the East Surreys were ordered forward into battle, the officers always threw a soccer ball in front of the infantrymen who then dribbled and kicked it as they advanced to the attack.

WHICH WAS THE LAST BATTLE FOUGHT BY OARED GALLEYS?

In the 1560s the Ottoman Empire, based in Turkey, was expanding. As an aggressive Islamic power, the Ottoman Empire threatened Europe both politically and culturally.

Pope Pius V organised a powerful Catholic league to resist the Moslems. In 1571 the combined fleets of Spain, Venice, Genoa and Naples clashed with the Ottoman ships at Lepanto.

Both sides consisted mainly of oared galleys. These ships had been used for centuries in the Mediterranean where their oars were useful when the wind died. The Christians, however, had a new type of ship called a galleass. This was a large ship armed with heavy guns. The battle raged for many hours but the Christians were victorious and Ottoman sea power was smashed.

WHO ASKED THE ENEMY TO SHOOT FIRST?

On May 11, 1745, a combined army of British, Austrian and

Dutch troops attacked the French position of Fontenoy, near Tournai.

The British infantry were given the task of attacking the French Guard. In steady ranks the redcoats advanced uphill towards the waiting French. When less than 100 yards (91 m) from the enemy, the British stopped and Lord John Hay stepped forward from the ranks. As the two masses of infantry watched, Lord Hay drank a toast to the French from his flask. He then took off his hat and cried "Tirez les premiers, Messieurs les Françaises!" ("You shoot first, gentlemen of France!").

This behaviour was not as suicidal as it may seem. The crude muskets then in use had an effective range of just 60 yards (55 m). If the French could be persuaded to open fire when the range was 100 yards (91 m), they would be wasting most of their bullets. The French knew this as well as Lord Hay. They did not fire.

Lord Hay returned to his troops and led them closer to the French before opening fire. The British troops rushed the French and sent them running from the field. But the effort was in vain. The Dutch on Hay's left failed to advance, so the British had to retreat. The French held on to Fontenoy.

WHO WAS OFFERED SEVEN FEET OF ENGLAND?

On September 25, 1066, two armies faced each other at Stamford Bridge in Yorkshire. On the eastern bank stood an army of Vikings led by King Harald Hardraada of Norway and Tostig, the rebel brother of the English King and the Earl of Northumbria. On the western bank stood the English army led by King Harold Godwinson.

Before the battle began in earnest, the three leaders met to try to reach an agreement. Harold Godwinson greeted his brother and Harald Hardraada. In the hope of avoiding a battle with his own brother, Harold made Tostig an offer. Harold said he could keep his earldom and have many other lands as well, if only he would rejoin his king.

Tostig was a great friend of Harald Hardraada. He asked what Hardraada would get. Harold Godwinson's answer is one of the most famous in history. He offered him "seven feet of England, or slightly more as he is rather taller than other men."

Battle commenced and in the savage hand-to-hand fighting that followed Tostig and Hardraada were killed. Harold Godwinson was victorious.

WHO PREVENTED THE FRENCH FROM INVADING ENGLAND IN 1805?

Throughout the summer of 1805, a huge French army under the command of Napoleon waited outside Boulogne. Napoleon was determined to invade Britain, but first

A shot rang out and Nelson fell to the deck

he had to control the Channel.

The French fleet was in Cadiz with the ships of Spain. If Napoleon was to invade Britain, the fleet had to reach the Channel and protect the craft carrying the army. Admiral Villeneuve, therefore, led his combined fleet out of port on October 19.

Two days later, the British fleet under Admiral Nelson found the French off Cape Trafalgar. Though outnumbered by 33 ships to 22, Nelson attacked at once. Nelson organised his ships into two lines and headed straight for the French and Spanish fleets.

Ignoring the usual formations, Nelson was determined on a battle in which captains could act on their own initiative. Nelson then hoisted his famous signal "England expects that every man will do his duty". He knew that the superior gunnery and tactics of his ships would beat the enemy.

As the heavy cannon thundered out and the smoke billowed around the ships, it became clear that Nelson was winning. Ship after ship, of the enemy fleet was surrendering. All through the battle, Nelson strode the deck of his flagship the *Victory*.

Suddenly, amid the smoke and the din of booming guns, a single musket shot rang out. The shot had come from the French ship

Redoutable, just 45 feet from the Victory. Nelson fell forward, clutching his chest.

Nelson was carried down to the sick bay. As the battle raged on, Nelson, the architect of victory, was slowly dying. Before he died, Nelson was given the news he longed to hear. Victory had been won. The combined fleets had been smashed. Britain was safe from invasion.

WHICH WARRIOR DEFIED AN ARMY?

King Richard the Lionheart was tall, muscular, blond, charming and the deadliest warrior in Christendom. Even hardened soldiers were amazed by his courage and tenacity on the battlefield.

In 1190 he led his army to the Holy Land to join the Crusade against the Moslems. After two years of hard fighting, Richard prepared to return home. Then he heard that the city of Jaffa was being attacked by the Moslems.

Richard at once loaded his troops aboard ship and sailed to Jaffa. As soon as his ship anchored, he leapt ashore and led his troops into the city. The battle which followed was ferocious.

It came to an end when Richard, with just 12 knights, charged into the heart of the Saracen army. Hacking to left and right with his axe, Richard killed several men. As the enemy fell back, one Moslem galloped forward to attack the King. In full view of the Sar-

acen army, Richard whirled to face the man. His axe rose and fell. The Moslem was dead before he toppled from his saddle.

With this vicious example in front of them, the Saracens edged back. While his own army was regrouping, Richard rode alone towards the Moslem army. He slowly trotted up and down in front of the silent Moslems. Richard challenged them to come and fight. Of all the thousands of Saracens, not one moved.

On his own, Richard the Lionheart was holding an entire army at bay. There was not another warrior like him in the world.

WHY DO TEXANS REMEMBER THE ALAMO?

In 1836, the American settlers in Texas had finally had enough. They had been allowed to settle by the Mexican government some years earlier. Now, however, the government of the dictator Santa Anna was imposing unacceptable terms and conditions. The Americans and many native Texans rebelled.

Before the Texans, under Sam Houston, had time to organise their forces, Santa Anna struck. He advanced north with a large army. The first determined resistance he met was at a small fortified mission called the Alamo.

Here 150 defenders waited to fight. Among them were two of the famous frontiersmen, Davy Crockett and Jim Bowie. For 12 days the Alamo held out against the massive Mexican army, until it fell on March 6, 1836. Every one of the defenders was killed in the assault.

This massacre became a cause for revenge by the Texans. "Remember the Alamo" became a war cry in the struggle. The sacrifice at the Alamo was not in vain. The Texans used the time gained to build up their army. A few weeks later, at San Jacinto, the Mexicans were defeated and Texas won its independence.

WHO SAID "I SHALL RETURN?"

In December 1941, the Japanese unleashed their armed forces on the world. The American Pacific fleet was virtually wiped out at Pearl Harbor. In the Philippines, nearly every American aircraft was destroyed on the ground.

Then the Japanese army rolled forward. It launched attack after attack on the Americans in the Philippines. General MacArthur, the American commander, believed that he could hold until relieved, but with the American fleet destroyed this was impossible.

As the Japanese attack developed into an overwhelming onslaught, MacArthur had to pull his troops back to the fortress of Corregidor. Soon it became clear that the Americans would have to surrender. MacArthur, however, was too valuable a general to lose. The President, therefore, ordered him

to escape to Australia, if he could. When MacArthur arrived in Australia he vowed: "I shall return." In the face of unbroken Japanese success it seemed a rash boast. After more than two years of fierce fighting, however, MacArthur lived up to his boast when he led American troops back into the Philippines.

WHO WAS "H"?

In May 1982 British forces landed on the Falkland Islands to retake them from the invading Argentinians.

One of the most important preliminary actions was the capture of Goose Green. The job was given to 2 Para and its Lieutenant Colonel, H Jones.

Colonel Jones, known as "H", was an unconventional and very popular officer who believed in leading from the front. After careful planning, Jones ordered his parachutists forward. The initial stages of the battle, carried out in the safety of darkness, went well for the British. As dawn broke, it became clear that the attack was slowing down.

Colonel Jones went forward to see the situation for himself. Summing things up "H" realised that a chain of Argentine trenches had to be taken. Together with his men Jones charged. The colonel was within three feet (one metre) of the enemy before he was shot dead.

His death spurred on 2 Para and they renewed the attack and

stormed into Goose Green. When the fighting ended some hours later, the odds against the British became clear. There had been 1,400 Argentinians in Goose Green and they had been overcome by a single battalion but at a heavy cost. The loss of Colonel H Jones was irreparable.

WHAT WAS THE BRITISH SQUARE?

During the 18th century the great fear of infantry was a cavalry attack. If the horsemen charged infantry from the front, they could probably be driven back with gunfire. If the cavalry managed to attack from the flank or rear, the infantry could be cut down and slaughtered.

The tactic devised to oppose a cavalry attack was the square. In this formation an infantry regiment would draw up in a square with men on each side facing outward.

From whichever direction the cavalry attacked, they would be met by a hail of fire. The problem was that on the field of battle, cavalry moved much faster than infantry. For the square to be effective, the infantry had to form square at a moment's notice.

The redcoated British infantry were amongst the most highly trained in the world. Time and again enemy cavalry would charge forward, only to find that the British rapidly formed square before the impact.

The greatest victory of the British square was at the Battle of Waterloo. After many hours of heavy fighting, the French Marshal Ney led a massive charge by 5,000 cavalry against the weary British. The British regiments hastily formed square and drove back the ferocious French assaults. Soon after, the French army broke and fled.

DID NAPOLEON EVER ACTUALLY LEAD HIS TROOPS IN BATTLE?

Yes. Long before he became the Emperor of the French, Napoleon Bonaparte was the General commanding the French army in northern Italy. In 1796, he was laying siege to Austrian forces in the city of Mantua when he learned that a fresh Austrian army was advancing towards him, along the Adige River.

Hoping to launch a surprise attack, Bonaparte decided to cross the Adige and its tributary the Alpone, at the town of Arcola. The Austrians, however, had posted a garrison in Arcola. At dawn on November 15, 1796, Bonaparte launched his attack.

The battle soon became centred on the bridge in Arcola. Time was running out for Bonaparte's surprise attack. Seizing a French tricolour in his hand, Napoleon leapt up. Urging his troops to follow, in one last attack, Napoleon ran forward. Surprised that their commander-in-chief was in the front line, the French army followed him.

Waving the red, white and blue flag over his head, Napoleon led his men across the bridge at Arcola. In the face of enemy fire, the French stormed forward. Though the battle rumbled on for two more days, it was Bonaparte's dash and bravery that eventually won the battle and drove the Austrians back.

WHAT WAS A SCHILTRON?

In 1297 Sir William Wallace was leading the Scottish resistance to English rule. While the Scots were successful in guerilla warfare, Wallace was considering how to face the English in open battle.

The English had a superiority of mounted knights. To try to defeat the knights, Wallace used the formation known as schiltron. He drew his infantry up in dense phalanxes so that their long spears faced outwards.

Confronted by an impenetrable hedgehog of spikes, the knights were helpless.

Wallace was eventually defeated, but Robert Bruce used the schiltron formation in his devastating victory over the English at Bannockburn in 1314.

Napoleon Bonaparte led his men across the bridge

WHAT WAS THE GREAT HELM?

In the Middle Ages, hand-to-hand warfare was fairly commonplace. This was mainly a matter of hacking at the enemy with sword or axe. At such times, it was best to be well protected against such vicious, close-range weapons.

The most vulnerable part of the body was the head, so this was the most heavily armoured.

In the 13th century the great helm came into its own. Basically the great helm consisted of a hollow cylinder of metal, covered at the crown.

To help the wearers withstand the crushing blows of heavy war axes and swords, these helmets were made of thick metal. They weighed on average some 15 pounds (7 kgs). Learning to fight while carrying such a weight on the head was an essential part of knightly training.

WHO CAPTURED 135 OF THE ENEMY SINGLE-HANDED?

On October 8, 1918, when the First World War was approaching its end end, an American patrol went forward in the Argonne area of France under the command of Sergeant Alvin York. It had orders to attack a railroad.

After penetrating the German lines, the patrol came under heavy fire and scattered. Sergeant York dived into cover and found himself alone. After picking off a few enemy troops, York was charged by a group of Germans. Drawing his automatic, he shot them all.

York then turned his murderous fire on to yet another group of Germans. One of them was a major. He cried out to York in English that he would surrender if only the American would stop shooting. York did so.

The German major surrendered with all his men. There were dozens of them. York called his handful of men together and began to escort the Germans towards the American lines. When the German major asked York how many American troops he had, York just grinned and said: "Plenty".

On the way back to the American lines, the strange procession came across several more German positions. Seeing so many of their comrades with raised hands, these Germans promptly surrendered as well. When Sergeant York reached his own lines, he had gathered together 135 prisoners. He had also, single-handed, killed 15 Germans and captured 35 machine gun nests. It was one of the outstanding events of World War I.

WHO WERE THE ORIGINAL VANDALS?

Today the word vandal means a person who destroys without purpose. Yet originally the word was the name of a tribe of barbarians who were active 1,600 years ago. It was the original Vandals who gave the modern word its meaning.

As the might of Rome fell into

decay, the barbarians swarmed over the borders. Most tribes were content with bribes or gifts of land. The Vandals were not.

Scorning all gifts they were offered by the Romans, the Vandals were only interested in plunder and destruction. In the early 5th century the Vandals swept through Gaul, leaving a trail of ruin behind them. Then they marched into Spain. Here they wrought havoc and bloodshed for 20 years.

Then the Vandal fighting force crossed to Africa to raid new lands. Here the Vandals captured a fleet and crossed to Italy. Their next act was to sack Rome.

Everywhere they went, the Vandals behaved atrociously. The Romans had become used to uncultured barbarians, but the Vandals were different. Most barbarians enjoyed luxury. They could be won over with treasure or soft living. The Vandals seemed to delight in destroying beautiful objects. They would destroy works of art and books for no reason at all. For nearly a century the Vandals roamed and destroyed almost at will.

In AD 533 the Vandals were finally smashed by the Byzantines. Their career of destruction was over.

WHAT WERE THE DEATH'S HEAD HUSSARS?
In 1740 Frederick II came to the throne of Prussia and set about creating a magnificent army.

The infantry was drilled to perfection. It was trained to march in precise formation and to deliver devastating volleys of musket fire. The cavalry was also specially trained. While the infantry was expected to be steady and dependable, the cavalry had to be dashing and brave. The bravest and most dashing were the hussars.

These light cavalry regiments were dressed in elegant uniforms. Resplendent in braided and fur-trimmed jackets, the hussars were mounted on the swiftest horses in the army. The daring charges of the Prussian hussars became legendary.

One regiment stood out above the others. It dressed in black and took as its badge a skull. The regiment became known as the Death's Head Hussars and struck fear into the enemy for many long years.

WHO WAS SHAKA?
Shaka was born in 1778, the illegitimate child of a chief of a small African tribe. Before he died, Shaka had become a ruthless conqueror of terrible power.

In childhood, Shaka was banished from his tribe, the Zulu, to grow up among the Mthetwa. Here he learned the skills of a warrior. In 1816 Shaka returned to the Zulu and became king.

At once he organised a small army along Mthetwa lines of age-group regiments. Shaka, however, trained his army in new ideas. He equipped them with a new, shorter spear designed for lethal stabbing at close quarters. He also ordered the men to kill without mercy. It was a far cry from the cattle-raiding warfare then practised by other tribes.

Shaka's first act in his path of conquest was to attack the Buthelezi tribe. The Zulu warriors used Shaka's new tactics and slaughtered the Buthelezi. Shaka and his Zulu warriors attacked tribe after tribe and conquered them all. The Zulu empire grew in territory, wealth and population. As the frightfulness of the Zulus spread, other tribes fled to land occupied by different tribes. These convulsions went on right across southern Africa, causing innumerable clashes and massacres.

By 1828, Shaka had built up an invincible army of some 20,000 warriors and a massive empire, but his rule became increasingly tyrannical and he was assassinated by his half brother, Dingane.

WHEN WERE CANNON FIRST USED IN BATTLE?

In the summer of 1346, an English army of some 20,000 men was marching across northern France. On August 26, a French army of nearly 80,000 men caught up with the English at Crecy.

The English king, Edward III, posted his small army skilfully. The massive French army would only be able to advance on a narrow front. In addition to his knights he had thousands of bowmen and four cannon. This was the first time cannon were used in a battle and nobody was quite sure what the cannon would do.

In mid-afternoon the French advanced. As soon as the French Army was within range, the bowmen let fly their arrows. Arcing through the air, the arrows seemed to fall like a blizzard on the massed French ranks. Thousands fell beneath the arrows, yet the ranks behind still pushed forward.

Then the cannon opened fire. They were noisy and frightening, but they did not seem to achieve much. It was the English bowmen and knights who slaughtered the French wholesale.

When night fell, the French army was in full retreat, leaving thousands dead on the field of battle. In the gathering dusk King Edward led his son, also called Edward but better known as the Black Prince, around the battlefield. It had been a glorious day for England but a tragic one for France.

WHAT DID THE MONGOLS DO IN KHOROSAN?

Before 1218, Khorosan was a rich and fertile country. The agricultural land was watered by an efficient irrigation system and supported several large cities.

Then the Shah of Khorosan murdered an ambassador from

Genghis Khan, leader of the Mongols. Genghis Khan's revenge was swift and terrible. In 1219, he led his ferocious mounted warriors into Khorosan from the east. Genghis Khan was intent on destruction and death on an unparalleled scale.

The army of the Shah was no match for the Mongols who roamed at will across the land. Thousands of peasants were butchered in their villages. Those that fled to the walled cities fared no better. City after city fell to the savage attacks of the Mongols. As each city fell to the conqueror, hundreds of thousands of men, women and children were massacred.

Even more terrible was the damage the Mongols caused to the countryside. With no peasants left to work the land, the irrigation systems fell into disrepair. The fertility of the soil was destroyed.

The Mongols changed Khorosan from a fertile, thriving country into an arid, wind-blown land of death. The land has never really recovered. Today it remains a testimony to the savagery of the Mongols.

General Robert E Lee

WHO WAS KNOWN AS "MARSE ROBERT"?

This was Robert Edward Lee, the commander-in-chief of the forces of the Southern Confederacy during the American Civil War.

Born January 19, 1807, of an old Virginian family (his father was known to fame as Light-Horse Harry Lee, one of George Washington's officers), Robert E Lee entered the military academy of West Point in 1825.

For his gallant services during the Mexican war of 1846, he was promoted colonel, and in 1852 he was chosen superintendent at West Point.

When the Civil War began in 1861, he commanded the first U S cavalry regiment, and was at once offered a high command by the Federal Government. Like many other officers born in a Southern State, he had to choose between North and South. He felt his first duty was to Virginia and so, reluctantly, he resigned his commission and joined the Confederate army.

Then followed three years of

magnificent generalship. In combination with General Thomas Jonathan "Stonewall" Jackson, he defeated the northern armies time and again.

"Marse" in the Deep South is a contraction of "Master" and Robert E Lee was known affectionately to his troops as "Marse Robert."

Finally, Lee was overwhelmed by the superior forces of the North under the command of General U S Grant. On April 9, 1865, Lee surrendered his army to Grant. The long war was over.

Respected by friend and foe alike, he was appointed president of Washington College, Lexington, Virginia, where he remained until his death, October 12, 1870.

WHO IN THE BRITISH ARMY ARE "THE DUKE OF CAMBRIDGE'S OWN"?

The 17th Lancers who led the fatal charge of the Light Brigade at the battle of Balaclava when the French and British on one side, and the Russians on the other, were fighting in the Crimean War. The 17th Lancers' lance-plate carried their badge of a skull and cross bones, signifying death, and the motto "Or Glory." This is why the 17th Lancers are referred to as "The Death and Glory Boys".

The badge was adopted by them because an officer of the 17th, then Light Dragoons, brought back to England the news of the death of General Wolfe on the Heights of Abraham, outside Quebec.

George Frederick William Charles, 2nd Duke of Cambridge, was born March 26, 1819. He joined the British Army in 1838 and became the officer commanding the 17th Lancers. During the Crimean War he led a division and succeeded Lord Hardinge as commander-in-chief in 1856.

WHO WAS ERIC BLOODAXE?

Eric Bloodaxe was a renowned warrior of the 10th century. He was a Viking who led a magnificent and violent life in northern Europe.

Eric, a son of Harald, king of Norway, was forced to flee from Norway when his father died and he went to York in 947. Here most of the people were Vikings and disliked being ruled from southern England. When they found the famous warrior Eric Bloodaxe in their city, they set him up as king and declared themselves independent.

At first, things went well. Eric defeated an English army in a savage battle. Eric was earning his surname with hard fighting. Then his followers deserted him. Eric took to the seas and followed a traditional Viking life, plundering raiding.

In 952, Eric returned to York. Again he was hailed as king. This time Eric Bloodaxe ruled for three years. He fought battles and ruled with a ruthlessness and strength which were amazing. In 954 Eric was betrayed and killed.

WHAT WAS THE HIGH TIDE OF THE CONFEDERACY?

By the spring of 1863 the American Civil War had been raging for two years. Though initially successful, the Confederate, or Southern, forces were growing weaker. The Union armies, on the other hand, were becoming stronger all the time.

The Confederate leaders decided to launch a huge attack to threaten Washington. On July 1, a Confederate brigade ran into a Union division at Gettysburg. Fighting broke out, and both sides sent for reinforcements. All day the battle raged, until the Union forces were pushed out of town. Next day, after reinforcements arrived for both sides, the Union troops were pushed even further back to a hill known as Cemetery Ridge, south of Gettysburg.

By July 3, nearly the entire armies of both sides were south of Gettysburg. Lee, the Confederate general, decided on a huge infantry attack on Cemetery Ridge while he launched a cavalry offensive in the Union rear. Early in the afternoon 15,000 Confederates marched forward to scale the hill.

The Union leader, Meade, had anticipated the attack and ranged his guns and troops at the spot where the Confederates attacked. The Southern troops under Brigadier General Pickett were in murderous gunfire. Still they advanced, but only 150 Confederates reached the crest of the hill. A counter attack soon threw them back down the slope.

By evening the battle was over. The last chance of victory for the South was lost. For this reason, Pickett's charge became known as the High Tide of the Confederacy.

WHO HEARD THE PIPES OF LUCKNOW?

In 1857, Northern India blazed in revolt. The Indian troops employed by the British mutinied. In an orgy of violence they massacred the British, killing men, women and children by the hundred.

At Lucknow was a force of less than 2,000 British and loyal native troops together with their wives and children. They barricaded themselves in the British Residency and awaited the inevitable attack. About 6,000 mutinous troops surrounded the Residency in early July and began a siege that was vicious and prolonged.

For weeks the siege dragged on, with casualties mounting daily. The British knew a relief column would be sent, but would it arrive in time? As artillery continued to pound the Residency, it seemed that only death awaited the British in Lucknow.

Then, according to the story, a young Scottish woman called Jessie was working to repair damage to the defences early one morning. Suddenly she stopped, turned to the men with her and told them to be quiet.

"Can ye nae hear them?" she asked. At first the men could hear nothing. Then one of them heard the sound. On the breeze came the sound of bagpipes. Rejoicing broke out along the walls and in the city. The British troops had arrived.

WHAT WAS BLITZKRIEG?

When the Second World War broke out, the Germans swept everything before them, thanks to Blitzkrieg.

This was a new form of warfare which the Germans had been developing for some years. Its name means "lightning war." Blitzkrieg depended on swift advances by tanks and armoured vehicles supported by devastating air power and infantry.

The medium bombers would be used first to bomb critical communication centres behind enemy lines. Stuka dive bombers would scream down to flatten tactical targets such as artillery batteries. Then the tanks would rumble forward, followed by infantry.

The speed of the German advances and their overwhelming assaults were successful. The Allies had to learn to counter Blitzkrieg during the bitter war years that followed.

WHO WAS KNOWN AS THE LEGLESS ACE?

The most remarkable pilot of the Second World War was, without doubt, Douglas Bader. In 1931 he was the star aerobatic pilot of the RAF, but in December he crashed his plane and had to have both legs amputated. He was invalided out of the air force.

When war broke out Bader was back in the RAF and began flying Spitfires. In itself this was a triumph of willpower over his disability but Bader went further. He fought magnificently over Dunkirk and was then given his own squadron.

On his first day in action as Squadron Leader, Bader shot down two German planes. His success was due to the use of new tactics which had been worked out. Bader kept his squadron tightly grouped and concentrated on disrupting German formations. As soon as the formations were broken, German bombers became relatively easy targets.

Bader's tactics were adopted throughout the RAF, and he was given five squadrons to command. On September 15, 1940, Bader led a massed formation of 60 fighters against enemy bombers and, together with other formations, caused such heavy losses that Hitler had to accept that he could not invade Britain.

In 1941 Bader was brought down over France and despite several attempts at escape, spent the rest of the war as a prisoner. In his brief months of war, Bader had overcome his handicap and had become one of the greatest aces of the RAF.

George Armstrong Custer

WHO WAS LONG HAIR?

The Indians of North America gave apt and often colourful names to themselves and others. The name Long Hair was given to one of their most implacable and courageous foes.

General George Armstrong Custer was a flamboyant and successful cavalry leader. He had long, golden hair and always wore dashing and colourful uniforms. After a brilliant career in the Civil War, Custer was sent westwards to harry the Indians, a task he did so well and with such style that the Indians feared yet respected him and gave him his nickname.

On June 25, 1876, Custer led the 7th Cavalry in a daring attack on hostile Sioux. This time Custer's dash and bravery counted against him. Catching up with the Sioux in the Valley of the Little Big Horn River, Custer advanced to deliver a surprise attack. He had not stopped to discover that he faced the main force of thousands of Sioux. Custer and his entire command were wiped out. Even after they had killed him the Indians did not take his scalp, but left his hair intact, as a sign of respect.

WHAT WAS A SAMURAI?

Until the middle of the last century Japan was a closed and highly traditional society. The Japanese elite were the Samurai warriors.

These men dominated the country and lived by a code known as Bushido. This demanded absolute loyalty to the samurai's superior, outstanding courage, and a total devotion to honour. Death in battle was the pinnacle of a military career, and suicide was preferred to surrender or retreat.

The samurai's weapon was a sword and the Japanese were master swordsmiths. They produced swords of incredible sharpness, without making the blades brittle. To make a samurai sword was expensive and accompanied by much ritual. Every samurai carried two such swords, one long and another short.

Dominance of the Samurai in Japanese society ended in 1867 when Emperor Meiji took over the government and opened up the country to the rest of the world.

WHAT WAS THE CHARGE OF THE LIGHT BRIGADE?

In 1854 a combined British, French and Turkish army was in

The few men remaining in the saddle finally reached the guns

the Crimea fighting the Russians. In an effort to drive the British and French from the Crimea, the Russians attacked their base at Balaklava.

After a hard battle the Russians began to retreat. The British commander, Lord Raglan, ordered the Light Cavalry Brigade to attack some guns the Russians were removing.

Lord Cardigan, commander of the light cavalry, misinterpreted the message. He thought he was ordered to charge Russian guns nearly a mile and a half away.

Placing himself at the very front of the Light Brigade, Cardigan led his men towards the guns. As the British cavalry galloped forward in their splendid uniforms, the Russian guns in front of them crashed out time and again, as did cannon on the flank and numerous small arms.

The firing cannons did not

daunt the British cavalry who continued forward. Men and horses were falling fast yet still the Light Brigade galloped towards the guns. The few men remaining in the saddle finally reached the guns and crashed through.

At the moment of victory, the Russian cavalry counter-charged and the British had to retreat up the valley. It was the most gallant, and most futile action in the war and cost the British heavily. Only 195 of the 673 men of the Light Brigade returned from the heroic charge.

WHAT WAS THE DAMBUSTER RAID?

In the spring of 1943, the Allied bomber offensive against Germany was in full swing. At night the British RAF bombed Germany, to be followed in the day by the Americans.

What was needed was a single blow against a major target. The most important targets of all were the Ruhr dams which provided the German industrial heartland with their vital water supply.

To achieve this, the inventor Barnes Wallis developed a startling new bomb which bounced across water and could be made to destroy dams. It had to be dropped accurately from a height of just 40 ft (12 m).

A special squadron of Lancaster bombers, Number 617, was formed under the command of Guy Gibson. Night after night the

men trained at flying at low heights across lakes.

On the night of May 16, the squadron took off for Germany. The first dam to be attacked was the Moehne. Gibson was the first to attack. He placed his bomb perfectly but the dam held. The second Lancaster was shot down, but the third, fourth and fifth bombers dropped their bouncing bombs on target.

Suddenly, the dam collapsed. A hole, a hundred yards wide had been made in the dam. Millions of gallons of water cascaded down the valley, destroying everything in its path. The next dam to be attacked was the Eder, which fell to just two bombs.

The damage caused by the destruction of the two dams was immense. The raid was a major blow to Germany.

WHICH ROMAN LEGION VANISHED?

The Ninth Legion, known as Hispana, had not enjoyed a very distinguished history. It came to Britain in the invasions ordered by the Emperor Claudius in AD 43. During the subsequent campaigns it seems that the Ninth marched northwards along the eastern coast.

When Boadicea launched her attack against the Romans in AD 61 the first Roman force sent against her was the Ninth. The two forces met somewhere north of London and the Ninth was slaughtered. Though it was soon reinforced and brought back up to strength the Ninth had an unfortunate record.

In AD 107 the legion is recorded as stationed at York. No Roman historian ever mentioned it again. Nobody knows what happened to the Ninth. The fact that its fate was apparently ignored seems to indicate that the end of the Ninth was not glorious.

Perhaps the legion suffered a further defeat and was never reformed. Another possibility is that it was disbanded for some reason. Whatever happened, the Ninth remains the only Roman legion to vanish from the records.

WHO WERE THE CONDOTTIERI?

In the 14th century Italy was split up into a large number of small city states. Many of these were ruled by dictators who could not trust armies recruited from their own citizens.

These dictators, therefore, began hiring mercenaries. At first the mercenaries were foreigners but later, Italians took to the business of fighting as well. The mercenaries treated this fighting as a real business.

They were known as condottieri, which means "contractors." Each company of mercenaries would be led by a condottieri who would find them employment and arrange the terms of the contract. Normally this would involve working for a city for a given period and at set rates of pay. The mercenaries were also allowed to keep any loot they might capture from the enemy.

In time, the business of the condottieri settled into an established pattern. They would be hired by a city to fight the condottieri hired by another city. Both groups of mercenaries would try to avoid fighting each other. Instead they attempted to out-manoeuvre the other and capture towns rich in plunder.

Warfare of this kind kept the people happy. Dictators had soldiers they trusted, the condottieri were employed, and the citizens did not have to fight, although they did run the risk of being plundered.

The system failed in 1494 when the French invaded Italy because the French were willing to fight, and they easily defeated the condottieri.

WHAT WAS THE HOME GUARD?

After the evacuation of British and French troops from Dunkirk in June 1940, German troops stood ready to the south of the English Channel.

This position had been foreseen. The British army had lost vast amounts of equipment at Dunkirk and more men were desperately needed. Throughout May, therefore, hundreds of thousands of British men joined the Local Defence Volunteers, later renamed the Home Guard.

It was believed that German paratroops would soon be dropping from the skies to take important areas prior to a large scale landing. The job of the Home Guard was to report any such landings and provide the regular army with local information. Many members of the Home Guard were quite prepared to go further and made ready to defend their home villages to the death. In the event, of course, the Germans never landed, but the Home Guard remained a vital part of the defence for some time.

WHAT WAS THE "FIGHTING MAN"?

During the Anglo Saxon period fighting was a very personal affair. The king would lead his troops into battle and would be surrounded by his personal war band, each of whom he knew well.

Beside him the king would have his standard by which he would be identified. On the field of battle, this standard, carried by a bearer, would mark the position of the king and the centre of the army. Some of these standards became famous. Perhaps the best known was "The Fighting Man".

This was the standard of Harold Godwinson, King of England in 1066. It was a beautiful piece of needlework, embroidered with a magnificent picture of an armed warrior. It was beneath this standard that Harold died at the Battle of Hastings.

WHAT HAPPENED AT RORKE'S DRIFT?

In January 1879, three British army columns invaded Zulu territory in southern Africa. On January 22, most of the central column, about 1,200 men, were killed by the Zulu army 20,000 strong.

The only outpost between the Zulus and British-held lands was Rorke's Drift. In the mission there, being used as a temporary storehouse and hospital, were Lieutenants Bromhead and Chard with just 140 men of the 24th Regiment.

Chard was the senior officer and as soon as he learnt of the disaster from fugitives, he ordered the men to start building barricades from biscuit boxes and sacks of grain. These chest-high defences were only just completed when 4,500 Zulu warriors appeared on a nearby hill.

A band of Zulus streamed forward towards the lowest section of the barricades. Every man inside Rorke's Drift, even those ill in hospital, were given rifles and began to blast away. The concentrated gunfire and hand-to-hand fighting with bayonets defeated the first Zulu rush.

Zulus with rifles then began a sniping fire, which was to continue all day. As the fighting continued it became clear that Chard could not hold the whole of his perimeter. He retreated to an inner line of defence. Then the Zulus set fire to the hospital. As dusk fell, fresh Zulu warriors streamed into

The hand-to-hand fighting defeated the first Zulu rush

the attack by the light of the burning building.

The fighting continued long into the night, the attacks only slackening at about 2 am. The next day found only some 70 men still able to man the defences, but the Zulus had gone.

The British began to clear up when suddenly the Zulus reappeared on a hill. The redcoats hastily remanned their defences but the Zulus moved off without attacking. One of the most amazing defences of the 19th century was over. In the action, 11 defenders won Britain's highest military decoration, the Victoria Cross, more than in any other engagement.

WHEN DID CAVALRY CHARGE AN AEROPLANE?

In March 1917 the Australian pilot, Lieutenant McNamara was on a bombing raid in the Middle East. Shortly after he dropped most of his bombs, McNamara saw another pilot, called Rutherford, who had been forced to land. Rutherford was obviously unhurt and was signalling for help.

McNamara managed to land, but on taking off again his undercarriage collapsed. Setting fire to the plane, the Australian turned to face a group of Turkish cavalry which was approaching. Just as McNamara was about to open up with Rutherford's gun, a bomb on his own plane suddenly exploded.

This stopped the Turks in their tracks.

A quick inspection of Rutherford's plane showed that it might be made to fly. The two men started the engine and jumped into the cockpit. As the engine roared into life, the Turks remounted their horses and charged at the plane. The plane slowly picked up speed, but the enemy cavalry were approaching fast. The Turkish cavalry were only yards away when McNamara managed to lift his plane into the air. For this exploit, McNamara was awarded the Victoria Cross.

WHO RODE INTO BATTLE WITH A POODLE?

The most dashing and heroic leader in the English Civil War was Prince Rupert. He was born as the son of the King of Bohemia, but his father lost his kingdom when Rupert was a toddler.

Rupert had grown up to be a bold adventurer who took part in many wars in Europe. When, at the age of 23, he heard that his uncle, King Charles I of Britain, faced civil war, Rupert rode at once to offer his sword.

One of Rupert's first victories was typical of his bravery and dash. Rupert was resting with 400 young cavaliers at Powick Bridge, near Shrewsbury, when a force of 1,000 Parliamentarian cavalry appeared. Rupert woke up, grabbed his sword and leapt into the saddle. Not even waiting to see if his men would follow him, Rupert galloped straight into the front ranks of the approaching enemy. Following his example, the other Royalists charged forward. The Parliamentarians were surprised and scattered in confusion, leaving 400 men dead. The Royalists lost only 4 men.

Later Rupert was to become the commander of all the King's cavalry, and wherever he went, he took with him his favourite dog. This was a poodle called Boy and it happily followed the prince into battle. Rupert's enemies tried to make out that the dog was the devil in disguise and directed much spite at the little dog. When Boy finally died, Rupert was heart-broken.

WHO WERE THE LADIES FROM HELL?

When the First World War broke out in the summer of 1914, the Scottish regiments in the British army were still clad in kilts. These were not the tartan costumes of previous years and the glamorous red coats had also gone. Military tactics demanded that they be replaced by drab khaki. In some instances, the Scots were still led into battle by their pipers playing wild and stirring music. The sheer ferocity of the Scots and their incredible fighting abilities greatly impressed the Germans. Because the Germans took the kilts to be skirts, they named the fierce Scots "the ladies from Hell."

WHO WERE SCARLETT'S 300?

During the Battle of Balaklava, at the time of the Crimean War, an amazing feat of cavalry fighting occurred. General Scarlett was leading a section of the Heavy Cavalry Brigade along the foot of a hill known as the Causeway Heights. Suddenly, the top of the hill was filled with a massive force of Russian cavalry. They began to march down the hill towards Scarlett and then stopped.

Undismayed, Scarlett ordered his men to wheel. He then addressed their ranks in view of the enemy before turning and giving the order to charge. Scarlett had only 300 men of the Scots Greys and Inniskilling Dragoons with him when he charged, yet he was attacking 3,000 Russians.

The British were heavy cavalry, big men on big horses and the sheer momentum of their charge carried them deep into the enemy formation.

To those watching it seemed as though Scarlett and his 300 had disappeared. Far from discouraged by this sight the 4th and 5th Dragoons drew their sabres and galloped to help. In their turn they plunged into the Russian mass, hacking away with their sabres.

The combined attacks of the heavy cavalry were too much for the Russians. Assaulted from different directions and ridden through, their formation was destroyed. They fell back, leaving the exhausted British cavalry in command of the hill.

WHAT WAS A STERN-CHASER?

In the days of sail, warships were armed with smooth-bored guns firing shot weighing anything from 6 to 42 pounds. These guns were fired through gunports cut into the ship's sides. If one ship was being chased by another, none of these guns could be brought to bear. But if a gun could be fired backwards, it might disable the other craft and stop pursuit.

To overcome this problem shipbuilders began to cut gunports in the rear of the ship. The design of sailing warships did not permit many of these. The largest ships would mount only four guns. Because such guns were used during chases they were known as chasers. Those at the front were bowchasers, those at the rear were stern-chasers.

WHAT WAS DRAKE'S RICHEST PRIZE?

For many years in the 16th century the Devon sailor, Francis Drake spent all his time pillaging the Spanish Empire. In his career Drake captured several towns, many ships and a huge fortune. His richest prize, however, was captured early in life. Drake led a fleet towards the Pacific in 1577. The only ship to arrive was the *Golden Hind* and in this Drake raided towns and captured ships along the coast of the Spanish possessions. Then he heard that the ship known as the *Cacafuego* was nearby.

After two weeks of searching, Drake found the ship. The Spanish captain could not believe that there was an English vessel in the Pacific for no ship, other than those of Spain, had ever reached that ocean. When Drake opened fire, however, the Spaniard soon surrendered.

The treasure aboard the *Cacafuego* was staggering. As well as vast amounts of jewels and precious stones, there were 13 chests of coins, 80 pounds of gold and no less than 26 tons of silver. Drake and his men were rich beyond dreams.

WHEN DID REDSKINS FIGHT BESIDE BRITISH REDCOATS?

In the middle of the 18th century, Britain and France contested for control of the trade routes into the heart of North America. Trouble flared into the open in 1754. The governor of Virginia sent a group of militiamen to build a fort at the confluence of the Allegheny and Monongahela rivers.

The French considered this to be interference in their lands and attacked. The militia were thrown out, and a vigorous counter-attack the next year was also beaten back by the French. In 1756 Britain and France began the Seven Years War which was to see much fighting in both Europe and America.

As part of their strategy, the British allied themselves with the Iroquois Indians. The redcoats were not used to fighting in dense forests but the Iroquois were. The redskins proved invaluable to the British in the following years of warfare, particularly in driving the French from the Ohio. The war ended in 1763 with victory for the British and their Indian allies.

WHY ARE POPPIES WORN IN BRITAIN EVERY YEAR IN NOVEMBER?

The First World War was one of terrible sacrifice and suffering. For nearly four years the armies on the Western Front faced each other across the desolate waste of No-Man's land.

The British army was positioned at the northern end of the line, in Flanders. The constant shellfire stopped any attempt at farming. This made conditions ideal for wild flowers to grow. The most prolific and colourful of these was the poppy. The nodding red heads of poppies carpeted the battlefields in contrast to the grim realities of war.

When the war ended on November 11, 1918 it was decided to make the poppy a sign of yearly remembrance. When we buy and wear poppies we remember the fallen of two world wars and contribute towards the relief of the wounded.

WHY DID GARIBALDI INVADE SICILY?

In the middle of the last century, Italy as a country did not exist.

The peninsula was divided up into a number of countries.

Many Italians, including an adventurer called Garibaldi, felt the whole of their country should be united but previous attempts at unification had been stopped by the Austrian army. In 1859 the northern kingdom of Piedmont, under its king Victor Emmanuel II, managed, with French help, to unite much of northern Italy.

Garibaldi believed that all Italy should be united, not just the north. He, therefore, gathered together 1,000 volunteers and set off to achieve his purpose. He decided to begin with Sicily. The people of this island, ruled by a king in Naples, had long been dissatisfied. Garibaldi decided to take advantage of this.

He landed with his 1,000 men at Marsala in May 1860. In a brilliant campaign, he quickly swept the island clear of Neapolitan troops. Garibaldi then led his men across the Straits of Messina to mainland Italy. Marching north, he quickly defeated the Neapolitans again and forced their king to flee.

As he marched north, Garibaldi was met by King Victor Emmanuel. Garibaldi then handed his conquests over to the king. Italy was declared to be a united kingdom the following year. Garibaldi had succeeded.

WHO WERE THE HITTITES?

The area now occupied by Turkey was known as Asia Minor in ancient times. It was here that a new power arose about 2,000 BC.

This new nation, known as the Hittites, built a massive capital city at Hattusas which had walls nearly four miles long. The Hittites seem to have been the first people to master ironwork and this may have contributed to their success.

The Hittites were a warlike nation. They produced iron weapons which were far superior to the bronze weapons used elsewhere. Chariot fighting was also brought to a fine art by the Hittites who used the chariot to defeat many enemies. One of the famous Hittite victories was the sack of Babylon. In 1286 BC, the Hittites clashed with the Egyptians at the Battle of Kadesh, which both sides claimed as a victory.

This was to be the high point of the Hittite Empire. It collapsed soon after due to a combination of internal decay and outside attack.

WHO WAS THE FIRST KING OF HAWAII?

In the 1780s, the island chain of Hawaii was divided into a number of tribal kingdoms. Each island had its king and the largest island, Hawaii, was divided between two cousins.

In 1782 Hawaii was united by one of these cousins whose name was Kamehameha. Eight years later Kamehameha attacked the island of Maui. Helped by two Englishmen, Kamehameha took over the island. The following year, Kamehameha enlisted the help of a European ship and cannon in a sea fight with the warriors of Oahu and Kauai. Again Kamehameha won. His career of conquest reached its climax in a battle on Oahu island in May 1795. In the battle, the warriors of Oahu were pushed steadily back until they were forced over a precipice to be dashed to the rocks below.

By 1809, Kamehameha had united the island chain, either by conquest or negotiation. This astounding career as a warrior and conqueror was followed by an equally successful life as a king and an administrator.

WHAT WAS THE LONGEST RANGE AIR STRIKE?

In the early days of aerial warfare weapons had to be improvised and many pilots in the First World War carried artillery shells which were dropped on the enemy. Proper bombing attacks had to await more sophisticated technology.

During the Second World War huge formations of bombers flew right across Europe to rain explosives on the enemy cities. The farthest a bomber has ever flown to drop its bombs, however, happened in the South Atlantic.

During the Falklands conflict between Britain and Argentina the British found it essential to attack the Port Stanley airfield. Huge Vulcan bombers took off from the

RAF base on Ascension Island. They headed south, refuelling in mid air. After dropping their bombs on the airfield, the Vulcan bombers returned to base after a journey of 8,000 miles.

WHO WAS LITTLE TURTLE?

In 1790 a confederation of Red Indians under the leadership of Chief Little Turtle was proving troublesome to the new United States of America. General Harmer was, therefore, sent to the northwest Territories to subdue the Indians.

His army of 1,100 was lured into an ambush and cut to pieces.

The next year Governor St Clair led an army of over 2,000 trained men to avenge the defeat. On November 4, St Clair was also attacked and thrown back after losing more than half his men.

General Anthony Wayne then took a hand. In 1794 he led an army of 1,000 men into the territory of Chief Little Turtle. He met the Indians in the depths of the forest, where Little Turtle had positioned his warriors behind a stockade of fallen timbers. After several days of inaction, Wayne attacked and threw the Indian warriors back. Wayne then destroyed Indian villages and crops until, in August 1795, Little Turtle surrendered.

The United States took over most of the present states of Ohio, Indiana and Michigan as a result of the war.

WHAT WAS NANA SAHIB'S TREACHERY?

In the summer of 1857, India blazed in revolt against the British. The native troops mutinied and slaughtered their officers.

At Cawnpore some 500 men, women and children were defending themselves against the mutineers. Then, just as their food was running out, the British received an offer from the Indian leader, Nana Sahib. He said that if they promised to leave, they would be freed and given boats on which to sail down the Ganges.

On June 27, the British walked out of Cawnpore. As soon as they had reached the Ganges, however, Nana Sahib ordered his men to open fire. More than 300 men, women and children were shot down. The rest were dragged ashore and murdered some days later. Just one boat with about 60 women and children and a few men escaped the slaughter.

All day and night the boat drifted down the river while Indians shot at it from the banks. Next day, the boat became stranded and a force of Indians threatened to attack. So 14 men clambered out of the boat and charged forward. They drove the Indians back but when they returned to the river, the boat had gone. It had been captured and its occupants taken to Cawnpore to be shot.

The 14 men had no choice but to try to walk along the banks of the Ganges. All the way they were shot at by snipers and once faced a full scale attack.

Only four men survived to tell the world of the horrific ordeal experienced by the British at Cawnpore.

WHAT WERE THE V-1 AND V-2?

When it became clear that Hitler would not be able to invade Britain, he placed his faith in secret weapons to bring the country to its knees.

The most spectacular of these were the V-1 and V-2 which came into action in 1944. The V-1 began crashing into London in the summer. They were simply small, pilotless aircraft packed with explosives.

Launched from ramps on the north coast of France they were pointed in the direction of London, given enough fuel to get them there and sent on their way. Because of their peculiar engine noise, the V-1s were called "doodlebugs".

At first the V-1 caused major damage. Some fighter pilots learnt the knack of flying alongside the doodlebugs and flipping them over with a wingtip. Soon anti-aircraft shells fitted with special fuses took such a heavy toll on the V-1s that only one in five ever reached London.

The V-2s were more dangerous. They were rocket-powered missiles against which there was no defence. They travelled so quickly that there was no warning when one would fall. Luckily the Allies captured the V-2 bases before too many could be launched.

WHAT IS THE EARLIEST RECORDED BATTLE?

We know from archaeology that warfare is as old as civilisation. Even the earliest cities have been found to contain weapons and other warlike material.

As the history of mankind emerges, we learn of wars and conquests which determined the futures of whole empires. No details of these struggles have survived. The earliest battle about which much is known is that of Kadesh.

The battle was fought in Syria between the forces of Pharaoh Rameses II of Egypt and Muwatallis, King of the Hittites. Though Rameses had about 20,000 men to the enemy's 16,000, the Hittites had a force of about 2,000 chariots. With these, Muwatallis surrounded the Egyptians who were all fighting on foot. Only some fierce fighting by Rameses II managed to save the Egyptians from disaster.

The result of the battle was rather inconclusive. A border was agreed between the two empires which was exactly what it had been before the fighting started.

WHO WAS THE SUPREME COMMANDER OF THE ALLIES?

In the summer of 1944, it became increasingly clear that the Allies

General Dwight D Eisenhower

needed a supreme commander to co-ordinate the huge forces being massed for the attack on Germany.

The choice fell upon General Dwight D Eisenhower. In some ways it was a surprising choice. When war had broken out, Eisenhower was only a lieutenant-colonel. Once fighting began, however, Eisenhower was soon promoted through the various ranks.

It was not his skills as a soldier that made him the choice of politicians for Supreme Commander. There were many far more brilliant soldiers serving as generals. Eisenhower was chosen because he was a magnificent administrator and also because he could calm tempers. Such brilliant commanders as Montgomery and Patton were ideal battlefield leaders but they argued incessantly with each other.

Eisenhower's chief achievement was that he was able to get so many generals to co-operate for so long. As Supreme Commander, Eisenhower was in command of the D-Day landings and the attacks which led to the eventual surrender of Germany. He handled his task brilliantly and upheld the trust placed in him.

After the war, Eisenhower became the Supreme Commander of NATO in Europe. In 1952 he was elected as President of the United States, a post which he held for eight years.

WHEN WAS THE FIRST TANK USED IN BATTLE?

The appalling conditions of trench warfare in the First World War had not been foreseen by most military thinkers. When they emerged, people were appalled and tried to find an answer.

Colonel Ernest Swinton was an officer who had an idea which would revolutionise warfare. Some years before warfare broke out, he saw a caterpillar tractor able to cross mud and ditches. He reasoned that such a vehicle would quickly cross No-Man's Land and get to grips with the enemy.

By the summer of 1915, Swinton had realised that his cat-erpillar tractor would have to be covered with armour plating. This would make it invulnerable to machine gun fire. The tractor would also be armed with cannon and machine guns.

Incredibly the army dismissed his ideas as worthless. It was Winston Churchill who poured Admiralty money into the idea.

While trying to think up a code name for the machine, Swinton decided that it looked like a large water tank. Rather than call it a "cistern," Swinton settled on the name "tank." By the autumn of 1916 the first of these weapons was ready to go into action. On September 15, tanks rumbled forward through the morning mist. Nobody knew how effective they would prove to be. In the event the tanks were superb. They thundered across the German trenches. The Germans who were not killed instantly, surrendered.

Because nobody knew what sort of tactics to use, nor what kind of support the tanks would need, the attack was not as effective as it might have been. However, there was no doubt that the effectiveness of the machine had been shown.

HOW DID KING EDMUND IRON-SIDE EARN HIS NAME?

Edmund was born in 980 and was the son of King Ethelred the Unready. Ethelred tried to get rid of the Viking attacks by paying the Vikings to go away. This, of course, only encouraged other Vikings to attack him.

Edmund was very different from his father. He was a man of action who knew that the only way to get rid of the Vikings was to defeat them in battle. In 1015, while yet a prince, Edmund launched an attack on a Viking force in northern England. Edmund's implacable opposition to the Vikings was already showing itself.

In April 1016, Edmund became king. Some English nobles wanted Canute, the leader of the Vikings, as king. The armies of Edmund and Canute met at Sherston in Wiltshire. For two days the battle raged, as the Saxons desperately attacked the Vikings.

The Vikings fell back towards the east and Edmund gave chase. Marching across the country with lightning speed, Edmund met and harried the Vikings wherever he could find them.

This energy and his skill as a warrior earned Edmund the name of Ironside. At Ashington, Edmund was defeated by treachery and had to agree to divide England with Canute. Edmund died a few weeks later and many thought that Canute had had him poisoned.

WHAT WAS A TRIREME?

The ancient Greeks were skilled mariners. They sailed far and wide through the area of the Mediterranean while on their trading and colonising activities.

To protect their trading ships, the Greeks developed various types of warships. The most successful of these was the trireme.

Triremes were long, narrow ships propelled by nearly 200 oarsmen seated in three decks. In battle the oars made the triremes very manoeuvrable. They could dart back and forth while other ships were still trying to turn. The principal weapon of the trireme was a metal-tipped battering ram with which they could sink other ships.

The most spectacular victory of the trireme came in 480 BC. A fleet of 200 Greek triremes smashed 800 Persian ships at Salamis.

WHO SANK THE GRAF SPEE?

When World War II broke out in 1939, the powerful German battleship *Graf Spee* was at sea in the South Atlantic. She quickly created havoc among merchant ships and sank over 50,000 tonnes of shipping.

The Royal Navy had to sink the *Graf Spee* as quickly as possible before she could completely wreck trade. On December 13, the British ships *Exeter* and *Ajax*, together with the New Zealand ship *Achilles* found the *Graf Spee* off the River Plate in South America and opened fire on her.

The German ship heavily outgunned her opponents. In little less than an hour the *Ajax* and *Exeter* were so badly damaged that they had to fall back. Unable to

fight on her own, *Achilles* also fell back.

The *Graf Spee* had suffered damage as well. This included a large hole in her bow which meant she would be unfit for the long voyage back home. Hoping to make repairs, the *Graf Spee* sailed into the Uraguayan port of Montevideo.

The Captain was only allowed to make a few repairs before being told he had to leave. Meanwhile the British had been sending radio messages and dropping hints which indicated that a large fleet of British warships was nearby. In fact no such ships existed.

On October 17, the *Graf Spee* steamed out of Montevideo. Convinced that he would be facing overwhelming opposition, the German captain scuttled his battleship.

HOW DID THE BYZANTINE EMPIRE FALL?

For more than a thousand years Constantinople had been the centre of the mighty Byzantine Empire. At one time, it had ruled nearly the whole of the Mediterranean and had been the most powerful force in Europe.

By the 15th century the Byzantine Empire had become much weaker. The continual attacks by the Moslems on this Christian empire had made such inroads that finally, all that was left was the city of Constantinople itself.

In the spring of 1453, the Sultan, Mahomet II, determined to capture this last Christian outpost. The Moslem army gathered outside Constantinople. Day after day Mahomet pounded the city and its famous triple walls with his huge cannon.

Finally, on May 29, Mahomet urged his troops to take the city. Within the walls the Emperor Constantine XI was bravely leading the resistance.

Wave after wave of Moslems surged up to a breach in the walls. Every time the Christians threw them back. Finally, a Moslem Janissary called Hassan charged wielding his scimitar and broke through the breach. Thousands followed him and within minutes the city was lost.

Constantine XI fell fighting the Moslems near the breach. Soon after, Mahomet rode into the city to see the fine palaces and churches pillaged by his troops. Despite the terrible damage caused during the siege, Mahomet did not destroy the city. He made it the capital of the Moslem Empire. Now called Istanbul, Constantinople is still the capital of Turkey.

WHEN DID ONE FIGHT 53?

In September 1591, a fleet of English ships was lying off Flores in the Azores. They were waiting for the Spanish treasure ships from Mexico. Suddenly Spanish ships were sighted. But they were not the treasure ships expected from the west. Instead 53 warships were bearing down from the east.

Lord Thomas Howard ordered his ships to flee. Sir Richard Grenville refused. He had sick men ashore and stopped to pick them up. By the time Grenville had his ship, the *Revenge*, away there was no room to outmanoeuvre the Spanish. His only chance was to sail through the Spanish fleet and then outdistance them.

With all sail set, the *Revenge* tore down towards the Spanish. She sailed past the first ships, but then the mighty *San Felipe* came up. This ship was so large that she took the wind from the *Revenge*. All chance of escape was gone.

Cannon crashed out from the *Revenge* sending shot into the *San Felipe* whose guns quickly replied. The Spanish captain tried to board the *Revenge* but his men were forced back. Then two more Spanish ships came up to join in the fight. They, too, were thrown back by the sheer ferocity of the *Revenge*. As dusk fell the battle raged on. The flash of cannon and musket fire marked the position of the *Revenge*, and the Spanish ships fighting her.

At 11.00 pm Grenville was mortally wounded and carried below. Still the fighting raged on. When dawn broke the *Revenge* was seen to be smashed to a hulk, but still her valiant crew fought on. She had sunk two Spanish ships and damaged several others. With powder and shot running low, the *Revenge* was finally forced to surrender. A few days later a storm sank the damaged vessel and several of the broken Spanish ships.

WHAT DID THE DUKE OF WELLINGTON SAY WHEN LORD UXBRIDGE LOST HIS LEG?

The Battle of Waterloo involved armies of many thousands of men and resulted in the utter defeat of Napoleon, Emperor of France.

The battle had raged all day, when the French army began to fall back from the British-held ridge. The Duke of Wellington, commander of the British army, was sitting on his horse talking to Lord Uxbridge, his cavalry general, about the course of the battle. Both were under fire at the time.

Suddenly, a cannon ball flew past, striking Lord Uxbridge in the knee. There was silence for a moment as both men recovered from the shock. Then Lord Uxbridge calmly announced: "By God, sir, I've lost my leg."

Looking down at the shattered leg, Wellington replied: "By God, sir, so you have."

WHAT WAS THE '15 REBELLION?

When George I, who was a German, became king of the United Kingdom in 1714, many Jacobites thought that their chance had come. Jacobites were the supporters of the direct descendants of King James II who had been driven out of the country by his rebellious subjects. They thought that King George would be unpopular and that the people might rally to James Edward, James II's son, who was in exile.

In 1715 The Earl of Mar raised the Jacobites of the Highlands in rebellion while a force of English supporters seized the town of Preston. It was to no avail. By the time that James Edward had arrived from France, the rebellion had all but collapsed.

Troops loyal to King George quickly recaptured Preston and the Highlanders melted back to the mountains. This Jacobite rebellion is called the '15 to distinguish it from the later and larger rebellion of 1745. This later rebellion was led by Bonnie Prince Charlie, son of James Edward, and came much closer to success before it, too, failed.

WHEN DID THE FIRST AERIAL BOMBING TAKE PLACE?
The first aerial bombardment was carried out by the Austrians against the Venetians in March 1849, when Oberleutnant Franz Buchatius launched several paper balloons, each carrying a 30 lb (14 kg) bomb which were allowed to drift with the wind across the city and release their charges in response to a time fuse.

WHEN WAS THE FIRST ATOMIC BOMB DROPPED?
The first atomic bomb was dropped on the Japanese city of Hiroshima at 08.15 hours local time on August 6, 1945, when a single bomb was released from a B-29 flying at 31,600 ft (9,632 m) above the city. About 71,000 people were killed and a further 68,000 injured in the explosion, which completely destroyed 49,000 buildings.

HOW POWERFUL ARE NUCLEAR WEAPONS?
Atom bombs like those dropped on Hiroshima and Nagasaki are called fission weapons and have a fixed explosive yield equivalent to the destructive power of about 20,000 tons of TNT. Thermonuclear, or fusion weapons (more popularly called hydrogen bombs) have an explosive yield of unlimited size. The largest in use today has an explosive yield equal to 20 million tons of TNT, although the vast majority have an explosive yield of between 500,000 and 1,000,000 tons of TNT equivalent.

WHO WAS CROWNED AS EMPEROR ON CHRISTMAS DAY 800?
The greatest and most powerful ruler of western Europe in the 8th century was undoubtedly Charlemagne, King of the Franks. Charlemagne had become king in 768. From the first this descendant of barbarian warlords showed himself to be a cultured and dynamic king.

He was a devout Christian and

led armies against the Moslems in Spain. He conquered the pagan Saxons, converting them to Christianity. He also took on the ferocious Avars from Hungary and steadily extended his rule until it covered a huge area of Europe.

Charlemagne was not only a warrior. He encouraged learning and art all over his territory. Frankish scholars developed a style of handwriting which forms the basis of our modern letters.

In 799 Pope Leo III appealed to Charlemagne to help restore the power of the Papacy. Charlemagne was so successful that the Pope crowned him in St Peter's in Rome on Christmas Day 800. The Pope gave Charlemagne the title of Emperor in recognition of his greatness.

HOW MANY AEROPLANES DID BRITAIN PRODUCE DURING THE SECOND WORLD WAR?

Between 1939 and 1945, Britain built approximately 128,775 planes and lost 45,000 in combat.

WHO PRODUCED THE MOST WARPLANES DURING THE FIRST WORLD WAR (1914-1918)?

France produced the greatest number, assembling 67,982. Next came Great Britain with a total of 55,093, followed by Germany which produced 45,704, of which nearly 21,000 were produced in 1918 alone. In all, the German and Austro-Hungarian aircraft fac-tories produced 51,135 planes compared with 154,302 produced by the allied powers, France, Great Britain, Italy and the United States.

WHO SAID "THEY SHALL NOT PASS"?

On February 21, 1916, a seven mile stretch of the Western Front erupted into battle. Without any warning the German artillery opened up. They rained a staggering 100,000 shells an hour down on the French. The Battle of Verdun had begun.

The French front lines were flattened and their troops slaughtered. The French reserves could not be brought up through the chaos in front of them. On February 25, the famous Brandenburg Regiment captured Fort Douaumont, the key to the French defences of Verdun.

Realising the extent of the unexpected German attack, the French poured troops into Verdun. General Pétain was placed in command of the sector. The determination of the French defenders was summed up in the phrase: "They shall not pass."

The terrible carnage of Verdun continued for weeks as the Germans attacked and the French counterattacked. All the time the artillery shells continued to fall and cause havoc. By the time winter fell nearly a million men had died around Verdun. Neither side had broken through the other's lines.

WHO WAS THE RED BARON?

The man known to friend and foe alike as the Red Baron was one of the most charismatic men of the First World War.

Baron Manfred von Richthofen began the war in a dashing cavalry regiment. When the war settled down into trenches, Baron von Richthofen transferred to the air service. Here he was able to use his marksmanship and hunting skills to the full.

On September 17, 1916, von Richthofen shot down his first victim. By the end of the year he had become a celebrity as one of the most successful air aces in the world. He was given a squadron to command and a legend really began to develop around him.

The Baron knew all the tricks of aerial fighting. He made sure that all the pilots in his squadron knew them too. His squadron, or Flying Circus as it became known, was greatly respected by the British and French. Von Richthofen then painted his plane blood red all over. He was so confident of his fighting ability that he wanted the enemy to know who exactly was flying that aircraft.

By the summer of 1917 von Richthofen had earned the name of Red Baron and had accounted for 56 enemy planes. On April 20, 1918, he shot down his 80th aeroplane. The Red Baron had become a legend and an example in the German air force.

The next day, the Red Baron was caught in the gunfire of Captain

Baron Manfred von Richthofen

Roy Brown. Machine gunners and infantry were also firing from the ground. Slowly the bright red plane glided down towards earth and made a perfect landing behind British lines. Eager to capture the Red Baron, British troops rushed forward. They found Richthofen sitting dead in his cockpit. His plane had landed when he was already dead. It was a dramatic end to a dramatic career.

There is still controversy as to who shot down the Red Baron, Roy Brown or the marksmen from the ground.

WHO WAS THE MONARCH WHO WAS KNOWN AS THE LION OF THE NORTH?

When Gustavus Adolphus became King of Sweden in 1611, his country was on the edge of European politics. Before his death in 1632, he had made Sweden a major power.

Gustavus Adolphus began his remarkable career by reforming the Swedish army. He encouraged the Swedish iron industry to produce better weapons. The infantry were equipped with a lighter, more reliable musket, the artillery was trebled in size and re-equipped with modern guns. The cavalry were retrained to deliver dramatic charges using sabres rather than pistols.

By 1629 Gustavus Adolphus had defeated both Poland and Russia. As a prize, Sweden gained large areas of Finland and some important ports along the north German coast. In 1630 Gustavus Adolphus threw his nation into the Thirty Years War. Within two years he had defeated the army of the Holy Roman Empire and had established his reputation as "The Lion of the North".

In 1632, Gustavus Adolphus was advancing on Vienna. His army was met by an Imperial force at Lutzen. In the following battle, the Swedes were victorious, but Gustavus Adolphus was killed. Without his personal command, the power of Sweden quickly crumbled.

WHOSE FAVOURITE MAXIM WAS "GIT THAR FUSTEST WITH THE MOSTEST"?

Nathan Bedford Forrest, a major general of the Confederacy during the American Civil War. He had received little education as a boy and no military experience before the war but he climbed the ranks to become one of the South's greatest officers.

WHAT WAS THE LAST PIECE OF ARMOUR WORN BY BRITISH INFANTRY?

When guns began to appear on the battlefield in large numbers, armour became useless. Cannon balls and musket bullets could pierce all but the heaviest armour.

Most armies discarded armour for infantry during the 17th century. The only piece of armour to remain was the gorget. This was a large metal plate which fitted over the shoulders and protected the throat. Gradually it became smaller until by the middle of the 18th century it was simply a crescent-shaped piece of metal worn round the neck showing rank. It was abandoned by the British army in

1830. A few cavalry regiments continued to wear breast and back plates after this date.

WHERE DID PAUL REVERE RIDE?

Paul Revere had a distinguished career as an officer in the American forces during the American War of Independence, but his moment of fame came on April 18, 1775.

Although fighting had not yet begun, American patriots were piling up war stores at Concord, Mass. On April 18, 1775, a British force of 800 men left Boston after dark to capture these stores. Paul Revere saw them and gave a prearranged signal by lanterns from a church steeple to his fellow patriots.

Revere then leapt on to his horse and galloped towards Lexington. All along his route, Revere alerted the minutemen, (men who only required a minute's notice to be ready for battle) and roused many patriots before his ride was over.

WHO THREW HIS SPEAR AT THE GATES OF ROME?

In 218 BC, Rome and Carthage went to war. Forestalling any Roman attack, the Carthaginian general, Hannibal, led an army, including elephants, over the Alps into Italy.

He quickly defeated two Roman forces in the Po Valley. On August 2, 216 BC, Hannibal's force of 50,000 men was confronted by a Roman army of nearly 80,000 soldiers. By skilful manoeuvring and a series of well-timed attacks from the rear, Hannibal managed to crush the Roman army. Only 3,000 Romans escaped the disaster.

For many years Hannibal marched up and down Italy, raising cities in rebellion against Rome and leading several successful actions. On one occasion, Hannibal actually reached the city of Rome. Riding up to the city, Hannibal flung his spear into the gates but without a siege train, Hannibal had to retreat.

Eventually the Romans defeated Hannibal but they never forgot the man who had flung his spear in the gates of Rome.

WHO WON A VC ON THE WING OF AN AIRCRAFT?

On the night of July 7, 1941, during World War II, a force of RAF Wellington bombers were raiding the German city of Munster. On the way back, the Wellington flown by Squadron Leader Widdowson was suddenly raked with gunfire by a Messerschmitt Me 110.

Though the German plane disappeared into the night, the Wellington was in trouble. The starboard engine was blazing and the hydraulic controls were destroyed. Widdowson struggled to keep the plane on a straight course and ordered his crew to try to put out the fire.

Led by Sergeant James Ward,

Sergeant Ward crept out along the wing

the crew aimed fire extinguishers at the flames but the jets could not reach them. Slowly, the fire crept along the wing towards the fuselage. Ward decided to try a desperate measure. Tying a rope around his waist, he climbed out of the aircraft.

He was at once caught in the airstream whipping past the wing. Kicking footholds in the flimsy covering, Ward slowly crept out along the wing. Each movement might have spelt disaster, for each time he lifted a hand or foot his hold was weakened. Eventually, Ward reached the fire and pulled

out the cockpit cover which he had thoughtfully brought with him.

Desperately Ward crammed the cover into the blazing hole. Almost at once the cover blew away into the night but Ward had prevented the fire spreading further along the wing. The fire, now contained, soon went out.

Widdowson managed to get the plane home safely, though the Wellington ended up in a fence. For his valour in putting out the fire, Ward was awarded the Victoria Cross, the highest military decoration in Britain.

WHO WERE THE VARANGIANS?

The Vikings did not only raid and trade with Western Europe. By sailing their ships along the rivers of Russia they reached the Black Sea and the Mediterranean.

The greatest power in the Eastern Mediterranean at the time was the Byzantine Empire. Though the two often clashed, the Byzantines were impressed by the fighting abilities of the Vikings. So much so that the Emperors began to recruit Viking mercenaries as Imperial bodyguards. This special force of warriors was known as the Varangian Guard.

For a hundred years the Varangians remained a powerful force in the Mediterranean. When their term of service in the Varangian Guard was over, many Vikings stayed on in the Byzantine Empire.

Others returned home laden with fine clothes and wealth, encouraging more of their fellow country-men to follow the road to join the Varangians.

WHAT WAS THE PENINSULAR WAR?

In 1808 Napoleon forced the King of Spain to abdicate. Napoleon then made his own brother, Joseph, King of Spain.

The Spanish immediately rebelled against this foreign domination. The Portuguese too, joined in the struggle against the French army of occupation and British troops were sent to help, under the command of Sir John Moore. The French suffered setbacks, until Napoleon took a hand personally. He quickly pushed the British out of Spain and defeated the armies ranged against him.

A vicious guerilla warfare then began. Spanish peasants took up arms and cut down any isolated French patrol they could find. The British returned under the command of Wellesley, later to be Duke of Wellington. The Peninsular War which followed was named from the fact that it was fought in the Spanish Peninsula. It did not end until Napoleon was forced to abdicate in 1814.

WHICH ENGLISH WARRIORS ESPECIALLY WON THE ADMIRATION OF THEIR VIKING FOES?

In the 9th century Britain was under almost constant attack from the fierce Vikings. One such attack was led by Olaf, a member of the Norwegian Royal family, with a fleet of 93 ships.

He landed at Maldon, in Essex, where he encountered opposition. The local Earldorman of Essex, who was the leader of local government, was a tall, grizzled old warrior called Brihtnoth. He had fought in many battles and was determined to face Olaf and his Vikings. He gathered his men around him and stormed down to Maldon.

The English arrived at high tide when the Vikings were cut off on an island by the tide. As the tide fell a causeway appeared. Brihtnoth sent his three best warriors, Wulfstan, Aelfhere and Maccus to hold the causeway. For some time they fought the Vikings off but eventually, the tide fell further and the Vikings were able to scramble ashore.

The battle raged for hours with war-cries booming out and swords and axes swinging. At last, Brihtnoth fell beneath the swords of the Vikings. Some of the English fled but one of the warriors sang out: "Thoughts must be the braver, hearts more valiant, courage the greater as our strength grows less."

The English who remained, grimly set themselves to kill as many Vikings as possible before they, too, were cut down. Though Olaf won the battle, and lost good men, he regarded highly the courage of Brihtnoth and his men, even though they had fought against him.

WHO WAS THE DUKE OF MARLBOROUGH'S WOMAN SOLDIER?

In 1706 the British fought the French at the Battle of Ramillies. One of many soldiers brought in for treatment of wounds was a trooper of dragoons. While the surgeons were preparing the soldier for treatment, they realised that "he" was a woman.

When the soldier recovered she revealed the truth. Apparently she was the wife of Christopher Walsh, another trooper in the same regiment, and had joined up nearly 13 years earlier to be with her husband. Obviously now that her secret was out, she could no longer serve in the ranks.

The Duke of Marlborough, who commanded the British army, decided that the brave woman should have a fresh wedding. This was held soon after and was attended by many officers and noblemen in the army. Mrs Walsh was then made a cook in her husband's regiment so that they could still be together.

WHO WAS TAMURLAINE THE MAGNIFICENT?

Born in 1336, Tamurlaine was made governor of the town of Kesh, in Turkestan, at the age of 24. Nine years later he rebelled and began his march to greatness.

Tamurlaine seems to have had an unquenchable lust for power, conquest and war. He certainly behaved as if his only object in life was to conquer others. Tamurlaine based his army on cavalry. He bred and trained vast numbers of magnificent horses for his army and gathered about him the best and most ferocious horsemen he could find. In his first campaign, Tamurlaine led 100,000 horsemen against the Mongols and savagely beat them.

In 1398 Tamurlaine charged down from the Himalayas to storm across northern India and capture Delhi. He then turned west and rode through Persia to defeat the Syrian and Egyptian armies. When he died in 1405, Tamurlaine had risen from a provincial governor to command vast areas of Asia. He was the greatest warrior of his time.

WHO WAS THE LAST BRITON TO BE KNIGHTED BY A BRITISH MONARCH ON THE FIELD OF BATTLE?

During the days of chivalry, kings led their armies into battle. If a squire fought particularly well, the king would knight him on the field of battle. Such knights, who gained their position for bravery, were called knights banneret, and were allowed special privileges.

By the 18th century, kings rarely risked their lives in battle but in 1743, King George II took the unusual step of accompanying his army to war. On June 27, the British ran into a superior French army at Dettingen in Germany.

The French attacked and though repulsed, captured a standard. Seeing the French making off with such a valuable prize, Trooper Thomas Brown of the 3rd Dragoons spurred his horse forward at the gallop. Hacking his way through the French, Trooper Brown grabbed the standard and then fought his way back. Though wounded no fewer than seven times, the trooper had rescued the standard.

King George saw the feat and promptly knighted Trooper Thomas Brown. It was the last time a British monarch created a knight banneret on the battlefield.

WHEN WAS THE LAST GREAT CAVALRY VICTORY?

Despite the technological advances of the 20th century, cavalry still formed a large part of most armies in the First World War. Though useless in the trenches of the Western Front, the cavalry came into its own in the Middle East.

In 1918 General Allenby was leading the British, as well as the Australian and New Zealand forces against the Turks. In the open desert Allenby, himself a cavalry office, used horsemen with considerable effect.

Following the victory at Meggido, the Turks placed a strong rear guard at the village of Samakh. Allenby sent forward a force of Australian Cavalry under Brigadier Grant to make an inspection of the village.

Arriving at dawn, Grant set up some machine guns to give covering fire and then ordered his cavalry to charge. Galloping through the grey morning light, the Australians charged forward. Ignoring heavy Turkish fire, in one bold dash they rode through Samakh and captured it. The Turkish retreat was thrown into confusion. A few days later peace was signed.

It was the last great victory for the cavalry in modern warfare.

Science and Technology

WHAT, TO DATE, WERE THE LAST WORDS SPOKEN ON THE MOON?

Eugene Cernan, commander of Apollo 17, said as he boarded his Lunar Module on the Moon: "We leave as we came and God willing as we shall return, with peace and hope for all mankind. God speed the crew of Apollo 17." He and his crew returned December 19, 1972.

WHO WAS THE FIRST MAN TO GO THROUGH THE SOUND BARRIER AND IN WHAT PLANE?

On October 14, 1947, Major Charles E Yeager broke the sound barrier for the first time, flying the Bell X-1 in California.

IF A MAN CAN JUMP 6 FEET (1.8 m) FROM THE SURFACE OF THE EARTH, HOW HIGH WOULD THAT SAME MAN JUMP FROM THE SURFACE OF THE MOON?

A man jumping on the surface of the moon would leap six times as high as he could on earth because the moon has only one-sixth the gravity of earth; therefore, the man would jump a height of 36 ft (10.97 metres).

WHICH COUNTRY LAUNCHED THE FIRST ARTIFICIAL SATELLITE AND WHY?

On October 4, 1957, the Soviet Union launched Sputnik 1, a 30 lb (13.6 kg) sphere designed to begin a series of missions in support of the International Geophysical Year.

WHICH TWO FAMOUS EXPERIMENTS, CENTURIES APART, DEMONSTRATE THAT A HAMMER AND A FEATHER FALL AT EQUAL SPEED IN A VACUUM?

Early in the 17th century, Galileo Galilei dropp d two spheres of unequal weignt from the leaning tower of Pisa and calculated the air resistance that prevented one reaching the earth sooner than the other and wrote a theory that the two would fall equally fast in a vacuum. In 1971, astronaut David R Scott demonstrated from the surface of the moon that indeed a hammer and a feather released at the same time arrive at the surface together.

action there is an equal and opposite action. It is not the exhaust pushing against air which propels the spacecraft in the opposite direction but purely the reaction brought about by the rocket's exhaust going in one direction.

HOW CAN ROCKETS WORK IN A VACUUM WHEN THERE IS NO AIR FOR THE EXHAUST TO PUSH AGAINST AND SO PROPEL THE SPACECRAFT FORWARD?

A rocket can work in a vacuum because it takes its own oxygen in special tanks to mix with fuel burned in the rocket engine. A rocket motor pushes a spacecraft forward by Newton's Third Law of Motion which states that for every

WHY ARE ASTRONAUTS WEIGHTLESS IN SPACE?

Astronauts are weightless in space because then they are continually falling between worlds, or they are falling around the earth and never reaching its centre; hence they are like riders in a rapidly descending lift where everything is falling at the same speed and there is no relative motion between the lift and its occupants.

US Senator E J Garn experimenting in space weightlessness

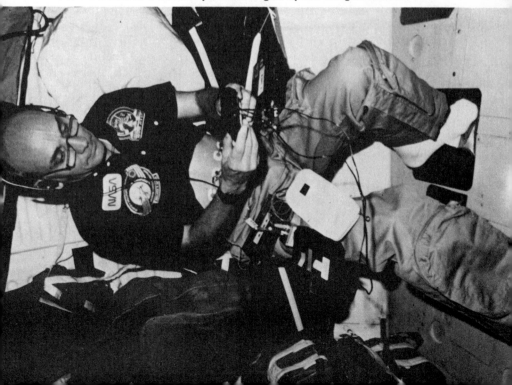

WHAT IS THE DIFFERENCE BETWEEN A BLACK HOLE AND A WHITE HOLE?

A black hole is believed to be formed when matter is compressed down so tightly because of gravity that it bends space and time and disappears into infinity, theoretically believed by some to emerge in another part of the universe through a white hole.

HOW OLD IS THE EARTH AND HOW DO WE KNOW?

The earth is believed to be nearly 5,000 million years old because rocks brought back from the moon have a maximum age of about 4,600 million years and are known to have been formed close to the origin of the solar system where the moon and all the planets formed. The age of rocks on earth (a living planet) are too new to give the information.

WHAT IS THE SPEED NEEDED TO REACH ORBIT AND THE SPEED NEEDED TO ESCAPE EARTH'S GRAVITY?

Orbital speed, defined as the speed needed to continue falling around the curvature of the earth and never coming any closer to it, is 17,500 mph (28,162 km/h). As speed is added the orbit gets progressively more elliptical until at 25,000 mph (40,232 km/h) the spacecraft breaks free of earth's gravity and leaves the vicinity of the planet.

HOW OLD IS THE UNIVERSE AND HOW DO WE KNOW THAT?

The universe is believed to be nearly 20,000 million years old because galaxies 12,000 million light years away are seen to be moving at more than half the speed of light. Therefore, because we see back in time 12,000 million years, we can calculate that nearly 20,000 million years ago matter was probably bursting out from the big bang close to the speed of light.

WHAT IS THE RELATIONSHIP BETWEEN AN AIRSICK PASSENGER IN A BOEING JUMBO JET AND A NAUSEATED ASTRONAUT IN ORBIT?

Because our sense of balance is determined by movement of fluid in the inner ear, any motion which disturbs our equilibrium causes the body to react in a way which we interpret as a feeling of sickness. An astronaut in space can be disorientated and get the same effect.

WHAT IS THE FASTEST PRODUCTION AEROPLANE IN THE WORLD?

The fastest plane flying today is believed to be the Lockheed SR-71 which has a classified top speed. It is, however, known to have flown for periods of at least 30 minutes at speeds something in excess of Mach 3, approximately 2,000 mph (3,219 km/h).

American Space-shuttle

WHEN DID THE SHUTTLE MAKE ITS FIRST FLIGHT INTO SPACE?

On April 12, 1981, carrying astronauts John Young and Robert Crippen, the first Shuttle equipped to fly into space (Columbia) was launched from the Kennedy Space Center in Florida.

WHO WAS THE FIRST AMERICAN TO ORBIT THE EARTH?

On February 12, 1962, astronaut John H Glenn Jr became the first United States citizen to enter earth orbit when he was launched from Cape Canaveral in Florida, a site later renamed the Kennedy Space Center. He remained in space for less than five hours, making three full orbits of the earth.

WHY IS PLUTO SO UNLIKE ANY OTHER PLANET IN THE SOLAR SYSTEM?

Pluto, which for most of its orbit is the outermost planet in the solar system, only infrequently dipping within the orbit of Neptune, is almost entirely composed of water, ice and frozen gases surrounding a very small rocky core. All other planets are either densely compressed balls of rock and gas or comprise solid terrestrial bodies like the earth. Moreover, Pluto is probably an escaped moon of Neptune knocked out of orbit around its giant neighbour by forces early in the evolution of the solar system.

WHEN DID AMERICAN ASTRONAUTS AND RUSSIAN COSMONAUTS JOIN UP IN THE SAME SPACECRAFT ABOVE EARTH?

On July 15, 1975, NASA astronauts Thomas Stafford, Vance Brand and Deke Slayton were launched aboard their Apollo spacecraft from the Kennedy Space Center. Just seven and a half hours earlier, cosmonauts Alexei Leonov and Valery Kubasov had been launched in their Soyuz spacecraft from Baikonur. After two days catching each other up, the spacecraft docked and astronauts joined cosmonauts via a docking module connecting the two vehicles.

WHAT WAS THE FIRST SPACECRAFT TO GO INTO ORBIT AROUND THE MOON?

Launched on March 31, 1966, the 3,528 lb (1,600 kg) Soviet space craft Luna 10 was the first man-made object successfully to enter orbit about another body in the solar system when it completed the first of many orbits of the moon several days later.

WHAT WAS THE FIRST SUCCESSFUL PLANETARY SPACECRAFT?

On August 27, 1962, the United States launched Mariner 2, weighing 447 lb (203 kg) towards the planet Venus. After several months of successful flight, it became the first man-made object to report details back to earth from instruments aboard a spacecraft, sensing the environment of another planet. It followed an unsuccessful attempt one month before to launch Mariner 1, which had failed to go into the correct trajectory.

WHEN WAS THE FIRST SUCCESSFUL LANDING ON MARS ACCOMPLISHED?

On August 20, 1975, the United States launched Viking I, a 7,585 lb (3,441 kg) spacecraft comprising an orbiter and a lander. Connected together, Viking I successfully entered orbit about Mars before releasing the lander to descend to the surface on July 20, 1976. The spacecraft successfully operated from the surface and was followed a few months later by a second Viking which also put a lander down on the Martian dust.

WHAT WAS THE FIRST MANNED SPACE MISSION KNOWN TO HAVE BEEN STRUCK BY LIGHTNING DURING LAUNCH?

During late morning on November 14, 1969, while flying straight up through a rain-lashed sky, the 2,900 ton (2,946,585 kg) Apollo 12 spacecraft and launch vehicle was twice struck by lightning just seconds after lift-off. The Apollo spacecraft computers were knocked out of action but the Saturn rocket responsible for putting the spacecraft in orbit about earth continued to operate without undue effect from the lightning strike. The Apollo computers were turned on again before reaching orbit. Apollo 12 was the second successful manned landing on the moon.

WHAT ARE THE ASTEROIDS AND WHERE DID THEY COME FROM?

Beyond the four inner planets of Mercury, Venus, the Earth and Mars, lies a vast and wide range of rocky and microscopic debris known as the asteroid belt. The width of the belt is greater than the distance from the sun to its inner edge, a distance that includes the orbits of all four inner planets. The asteriod belt is believed to be many millions of miles thick and may be the remnants of an old planet originally formed at that distance but broken apart by violent forces early in the solar system's history.

WHO WAS IGOR SIKORSKY?

He was a Russian refugee who fled from the Revolution in 1917 and who in 1925 was a celebrated aircraft designer working on Long Island, New York.

Across the years he designed many famous aircraft but perhaps he is best known for the advances he made in helicopter design. The first successful single-rotor helicopter was a Sikorsky VA-300.

WHAT IS THE OUTERMOST PLANET AND IS IT ALWAYS SO?

The outermost planet is generally considered to be Pluto, yet because its orbit is a huge ellipse, the inner part of which comes inside the orbit of Neptune, at some times it is closer to the sun, as it is for a part of this century.

WHO MADE THE FIRST NON-STOP TRANSATLANTIC FLIGHT FROM WEST TO EAST AND WHEN?

On June 14, 1919, Captain John Alcock and Lieutenant Arthur W Brown took off in a Vickers Vimy from Newfoundland and landed heavily in a bog in southern Ireland 15 hours 57 minutes later.

WHEN AND WHERE WAS THE FIRST SUCCESSFUL LAUNCH OF A LIQUID PROPELLANT ROCKET?

On March 16, 1926, Robert H Goddard first launched a liquid propellant rocket from a primitive firing site at Auburn, Mass, USA. It reached a height of 41 ft (12 m), travelled a ground distance of 184 ft (56 m) and landed in a patch of old cabbages 2.5 seconds after launch, having averaged 60 mph (97 km/h).

WHAT IS THE HIGHEST FLYING PLANE IN THE WORLD?

The plane known to have flown the highest is the North American

This photo was taken by Viking Lander 1 from its position on Mars. The big boulder, nicknamed Big Joe, is approximately six and a half feet (approx. two metres) across and 23 to 26 feet (10 to 15m) from the Lander

Aviation X-15 which reached a height of 354,000 ft (approximately 67 miles or 108 km) in 1963. However, the Shuttle, which is launched like a rocket but lands like a plane, has reached a maximum altitude of just over 200 miles (322 km) in orbit.

WHAT WAS THE FIRST MILITARY AEROPLANE?

The first military aeroplane was delivered to the United States Army in August 1909. It was built by Wilbur and Orville Wright who achieved the first powered flight six years earlier.

DO WE KNOW IF THERE IS LIFE ON MARS?

Nobody knows for sure whether there is life on Mars. The only real attempt to find out was the United States Viking programme which successfully landed two spacecraft on the surface of the planet in 1976. Each lander carried special instruments to search for signs of life using a variety of well-tried techniques. A sampler was used to dig soil and deposit small quantities in funnels and hoppers which fed directly to the inside of the spacecraft and on to the tiny conveyor belt which transported material to each biological instrument. After many years of analysing the surface samples and having that information sent back to earth, scientists have deduced that it is still an open question, seeing signs of life in the results that they achieved but being quite unable to identify positively any living organism.

WHAT WAS THE FIRST OBJECT TO HIT THE MOON?

On September 14, 1959, the Soviet Union succeeded in hitting the moon with Luna 2, an 860 lb (390 kg) probe launched September 12. It crashed 268 miles (431 km) from the visible centre.

WHAT WAS THE FIRST AMERICAN SATELLITE?

On January 31, 1958, a 31 lb (14 kg) satellite was launched by a Jupiter C rocket from Cape Canaveral in Florida, the first United States satellite placed in orbit. It was the third object in space, following Sputnik 1 and Sputnik 2 launched by the Soviet Union in October and November 1957.

WHEN WAS THE TELESCOPE INVENTED?

In 1608 the Dutch spectacle maker Hans Lippershey discovered that two lenses, one in front of the other, could produce a magnifying effect. One year later, Galileo Galilei heard of the discovery and made what is believed to be the world's first telescope, going on to discover the moons of Jupiter, craters on the moon, and observe for the first time separate stars in the Milky Way.

WHAT IS HALLEY'S COMET?

Seen in England during the spring of 1066, where it was regarded ominously as the precursor of a Norman invasion, Halley's Comet (as it was later called) appeared in the Bayeux Tapestry, famous for its depiction of the end of Saxon rule in England. The comet makes a close pass around the sun once every 76 years, and last appeared during early 1986 when it was analysed by several spacecraft from Russia, Japan and Europe. The comet derives its name from Edmond Halley (1656-1742) who became the first astronomer to establish its orbit.

WHAT MAKES THE SUN SHINE?

Basically, the sun is a continuous hydrogen bomb explosion with hydrogen atoms converted into helium atoms at the rate of 700 million tons (711 million tonnes) per second. A series of nuclear reactions fuse four hydrogen atoms, creating one helium atom with a consequent loss of energy. Each second the sun burns, it reduces its weight by 4 million tons (4,064,000 tonnes) of energy, equivalent to the output in light, heat and radiation. The sun is composed of 73% hydrogen, 25%

helium and 2% of other elements like carbon, oxygen, nitrogen and iron. Presently, the sun is estimated to be almost 5,000 million years old and has about the same length of time left before it dies.

WHAT WAS THE FIRST COMMUNICATION SATELLITE?

The first truly commerical communication satellite, called Telstar 1, was launched into a low earth orbit 592 miles (953 km) at the low point by 5,300 miles (8,529 km) at the high point on July 10, 1962. The first pictures were relayed from the United States to Britain and France just 15 hours after launch and two weeks later millions of Europeans and Americans watched as a conversation was conducted by people on opposite sides of the Atlantic.

HOW POWERFUL ARE COMMUNICATION SATELLITES TODAY?

Today, powerful communication satellites high above the earth in stationary orbit, a path aligned with the earth's equator in which they appear to remain over one spot on the surface, provide more than 60% of international communications. The most powerful satellites for international duty are called Intelsat 5, with each capable of handling 15,000 simultaneous, two-way telephone calls at any one time. Several of these satellites are located over the Atlantic, Pacific and Indian Oceans. They will soon be replaced by satellites capable of carrying three and four times this capacity.

WHEN WAS THE WORLD'S FIRST OPERATIONAL WEATHER SATELLITE LAUNCHED?

In April 1960, the United States launched Tiros 1, the world's first operational meteorological satellite. Tiros 1 weighed only 283 lb (128 kg) and had two low-power cameras. Today, satellites of the Tiros-N series weigh almost 4,000 lb (1,814 kg) and have a complex array of picture-taking equipment with many special sensors to record the temperature of clouds, the temperature of the lower atmosphere and significant pieces of information about the condition of weather systems. They are assisted by other, equally powerful satellites in stationary orbit, 22,300 miles (35,881 km) above the equator.

WHY WAS THE SECOND WORLD WAR RESPONSIBLE FOR THE WIDE-SPREAD USE OF REFLECTING ROAD-STUDS POPULARLY CALLED CATSEYES?

Percy Shaw, the British inventor first designed catseyes in 1934 but it was not until the blackout was imposed in Britain at the outbreak of war in 1939 that it was realised how indispensable they were for the safety of drivers of all types of vehicles at night. Production then rocketed.

WHO INVENTED THE PARKING METER?

Carl C Magee of Oklahoma City. It was in 1936 that his application to the US Patent Office was granted.

HOW MANY SATELLITE LAUNCH SITES ARE THERE IN THE UNITED STATES?

The United States has developed four satellite launching facilities. Two are close together at Cape Canaveral and comprise one facility run by the Air Force, called the Eastern Missile Test Range, and the other by NASA, called the Kennedy Space Center. The United States Air Force operates a major launch facility on the West Coast of America called the Vandenberg Air Force Base and NASA operates a small satellite launching facility at Wallops Island on the Atlantic coast of Virginia.

HOW MANY SATELLITE LAUNCHING SITES DO THE RUSSIANS OPERATE?

The Russians operate three main satellite launching centres. By far the biggest is located at Baikonur in Kazahkstan and has been used to launch many satellites since the first in October 1957. The second is located near Volgograd and is known as Kapustin Yar, from where smaller satellites are sent

into space. The third site is south of Archangel and is a major military launch facility known as Plesetsk, from the town which lies a few miles away.

WHAT IS THE MOST ACTIVE VOLCANO IN THE SOLAR SYSTEM?

In a state of almost continuous eruption, a massive volcano on the Jupiter moon, called Io, was observed by the cameras of Voyager 1 from a distance of more than 2.5 million miles (4 million km). The huge plume seen bursting over the horizon of the planet's rim has been identified as a continuous outpouring of sulphur dioxide from a turbulent interior.

WHAT WAS THE FIRST OBJECT TO LAND A PACKAGE OF WORKING INSTRUMENTS ON THE SURFACE OF THE MOON?

The Russian Luna 9 which landed gently on the surface of the moon January 31, 1966, was the first instrumented spacecraft to set a package of sensors down on the lunar surface. The lunar spacecraft weighed 225 lb (102 kg) and took the form of a sphere with petals unfolded from the top to stabilise it on the surface. It carried a 3.3 lb (1.5 kg) TV camera inside layers of shock-absorbing material and within seven hours of landing had sent back the first pictures ever transmitted from the surface of the moon.

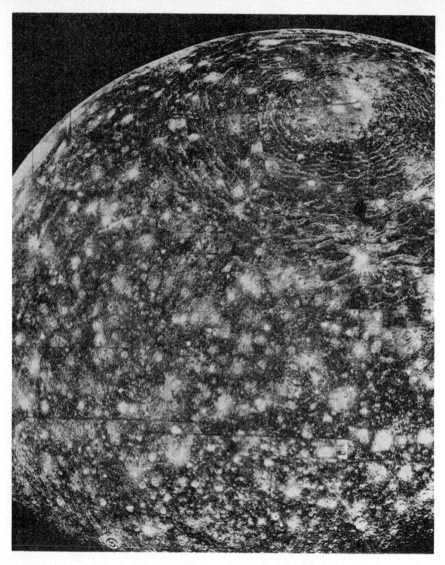

A photomosaic of Callisto, a Galilean satellite of Jupiter

HOW MANY PLANETS HAVE BEEN EXPLORED BY SPACE-CRAFT?

Of the nine planets in the solar system only Neptune and Pluto have not been closely inspected by spacecraft flying past. Neptune will be inspected at close quarters when the Voyager spacecraft reaches the planet in early 1989 and makes a pass just a few thousand miles above its cloud tops. Of the eight planets apart from Earth, only Venus and Mars have been inspected from the surface. There are plans to retrieve samples from the surface of Mars and bring them back to earth using automatic robot spacecraft. This event may take place in the late 1990s. Although the moon is a natural satellite of the earth and not a planet at all, astronauts have visited the surface and returned samples to earth from six successful missions.

WHAT WAS THE FIRST SUCCESSFUL FLY-BY MISSION TO MARS?

Launched on November 28, 1964, the 575 lb (261 kg) United States spacecraft called Mariner 4, was launched from Cape Canaveral using an Atlas-Aegina rocket. Mariner 4 was launched into an enormous orbit of the sun, part of which intersected the planet Mars. The spacecraft passed the red planet across the region of the equator on the evening of July 14, 1965, becoming the first successful space mission to report back from the vicinity of Mars.

WHO WERE THE FIRST MEN TO DIE IN SPACE?

On June 6, 1971, Soviet cosmonauts Georgi Dobrovolski, Vladislav Volkov and Viktor Patsayev were launched aboard the Soyuz II spacecraft to dock with the world's first space station,

Salyut 1, previously launched. On June 29 they separated from Salyut 1 in an attempt to return to earth but a sudden loss of pressure inside the capsule asphyxiated them before they started the return flight. The crew were not carrying pressure suits, in order to make sufficient room in Soyuz II for three rather than two cosmonauts, and there was no way they could save themselves without oxygen to breathe.

WHAT IS GEOSTATIONARY ORBIT?

Geostationary orbit is achieved when a satellite is placed 22,300 miles (35,881 km) above the surface of the earth in a path which carries it in the plane of the equator. At this distance a satellite takes exactly 24 hours to travel once around the earth and therefore seems to keep pace with a point on the surface over which it is positioned.

HOW MANY STARS ARE THERE IN THE MILKY WAY?

The galaxy called the Milky Way is a broad band of stars visible on a clear night. It is a pattern created by looking along the local arm of our spiral galaxy of which the solar system is a member. Altogether, although we can only see just a few thousand stars with the naked eye, the galaxy of which we are a part may have up to 200 million stars.

HOW OLD ARE THE CRATERS ON THE MOON?

Scientists believe that the moon's craters go back a long way towards its origin, about 4,800 million years ago. It is believed the craters were formed by the constant impact of rocks and boulders left over immediately after the formation of the sun, the moon and all the planets. The early, very intense, period of bombardment was over by about 3,000 million years ago.

WHY ARE THERE NO CRATERS ON EARTH LIKE THERE ARE ON THE MOON?

Craters have been formed on earth but they have been rubbed out by the constant weathering and movement of rock surfaces. This does not happen on the airless, lifeless moon, where they are preserved for much longer.

WHAT IS THE DIFFERENCE BETWEEN AN ATOM BOMB AND A HYDROGEN BOMB?

An atom bomb releases energy generated by the breaking apart (fission) of plutonium or uranium nuclei. A hydrogen bomb releases energy created when atoms of an isotope of hydrogen are brought together (fused). It takes an atom bomb to create the conditions to operate a hydrogen bomb, so a fission device is installed to trigger a fusion, or thermonuclear, explosion, duplicating conditions for a fraction of a second similar to those that go on at the centre of our sun.

WHAT IS THE WORLD'S LARGEST AIRCRAFT CARRIER?

The United States Navy aircraft carrier *Enterprise* is the world's biggest floating airfield, with a length of 1,123 ft (342 m) and a maximum width across the flight deck of 248 ft (76 m). With a crew of 4,900 (some carriers have a complement of 6,300), the carrier can support nearly 100 fighter and attack planes. Like others in its class, *Enterprise* is powered by a nuclear generator which needs refuelling only every 13 years.

WHAT IS A SUPERNOVA?

A supernova is a massive release of energy when a large part of an old and dying star is blown outward from the inner core, leaving a tiny portion of its former size to cool down into what astronomers call a neutron star. The most famous supernova is the Crab Nebula, the explosive remnants of a star that blew up in the 11th century.

HOW LONG HAS OUR NEAREST STAR, THE SUN, BEEN AROUND AND HOW MUCH LONGER WILL IT CONTINUE TO SHINE?

Astronomers believe our sun is nearly 5,000 million years old and was created out of swirling gas and dust, forming planets as a result of this process. By careful calculation of the amount of energy it is releasing every day, astronomers also believe the sun will continue to shine for at least a further 5,000 million years. Meanwhile, the sun will very slowly start to increase its output until it expands at the end of its life into a huge gaseous ball engulfing the orbits of Mercury, Venus and Earth immediately before it collapses into what astronomers call a White Dwarf.

WHERE DOES NATURAL LIGHT COME FROM?

In all the universe, most natural light comes from the thermonuclear reactions inside stars like our Sun. In a process called nuclear fusion, hydrogen atoms fuse together to build heavier elements like helium and eventually oxygen and iron. When they do this they release energy in the form of radiation, some of which is transmitted in the form of light which radiates outward at about **186,300** miles (299,757 km) per second.

WHAT WAS THE WORLD'S MOST POWERFUL SPACE ROCKET?

Built to push Apollo spacecraft to a speed of 25,000 mph (40,232 km/h) and send them on their way to the moon, NASA's giant Saturn V launch rocket which first flew in November 1967 is the most

Apollo 8 spacerocket lifts off

powerful rocket so far used to put payloads into space. It was powered by five huge engines in the first stage, developing a total lift-off thrust of 7,500,000 lb (3,402,000 kg) and upper stages which added a further 1,300,000 lb (598,680 kg) of thrust. Twelve rockets of this type were used to launch Apollo vehicles, while a thirteenth, the last in the series, with just two stages stacked on top of one another, was used to launch the NASA Skylab space station in May 1973.

HOW DO THE SOVIET AND AMERICAN SPACE PRO-GRAMMES COMPARE IN SIZE?

The United States launches about 20 to 30 satellites each year, while the Soviet Union launches between 75 and 120. The Soviet Union has larger facilities than the United States, spends about three times as much on its space programme, and relies more heavily on satellites to support its military operations than does the United States. The United States operates fewer types of rocket, while the Soviet Union has developed a broad base of launch capacity developed from its original rockets in the 1950s.

WHEN WAS THE FIRST RUSSIAN ROCKET LAUNCHED?

The first liquid-propellant rocket launched by the Soviet Union was called GIRD 09 and was launched on August 17, 1933. It was powered by oxygen and jellified petrol and reached an altitude of about 1,312 ft (400 m). The first fully liquid rocket, the GIRD X, reached a height of 262 ft (80 m) on November 15, 1933.

WHO MADE THE FIRST SPACE WALK AND WHEN?

On March 18, 1965, Soviet cosmonauts Pavel Belyaev and Alexei Leonov were launched aboard the Voskhod 2 spacecraft from Baikonur. Soon after entering orbit, Leonov went outside his capsule via a special air lock, to become the first man to walk in space, remaining there for about ten minutes.

HOW OLD IS MANKIND?

The earth and the solar system are about 4,700 million years old. The first signs of life probably appeared more than 3,500 million years ago, but the first signs of early mankind date to no more than 5 million years ago.

WHEN WAS THE FIRST GERMAN LONG-RANGE V2 ROCKET FIRED?

The first V2 was successfully launched on October 3, 1942. As an operational weapon it had a range of nearly 200 miles (322 km), carrying a one-ton warhead to a peak altitude of 60 miles (97 km) and a speed of 2,200 mph (3,540 km/h). Of about 1,600 V2s launched against England only 1,115 arrived, and most of those fell within an 11 mile (17.7 km) radius of their target.

WHAT IS THE LARGEST VOLCANO KNOWN TO EXIST ON ANY WORLD IN THE SOLAR SYSTEM?

Examined closely by several orbiting spacecraft, Olympus Mons is the largest volcano ever observed and lies just above the equator in the northern hemisphere of Mars. It is almost 400 miles (644 km) across and stands 18 miles (29 km) above the plain on which it has built its dome through millions of years of volcanic eruption. The rim of the lava tube is more than 40 miles (64.3 km) across.

A photo of a Martian Canyon floor

WHAT IS THE LARGEST CANYON OBSERVED ON ANY PLANET IN THE SOLAR SYSTEM?

Dwarfing the Grand Canyon in the United States, the Valles Marineris is a complex of steep walled canyons extending along the equator on Mars. Gullies and clefts in the walls of this enormous fault extend to a width of almost 450 miles (724 km) and in places the depth is estimated to exceed five miles (8 km), more than five times the depth of the Grand Canyon.

HOW FAR AWAY IS THE MOON AND HOW LONG HAS IT BEEN THERE?

The earth and moon formed together about 4,800 million years ago. At one time the two were much closer together, earth's day being shorter, and tides much higher. The moon is now about 240,000 miles (386,232 km) away from earth and is very gradually spiralling further out and as a result, slowing earth's rotation. In many, many millions of years the earth's day will be about 40 hours long.

WHAT IS A VAMP?

Vamp stands for Variable Anamorphic Motion Picture and is, in fact, a flight simulator. Introduced in 1970, it is a device for creating the effect of flying without leaving the ground.

A trainee pilot is confronted by the controls of an aircraft and a wide cinema screen which shows how well he is piloting his imaginary aircraft.

VAMP uses 70 mm colour films (the ones you show at home are only 8 mm) which show almost any landing and take-off at an airport.

They are selected for showing by a computer which responds to the controls the trainee is operating. For instance, if the pilot veers to the right, the scene also shifts in that direction. If the computer calls for a sudden crosswind, the image changes accordingly. The perspective of the original scene is changed so that the picture the pilot sees is exactly the same as he would really see if he were flying at the position, attitude and altitude of the simulated aircraft.

Further realism is achieved by altering weather conditions. A mechanical device can produce a cloud, fog or haze faster than a flash of lightning.

During an approach and landing the ground can be made to glow from the lights of the runway. It all sounds so marvellous that one wonders how it was achieved. The answer is that special films of the various landings and conditions were made by a camera slung beneath a helicopter.

The top picture opposite shows a very realistic view as the pilot is about to touch down on the runway. The complete simulator unit with the visual system in position is illustrated in the lower picture. The cockpit itself is the black-nosed lower area. The VAMP system with its projector and computers is in the hump mounted above the cockpit, towering nearly 20 feet (6 km) high. The whole assembly can be tilted in any direction as it is "flown".

Today Pan Am Airlines are using a Boeing 727 VAMP.

WHY IS EDWIN LAND FAMOUS?

Because in 1947 he invented the very popular Polaroid camera.

WHAT IS POLYTETRA-FLUORETHYLENE?

It is a plastic, used for the production of non-stick pots and pans. It was first discovered by Dr Roy Plunkett when he was working for the American chemical firm of Du Pont.

FOR WHAT ARE WILLIAM SHOCKLEY, JOHN BARDEEN AND WALTER BRATTAIN FAMOUS?

It was they who were responsible for transistors. It was at the Bell Telephone Laboratories in the U S in 1948 that a transistor was first

185

successfully demonstrated.

It revolutionised the construction of radio sets inasmuch as the transistor is capable of doing virtually all the jobs of a conventional radio valve. It is smaller and more reliable than a valve.

The first transistors could not amplify as could the valve but Shockley, Bardeen and Brattain finally managed to overcome this drawback.

WHO INVENTED THE ELECTROCARDIOGRAPH?

Willem Einthoven in 1903. For his wonderful achievement, he was awarded a Nobel prize in 1924.

The electrocardiograph is an instrument which is used in the examination of people suffering from heart disease. It indicates how serious is their illness and maintains a check on recovery subsequent to a heart attack. In essence, it detects the amount of electricity which passes through the heart muscle as it pumps blood through the body.

Einthoven's successful invention stemmed from the discovery by two German scientists in the mid-19th century, that a frog's heart creates an electric current.

HOW DOES AN AEROSOL WORK?

The word aerosol once meant simply a mist of tiny drops of liquid floating in the air. Fog is an aerosol. The word now also refers to the spray-cans that we use to spray many kinds of liquids: paints, deodorant, shaving foam, fly killer, oil and many others.

The aerosol we use was invented in 1941 by Lyle David Goodhue, an American scientist.

When the press-button is operated a valve opens allowing some of the pressurised liquid inside to be released in the form of a fine spray. The liquid streams out because it is forced up a tube from the bottom of the can by gas under pressure which occupies the space above the liquid.

ARE AEROSOL SPRAYS HARMFUL?

Aerosol sprays were generally believed to be harmless to people and other living things. It is now understood that they are damaging the ozone layer high in the earth's atmosphere because they are now being released into the air in large quantities.

Ozone is a form of oxygen which prevents some of the ultra violet sunlight from reaching the earth's surface. If this layer were damaged or destroyed the increase in ultra violet rays could be dangerous.

WHAT WERE THE FIRST NUCLEAR POWER STATIONS TO OPERATE FROM THE SURFACE OF ANOTHER WORLD?

During six Apollo lunar landing missions between 1969 and 1972, the moon-walking astronauts laid out an array of scientific experiments to monitor activity on and below the surface. On five of these flights, the astronauts used a complex set of equipment which they left after returning to earth, powered by a radio isotope thermoelectric generator (RTG). From the heat that was produced from the radio-active decay of the plutonium core, electricity was produced to power these miniature research stations for several years after the crew left the moon.

WHAT WAS THE FIRST LIVING THING TO BE PLACED IN ORBIT?

On November 3, 1957, the Soviet satellite Sputnik 2 was launched with the dog Laika inside, the first living thing to go into orbit. There was not enough oxygen to keep the dog alive and it was asphyxiated before the capsule it was strapped in burned up as it fell back through the atmosphere just over 13 months later.

WHAT ARE THE ADVANTAGES OF FOUR-WHEEL DRIVE?

In most cars the power from the engine is used to drive either the front wheels or the back wheels. This contact with the road provides sufficient grip on all normal road surfaces. But when the road's surface is slippery such as when covered by snow or ice, two wheels may not get enough grip and one or both may spin.

With all four wheels being driven the whole weight of the car is being used for traction and a better grip is obtained all round.

Military vehicles and those designed to travel over rough country are usually equipped with four-wheel drive. For running on normal roads, these vehicles are driven by two wheels as four-wheel drive is unsuited to prolonged higher speeds. An extra gear lever is used to engage four-wheel drive which usually operates at a lower gear ratio.

A very well-known vehicle with four-wheel drive is, of course, the American jeep which was used so extensively during the Second World War.

HOW WAS ONE MILLION POUNDS WORTH OF TREASURE RECOVERED FROM THE BOTTOM OF THE SEA?

It was on May 20, 1922, off the French coast that the P and O liner *Egypt* was rammed accidentally by a French cargo steamer in thick fog. In only 18 minutes *Egypt* had sunk to the bottom of the sea with the loss of 71 members of her crew and 15 passengers.

Down with her went one million pounds worth of gold and silver bars still securely locked in her strong-room.

Because of the fog, the location of *Egypt* was known only approximately and the sea in the area was so deep that any normal diving suit would be crushed by the immense pressure. It was not until

An observation chamber is lowered to inspect the sunken wreck of *Egypt*

1930 that the sunken vessel was finally discovered. By then an observation chamber was available. Explosive charges were lowered to blast through the ship's sides and decks. When the explosive was in place, the charge was detonated. A diver was lowered in the observation chamber to supervise grabs which removed twisted and blasted steel plates.

It was painfully slow and laborious work and in fact it was not until two years later in 1932, that the strong-room was reached.

Through a hole made in its roof grabs were lowered and the first of the treasure was triumphantly hauled to the surface.

It was many months before the operation was completed but when the divers finally surfaced, over one million pounds' worth of *Egypt's* lost treasure had been recovered.

WHAT DOES "LASER" MEAN?

It is short for Light Amplification by Stimulated Emission of Radiation. It is an intense narrow beam of light with all the light waves being exactly in step. It was in the Hughes Laboratory at Malibu, California, in 1960, that Theo Maiman discovered the laser.

WHAT ARE LASERS USED FOR?

Laser beams can be used for an amazing variety of jobs. In engineering, for instance, powerful lasers can be used to cut or weld metals. In medicine surgeons can use lasers instead of knives to perform delicate operations such as the refixing of a retina in the human eye.

Surveyors use lasers for aligning and measuring distances very accurately. The distance from the Earth's surface to the moon at any given time can be measured accurately to within a few centimeters.

The military uses for lasers are many, from aiming guns at a target to guiding missiles. Lasers are also used to send information similar to radio waves. They are used for compact and video disc systems to receive sound and pictures from the discs without actually touching and therefore wearing them. There are many more uses for lasers such as holography and as modern technology advances, still more uses will be found.

WHAT IS HOLOGRAPHY?

It is the word given to the making and using of holograms which are a form of photography made possible by the use of lasers.

"Holos" is a Greek word which means whole and hologram means "complete picture".

Photographs taken with an ordinary camera are two-dimensional and are viewed only from the standpoint of the lens. Holograms are three-dimensional photographs of scenes and objects as you would actually see them in real life. For example, supposing you have a photograph taken with an ordinary camera, of a person standing in front of a tree. No matter from which direction you look at the photograph, it always looks the same. But if the picture is a hologram, from whichever direction you look, the person will be standing in a different position in relation to the tree just as if in reality, you were looking at the scene and moving your head from one side to another.

WHEN WAS THE AEROPLANE FIRST USED IN WAR?

The first use of aircraft in war was when the Italians used a Bleriot monoplane on October 14, 1911, to reconnoitre the Turkish lines in Tripolitania.

HOW HAS THE SPEED OF FIGHTER PLANES INCREASED SINCE THEIR INVENTION?

When the First World War ended in 1918, most fighter planes had a maximum speed of around 140 mph (225 km/h), but by the end of the Second World War in 1945, this had increased to an average of 400 mph (644 km/h), although some German jets could reach 540 mph (869 km/h). By the 1960s, during the Vietnam War, fighters had achieved a top speed of around 1,300 mph (2,092 km/h), although combat was still usually carried out at about 300-500 mph (483-805 km/h).

WE HAVE ALL HEARD LOTS ABOUT IT, BUT WHAT EXACTLY IS A COMPUTER?

The simple description of a computer is an electronic machine able to carry out steps of a task under the control of stored instructions.

Consider a simple task such as boiling a kettle of water. There are a number of steps you need to take — you pick up the kettle, remove the lid, put the kettle under a tap, fill it with water, plug it in, switch on and so on. However, if you forget to fill the kettle with water, your task will go wrong! Computers also do things wrongly, but only when given the incorrect instructions. When all of the instructions are correct, computers are very good at carrying them out and they do so quickly.

The two main features of computers which make them different from other types of machine are that they can carry out instructions extremely quickly and they can hold or store vast amounts of information.

As an example of speed: an average person may take one or two minutes to add up 10 numbers. In the same time, some computers can add up millions of such numbers. As an example of the amount of information (data) which can be held: hundreds of telephone directories may be held on one storage device, and any piece of information in any of the directories can be looked up extremely quickly.

Another major benefit of computers is that once given the correct instructions, they can do things extremely accurately — imagine if you had to add up millions of numbers. You would soon become tired or bored, and so make lots of mistakes.

So, to summarise, a computer is an electronic machine which can do many repetitive tasks very accurately, using sets of instructions.

In fact, there is much more to a computer than this, and many books are available which explain, in more detail, how a computer actually works and how it is used.

WHO INVENTED THE FIRST COMPUTER?

The name of the man generally thought to have invented the world's first computer was Charles Babbage (often called the "father of the computer"). He designed a machine which he called an Analytical Engine in 1834. This used toothed wheels to do calculations and punched cards for storing information. It was the first ever machine to have input, processing and output devices, and also the first machine which could carry out instructions, meaning that it could be programmed.

However, his machine was impossible to build in those days, but Babbage's ideas and inventions later became what we now call computers.

Throughout history, many

**Two young students enjoy the complexities of an IBM Computer
(photo: IBM)**

people have helped us to develop computers, and various inventions have helped (for instance, transistors and micro chips). Centuries ago, devices such as the abacus were invented to assist people to do calculations. These ideas were evolved and machines became more complex and clever until computers, which started being produced during the 1950s.

Computers at that time were large, cumbersome and much slower than the modern versions. Today, they are smaller, more powerful and cheaper than in the early days, and they continue to improve very rapidly. Nowadays, you can buy a computer the size of a wristwatch.

WHAT ARE THE THREE MAIN TYPES OF COMPUTER?

These are called Mainframe, Mini and Micro.

Mainframe computers are the largest type. They are very complex and expensive and normally have many different input and output devices connected to them, which usually means that they are housed in special computer rooms. These computers often have special operating requirements; it is usually necessary to provide clean air, and a certain temperature and humidity level. Many mainframe computer rooms are specially controlled with air conditioning systems. A mainframe computer can do many jobs at the same time and can process large amounts of information.

Mini computers are smaller versions of mainframes, and are usually about the size of a wardrobe or fridge-freezer. They do not always need special rooms or air conditioning, and are not as expensive or as powerful as a mainframe.

Micro computers are the smallest type of computers and usually fit quite easily onto a desk top (they are about the size of a typewriter). They are often referred to as "Home Computers" or "Personal Computers" (PCs). Micros usually only process one program at a time and can only deal with small amounts of information. They vary in power depending on the make and model.

HOW IS INFORMATION STORED ON A COMPUTER?

Information (commonly called "data") is usually stored in one of two ways:-

1. Main Memory
This is an area inside a computer which can hold a certain amount of data (depending on the size and type of computer).

2. Storage Devices
These are usually items such as magnetic disk or tape. The majority of information held on a computer is stored in this way. Magnetic tapes are reels of tape about one inch wide, and magnetic disks look like several LP records on top of each other. In both cases, characters (numbers, letters and symbols) are stored and the computer can "read" the information or "write" to the storage disk or tape.

Micro computers often use cassette tapes to store data in a similar way.

WHAT IS A COMPUTER PROGRAM?

A computer program is a series of instructions given to a computer to enable it to carry out the required task the computer can understand. The computer will then do exactly as instructed. This is important to remember, as a computer cannot "think" — it will do only what you tell it to do in your program code. The code in which programs are written is called a Programming Language, and there are many such languages in use today.

ARE COMPUTERS EXPENSIVE?

The answer to this is YES and NO! The very large computers (called mainframes) often cost several million pounds. They also need special rooms and lots of other items and equipment, such as special floors raised from the ground to enable yards of cable to be stored, and special telephone lines to enable them to connect to computers in other parts of the country, or abroad. Also mainframes need many people to operate them and to ensure that they are being used properly. Large companies use this type of computer and need to make sure that their money is well spent!

At the other end of the scale, micro computers can be fairly cheap, so that most people can afford to buy one to use at home. Nowadays, many school children too, have a home computer.

So a computer can be as expensive or cheap as you wish to make it, depending on what you need it for.

WHAT IS MEANT BY "HARDWARE" AND "SOFTWARE"?

Computers are generally made up of a processor and other devices (usually called input and output devices).

HARDWARE is the name given to these physical components or units which, when linked together, form what it called a hardware "configuration". An example of this might be a central processor (to carry out calculations or processing), a visual display unit to input information to the computer, and to display the results on the screen (this would be called an input/output device), and a printer to print the output on paper (an output device). Hardware devices can be used alone or linked up in various types of configuration.

SOFTWARE is the programs (or instructions) which control what the computer does. Software is program code written by people and can be of two main types:

SYSTEM SOFTWARE (an example would be an operating system), which controls what and when the hardware carries out its tasks, and APPLICATION SOFTWARE which consists of programmes written to do a particular job, for example, to book a holiday or to carry out a calculation. Computer games are examples of application software.

WHAT IS A PERIPHERAL DEVICE?

A Peripheral Device is a unit attached to a computer. We need to be able to get things into our computers (this is called "input"), and also out from them (this is called "output"). There are a number of units or devices to help us with input and output, such as:

VDU (Visual Display Unit)

A screen (commonly referred to as a terminal) with a keyboard similar to a typewriter. Using a VDU, we can type things into the computer (such as program code), and see our results displayed on the screen. You can often see VDUs in shops or offices (have a look in your local travel agent, for instance).

PRINTER

Printers are used to provide us with information on paper. They can be small and look similar to a typewriter giving printout letter by letter, or large (the size of a small car) giving printout line by line (these are very fast — up to 20,000 lines of print per minute).

YOU HAVE PROBABLY HEARD OF "BITS" AND/OR "BYTES", BUT WHAT ARE THEY?

A "bit" is a binary digit or number made up of either a 0 (zero) or 1 (one). Binary is the numbering system which most computers use. Binary is used because it has only 2 possibilities (0 or 1). Hence, inside a computer a switch can be ON (1) or OFF (0).

Similarly a spot on a magnetic tape can be magnetized (1) or not (0), and so on. In this way, computers build up "codes" by which they can understand the information which they are given.

A "byte" is usually a set of 8 "bits", which make up the code for one character (letter, number or symbol). Data on most computers is grouped into bytes. For instance, on some computers, the byte "10000001" means the letter "A" in the computer's own code. Each 0 and 1 is a "bit", and all eight bits are called a "byte".

WHAT IS MEANT BY A HIGH-LEVEL PROGRAMMING LANGUAGE?

A High-Level Programming Language is a language where the code is understandable to us (for example, English sentences are used, or mathematical symbols).

There are also Low-Level Programming Languages, where the code is less understandable to us, but closer to the computer's own internal code.

In the cases of both High-Level and Low-Level Languages, the computer "translates" the code entered by the Programmer into a set of instructions which can be performed to carry out the required functions.

For High-Level Languages, the translation process is called a "Compiler".

For Low-Level Languages, it is called an "Assembler".

Examples of High-Level Languages are: COBOL, FORTRAN, PL1, RPG, ALGOL, BASIC, PASCAL.

Examples of Low-Level Languages are: ASSEMBLER, PLAN.

Of course, there are many hundreds of computer languages in use. It is also important to note that the code may vary slightly from computer to computer.

Most books about computers explain what the various programming languages are used for and books on this can be found in your local library.

WHAT IS MEANT BY COMPUTER GRAPHICS?

Computer graphics is the careful arranging of dots (called "Pixels") on the screen of a computer to produce a variety of pictures and diagrams such as graphs and drawings. The use of graphics can be clearly shown in computer games.

The way graphics are created on the computer's screen is by the placing of a dot (pixel) at a particular point on the screen, together with hundreds or

IBM has designed this Personal Computer for first-time and advanced users (Photo: IBM)

thousands of other dots which form a picture, or part of a picture or diagram.

Computer graphics can be great fun! Most computer games use animated figures which move about on the screen (often controlled by a joy stick). You can play against the computer, or try to obtain a high score, or play against one or more of your friends. The pictures and diagrams and figures in these games are all examples of graphics, and their movements are controlled by a computer program, which responds to the information input or the movements of a joystick. Many thousands of games can be purchased on cassettes to play on a home computer.

WHAT IS A PROGRAM LOOP?

A series of program instructions that are repeated until a specified condition is satisfied. This is an example of how computers can do repetitive tasks quickly.

WHAT IS A COMPUTER GAME?

Computer games are usually one or more computer programs which, when loaded, will act upon the response of the person playing the game.

There are different kinds of games; educational games which teach skills in a variety of subjects (for example, spelling), and pure fun games (we all know space invaders!).

It is quite easy to write your own computer games, once you have mastered a programming language. The language called BASIC is a good way to start and there are many books to help you both to learn how to use BASIC and to write games. All you need is a micro (or home) computer and two or three books.

WHAT IS THE MEANING OF THE LETTER "K" WHEN USED WITH COMPUTERS?

"K" means KILOBYTE, a unit of storage commonly used in a computer. A kilobyte or a "K" usually means one thousand bytes (Kilo means a thousand). In fact, to be strictly accurate, one "K" equals 1024 bytes, but people conveniently refer to a "K" as roughly 1000 bytes (as it is easier to think in chunks of 1000, rather than 1024).

The storage size of a computer is often referred to as having a number of "K". For instance, you may see micro computers in the shops showing that they are 48K or 256K machines. This means that the main memory of that computer has 48,000 or 256,000 "bytes" of storage — the higher the number, the more powerful is the computer.

Larger computers are often referred to as having MEGABYTES or GIGABYTES of storage. A Megabyte is a million bytes (mega means a million). A gigabyte is a thousand-million bytes (giga means a thousand-million, or a billion). You will not find home computers with Mega or Giga bytes of memory, these are only the large mainframe computers used by companies, but perhaps in the future, small computers will be able to hold much larger amounts of information. Micro computers that you can buy today can hold as much information as very large computers did in the early days of computing.

WHAT DOES ROM AND RAM MEAN?

Both ROM and RAM are examples of computer "memory" which is the part of a computer where information is stored and remembered. Information can be put into memory (write), or taken from memory (read).

ROM is short for "Read Only Memory" which is memory which can only be read and not written to. Usually the computer stores the instructions to make it work properly in its ROM and these instructions must not be changed (permanent instructions).

RAM is short for "Random Access Memory", which is memory that can be accessed and altered at any time (temporary information).

HOW ARE COMPUTERS USED AND BY WHOM?

Computers are used for a great variety of purposes. Their major benefits are that they can hold lots of information (or data), and "process" it very quickly. For example, a computer can do millions of calculations in a very short time (often fractions of a second). If we were to do them, it might take several minutes or hours (or even days or weeks), and we would probably make errors as we became tired.

All kinds of people now use computers in their work:

The Police

The police force keep records on computer of accidents, criminals, robberies, descriptions of people, all in an effort to help them fight crime. Where international crime is involved details and pictures can be sent overseas, in minutes.

Travel Agents

When you book a holiday, you need a hotel, perhaps a flight to another country and other arrangements. Availability of hotels and flights is held on a computer, and the travel agent can reserve your room or seat when you confirm your holiday.

Car Design

Car makers can design how a car will look or how fast it will go by using computers to assist them to work out the best shape and size of a car.

Space Travel

Rockets and spacecraft are designed with the help of computers, and computers help to track the speed and route and to gather and hold important information from space itself, or other planets.

WHAT IS THE CPU?

CPU stands for Central Processing Unit, which is the nerve centre of the computer. It controls and coordinates the activities of the many other parts of the computer.

WHAT CAN A COMPUTER *NOT* DO?

It cannot think! Computers are responsive to instructions, whether correct or wrong. However, they cannot think or reason.

It is worth remembering this, and next time you hear someone say: "That computer has gone wrong again", you can correct them by saying: "No, it is not the computer that has gone wrong, but rather somebody has given it wrong instructions or information".

Unfortunately, many people have the wrong impression of computers and tend to blame things on them. After all, computers are machines, and humans make them. As with any machine, if it is operated incorrectly or, given wrong instructions it will not give the results expected.

Remember: Computers do EXACTLY as they are told.

WHAT DOES GIGO MEAN?

GIGO is short for GARBAGE IN GARBAGE OUT. Wrong information fed into the computer means that wrong information will come out.

HOW ARE COMPUTERS USED AT AIRPORTS AND ON AIRCRAFT?

Computers at airports are used to allocate tickets and display timetables. When passengers book in for a flight, computers give information about the seats on the various aircraft using the airport on a particular day.

Within the airport terminal computers are used to display the departure and arrival time of aircraft. Information such as delays or problems with aircraft can also be displayed on screens like T V screens, enabling passengers to see details of their flights.

Computers assist air traffic control, in ensuring that flights take off and land safely, and stop at the correct airport area.

Automatic landing and monitoring of engines during flights, involves computers. In fog they help guide the aircraft. During flights computers will give "early warnings" of low fuel level and engine difficulties etc, enabling the pilot to take any necessary action. Most of the dials in the cockpit of an aircraft are linked to a computer.

The aircraft industry constantly employs computers to assist in the study and improvement of future air travel.

WHAT IS A COMPUTER SYSTEM?

This is a set of related programs which together perform a particular task.

HOW ARE COMPUTERS USED IN SPORT?

Computers are used in sport in a variety of ways.

Accurate timing of athletic races such as the London Marathon, and car races like the British Grand Prix are controlled by computers. In the case of the London Marathon, competitors can find out not only where they finished overall, but also where they finished in their age-group. For car races lap times are easily recorded.

The Olympic Games benefits from the use of computers. Apart from timing, they can control the sale of tickets for all the different events on each day, and can arrange when each event is held to ensure that nobody has to run two races at once. Also it can record and print all the results and lists of world records can be kept up-to-date.

Large displays shown at football stadiums are often controlled by computers. These show examples of graphics to "liven-up" the display with pictures when, for instance, a goal is scored.

Computers are used to plan fixture lists for a season. Most sports need to print fixture lists and computers help in planning matches so that teams play home and away on alternate weeks and help ensure that teams with nearby pitches do not play at home on the same day.

HOW ARE COMPUTERS USED TO CONTROL TRAFFIC ON OUR ROADS?

The most obvious example of computers in traffic control is the control of traffic lights. At certain times of the day traffic is heavier than at others. From a central control building traffic lights can be changed to remain green longer or shorter, to speed-up traffic flows. "Pads" on the road surface can also send messages to the computer when cars pass over them, and so control when the traffic lights change.

Traffic is also checked by video cameras mounted on lamp-posts. Information from these cameras is relayed back to the control centre and traffic lights can be adjusted for the best situation. Use of computers in this way is particularly important in the rush hours, when they assist in the smooth flow of traffic.

In London, the police control centre is at Scotland Yard.

This picture illustrates how small a micro-chip is when placed beside a fountain pen nib (Photo: IBM)

WHAT IS A MICRO-CHIP?

A micro, or silicon, chip is a small electronic circuit mounted on a substance which is called silicon. The micro-chip can control the many different functions within a computer. Typically, a micro-chip will be the size of your little fingernail or even smaller.

199

About Ourselves

WHY CAN WE SEE OUR BREATH ON A COLD DAY?

The air which we breathe out is a gaseous water — or water in the form of gas (like steam).

This breath is warmer than the air outside and on a warm day is not seen as it is exhaled, but on a cold day mist and steam can be seen coming from the mouth. This is because the gaseous water has suddenly been turned so cold that it forms a little cloud consisting of drops of water, as do all clouds.

What we really see on a cold day is our breath being turned into a liquid, by the cold.

WHAT CAUSES A DIMPLE?

To understand this, we should first realise that our skin is in two layers. There is the outer layer and the inner one which carries nerves and blood-vessels.

Beneath the skin is a loose layer of tissue which contains fibres that run in all directions. A few of these fibres are attached to the under-surface of the skin so that, although we can move the skin about very freely, there is a limit to this movement. Where there is a dimple, the number of fibres are increased and they are rather short. Therefore, their pull on the skin is greater and it is this which causes a dimple.

WHY DOES A HAIR-CUT NOT HURT?

All our senses are controlled by our nerves, which carry their messages to the brain. Therefore, any part of us that has nerves also has a sense of feeling. We might fall and cut ourselves, or have a tooth that aches. We are made well aware of pain because the damaged parts contain nerves. Our hair, however, does not contain nerves and so there can be no sense of hurt when it is being cut.

WHY DOES WATER NOT SOAK INTO OUR SKIN?

Our skin is a true waterproof, for nothing can enter it from the outside. Of course, it will allow water to come out in the form of sweat. Our skin contains millions of tiny tubes which carry sweat from the inner (true) skin to the finer skin on the surface of the body.

With the sweat glands exerting pressure upwards, water cannot make its way down into the skin and so this forms the perfect water-proofing.

WHY DO WE PERSPIRE?

Perspiration, or sweat, is the means whereby the temperature of our bodies is controlled. It is not good for the body to get too hot and so excess moisture is forced out through the pores of the skin to cool us down when it evaporates into the air.

If we could not perspire we should probably become ill. The sweat glands receive messages from nerve cells which dictate when to make sweat and when to stop doing so.

WHY DO WE BLOW ON OUR HANDS TO WARM THEM AND ON HOT THINGS TO COOL THEM?

It does seem strange that we have to blow on things not only to make them warmer but to make them cooler. There is, of course, a very good reason for doing this.

When we blow on our cold hands we are using the breath from our body and this is much warmer than the outside air.

Therefore we feel that warmth when we blow.

When we blow to cool things, though, the position is reversed. The heat from tea or coffee, for example, is much warmer than our breath. So to make sure we can drink a cup of hot tea or coffee without burning the mouth, we blow on it.

As our breath is much colder than the heat from the hot drink, we are really using cooler air to blow away that heat.

HOW MANY HAIRS GROW ON THE HUMAN HEAD?

The number varies because some people have much thicker hair strands than others but the average number is 144,000.

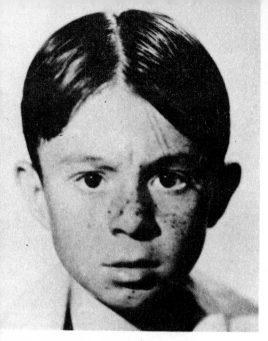

WHY DO WE SEEM TO HEAR THE SOUND OF WAVES IN A SEASHELL?

A seashell is shaped so that it picks up sounds and echoes them back to the ear. It even picks up sounds so slight that we might not hear them at all without the shell and they sound like a vague roaring. Imagination does the rest. Because of the shell we think of the sea and fancy we can hear the sound of waves on the shore.

HOW DO WE CATCH A COLD?

Despite much research, nobody is completely certain why some people catch colds while others do not. Cold research clinics take volunteers in the hope of finding the cause and cure of the common cold but the strange thing is that while some of the volunteers do catch cold, others simply do not become infected. Their natural resistance to the cold germ is so great.

WHAT ARE FRECKLES?

In most cases, freckles are caused by the action of the sun on cells in the skin. These cells produce a colouring matter, called pigment, which forms the spots we call freckles. When the sun's strength fades on the approach of winter, the freckles disappear.

There are, however, young people who naturally have freckles all the time.

WHAT IS MEANT BY A ROMAN NOSE?

A Roman nose is a thin, high, straight nose with a pointed tip, rather like an eagle's beak. It is supposed to be very aristocratic and was wrongfully believed to be characteristic of the Ancient Romans.

WHAT HAPPENS TO THE CARBON DIOXIDE WE EXHALE?

Carbon dioxide is a poisonous gas which is breathed out by humans and other living creature. It is also given off in chemical fumes and smoke. It is heavier than air and in confined spaces will stay nearer to the ground.

We all know how sleepy we become in a room where there is little ventilation. This is due to the carbon dioxide breathed out growing more powerful than the amount of oxygen in the air.

You might think that with so much of this heavy, poisonous gas being produced every minute of the day, that air would become foul and our oxygen be cut off. However, Nature has provided a way of overcoming this, for all green plant life takes in carbon dioxide and releases oxygen and the balance of the gases is thus maintained.

Were it not for trees and plants, we and all other animals could not survive.

WHY IS SEA AIR GOOD FOR US?

Because it is purer and fresher than air which blows overland. There are few, if any, particles of dust and dirt in sea air and this enables the health-giving rays of the sun to reach us more freely and powerfully. Sea air also contains vital salts and traces of iodine.

IS SOAP AND WATER GOOD FOR THE SKIN?

Yes. On all normal skin, good soap cleanses by combining with water to make a lather which penetrates the pores and roots out the dirt. Perfumed soaps can, however, cause allergies. Soap is made of fats and alkalis and the best soap contains rather less alkali and has special antiseptics which help to rid the skin of harmful bacteria. Good soap will not injure delicate skin.

WHAT IS HEART-BURN?

There are times when the stomach is upset and we get a burning feeling in the chest and throat. This is what we call heart-burn. It is a form of indigestion. It could be due to eating foods that do not agree with us, or which we have not digested properly. As a result too much acid is formed in the stomach and this causes the burning sensation.

WHY DO WE GET ELECTRICITY IN OUR HAIR?

When we comb our hair it sometimes happens that we can hear faint crackling. The reason is that combing can create a little electricity. Electrons are taken from the atoms of the comb and are added to other atoms of the hair. It is this passing of the electrons which creates electricity.

WHY DO SOME PEOPLE WALK AND TALK IN THEIR SLEEP?

Our mind controls our actions and movement; yet while there are acts we are aware of doing, there are others performed without our knowledge.

We breathe, walk, sit, stand and so on without really being aware of doing so, because these acts are so natural that we do not have to think about them.

Sometimes it happens that some of these movements may be carried out by a person who is asleep. This is because while one part of the mind is at rest, the other part is active.

It is this wakeful part of the mind which has an effect on sleep. The acts of walking and talking are so commonplace that the mind does not need to be *aware* of doing them. That is why, in disturbed sleep, some people walk and talk.

WHY DO OUR EYES CLOSE WHEN WE ARE ASLEEP?

Effort is needed to keep our eyes open; the small muscles of the eyes keep the lids open without our realising they are working. When we get sleepy we relax that effort and our eyelids drop because of their weight.

In other words, we cannot sleep with our eyes open because we cannot hold up our eyelids while we are asleep.

There is also another reason and it is that light keeps us awake by exciting the brain. So when we want to sleep, one of the first things we have to do is to shut off the brain from the outside world. This is why it is easier to go to sleep at night when it is dark.

WHY DO WE SHIVER WHEN WE ARE VERY COLD?

We shiver because cold excites or disturbs our nervous system. One reason for shivering is that it makes us seek protection from cold by getting dressed quickly. It is thought that another reason for shivering is a jerking of the muscles, as they try to make their own warmth by movement.

WHY IS YAWNING INFECTIOUS?

A yawn is a very deep breath and the usual cause of it is that we are tired and our breathing has fallen below what is needed, so we are trying to make it up quickly. The yawn that comes when we see someone else yawning, though, is due to what is called *suggestion*.

One example of suggestion is when we become afraid because we see someone else showing fear. Another is when we laugh because everyone around us is laughing.

The power of suggestion makes a yawn very catching.

WHY IS THE LUMP ON THE FRONT OF THE NECK KNOWN AS THE ADAM'S APPLE?

The lump in the front of the neck is part of the larynx, a section of the throat containing the vocal cords, which enable us to speak and sing. Its popular name, Adam's Apple, is very old and comes from a strange notion that when Adam ate the apple in the Garden of Eden, a piece of it was caught in his throat and formed the lump.

WHY DO OUR FACES TURN RED WHEN WE DO SOMETHING WRONG?

When our faces turn red because of some act that we know to be wrong, it is probably because we are ashamed. Another reason for blushing, as it is called, may well be from anger or shyness.

All these emotions disturb the nervous system which controls the flow of blood to the surface of the skin and it is then that our faces flush.

WHY DO WE SAY "TO SLEEP LIKE A TOP"?

This saying has its origin in the days of the pegtop and humming top, toys which at one time few boys and girls would be without.

Any such top would spin at so fast a rate that it would remain quiet and steady. It was then said to be asleep.

WHY DO WE SNEEZE?

Usually a person will sneeze because there is something in their nose that should not be there. The nose is the proper channel for breathing in air and when anything interferes with this channel, the brain transmits a message to breathe out violently through the nose. We call it a sneeze.

We sneeze when pepper is being sprinkled because it irritates the lining of the nose and that is what may be called "useful"sneezing. There is another kind of sneezing which is not useful and is due to the way the nerves of the brain are connected. For instance, we sneeze at a bright light, usually the sun, though this action seems to

serve no useful purpose.

Many people suffer from hay fever in the late spring. This is a time when pollen is in the air and hay fever sufferers keep sneezing because they are allergic to pollen.

WHY DO WE CRY WHEN PEELING ONIONS?

The smell, flavour and "sting" of an onion all come from an oil which it contains. Called *allyl*, it is what is known as a volatile oil which means it evaporates or escapes quickly into the air.

When we peel onions, this oil excites the nerves in the nose and eyes and these nerves convey a message to the brain to make tears flow quickly to protect the eyes or, as we say, make our eyes water. This can be avoided if we peel onions under water, either in a bowl or under a running tap.

HOW MUCH DOES A HUMAN BRAIN WEIGH?

A little over three pounds (1.36 kg).

WHY DO WE BLINK OUR EYES?

Blinking takes place every few seconds to keep the eyes clean and moist. We wash our eyes whenever we blink. Above each eye is a tear-gland slowly making tears all the time we are awake. When we cry we make more tears than the eyes need for keeping clean, so most of them spill over the edges of the lower eyelids and run down our cheeks; the rest run down into the nose when we have been crying a great deal.

WHAT DOES "SECOND WIND" MEAN?

Have you ever run until you felt it difficult to draw another breath and then, as if by a miracle, you find that you can keep on running at a steady pace? When that happens, you have got your "second wind".

This is the name given to the return of normal breathing after a temporary loss of breath during a long period of exertion, such as running.

What has happened is the heart has adjusted itself to a new rate of breathing. When the runner's heart and lungs have become accustomed to the extra energy given out by the body, he is said to have got his "second wind".

WHAT DOES "MAKE YOUR MOUTH WATER" MEAN?

When you are chewing your food, certain glands inside your mouth get to work.

They are called salivary glands and they provide moisture with which to soften the food and help its digestion.

These glands are working all the time and when you are hungry, or see someone eating something you like, the glands make a lot of extra saliva or water, as it really is, and so your mouth waters.

OF WHAT USE ARE OUR EYEBROWS?

Eyebrows keep the perspiration from our forehead from running down into our eyes. The perspiration that forms when we get hot is trapped by the eyebrows and turned aside, and the moisture runs down our temples on the sides of our face, otherwise it would blur our vision and make us feel uncomfortable.

HOW DO "GOOSE PIMPLES" FORM?

This is another term for gooseflesh, because cold or fear causes the skin to look like that of a plucked goose. What happens is that when we are cold or receive a fright or shock, nerves which control the tiny muscles at the roots of the hair are disturbed.

As a result, these muscles cause the hair to stand on end and produce the effect we call "goosepimples". It is a very faint trace of a reaction seen best in cats when their fur stands on end if they are angry or scared.

WHY DO WE GET "PINS AND NEEDLES"?

Pressure on certain nerves causes a limb to become numb or "go to sleep". This is what happens if you sit on a chair awkwardly. The edge presses heavily on your leg and affects the nerves that serve the foot. When the pressure is removed, the power of the nerves returns with the tingling sensation that we refer to as "pins and needles".

WHAT CAUSES HICCOUGHS?

Between the chest and the abdomen there is a wall of muscle called the diaphragm which at times will very suddenly shrink. This action causes the closing of the glottis, the name given to the opening which allows air to pass into the windpipe. As the air being breathed strikes the glottis it creates the curious, disturbing sound we call hiccoughs or hiccups.

There are several suggested cures for hiccoughs, but the most successful seems to be that of hold the breath for several seconds.

WHY DOES HAIR TURN GREY?

The colour of our hair depends on the amount of pigment (colouring matter) in it. Dark hair contains more of it than fair hair. This colouring matter is produced in our bodies and is controlled by the nervous system. If anything goes wrong with this control through illness but more often by wearing out in old age, then the hair turns grey or white.

WHY ARE FINGERS OF DIFFERENT LENGTHS HELPFUL TO US?

In the earliest days of life on Earth, hands helped Man when he stood or walked about. They were used much as an ape uses them now.

If we put our hands on a table as if about to walk on the tips of our fingers, we can see what a well-balanced support is formed. We no longer need our hands for walking, of course, but the unequal lengths of our fingers still help us in many ways to maintain balance and grasp and use tools—the main thing man can do that makes him special.

WHY DON'T WE LAUGH WHEN WE TICKLE OURSELVES?

When we are tickled, we laugh and wriggle. This is what is termed a reflex action, an action which takes place without any thought on our part.

Balancing ourselves when we walk is another example of reflex action.

We retain our balance automatically, without thinking about it, but when we try to tickle ourselves, the brain knows that we are going to do it and so there is no reflex action.

WHAT ARE MILK MICROBES AND ARE THEY INJURIOUS TO MANKIND?

A microbe is a microscopic living organism, especially a bacterium which produces disease. Milk microbes, however, are good for mankind.

It is well known that milk is a very good liquid in which to grow microbes. Those which get into it grow very quickly. On one hand, milk microbes are a welcome addition to milk while the microbe known as tubercle bacillus is definitely dangerous as it is the cause of tuberculosis, which is a killer disease if not treated in time.

Milk microbes exist in great numbers in cowsheds and get into the milk soon after cows have been milked. The amazing fact about that is that as the milk microbes grow and multiply in the milk they prevent microbes which are harmful to us from growing there.

As time goes on, milk microbes turn milk sour but although sour milk is unpleasant to taste, it does not harm us.

Milk microbes are good for us and when sour milk is taken into the body, they protect us by keeping at bay the microbes which could be injurious.

Milk microbes help us in another way. Cream is obtained from milk and it is from cream that we get butter. Without the proper microbes of milk, butter cannot be made. The milk microbes cause the cream to ripen so that butter can be made from it. Without butter there would also be no cheese.

WHY DO WE GET CRAMP?

Cramp is really a spasm, or contraction of one or more muscles in a limb, or some other part of the body, due to over-production of acid in the muscle. We have all felt a sudden pain while playing some game or other and when running or swimming, when we are seized by cramp in a muscle. Working muscles too hard can cause it, as can cold.

A brisk rubbing over the surface will relax the muscle and relieve the pain. Cramp can also occur due to lack of salt (NaCl) in the body. To be seized with cramp when swimming, however, is very dangerous because we need to get out of the water before the cramp can be treated. This is one of the reasons why it is dangerous to stay too long in water, especially cold water, or to swim beyond our depth.

HOW MANY MUSCLES ARE THERE IN THE HUMAN BODY?
There are at least 500, of various shapes, sizes and functions.

MILLIONS OF PEOPLE WEAR SPECTACLES BUT HOW DID THEY DEVELOP?
Although some Ancient Roman writers made reference to eyeglasses of beryl gemstone worn by the Emperor Nero, the earliest framed lenses to correct defects in vision were made in China in the 10th century. They did not appear in Europe until the later 13th century and are first recorded in Britain in 1326.

These early spectacles were held in the hand or perched on the bridge of the nose. Rigid arms to connect with the ears and fasten the lenses were invented by Edward Scarlett, a British optician, in 1724.

The manufacture of spectacles then increased greatly and the quality of the lenses used also improved.

BY WHAT NAME IS A POLY-GRAPH BETTER KNOWN?
A polygraph is commonly called a lie-detector.

In fact the word polygraph has two other meanings. It is a machine which will produce several copies of drawings or documents and it also applies to an author of many books or many types of books.

It is, however, as a lie-detector that it is more generally known. It is used for this purpose by police forces all over the world. It records a suspect's changes in blood pressure and reflexes during an interrogation. Experts can see from examination of the graph produced by the polygraph if the suspect might have been telling the truth or not.

WHY ARE SOME PEOPLE SAID TO BE DOUBLE-JOINTED?
Joints are the places where two or more bones meet. Some bones are fixed together so that there is little or no movement between them. Most joints, however, allow movement between the bones.

"Double-jointed" does not mean

that a person has two joints between the bones but that the joint is unusually flexible and allows a much greater degree of motion of parts of the body such as arms, legs and fingers.

ORBIT IS A WORD OFTEN HEARD WHEN SPACE TRAVEL IS BEING DISCUSSED BUT WHAT IS A HUMAN ORBIT?

It is the eye-socket.

WHEN DID THE THEORY OF EVOLUTION FIRST BECOME KNOWN TO THE WORLD?

In 1871 when Charles Darwin's book *The Descent of Man* was first published. It caused an uproar at the time because his theory was contrary to what had been written in the Bible. The idea that mankind and the apes had evolved from the same original creature (the "missing link"), over millions of years, rather than been created and placed on earth, offended many people. Today Darwin's theory is widely accepted although the closeness of mankind's connection with the ape is still debated.

WHEN DOES ADOLESCENCE TAKE PLACE?

Between the ages of about eleven and eighteen years.

It is the time when a child's body gradually changes into that of an adult.

WHY DO PEOPLE GO BALD?

This is something which cannot yet be fully explained. It has been said that hats and caps which fit tightly restrict the blood vessels, so that the flow of blood to the scalp is checked; but people who have never worn hats have also become bald.

Sometimes when people have an illness or are under stress, they lose more hair than usual when combing or brushing, but this hair usually grows again.

Baldness occurs more in men due to excess of male sex hormones. Until scientists have learned more about the reasons for baldness, its prevention and cure will remain a problem.

WHY DO WE DREAM?

During sleep the conscious mind, which controls our emotions and

210

actions when we are awake, is at rest. This allows the sub-conscious mind to express some of our innermost desires, free of all inhibitions. But the conscious mind still exerts some controlling influence, so it is able to prevent the thoughts being expressed in straightforward terms. They then become the strange thoughts we know as dreams.

WHAT IS A NOSE-BLEED?

The proper medical name for a nose-bleed is *epistaxis*. It may be caused by an obvious injury or by a slight knock to a blood vessel that has been weakened by previous nose-bleeds.

They are a common symptom of many fevers and may also be caused by high blood pressure.

The bleeding may be stopped by pinching the nose for a few minutes, but a serious nose-bleed should receive expert attention.

HOW MANY TIMES DOES THE HEART BEAT IN A MINUTE?

The normal rate in adults is between 70 and 75 per minute, while in young people it is higher.

The rate varies, however, with a person's age and the state of their health.

DO ALL OUR JOINTS MOVE?

No. There are 230 joints in the body and all play their part in allowing the skeleton to maintain its shape and, in some cases, to move.

Some of the body's joints, however, do not move at all—the cranial bones of the skull, for example. Other joints, such as the elbow joint, allow movement in one direction only.

WHAT DOES THE WORD "MUMPS" MEAN?

The word "mump" is a verb which means to look sullen or glum or very serious. Mumps is a short name given to the painful disease, (the proper name of which is parotitis, a viral infection of the salvary gland) because it describes the look of those who are suffering from it.

WHAT MAKES BLOOD RED?

A red substance called haemoglobin containing iron which is present in the red blood cells.

WHAT IS THE DIFFERENCE BE-TWEEN THE POSITION OF THE HUMAN BRAIN AND THAT OF OTHER ANIMALS?

The human brain is at the top of the head, behind the forehead. The brains of other animals are behind their faces.

Compared with the brain of an animal, the human brain has become enormous and room has had to be found somewhere for it. It is the size of our brain that more than anything else distinguishes us from other animals.

Across the millions of years of evolution, the topmost section of the brain has grown so much that it has doubled over upon itself forward instead of growing straight up. The human skull, therefore, has had to grow forward to contain it.

The skull has grown over the face unlike other animals whose skulls are entirely behind their faces.

IS THE WAX IN OUR EARS OF BENEFIT TO US?

Yes. It prevents particles of dust from settling on the ear-drum.

WHAT IS MORE IMPORTANT IN KEEPING US ALIVE, FOOD OR WATER?

Water. We can live for some weeks without food but only a few days without water.

WHY DO MANY PEOPLE WEAR WHITE CLOTHES IN HOT COUNTRIES?

The warmest clothes we can wear are those best able to prevent the heat of our bodies from escaping. This depends partly on the weight of the clothes and partly on the kind of material and the way it is used. Dark clothing is also warm because it absorbs most of the light and heat that falls on its outside surface. White clothing absorbs little of this light and heat and so it is the coolest of all. That is why it is often worn in hot countries, especially by white people, who feel the heat much more than dark-skinned people.

WHY CAN WE HEAR BETTER ON LAND THAN ON WATER?

Sound consists of waves of different lengths transmitted through the air. Should these waves strike an obstacle, they are interrupted and broken up.

On land there are many such obstacles, for instance houses, trees, undulating ground and mountains. These prevent sound waves from travelling for any great distance.

On the sea or on a great lake, though, the surface is quite level and there are no such obstacles. This is why the sound waves can travel for long distances.

WHAT IS A BLIND SPOT?

That part of the eye which is insensitive to light and, therefore, has no power to see. It occurs where the optic nerve enters the back of the eye and has a diameter of above one-twelfth of an inch (2 mm). Just beside it is the yellow spot, the part of the eye in which vision is most acute. Everyone possesses these blind spots, but they are seldom noticed because part of the sensitive area of one eye compensates to some extent for the blind spot of the other.

WHAT ARE ENZYMES?

The word "enzyme" was coined by the German physiologist Willy Kuhne in 1878, to describe certain fermenting agencies produced by living cells. The word means "in yeast" because they are to a marked degree active in that substance; but their chemical composition is still uncertain. Their interest for the general public arises from the fact that they play an important part in the digestive processes. Digestion means the breaking-down of food substances into such a form that they will be capable of passing readily through the walls of the intestine into the blood and lymph vessels.

This breaking-down is begun by the chewing of the food in the mouth. When it is swallowed, enzymes are called into action in the upper parts of the digestive tract.

WHAT MAKES OUR HAIR STAND ON END?

When someone is terribly frightened, his hair may stand almost erect. This is something that can be felt as a tingling sensation down the back of the neck. It is caused by a series of small muscles that stretch from the surface of the skin to the root of the hair.

This strange effect can be seen more easily in animals, such as a cat which will be seen with an exceedingly bushy tail after a scare. When this affects the entire coat, it makes an animal appear larger and more daunting to its enemies.

WHAT IS THE LARYNX?
The upper part of the windpipe. It is a box-like formation of muscles and cartilage which contains the vocal cords.

IF YOU PRESS A FINGER ON THE BACK OF YOUR HAND IT LEAVES A WHITE PATCH. WHY?
Because the blood flow is interrupted immediately under the point of pressure.

WHY ARE WISDOM TEETH SO-CALLED?
Because by the time a normal person has them, he is an intelligent adult.

WHY IS IT BETTER TO BREATHE THROUGH THE NOSE?
Air breathed through the nose enters the lungs more slowly and at a temperature that does not irritate the lungs. Also membranes in the nose filter the air.

WHAT IS CHLOROFORM?
It is a colourless, volatile liquid with a sweetish smell. Inhalation of it can render a person completely insensible. It was often used in hospitals to make patients insensible for operations.

Choloroform was discovered at the same time by two chemists in 1831. Four years later it was analysed and described by Jean Dumas, a famous French chemist.

Somehow a chemist in Liverpool obtained some of the liquid and sent it to Sir James Young Simpson, an Edinburgh doctor, who had been experimenting rather unsuccessfully in an effort to find a better anaesthetic than ether.

It was Sir James Young Simpson who first introduced the use of chloroform in England after daringly experimenting with the drug on himself.

WHAT IS THE CAPACITY OF THE HUMAN STOMACH?
About four pints (1.9 l). The stomach is a crescent-moon shaped organ situated between the end of the gullet and the entrance to the small intestine. Its walls can be distended and its size varies according to the amount of food it contains.

CAN THE FACT THAT SOME PEOPLE ARE "LEFT-HANDED" BE EXPLAINED?
Not with certainty. Some authorities declare that people are born with strongly-developed tendencies towards either right- or left-handedness. Others assert that either tendency is merely acquired. Neither party, however, has been able to prove its case. The former state that the left side of the brain, which controls the right hand, is more highly developed than the right side, which controls the left hand. This, though, has not been proved and no explanation

why one side of the brain should be superior to the other is available.

It is often surmised that the reason for the right hand being the superior is that our distant ancestors acquired the habit of using the right hand to wield weapons while protecting their hearts with the left and in course of time, therefore, children began to be born with a tendency towards right-handedness.

It is estimated that fewer than 10% of people are left-handed.

WHAT IS THE CLAVICLE?

The collar bone.

WHAT IS THE SUBSTANCE INSIDE OUR BONES CALLED?

Marrow

WHEN WERE ANAESTHETICS FIRST USED?

As far back as the thirteenth century doctors were trying to induce anaesthesis for medical purposes. However, it was not until the nineteenth century that the problem of artificial anaesthesia began to receive serious scientific attention.

It was in 1800 that Sir Humphry Davy discovered that nitrous oxide (often referred to as "laughing" gas) could be used as an anaesthetic. That ether could effect the same result was demonstrated by Michael Faraday in 1818. It was 26 years later that an American, Dr Crawford D Long, carried out an operation on a patient to whom ether had been administered.

A few years later nitrous oxide began to be used as an anaesthetic in dental operations.

In 1847 the use of ether became established in England. In that same year Sir James Young Simpson began to experiment with chloroform.

WHAT ARE FLYING FLIES OR "FLOATING BODIES"?

Those curious little floating images which everybody sees before their eyes at some time. The medical term for these is *Muscae volantes* (Latin for flying flies). They are caused by the presence in the body of the eye of very tiny opaque particles, in the shape of spots or straight, looped or twisted fibres, which cast their shadow, greatly magnified, upon the retina. The mind projects these images into space, so that we appear to see them floating in the air when we look at a brightly lighted surface.

WHAT IS TREPHINATION?

In several countries in ancient times, it was thought that madness, headaches and epilepsy were caused by evil spirits in the brain.

So that the evil spirits could be released from the brain, holes were bored through the skull. It might be thought that patients submitting to such operations would inevitably die — but not so.

Several patients survived the operation. In fact some underwent the operation called trephination two or three times.

WHAT IS PHYSIOTHERAPY?

It is the treatment of illnesses and infirmities by physical methods rather than by medicines. These methods include the use of infrared rays (heat lamps), ultra violet rays (light lamps), radio-waves (short-waves), X-rays and atomic radiations, shock-treatment such as the passing of electric currents through the brain, massage, baths, swimming and exercises.

Another means of treatment is to give patients work to do to restore restricted movements or to take their minds off their illness.

WHAT IS RHESUS?

It is a blood group. People whose blood contains this group are referred to as being Rhesus positive. Those who lack it are called Rhesus negative.

WHAT IS THE HEART'S BASIC FUNCTION

Primarily, of course, to preserve life for in simple terms it is the body's blood pump. It circulates the blood to ensure that all the cells of the body are regularly supplied with food and oxygen and regularly cleared of poisonous products.

OF WHAT USE IS THE APPENDIX?

None that doctors can discover. It is generally believed that many thousands of years ago this organ had a definite function to perform in the process of digestion, but as man's diet gradually changed, it became less ˙and less important until today when it is worse than useless, being the cause of the illness known as appendicitis.

It is possible, however, that the appendix may still have a use which nobody has been able to discover. It may be of importance in the immune defence mechanism. Even doctors do not claim to know everything about the human body.

The appendix is from two to four inches (5-10 cm) long. Appendicitis was once a serious illness and many people died of it before a doctor arrived.

A surgical operation is necessary when appendicitis is diagnosed but today it is a very quick and safe operation.

SHOULD WE BRUSH OUR TEETH UP AND DOWN OR FROM SIDE TO SIDE?

Up and down.

WHAT IS THE THORAX?

The chest.

HOW MANY RIBS HAVE WE?

We have 24 ribs.

WHAT CAUSES THE WHITE MARKS WHICH SOMETIMES APPEAR ON OUR FINGER NAILS?

These are caused by calcium collecting under the nails.

WHAT IS THE FUNCTION OF OUR LUNGS?

They supply the blood passing through them with oxygen.

OF WHAT USE IS THE EARDRUM?

It receives sound vibrations which go to the inner ear and from there as impulses to the brain.

WHY DO WE GET SUN-TANNED?

Under the skin are cells of colouring matter called pigments In strong sunlight these multiply and spread over the skin.

WHAT ARE OUR TOE NAILS AND FINGER NAILS MADE OF?

A horny substance called keratin.

HOW MANY BONES ARE THERE BETWEEN KNEE AND ANKLE AND WHAT ARE THEIR NAMES?

There are two bones. The tibia and the fibula.

WHICH IS OUR BIGGEST BONE?

The thigh bone. In an adult it is 20 inches (approx .5 m) long.

HOW MANY BONES ARE THERE IN THE HUMAN WRIST AND FINGERS?

In the wrist there are eight pieces of bone all beautifully jointed. Beyond the wrist there are five long bones. Then there are two bones beyond the first of the five. These are the thumb bones. The other four bones each have three bones beyond them and these are the bones of the four fingers.

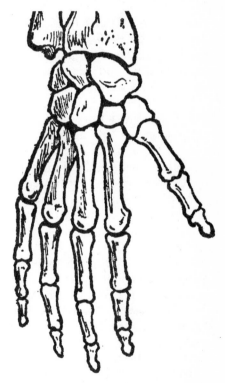

HOW MANY BONES ARE THERE IN THE ARM FROM ELBOW TO WRIST AND WHAT ARE THEIR NAMES?

Two bones. The ulna and the radius.

Famous People

HOW DID A FUTURE KING TURN THE TIDE OF BATTLE?

Joachim Murat was one of the most dashing and exciting generals of the Napoleonic Wars. From a dismissed junior officer, Murat rose to become a king.

He achieved this dazzling success by gallantry in the service of Napoleon, before the Emperor's own rise to power. As Napoleon climbed to the heights of Imperial power, he took Murat with him.

Possibly Murat's greatest action came at the Battle of Eylau on February 8, 1807. Napoleon's army of 45,000 men was in danger of being defeated by a Russian army of nearly 70,000. As the French infantry fell back, Napoleon sent an order to Murat. Leaping into the saddle, Murat ordered more than 10,000 French cavalry to follow him. Waving a riding crop over his head, Murat galloped through a snowstorm to lead his men in a crashing charge on the Russian left. Murat's charge turned the battle into a French victory. Later Napoleon was to re-ward Murat for his constant bravery and support by giving him the Kingdom of Naples.

WHERE DID KING OLAV OF NORWAY SPEND WORLD WAR II?

When the Second World War broke out King Olav V of Norway was a very popular and successful Crown Prince.

In 1928, the young Olav had led the Norwegian yachting crew to a gold medal in the Olympic Games. He was also a magnificent skier. Olav made a highly successful visit to America in 1939, the same year that Britain and France declared war on Germany.

After Hitler's armies overran his country in 1940, Olav fled with his father, King Haakon, to Britain. Olav's wife and children were sent to safety in America, but he stayed in Britain. Olav worked tirelessly for his nation. He helped train and lead the Norwegians who had escaped the Germans into an efficient fighting force.

King Haakon and Olav returned

home immediately after the war, but they never forgot the friendship of Britain. King Haakon sent a Christmas tree to London each year, a tradition continued after Haakon's death by King Olav.

WHO WAS THE FIRST PRINCE OF WALES?

Edward, the son of King Edward I of England. In 1276, the Welsh prince of North Wales was Llewelyn ab Fruffydd. In that year, after fighting valiantly against the forces of the invading Edward I, Llewelyn surrendered and was imprisoned for about five years. He rebelled and was killed in a fight near Builth.

His defeat did not, however, result in a conquest of Wales. The English king had conquered only the northern part of the country and the Welsh lords retained much of their power. This, though, did not prevent Edward naming his son as Prince of Wales in 1301. The young Edward was born in Carnarvon in Wales on April 25, 1284.

WHO INVENTED GUNPOWDER?

During the Middle Ages, science was not the highly organised study that it is today. Most scholars merely believed what was written in ancient books, rather than trying to find out the truth for themselves.

One man who did attempt to discover things for himself was an

Roger Bacon conducted experiments with lenses and chemicals.

English monk called Roger Bacon. Born around 1214, Bacon settled at Oxford to carry out his experiments and write up his work.

He conducted experiments with lenses and chemicals at his workshop and taught science to students at Oxford. While experimenting with lenses, Bacon produced a magnifying glass. It was his experiments with alchemy that produced his most famous invention. He discovered that a mixture of charcoal, saltpetre and sulphur would explode if set on fire. He had discovered gunpowder. This invention proved to be the most dramatic of Roger Bacon's discoveries.

WHICH SCIENTIST SPLIT THE ATOM?

At the end of the last century scientists believed that every object was made up of millions of. tiny objects called atoms. They also believed that each type of atom was completely different from another. One scientist disagreed. His name was Ernest Rutherford.

Rutherford was born in Nelson, New Zealand, in 1871 and rapidly showed a talent for chemistry. While other scientists thought that atoms were the smallest particles possible, Rutherford believed that each atom was made up of smaller particles. He maintained that it was the way in which these were put together which determined the type of atom.

While working in Canada, Rutherford was able to show that a radioactive chemical gradually changes into a quite different chemical. He went on to demonstrate that this is because radioactive atoms are losing tiny particles, so atoms must be made of several small objects. He had split the atom into component parts. His theory was vindicated. In later years Rutherford successfully predicted the many uses of radioactive materials.

He died in 1937.

BY WHAT NAME IS KAROL WOJTYLA BETTER KNOWN?

Karol Wojtyla was born on May 18, 1920, in the Polish town of Wadowice. Today he is far better known as Pope John Paul II.

Karol Wojtyla grew up in a different period. No sooner had he gone to university than the Germans invaded his country and closed the University. Wojtyla managed to continue his studies in secret, and was ordained as a priest in 1946.

Wojtyla rose steadily through the church as his abilities and talents came to the notice of his superiors. In 1963, Wojtyla was made Archbishop of Krakow. In the following years he opposed the repressive Communist government of his country, but was astute enough to keep the Church out of serious trouble. At the same time, his writings and abilities brought him world renown in Church affairs.

When Pope John Paul I died unexpectedly, Wojtyla attended the Conclave of October 1978 and was elected Pope. Since his election John Paul II has shown himself to be a firm and popular church leader. He has travelled extensively, taking the teaching of the Roman Catholic church into the lives of millions.

WHO UNITED GERMANY?

In the middle of the last century many Germans wanted to unite the various small states that make up what we know as Germany today. Only one man had the position and the ability to do it. His name was Otto Bismarck.

Born into the Prussian gentry, Bismarck looked for a career in politics. His astute and realistic attitude, together with his unwavering support for the King of Prussia, soon won him high office. In 1862 Bismarck became leader of the government.

He took immediate advantage of European politics to engineer a war against Austria. The complete defeat of Austria in 1866 gave Prussia dominance in Germany. Bismarck set about uniting many of the German states under Prussian leadership. These plans were partly disrupted by France, wary of the growing power of Prussia.

In 1870 France and Prussia went to war. France was utterly defeated and Bismarck was free to proclaim his King to be Emperor of Germany. Germany was united at last.

WHO IS THE DUKE OF CORNWALL?

The Duchy of Cornwall is one of the most important titles in Britain. Not only is it high in the order of noble precedence, but it brings with it thousands of acres of land.

The man who holds this Duchy, however, is rarely known by the title of Duke of Cornwall. We know him better as Prince Charles, eldest son of Queen Elizabeth II and his title of Prince of Wales takes precedence over that of Duke of Cornwall. Nonetheless the Duke of Cornwall is an important title.

It is as Duke of Cornwall that Prince Charles is entitled to sit in the House of Lords.

The vast lands he owns through the title provide the money for Charles' household and his public life. Prince Charles receives no money from the Civil List. In fact he pays a large proportion of the income of the Duchy of Cornwall to the government in the form of income tax.

WHO WAS THE "PHILOSOPHER" EMPEROR?

When Antoninus, Emperor of Rome, died in AD 161, he was succeeded by his nephew, Marcus Aurelius, a man not very well known. Throughout his uncle's reign Marcus Aurelius had spent his time studying and philosophising. Though he had led a quiet life, Marcus Aurelius had a reputation for good judgment and tolerance which was guaranteed to make him a popular Emperor.

As a Stoic philosopher, Marcus Aurelius believed he had a duty to Rome. He therefore abandoned his quiet life and threw himself into being a good Emperor. He overhauled the system of justice, making it more humane and practical. Marcus also re-organised the government of the Empire and introduced many wise social reforms. His reign is noted for its moderation and wisdom, traits which can be traced back to Marcus' philosophical training.

Ronald Reagan when he was a famous film star

of the United States, Ronald Reagan earned a living in a variety of ways, one of which was as a radio announcer.

In 1937, however, Ronald Reagan became an actor when he signed a contract with Warner Brothers. Ironically his first role was as a radio announcer. Later films were to cast him in a variety of parts, from secret agent and army corporal to football player and pianist. Reagan made several films for Warner Brothers before the war broke out, when he joined the Army Air Force.

With the fighting over, Ronald Reagan returned to a $1,000,000 film contract. In all he made a total of 53 movies before leaving Hollywood to pursue a political career. While he featured in more films than many other actors, Ronald Reagan will probably be best remembered for his two terms as President of the U S rather than for his acting.

Though no soldier, Marcus led his soldiers into battle against the barbarians threatening the Roman frontiers. It was on one of these campaigns that Marcus Aurelius died in AD 180. After his reign, Rome began its long period of decline.

HOW MANY FILMS DID RONALD REAGAN MAKE BEFORE HE BECAME PRESIDENT?

Long before he became President

WHY IS BOADICEA SO FAMOUS?

Boadicea, or Boudicca, tore a path through history with her bloody revolt against Rome. In following her cause of revenge, Boadicea created the glamorous image of a warrior queen.

When Boadicea's husband, King Prasutagus of the Iceni, died in AD 60 he left half his East Anglian kingdom to his daughters and half to the Emperor of Rome. When the Romans arrived they promptly set about looting the palace and seizing everything. Boadicea objected and she and her daughters were savagely beaten.

Vowing revenge, Boadicea raised her tribe and attacked the Romans. Other tribes, which had also suffered under Roman rule, rallied to her cause. Riding in her chariot and urging on the warriors, Boadicea massacred the Roman 9th Legion which had been sent against her. She then moved on to capture and plunder the Roman cities now known as Colchester, St Albans and London.

Soon after these victories the main Roman army in Britain arrived under the command of Suetonius. Boadicea's undisciplined warriors were heavily defeated. Boadicea killed herself rather than be taken prisoner.

HOW DID MIKHAIL GORBACHEV BECOME LEADER OF THE SOVIET UNION?

On March 12, 1985, Mikhail Gorbachev became General Secretary of the Central Committee of the Communist Party of the Soviet Union. In effect this made him the leader and most powerful man in Russia.

Gorbachev's origins were far from the seat of power, and he had to climb through the party structure by his own ability to gain his present position. He was born on March 2, 1931, in a small village north of the Caucasus Mountains. He came from a family of agricultural workers, but early in life Gorbachev showed that he would not follow the same career.

He joined the Communist party at the age of 21 and soon became involved with full-time party work.

Gradually, Gorbachev worked his way up through the ranks of the local party. By 1970 he was the most important party official in his home territory of Stavropol.

From there he was elected to the Central Committee. It was this Central Committee which, in turn, elected Gorbachev to power in 1985. The long road from farm worker's son to leader of millions was complete.

WHO WAS THE FIRST POPE?

After the Crucifixion and Ascension of Jesus, his followers journeyed far and wide, spreading the word of Christ. Perhaps the greatest of these followers was Saint Peter.

Always recognised as the foremost of the disciples, Peter became the leader of the Christian church after the Ascension. Peter travelled extensively and was prominent in preaching the Faith to non-Jews. He eventually settled in Rome where he began organising the first Christian community in the heart of the Roman Empire. In this Peter was very successful and there was soon a flourishing church in Rome. Unfortunately, the followers of the new religion were viewed with deep suspicion by the pagan Romans. In AD64 the Emperor Nero ordered a persecution of Christians. Peter was one of the first to die.

Before his death, Peter appointed St Linus as his successor as leader of the Church of Rome. From that day to this there has been a continuous line of Bishops of Rome. St Peter, therefore, is regarded as the first pope.

WHAT GREAT DISCOVERY DID MARIE CURIE MAKE?

While the young Polish scientist Manya Sklodovska was studying in Paris she met and married the man who would give her the name by which she is well-known. She became Madam Marie Curie.

Over the next few years she and her husband, Pierre, studied the new phenomenon of radioactivity. Some materials were found to emit invisible rays which penetrated solids and affected photographic plates. One of the most highly radioactive substances known was an ore called pitchblende. Marie determined to find out what caused the radioactivity.

She bought a ton of pitchblende and, with the help of her husband, started work. It took nearly four years, but in 1898 they found the cause. Glowing in their laboratory was a minute particle of a new element which Marie called radium. The cause of radioactivity had been isolated and could now be studied. Marie's contribution to modern science was immense.

WHICH ROLE MADE CHARLIE CHAPLIN FAMOUS?

When Charlie Chaplin made his first film in 1914 he was already well established as a music hall star. His successful career in his native Britain came to an end just before the First World War, when he went to America on tour. He stayed there and was soon working in films.

It was in Chaplin's second film that he first introduced a character he called "the little fella". The obstinate down-and-out who struggled against those in authority soon became known to the audiences as "the tramp".

In 1915 Charlie Chaplin made a film called The Tramp. He shot to stardom. The character struck a sympathetic chord with the public and enormous success followed. The masterpiece of the tramp character is often thought to be a film called The Kid, which was a full-length feature film. Even after 70 years the films of Chaplin's tramp are still shown and delight their audiences.

WHICH EMPRESS OF GERMANY NEARLY BECAME QUEEN OF ENGLAND?

When King Henry I died in 1135 his only legitimate child was Matilda. She had been married to the Emperor of Germany, but after being widowed had married Geoffrey of Anjou.

As soon as he learnt that the king was dead, Count Stephen of

Boulogne, a nephew of King Henry, claimed the throne. Stephen was well liked and generous, while Geoffrey of Anjou was thoroughly disliked. When the Empress Matilda arrived to claim her throne, Stephen was already king. Civil war flared up almost at once. Some barons supported Stephen, while others declared for Matilda. The war raged across England and bands of warriors roamed at will. At times it seemed that Matilda would gain the throne, but she always failed.

Finally, in 1153, a peace was arranged between Stephen and Matilda. It was a compromise in which Stephen was to continue as king but Matilda's son, Henry, would inherit the throne after Stephen's death.

WHICH ROYAL FAMILY CAME BACK TO ITS THRONE IN 1975?

Following the Civil War of the 1930s, Spain was ruled by General Franco. After 30 years of government by Franco, it was clear that he would have to choose a successor. It would not be an easy choice. Whoever followed Franco would have to be acceptable to everyone in Spain and be able to introduce reform without upsetting the traditionalists.

In 1969 Franco announced that he had chosen Don Juan Carlos. As a member of the ancient royal family of Spain, Juan Carlos would have considerable support. His long service in the armed forces meant that the powerful generals knew him. He was also committed to a programme of limited social reform.

When Franco died in 1975, Juan Carlos became King Juan Carlos. Power was transferred smoothly and easily without any of the trouble which some had expected. Spain settled down to a peaceful life under her new king. Spain thus became unusual in regaining her monarchy many years after it had been abolished.

WHO CREATED MICKEY MOUSE?

Mickey Mouse is probably the best known cartoon character of all time. His manic adventures, which spread over 130 films, have brought him fame and popularity all over the world.

Mickey was created in 1928 by a young American artist, Walter Elias Disney, who had been working in cartoons for some years. He thought up the idea of a cartoon mouse that he wanted to call Mortimer. His wife persuaded him to change the name to Mickey Mouse. The first film to star Mickey was Steamboat Willie, the first sound cartoon. It was this character which established the fortunes of his creator, Walt Disney.

Disney, born in Chicago in 1901, showed his imaginative flair early in life. When Mickey was created, Disney was working in a converted garage. Soon he had to take on staff and expand into a massive studio just to keep pace with the success of his characters. Today, long after the death of Walt Disney himself, the studios he began continue to produce loveable and popular cartoons.

WHEN DID A WOMAN SAVE CANADA?

In 1813, American troops crossed the border into Canada and began an invasion they had planned for some time. As the Canadian forces fell back, they had to leave a woman called Laura Secord and her husband behind. James Secord had been wounded in the fighting and was too ill to move.

When the Americans arrived, Laura Secord was forced to invite some of them into her house and feed them. One day, she heard two American officers discussing a surprise attack that they were about to launch on the Canadians. Laura had to get news to the Canadian army, but was at a loss to know how until an idea came to her.

She led her cow out into the field and began to milk it. Suddenly the cow kicked over the milk bucket. The American troops roared with laughter. Laura tried to milk it again. Again the cow kicked out and this time bolted for the woods. Laura followed at the run. Laura had been deliberately pinching the cow's udder so that it would bolt.

Laura Secord's cow kicked over the milk bucket

Now she was away from the eyes of the American troops, she began to make her way towards the Canadian army. Having crossed swamps and creeks, Laura was suddenly pounced upon by a group of Indians. To her great relief, they turned out to be friendly and led her to the army. Forewarned of the attack, the Canadian army was able to beat the Americans. Canada had been saved by the news brought by a single brave woman.

WHICH QUEEN WAS KNOWN AS GLORIANA?

When Queen Mary I of England died in 1558, she left her country a poor and divided nation. Her religious persecutions and those of her brother, Edward VI, had split the country and disrupted trade.

Mary's successor was her younger sister, Elizabeth. Over the 40 years of her reign, Elizabeth was to make England a rich and united nation. One of her first actions was to reach a compromise over religion which satisfied most of her subjects. She then encouraged trade with foreign countries.

At home Elizabeth presided over the growth of a healthy economy and a thriving culture which encouraged artists and writers of high calibre. The startling success of her reign was in such contrast with her predecessors that Elizabeth gained the name of "Gloriana" from her subjects.

WHICH PRINCE SAILED TO WAR IN 1982?

In centuries gone by, princes and kings were expected to lead their men into battle. In the 20th century such behaviour has become increasingly rare.

When Argentina invaded the Falklands in April 1982, the stage was set for a modern prince to fight a modern war. At the time Prince Andrew, second son of Queen Elizabeth II, was serving as a helicopter pilot in the Royal Navy. When his ship was ordered south as part of the task force, Prince Andrew sailed with her. Over the following weeks, Prince Andrew flew dozens of missions and faced the fire of the Argentinians. At one time he had the unenviable job of deliberately acting as a decoy so that enemy missiles would not sink the aircraft carriers of the fleet.

When it was all over, Prince Andrew returned home with his ship to his family and friends.

WHO WAS CATHERINE DE MEDICI?

When Henri, second son of the King of France, was looking for a wife, he chose Catherine de Medici. It was a fateful decision.

Catherine, the daughter of the rich and powerful Lorenzo the Magnificent, ruler of Florence, was clever and astute. In 1547 Henri became king and Catherine queen. During the reign of her husband Catherine played little part in politics. When Henri died, however, he was succeeded by the young Francis II and Catherine became regent.

She thought her job as regent was to concentrate power in the hands of the king and to put down rebellious nobles. When Francis died in 1560 his younger brother, Charles IX, came to the throne. The government was still controlled by Catherine. She became involved in political intrigues to attain her ends. The passions of the religious wars proved too strong and France was torn by civil war. Continuing her regency into the reign of Henri III, Catherine held on to power until her death in 1589.

WHICH BLIND WOMAN BROUGHT HOPE TO OTHERS?

In 1880 a cheerful little girl was born to the Keller family in Alabama. They named her Helen. When only 18 months old Helen suffered a terrible illness which left her blind and deaf.

In desperation, her parents contacted the great expert Samuel Howe. He suggested a lady named Annie Sullivan as a teacher for Helen.

When Annie Sullivan arrived she found Helen was an impossible child who threw tantrums and hit anybody who came near her. Slowly Annie set to work. After gaining Helen's trust, Annie slowly taught her how to read braille. Suddenly Helen became

aware of the world around her. She learned to read braille in several different languages. Most surprising of all, Helen learnt to speak by touching Annie's throat when she said words.

After going to school and passing her exams, Helen began to give lectures to encourage other handicapped people. During the First World War, many men were blinded by poison gas. Helen Keller visited these men to show them how blind people could enjoy life. She became a tireless worker for the blind and deaf.

WHICH FRENCH MARSHAL WAS INVITED TO BECOME KING OF SWEDEN?

When Napoleon, Emperor of the French, created 18 of his best generals Marshals of France, perhaps the most determined was Jean Baptiste Bernadotte.

Bernadotte led his troops in many successful battles over the following years, including the glorious victory of Austerlitz. In 1809, Bernadotte quarrelled with Napoleon and resigned his command. The following year Bernadotte was elected as Crown Prince of Sweden and heir to the ageing Charles XIII.

Bernadotte took his new duties seriously and pledged himself to the Swedish crown. When Napoleon invaded Swedish Pomerania in 1812, Bernadotte instantly abandoned his old master and joined the Tsar of Russia against Napoleon. In 1813 Bernadotte led Swedish troops against Napoleon at the Battle of Leipzig.

When the war was over, Bernadotte settled down to rule Sweden. He became king as Charles XIV in 1818 and ruled his kingdom efficiently until his death in 1844. The descendants of Bernadotte still occupy the throne of Sweden.

WHO WAS LENIN (REAL NAME ULIANOV)?

Lenin was a ruthless man, totally committed to Communism.

He was born the son of a Russian school teacher. While at university he and his brother became involved in revolutionary activities. Arrested and tried, Lenin was sent to Siberia and his brother was executed.

Lenin became a prominent leader of the Communists and had to flee from his country to escape the Tsar's police. In 1917 the Germans sent Lenin to Russia as they believed he could overthrow the government and withdraw Russia from the war.

When he arrived, Lenin set about organising the Communist revolution. Aided by his friend, Trotsky, Lenin led the first outbreak of violence on October 25, 1917. Within a short time, the Communists had control of the government. Lenin had to contend with a civil war for some time, but eventually peace came to Russia.

He was starting to reorganise the state along Communist lines when he died in 1924.

Lenin's real name was Vladimir Ilyitch Ulianov.

WHICH PRIME MINISTER WAS KNOWN AS "WINNIE"?

When Britain went to war in 1939, it soon became clear that Prime Minister Neville Chamberlain had neither the character nor the ability to lead the country.

In May 1940, Winston Churchill, a man with a powerful personality, was called in to form a government. He set about his task with a will. Not only did Churchill put Britain on a war footing, but he also raised the spirits of the country. By making moving and dramatic speeches on the radio, he made sure that his message reached the hearts and minds of the British people.

Known affectionately as "Winnie", Churchill was able to meet every event, be it disaster or victory, with indomitable courage. He entirely caught the mood and imagination of Britain during the war. Serving again as Prime Minister during the early 1950s, Churchill had to retire on health grounds and died in 1965.

WHICH PARTNERSHIP CREATED A MAGNIFICENT CAR?

Rolls-Royce make what are reputedly the finest and most prestigious cars in the world. This highly successful company was born out of the partnership of two very different men.

Frederick Royce was born in 1863, and early in his career showed a flair for engineering. He worked for the Great Northern Railway and the City of Liverpool before starting his own company. From his earliest days, he decided to strive for excellence and not to accept second best.

One day, he bought a French car and decided he could improve it. In 1904 he produced his first car, a very quiet and smooth-running vehicle. This car came to the notice of the rich and flamboyant Charles Rolls. As a keen racing driver, Rolls was anxious to spread the use of the motor car in Britain. He persuaded Royce to expand the car-making business. With Rolls putting up the money, they produced magnificent luxury cars under the name of Rolls-Royce. They built a large new factory in Derby and were soon selling as many cars as they could produce.

Always one to try something new, Charles Rolls was killed flying an aeroplane in 1910. But the company he had started went from strength to strength and still produces what are acknowledged to be the finest cars in the world.

WHO WAS THE GREATEST GREEK SCULPTOR?

The great age of Greek art was during the 5th and 4th centuries BC.

In that time Greek artists escaped the rigid formulas of the past and produced work of unsurpassed beauty.

One of the most famous, and arguably the greatest, of the sculptors working at this time was Praxiteles who worked mainly in Athens during the 4th century. Ancient writers never tired of praising his work and many other artists copied his work. These copies have been found throughout the Roman Empire and show the talent of Praxiteles.

No original statue by this great sculptor was found until 1877. Then archaeologists excavating the ancient site of Olympia came across a magnificent statue of the god Hermes with the infant Dionysus. The beautiful work carried the signature of Praxiteles. This statue is now on show in the museum at Olympia.

WHAT HAPPENED TO AMELIA EARHART?

During the 1920s and 30s, Amelia Earhart was one of the most famous women in the world. She was one of very few woman pilots and broke many records.

She flew higher than any other woman and was the first woman to fly solo across the Atlantic. In 1937 Amelia Earhart decided to attempt another great feat of aviation. She was going to fly around the world. Taking with her the experienced navigator Fred Noonan, she set off from California on May

Amelia Earhart was the first woman to fly solo across the Atlantic

20, 1937. By July 2, Amelia had flown across Africa, India and Indonesia. Then she set off across the Pacific. The first leg of the trip was from New Guinea to Howland Island.

Earhart and Noonan took off at 10 am and expected to reach Howland some seventeen hours later. They never arrived. A few radio messages were heard asking for a radio fix, but static was so bad it was impossible to get a bearing. A massive search was launched with naval ships and local boats taking part, but no trace of Amelia Earhart, Fred Noonan or their plane was ever found. It is presumed that something went wrong with their navigational equipment and they crashed into the ocean.

WHAT DID PYTHAGORAS DISCOVER?

The ancient Greek philosopher, Pythagoras, was born at Samos in the 6th century BC. He later moved to Crotona in Italy and it was here that he did most of his teaching.

Pythagoras believed that numbers were the basis of the universe. Not only could objects be measured with numbers, he taught, but they were the sum of those numbers. Though this idea proved to be wrong, it led to many important discoveries.

While investigating the numbers of a stringed musical instrument, Pythagoras discovered the octave. This is still the basis of all music. It was when investigating geometrical shapes such as triangles, Pythagoras proved the theorem which still bears his name. This states that in a right-angled triangle the square of the hypotenuse is equal to the sum of the squares of the other two sides. For these two discoveries, if for nothing else, Pythagoras has become famous.

WHO WAS FRANK LLOYD WRIGHT?

Like so many areas of the arts, architecture has changed radically in the 20th century. From a style reminiscent of the past, architecture has progressed to embrace a wide range of imitative styles. One of the most influential figures in this movement was Frank Lloyd Wright.

He was born in America in 1869. His experiences as an architect enabled him to make great use of modern materials, such as concrete, in highly imaginative ways. The smooth curves of the Guggenheim Museum in New York exemplify the type of work produced by this highly original man.

WHICH ENGLISH CHILD STAR BECAME A TALENTED INTERNATIONAL ACTRESS?

It is always difficult for child prodigies to carry their fame and ability into adulthood. Most fade from public view. Elizabeth Taylor, on the other hand, has become even more famous as an adult actress than she was as a child star.

Born in London in 1932, she played in her first Hollywood film ten years later. Her most famous film as a child was *National Velvet*, still popular today. By the early 1950s she had started to play roles as attractive young women and she was recognised as a great screen actress. In 1960, she won the title role in the multi-million dollar epic *Cleopatra*. Elizabeth Taylor has since gone on to star in several more successful films.

WHAT DID ELEVEN YEAR OLD MARY ANNING FIND?

At the beginning of the last century man's knowledge of the distant past was very limited. Nobody knew that giant dinosaurs had roamed the earth.

In 1810 an eleven year old girl called Mary Anning was walking by the sea in Dorset. Suddenly she spotted some bones embedded in the rock. Using a hammer and chisel Mary and her brother managed to reveal the 30-foot skeleton of a strange animal. The children were puzzled and wrote to ask scientists for help.

What Mary Anning had found was the first known skeleton of an *Ichthyosaurus*, a giant reptile which lived in the seas millions of years ago. Such discoveries as this started scientists on the road to accepting modern views of geology and extinct life.

WHICH POPE INTRODUCED OUR MODERN CALENDAR?

By the middle of the 16th century it was becoming increasingly obvious that there was something wrong with the calendar.

The longest day of the year was supposed to be June 21, but in fact it fell ten days earlier. More importantly for such a religious age, was the suspicion that this might mean that religious festivals were being held on the wrong day.

In February 1582 a papal commission reported on the problem. They had been working for some years at the Villa Mondragone on complicated chronological data. The pope who read the report was Gregory XIII. He at once realised its significance and introduced the new calendar, which the report recommended, within a month. It is this Gregorian calendar which we still use today.

WHICH FAMILY MADE THE WALTZ THEIR OWN?

In 1825 a young musician set up a dance orchestra in Vienna. His name was Johann Strauss and he was to become the most popular musician in Europe. His orchestra began playing dance music, mostly his own compositions. Soon it was playing to packed dance halls every night, and Strauss went on long international tours. In all he wrote 180 pieces of dance music.

All three of Johann's sons, Joseph, Edward and Johann the younger, went into the music business, even though their father disapproved at first. Johann the younger was by far the most successful. He took over his father's orchestra and wrote such masterpieces as the concert waltz, *The Blue Danube*, the operetta *Die Fledermaus*, and more than 400 dance pieces before his death in 1899.

WHAT DID CONFUCIUS TEACH?

Thought to have been born in 551 BC, Confucius established perhaps the most important philosophical school of the Far East.

He was born into a noble family and he entered the civil service of the Chinese Empire at a young age. Confucius rose rapidly and by the age of 55 was the most important official in China.

In such a position he was able to put into practice the ideas he had been developing all his life. Confucius taught that man should follow a highly moral life, adhering to the virtues of life, such as modesty and compassion for others. He applied these ideas to government and achieved many humane reforms.

After leaving government, Confucius went to live in the country. Here he completed five sacred books and passed on his ideas to anyone who would listen to him. By the time he died in 478 BC, Confucius had spread his ideas far and wide. He is still revered by millions in the Far East.

WHAT DID A GIPSY WOMAN TEACH LADY MONTAGU?

In March 1718, Lady Mary Montagu took the greatest risk of her life. If she had been wrong, her son would have died.

Lady Montagu was in Constantinople with her husband who was the British ambassador to Turkey, when smallpox broke out. To Lady Montague's amazement, nobody was particularly worried. When she asked why people were not concerned about the killer disease, she was told that it was because of a gipsy treatment that prevented the disease.

She called in an old gipsy woman and asked her to treat her son. As Lady Montagu watched in trepidation, the gipsy dipped a needle in pus from a smallpox sore and then stuck it into the Englishwoman's son's arm. A few days later, the boy became mildly ill but soon recovered and never caught smallpox.

Lady Montagu realised the benefit of this treatment, which is today known as inoculation. She tried to introduce the idea into Britain. At first it caught on, but then somebody who had been inoculated died of smallpox. The practice was abandoned, but the idea of inoculation was not forgotten and is today widely practised. Edward Jenner later discovered a safer form of inoculation against smallpox, using the same technique but involving the milder disease, cowpox, which prevented infection with smallpox.

WHO IS SAID TO BE THE MOST POPULAR ACTOR OF RECENT YEARS?

With a string of successful films behind him, all of them huge box office hits, Paul Newman has become so popular that few others can approach his fame.

He was born in Ohio in 1925 and though he worked in TV and theatre, he did not appear on film until 1954. In his films made in the 1950s, Newman established his screen personality as a charming loner. In films such as *Butch Cassidy and the Sundance Kid* and *The Towering Inferno*, he played characters who disagree with those in authority. Newman manages to combine success with privacy in a way other actors do not, and seems set to continue his popularity well into the future.

WHAT DID VANBRUGH BUILD?

Sir John Vanbrugh certainly led the most exciting life of any architect of his time.

He was born in 1664 and, after studying architecture, joined the army. While in France, Vanbrugh was arrested as a spy and imprisoned in the infamous Bastille. After his release, he returned to Britain to take up the safer occupation of architect.

Vanbrugh specialised in the Baroque style then fashionable, and designed on a grand scale. His two most famous buildings are the magnificent Blenheim Palace and Castle Howard.

Lady Mary Montagu called in an old gipsy woman to treat her son

Blenheim Palace was the gift of the nation to the Duke of Marlborough. The scale of the work was truly enormous and Vanbrugh decorated the house and its outbuildings with Doric and Corinthian columns. Vanbrugh included columns in his designs for Castle Howard in Yorkshire, where he also constructed follies in the grounds. Both buildings remain tributes to Vanbrugh's skill.

WHICH DUTCHMAN WAS THE GREATEST SCHOLAR OF THE RENAISSANCE?

When Desiderius Erasmus joined the priesthood in 1492 there was little to distinguish him from other young priests. Within a few years, however, he revolutionised European learning.

Erasmus was not only well-read, but well-travelled. In search of the writings he wished to read, Erasmus visited Paris, Oxford, Cambridge and several towns in Italy and Germany. The works he produced were profound. He edited many standard works dating from ancient Rome or Greece, giving new insights into old learning. He also studied the New Testament and almost single-handedly founded Biblical criticism. Erasmus also wrote on how priests, bishops and congregations should behave.

Before his death in 1536, Erasmus had completely revised the methods and purpose of study. In so doing, he had laid the foundations for modern scholarship.

HOW LONG HAS ELIZABETH II BEEN QUEEN OF BRITAIN AND THE COMMONWEALTH?

When he opened the Festival of Britain in 1951, it was clear that King George VI was a sick man. The king, who had gallantly led Britain through her darkest hours of World War II, was dying.

Early in 1952 Princess Elizabeth and her husband, Prince Philip, left on a tour of the Commonwealth, which the king was too ill to make, as representatives of King George and Queen Elizabeth. While in Africa, in February 1952, they were told that the king had died. Elizabeth was now Queen.

Abandoning the tour, Queen Elizabeth II and Prince Philip returned to Britain to attend the state funeral of King George VI. The following year a magnificent coronation was held amid great national rejoicing.

Ever since she became queen, Queen Elizabeth II has devoted a considerable amount of time and energy to meeting her people, and has worked tirelessly for the good of the nation and the Commonwealth. She has never shirked her duty and has become one of the most popular monarchs of recent years.

WHO PAINTED THE FIRST CUBIST PAINTING?

Born in Malaga, Spain, in 1881, Pablo Picasso proved to be one of the most imaginative, versatile and successful of modern artists.

After studying fine art in Barcelona, Picasso moved to Majorca where he spent some time working with ceramics. In 1903 he moved to Paris where he became established as a portrait painter. In 1906 he painted, in a startling new style, a picture which he called *Les Demoiselles d'Avignon*. It was the first cubist painting. Soon a whole school of Cubism had grown up and many artists worked in the style. Picasso though, soon tired of this and moved on.

In the course of his life, Picasso touched on so many different types of art that his work can be split into periods. In his Blue Period, for instance, Picasso produced lovely, sentimental pictures. He died in 1973 after a lifetime of work.

WHICH KING OF FRANCE BECAME A SAINT?

While King Louis IX of France was still a child his mother, Blanche of Castille, made sure he had a thorough religious education.

In 1226, when Louis was 12 years old, his father died and he became king. Blanche, however, made sure that his education continued, while she assumed the reins of power. Ten years later Louis took over the government. His personal piety soon won him the admiration of his contemporaries and the love of his subjects.

After putting down a rebellion incited by England, Louis set off to lead the 7th Crusade in 1248. The venture was a failure. Louis himself was captured by the Moslems and was ransomed. He returned to France in 1254 where he forced King Henry III of England to renounce his claim to Normandy. Five years later Louis set out on another crusade, but died while on campaign.

His sanctity and piety were legendary, as was his devotion to the church. These gifts were responsible for his being made a saint soon after his death.

WHO WERE THE GREATEST COMEDY TEAM IN THE CINEMA?

Many film producers and actors have tried to make the audience laugh. No team has ever managed this better, or more lastingly, than Laurel and Hardy.

Stan Laurel and Oliver Hardy both had moderately successful careers as comedians before they made their first film together in 1927. It was called *Putting Pants on Philip* and was an instant success. They made several more short movies before sound arrived. Unlike many other Hollywood greats, Laurel and Hardy moved into sound film without any difficulty. A string of hilarious short movies was crowned by a number of full-length films in the 1930s. Their easy style of humour even now make Laurel and Hardy irresistible. Their films remain firm favourites with the public.

Grace Kelly

WHAT DID FATHER DAMIEN ACHIEVE?

Devotion to duty and a disregard of peril are virtues exemplified by the life of Father Damien.

Father Damien's name was actually Joseph de Veuster and he was born in Holland in 1840. At the age of 18 he decided to dedicate himself to a religious life. He joined a missionary order which sent him to Hawaii in 1864, where he was ordained as priest.

In 1873, Father Damien volunteered to go to the leper colony on the island of Molokai. Nobody dared minister to the lepers for fear of catching the terrible disease. Father Damien did not consider the danger to himself. He felt compelled to help the people abandoned to their fate by society.

The religious comfort which he brought to people who were dying is difficult to imagine. His courageous devotion eventually caused his own death. He was diagnosed as having leprosy in 1885 and died four years later.

WHICH HOLLYWOOD STAR BECAME A PRINCESS?

On November 12, 1929, a daughter was born to a wealthy family in Philadelphia. Her life was to bring her glamour, fame and eventually a fairytale-like romance which made her a princess.

Grace Kelly took up an acting career and after working on the stage for some time, she was given a small film part in 1951. She went on to achieve fame in the western *High Noon* and a series of thrillers directed by Alfred Hitchcock, one filmed in Monaco, where she met her future husband.

After starring in 11 films, Grace Kelly's Hollywood career was cut short when she married Prince Rainier of Monaco. For many years Princess Grace played an important role in the life of the Principality. Her tragic death in a car crash in 1982 was a great disaster to Monaco and its prince.

BY WHAT NAME IS TEMUJIN BETTER KNOWN?

Temujin was the son of a rather unimportant Mongol chieftain who died soon after his son was born. As soon as he was adult, Temujin embarked on a career that was to make him feared across Asia and Europe.

His charismatic personality and skill as a warrior quickly won him many followers. By making skilful alliances among the nomadic tribes of the Asian grasslands, Temujin made himself a powerful leader. By 1206, when he was 44, Temujin had reached such power that the tribes elected him as their leader. It was then that he took the title by which he is best known. He called himself Genghis Khan, which means universal ruler.

He launched the warriors of his newly united tribes in a ferocious attack against China. In a few short years he had massacred thousands and conquered vast areas. He had to break off the attack on China when the Shah of Khorasan insulted him. After devastating Khorasan, Genghis Khan returned to China to continue the conquest. When he died in 1227, Genghis Khan had conquered the largest empire yet seen. His successors made it even larger.

WHO WAS THE GENIUS OF THE RENAISSANCE?

Born in 1452 in the little Italian village of Vinci, Leonardo da Vinci was possibly the greatest genius of all time.

His talents first showed themselves in painting. He became a member of the Florentine Painters Guild at the age of twenty and became a Master just six years later. His work Mona Lisa hangs in the Louvre in Paris, and is the most famous painting in the world.

Leonardo's work was not restricted to painting. He worked on the most profound mathematics, fluid dynamics, astronomy, anatomy, technological invention, warfare and philosophy. In many of these areas Leonardo was so advanced in his thinking that nobody could understand him. After his death many of Leonardo's papers were lost or filed away, and some of his work had to be rediscovered by other scientists some years later. He was certainly the greatest genius of his time.

WHY WAS THE MONK RASPUTIN MURDERED?

In 1907 a shabby monk appeared at the court of the Tsar of Russia and announced he could cure the heir to the throne. The young Crown Prince suffered from haemophilia and his mother eagerly seized any chance to ease his suffering.

The monk was Gregory

Rasputin and he was a remarkable man. Venerated by many peasants as a saint, Rasputin believed that in order to repent to God he first had to sin. He therefore sinned on a grand scale, indulging in drunken orgies at every opportunity.

When Rasputin seemed to be healing the Crown Prince, he gained an almost hypnotic power over the Tsarina. Through her, he gained political power over the government.

By the end of 1916 his disgusting behaviour and misuse of power had become too much for Russian nobility. On December 15, Rasputin was invited to a meal by some nobles. They fed him poisoned food, but this had no effect on Rasputin so they shot him. Rasputin's death came too late for Russia. The inept government of Rasputin and the Tsarina had set the scene for the Revolution which broke out a few months later.

WHICH FILM STAR WAS A KARATE EXPERT?

In 1971 a film launched a new star on to the movie screens of the world. In just four films, including *Fists of Fury* and *Enter the Dragon*, Bruce Lee established himself as the leader of a growing interest in Oriental martial arts. Lee had played in domestic Hong Kong films since he was a boy but had attracted little notice elsewhere. Lee himself was a skilful Karate fighter who developed his own style. This expertise was used to the full in his films, together with Lee's incredible fitness. When Lee dropped dead just one year later, martial arts films had lost their leader and rapidly faded. Lee was a remarkable, if short-lived, figure in the film world.

WHICH KING OF BRITAIN SERVED UNDER NELSON?

Nelson was the greatest seaman of his time and led the Royal Navy to some of its most spectacular victories. Young men eager to learn the art of naval fighting were sent to serve under him.

One of these was a young officer of 17 years, Prince William, third son of King George III. When both his elder brothers died before him without leaving surviving children, William inherited the throne in 1830. Because of his years of service in the navy and lifelong interest in the sea, King William IV became known as the Sailor King.

As a king he was cautious and disliked radical innovations. When he applied this to politics, William quarrelled with his ministers and disagreed with the public. He died in 1837 and was succeeded by his niece, Victoria.

WHAT DID HENRY MOORE DO?

Henry Moore was born in 1898, but had to wait until he had passed his fortieth birthday before he found fame and fortune.

When he unveiled his sculpture *Reclining Figure* in 1939 it caused a sensation. Moore's highly original style simplified the human form in order to emphasise ideas. His numerous depictions of a mother and child seem to embody the tender emotions between the two. His work *King and Queen* sums up the dignity and elegance expected of such figures. Moore continued producing such works until his death.

WHO WAS TITIAN?

Titian was perhaps the greatest artist of Venice. He worked in the late 15th and early 16th centuries, producing work remarkable for its colour and magnificence.

He was born in Pieve but soon showed such artistic flair that his parents sent him to work in Venice. Here he learned the basics of art which he went on to adapt and develop in his own style.

When he became the official state painter of Venice, Titian painted portraits of noblemen and undertook many of his finest pictures. Perhaps the greatest is *The Assumption of the Virgin* which he produced in 1518.

In his later years Titian produced many works for the Emperor Charles V and King Philip II of Spain and many of his paintings are still in Spain. When he died in 1576, he was the acknowledged master of the colour technique he had made his own.

WHERE DID MOSES LEAD HIS PEOPLE?

By the middle of the 13th century BC, the Jews in Egypt had lost their position of privilege. They were treated little better than slaves.

One Jew, who had been brought up as an Egyptian nobleman, was determined to help his people. His name was Moses. After fleeing Egypt when he got into trouble, Moses had a vision of God who told him to rescue the Jews.

Moses returned to Egypt and led the Jews out of bondage. Evading an army sent after them by the Pharaoh, Moses and the Jews pushed onwards. They were looking for their promised land — a land of milk and honey. For forty years Moses led the Jews through the Sinai and Middle East. He gave them a code of laws to live by and inspired them. Soon after his death, the Jews found their land in Canaan.

WHICH ACTORS BECAME FAMOUS AS JAMES BOND?

James Bond is a character created by Ian Fleming. Bond is a secret agent who is the hero of a number of spy novels written in the 1950s and 1960s.

In 1962 the first James Bond film was produced. In the lead role of the secret agent licensed to kill was the relatively unknown actor, Sean Connery. Five Bond movies later, Connery was an international star. He left the James Bond series and has since made a career for himself in other films.

The next actor chosen for the James Bond character was Roger Moore. Like Connery, Moore has earned international fame as James Bond and his career has benefited enormously. Sean Connery and Roger Moore have been replaced as James Bond by Timothy Dalton.

WHY WAS ARTHUR WELLESLEY MADE DUKE OF WELLINGTON?

When Arthur Wellesley was a boy he was so dull that his mother sent him off to join the army. She was convinced that he would not have much success in life.

Once in the army, Wellesley soon proved himself to be a superb officer. In India he won a dramatic series of battles and came home famous. In 1808 he was given command of an expedition sent to Spain. His mission was to help the Portuguese and Spaniards fight the occupying French troops.

Finding the French on the verge of victory, Wellesley set about organising his defences and his armies. Over the following years, Wellesley won a number of spectacular victories and caused a tremendous drain on French resources. For these services to his country Arthur Wellesley was created Duke of Wellington. He fought his last battle at Waterloo in 1815 and thereafter found a career in politics and army administration. From 1828 to 1830 he was Prime Minister of Britain.

WHAT TYPE OF BUILDINGS DID LE CORBUSIER DESIGN?

Born in 1887, near Neuchatel in Switzerland, Charles Edouard Le Corbusier was the greatest exponent of "engineer-building."

This style maintains that architecture should ignore detail and concentrate on proportion and function. By the mid-1920's, Le Corbusier was rejecting the idea of styles in architecture and stressing idealism and balance. His buildings are often large and rectangular with little aesthetic appeal.

Among his more famous buildings were the Maison Laroche at Auteuil and the Unite d'habitation in Marseilles. He also became interested in town planning, producing an idealised plan early in his career and designing the town of Chandigarh in India. After his death in 1965, Le Corbusier's ideals became increasingly unpopular and are now being superseded by new ideas in architecture.

WHO WAS "THE MASTER OF MARBLE"?

Born at Caprese, Italy, in 1475, Michelangelo Buonarroti became a giant in the world of art.

One of his most famous works is the painting of the Sistine Chapel in the Vatican which he began in 1508. On the chapel's ceiling, Michelangelo executed a huge and magnificent mural

It remains the masterpiece of

242

High Renaissance art. Nearly 30 years later, the great artist painted *The Last Judgement* on the wall of the chapel.

Michelangelo also worked in architecture, but he always believed that sculpture was his true art. Among the many fine works which he created are his *Pieta* of 1498 which can be seen in St Peter's Cathedral in Rome and the incomparable *David* which stands in a museum in Florence. Even today, these sculptures, and several others, remain untouched as expressions of pure sculpture. They fully earned him the reputation as the master of marble. There can be little doubt that Michelangelo was a genius of art.

WHO WAS THE FIRST MAN TO SWIM THE ENGLISH CHANNEL?

During the 19th century there was an upsurge of interest in sports of all kinds. One of these was swimming, in particular long distance swimming.

The captain battled gallantly against the current for hours

Captain Matthew Webb of the Merchant Navy was one of the most famous of the early swimmers. When still a boy he rescued his brother from the River Severn and later saved another man from drowning in the Mersey.

In August 1875, Captain Webb strode into the sea at Dover and began to swim. He was determined to reach France. Using breast-stroke, Captain Webb made his way out to sea, only to be swept down the coast by the tide. Gallantly battling against the current, Captain Webb continued swimming. Twenty-one hours and forty-five minutes later, he walked ashore at Cap Griz Nez in France.

Since that epic swim, many other long-distance swimmers have made the journey. There have even been organised races across the Channel. But none has achieved the fame of the first man to swim the Channel.

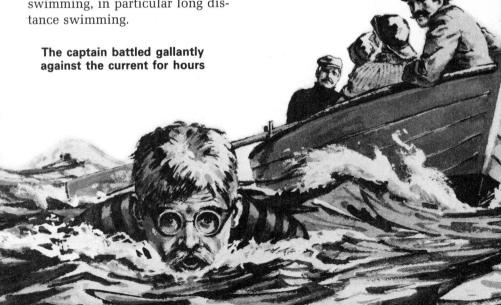

WHO WAS THE KING OF ROCK AND ROLL?

When Elvis Presley cut his first commercial disc in 1954, entitled *That's Alright, Mama*, there was little to indicate the stupendous success that he was to achieve.

With his good looks, wonderful voice and powerful personality, Elvis was to shoot to the top of the world music scene. He remained unchallenged for years and since his early death his following has barely diminished. Two years after his first record, he hit the number one slot with his rendition of *Heartbreak Hotel*. The unique style he brought to songs was the gift which kept him at the top. Soon he was being called the King of Rock and Roll, an accolade he fully deserved.

As well as his records and tours, Elvis starred in a number of fine musical films. He made his home in the deep south where he was born and today his Gracelands Mansion in Memphis is a museum to his life and works.

WHO WAS THE GREATEST SWASHBUCKLING FILM STAR OF THEM ALL?

Making a swashbuckling film is not an easy thing to do. One of the greatest problems is to find a leading actor who is larger than life, dashing and able to perform the part well enough to be believable.

Perhaps the greatest such actor was born in Hobart, Tasmania in 1909. Errol Flynn spent his early adult years drifting around the Pacific finding a living in a variety of ways. In 1933 he played in an Australian film. Two years later he reached stardom in Hollywood when he starred in the swashbuckling movie *Captain Blood*.

Flynn's obvious skill at playing dashing heroes brought him a rush of films such as *The Adventures of Robin Hood* and *They Died With Their Boots On*. He played his parts cleverly with due sensitivity and humour without missing the heroic stance. After a turbulent career, he died in 1959. His films are still regarded as the best of their type.

WHO LED THE LONG MARCH?

In 1934 it seemed that the Chinese Communist forces of Mao Tse-Tung had been defeated. In the Kiangsi Mountains of China, the Communists had faced five massive attacks by the Nationalist forces of Chiang Kai-shek.

In order to reorganise his troops, Mao decided they must escape. He therefore ordered them to start on a 6,000 mile march to the far north-west of China. They set out in October and did not reach their goal until a year later.

This Long March, as it became known, was the salvation of the Communist forces in China. On their way, they explained to the people they passed how Communism would help them. When the Communists reached the northwest provinces they began recruiting and re-equipping. The area controlled by Mao steadily expanded. After the Second World War, Mao launched his final bid for power. In 1949 he threw his enemies out of China and proclaimed the People's Republic of China.

WHY WAS THE WELSH PRINCE HYWEL CALLED "THE GOOD"?

In the 10th century Wales was ruled by a number of princes, each of whom jealously guarded his independence and warred with the others. One of these princes was Hywel, Prince of Ceredigion.

In 928 Hywel went on a pilgrimage to Rome. He was away for months and he saw much that interested him. When he came back he asked all the other Welsh princes to come to a conference.

Most of the princes arrived, eager to hear about Hywel's journey. He told them that in many European countries there was a written list of laws which everybody obeyed. Hywel thought that Wales ought to have such a list as well. The princes agreed with him and for several weeks they sat and discussed which laws to have and how to word them.

They all agreed to enforce the laws in their own lands. Because it was Hywel who had called the conference and who had formulated most of the laws, he became the most respected prince in Wales. He was called Hywel the Good because of his sense of justice and reigned until 950.

WHO WAS THE BLIND POET OF GREECE?

The two great epic poems of ancient Greece are The Illiad and The Odyssey. They deal with the siege and fall of Troy and the wanderings of the hero Odysseus on his journey home.

They are masterpieces of writing. The stories and tales contained within them are full of interest and excitement, while the style is absorbing. The works were important as they had a profound effect on later writers. The ancient Greeks believed that the poems had been written by a blind poet called Homer.

Homer is supposed to have lived sometime before 750 BC and to have been a native of the island of Chios. He is said to have spent his life travelling from country to country telling his tales and stories. Many recent scholars think that, rather than write the poems himself, Homer was responsible for writing down the stories which had been passed down orally for generations. Some even doubt that Homer, the great blind poet of Greece, ever existed.

WHO WAS RUSSIA'S GREATEST COMPOSER?

In 1863, at the age of 23 Peter Illyich Tchaikovsky gave up work to write music. Almost at once he met with success, being appointed as Professor of Harmony at the Conservatoire of Moscow, a post which he was to hold for years.

Despite this his early work was not well received by the public. His first three operas were dismal failures. Undeterred, Tchaikovsky turned to symphonic poems and achieved some recognition. It was a fourth opera, *Eugene Onegin*, which established him as a popular composer.

He then began to receive a regular allowance from a wealthy widow who admired his work. With his financial situation secure, Tchaikovsky could turn to composing with all his energy. He wrote the overture *1812*, *The Sleeping Beauty* ballet, a number of symphonies, operas and other works. When he died of cholera in 1893, Tchaikovsky was recognised as the greatest Russian composer.

WHOM DID HOLBEIN PAINT?

Hans Holbein was born in Augsburg in 1497, but moved to Basle in 1515. Here he began to earn a living as an artist. He painted some portraits and designed house decorations.

In 1526 he left Basle with a letter of introduction to Sir Thomas More, an important politician in England. It was here that he was to produce some of his best work and where he would achieve fame.

Holbein began by painting a group portrait of Sir Thomas More and his family. He then moved on to paint a number of portraits for other people, before coming to the notice of King Henry VIII. In 1536

he became court painter. Portraits of the royal family and other courtiers became the main work for Holbein. He was even sent abroad to paint portraits of foreign notables so that Henry would know what they looked like. His success as a portrait painter continued undiminished until his death in 1543.

WHERE DID BONNIE PRINCE CHARLIE LEAD HIS CLANSMEN?

As grandson of the deposed James II, Prince Charles Edward Stuart believed that he was rightful heir to the thrones of England and Scotland.

In 1745 he landed with a handful of men on the west coast of Scotland, determined to wrest the throne from King George II. Almost at once many of the Highland clans rallied to his cause. He unfurled his standard at Glenfinnan, where a fine memorial now stands. Charles won much of his support by his audacity and his charm. It was this which earned him his name Bonnie Prince Charlie.

Marching south with an army of Highlanders, Charles captured Edinburgh and held court in the ancient palace of Holyrood. He then went on to smash an army loyal to George and to march into England. By December Charles had led his clansmen as far as Derby. Here Charles was forced to turn back. At Culloden Moor on April 16, 1746, Charles' force was

The princess was awakened to be told she was now Queen of England

caught by a larger army and practically annihilated.

Bonnie Prince Charlie went on the run and finally fled to France. He took to drinking heavily and died a lonely man in Rome in 1788.

WHEN DID A GIRL BECOME QUEEN OF BRITAIN?

When, in 1819, Alexandrina Victoria was born as daughter to the Duke of Kent, few thought she would become one of Britain's greatest sovereigns. Her father was the fourth son of King George III and so remote from the line of succession.

After the Duke of Kent died, his wife quarrelled with the Royal Family and moved away from court. Her daughter was, therefore, brought up far from the dignified atmosphere of royalty. When Victoria's uncle, William IV, became king and all his brothers died childless, Victoria became heiress to the throne. On June 20, 1837, King William died.

Princess Victoria was woken up in the middle of the night by a pair of grave-faced men. They broke the news of her uncle's death and then fell on their knees before the 18-year old girl and saluted her as queen. The coronation ceremony which followed was full of pomp and ceremony and overawed many foreigners who came to see the new queen. Queen Victoria reigned for 63 years and died in 1901, a greatly respected and much loved sovereign.

WHICH ARTIST IS NAMED AFTER HIS HOME TOWN?

Born in about 1450, Hieronymus Van Aeken was to become one of the most unusual and controversial painters in Dutch history. He is better known as Hieronymus Bosch, a name he adopted from his home town of Hertengebosch.

The paintings of Bosch, while realistic in one sense, are masterpieces of nightmarish fantasy. Monsters and demons fill his paintings together with fantastic structures and devices. All these interact with beautifully painted people. Among the more famous of his pictures are *The Garden of Earthly Delights* and *St Jerome*. It seems obvious that the majority of Bosch's work is allegorical, though it cannot all be understood today.

His work was greatly admired in his day and inspired a wide, but short-lived, vogue for fantastic paintings. After his death in 1516, much of his work was lost or forgotten. It is only recently he has been appreciated again.

WHICH RUSSIAN LEADER WENT TO DISNEYLAND?

When Stalin, dictator of Russia, died in 1953, political disputes followed which only ended when Nikita Krushchev became First Secretary of the Communist party. Coming from peasant stock, Krushchev had joined the Communists before the Revolution and worked his way up through the party structure by sheer determination.

After coming to power, Krushchev amazed the world by condemning his predecessor, Stalin, as a murderer and abuser of power on a massive scale. This abrupt change from official hero worship to public denunciation was just the first of the surprises Krushchev had in store.

At one famous meeting of the United Nations he flew into a terrible rage and started shouting and banging on his desk, before leaving the hall.

In an effort to ease the Cold War Krushchev went to the United States with his wife and even visited the massive fun park of Disneyland in California.

Krushchev's unusual brand of Soviet leadership came to an end in 1964 when he was suddenly deprived of his office and replaced by Brezhnev.

HOW DID BRIAN BORU DIE?

When Brian Boru inherited the Irish Kingdom of Munster in 978 he was already more than 40 years of age, but he dreamed of uniting Ireland and set about the task energetically.

From his powerbase in south western Ireland, Brian launched a lightning attack on the King of Leinster. After a quick victory, he forced the King of Leinster to accept him as overlord. By 1001 Brian had defeated all the kings of Ireland. He assumed the title of King of Ireland and was known as Boru, which means tributetaker.

In 1014 he had to face a powerful coalition of rebellious Leinster and Viking warriors. On Good Friday 1014 the army of Brian Boru met that of his enemies at Clontarf. Brian was an old man by this time and did not take an active part in the fighting.

At last it became clear that Brian's forces were winning. But towards evening a group of Vikings reached Brian Boru's tent. They entered and killed him while he prayed. After Brian's death Ireland once again broke up into a number of warring kingdoms; unity had gone.

WHY IS JEAN BART FAMOUS?

Jean Bart was one of the most dashing and successful Frenchmen ever to take to the seas.

He was born in 1651 in the port of Dunkirk and grew up in a maritime environment. At an early age he joined the Dutch navy, but enlisted in the French navy at the age of 21. Over the next 18 years, Jean Bart earned a great reputation as a privateer. In the seemingly endless series of wars, Bart attacked and captured many Dutch and British ships, doing enormous damage to their trade.

In 1689 he was captured by the British, but promptly escaped to France. Taking command of a ship, he began raiding the coast of Scotland. By this time he had won such a reputation that King Louis XIV made him an admiral. In 1702, Jean Bart died at his home town of Dunkirk.

WHY IS CATHERINE CALLED "THE GREAT"?

In 1745 the German Princess Catherine of Anhalt-Zerbst married the heir to the throne of Russia. When her husband became Tsar as Peter III, Catherine had him murdered and seized power herself.

She set about modernising Russia. In particular she tried to give the peasants more freedom. This was stopped by a combination of opposition from the nobles and peasant rebellions. Repression then became the hallmark of Catherine's domestic policy, though she did revise the law.

In her foreign policy, Catherine was always uncompromisingly aggressive. After a war with Turkey she gained the right to protect Turkish Christian subjects, the Crimean peninsula and the Black Sea coast. This gave Russia a port which did not freeze in the winter. Turning her attention to eastern Europe, Catherine connived with Austria and Prussia to attack and divide Poland.

It was these foreign conquests and her dominating personality which earned Catherine the name of the Great, by which she is best known today.

WHO WAS CALLED THE BRAVEST OF THE BRAVE?

When Napoleon, Emperor of the French, created his marshals in 1804, one of the men he chose was Michel Ney. During the Revolutionary Wars, Ney earned such a reputation for gallantry that he was dubbed the Bravest of the Brave.

As marshal, Ney distinguished himself at the crucial battles of Eylau and Jena and was sent on a diplomatic mission to Switzer-

land. In 1808 he led French troops into Spain where he served for four years. On his return Ney followed his emperor to Russia. During the terrible retreat from Moscow, Ney commanded the rearguard. He did this so well that he personally led many Frenchmen to freedom who would otherwise have been taken prisoner or perished. He stood by Napoleon until the Emperor abdicated in 1814 and then made his peace with the reinstated King of France.

When Napoleon escaped in 1815, Ney joined him at once. He fought bravely through the campaigns which followed. At the Battle of Waterloo he led a tremendous charge of cavalry at the British centre. Despite his undoubted bravery, Ney failed. He was arrested and shot for his part in the campaign by the returning king.

WHO EXPLORED THE GREAT RIVERS OF CANADA?

In the 1780s the isolated trading outpost of Fort Chippewayan was commanded by a Scot named Alexander Mackenzie.

Fort Chippewayan stood on the edge of Lake Athabasca, beyond which lay virtually unknown territory. Mackenzie loved exploration and began to wonder if any of the mighty rivers near him led to the Pacific. In June 1789, after months of preparation, he set off with a small group of Indians and French Canadians.

**Canoeing down the Slave River, Mackenzie and
his companions reached the Great Slave Lake**

Canoeing down the Slave River, they reached the Great Slave Lake. Then they found a river flowing out of the lake to the northwest. Eagerly Mackenzie took his canoes down this river. The great river seemed to flow endlessly. For weeks they paddled downstream. After a trip of more than 1,000 miles, Mackenzie reached the sea. It was not the Pacific, however, but the Arctic Ocean. Mackenzie turned for home in disappointment. Today the mighty river down which he travelled is called the Mackenzie River.

Two years later, Mackenzie became the first man to cross the continent when he followed the Parsnip and Fraser Rivers across the Rocky Mountains. These trips of exploration were invaluable for the later settlement of the Canadian west.

WHICH COMPOSER WAS A CHILD PRODIGY?

In 1763 a seven year old child was giving harpsichord, violin and organ recitals of his own compositions to the nobility of Europe. Wolfgang Amadeus Mozart was an instant success.

As Mozart grew into adulthood, his early promise turned into true genius. He produced over 40 symphonies, several operas, 21 concertos and two dozen string quartets. Unfortunately he proved temperamental and completely incapable of managing his affairs. Alternating bouts of public adoration with periods of extreme poverty, Mozart still managed to keep up his phenomenal output.

While working on an opera called The Magic Flute, Mozart was visited by a mysterious stranger who asked him to write a requiem. For some reason Mozart was convinced he had been asked to write his own requiem by a supernatural being. A second visit from the stranger terrified Mozart who died soon afterwards of typhus. The stranger turned out to be a servant of Count Walsegg who had the requiem finished by another composer. The tragic death of Mozart at the age of 35 cut short the brilliantly creative life of possibly the greatest composer.

WHO WAS GOOD KING WENCESLAUS?

In the early 10th century Christianity was beginning to make converts in central Europe. One of the most important of these was Duke Wenceslaus of Bohemia.

Fired by his new faith, Wenceslaus built many churches throughout Bohemia and helped in the conversion of his subjects. Paganism was still a powerful force in Bohemia, however, and Wenceslaus faced strong opposition. In 929, he was killed in a brawl with his younger brother, who supported paganism.

The dead duke was at once hailed by the Church as a martyr and later became a saint. On the thousandth anniversary of his death, the crowned and veiled skull of Duke Wenceslaus was carried through the streets of Prague by six bishops.

WHICH ENGLISH KING WAS KILLED ON SENLAC HILL?

On October 14, 1066, a large army of Englishmen was drawn up for battle on Senlac Hill. Marching northwards from Hastings to meet it was a mixed army of Normans and Frenchmen.

The English army was led by their king, Harold Godwinsson. Harold was a well-known warrior and governor before he was elected king by the Witan earlier in the year. Facing him was William, Duke of Normandy, who said that King Edward of England had promised him the crown before dying.

The battle began in the morning and raged all day. The Normans made repeated attacks up the hill, only to be thrown back time and time again. Losses on both sides were heavy.

According to the chronicles, Harold fought with his massive battle axe until the end, when he was cut down by four Norman knights. One of the bravest and most determined of English kings had died in battle on Senlac Hill.

WHO KILLED THE RED COMYN?

The Red Comyn was the colourful name given to Sir John Comyn, an important Scottish nobleman of the later 13th century. He was given the name to distinguish him from his father, also called John, who was called the Black Comyn.

In 1296 King Edward I of England gained control of Scotland after defeating the Scottish king. Many Scottish nobles despised the English governor and plotted to rebel. Two of the most important of these nobles were the Red Comyn and Robert Bruce. Both were descended from Scottish kings and both claimed the throne.

The two men met in the church of the Franciscans in Dumfries to come to an agreement. Suddenly an argument flared up. Robert Bruce whipped out his dagger and stabbed the Red Comyn to death. The murder of a man in a church was a terrible act and it cost Bruce many friends. Eventually, however, he regained Scottish support and 12 years later defeated the English at Bannockburn.

WHO WAS IVAN THE TERRIBLE?

The man who has come down through history as Ivan the Terrible truly earned his name, but in his early years he was far from terrible.

In 1533, Ivan became Grand Duke of Moscow at the age of 3. When he was 14, Ivan dismissed the regents who had been ruling in his name. He had himself crowned Tsar, or Emperor, of Russia, the first man to claim the title. Later, he invaded and conquered Kazan, Astrakhan and Western Siberia, expanding Russia eastwards. Another series of wars in the west ended in failure and the loss of the Baltic coast.

After his wife died in 1560, Ivan became increasingly cruel and paranoid. He persecuted his powerful nobles, ordered the strangling of the Bishop of Moscow and even killed his own son. Ivan also turned on his subjects. When he suspected a plot was being hatched at Novgorod he marched his army to the city and killed everybody he could find. Despite these excesses, when he died in 1584, Ivan left a strong and united Russia.

WHAT TYPE OF PAINTING DID JACKSON POLLOCK PRODUCE?

Jackson Pollock was born in 1912 and soon showed an artistic flair. At first he painted in a realistic style and produced several paintings which failed to make much of an impact.

Pollock then turned to an entirely new style which he created himself. He believed that he had to give his subconscious command of his paintings. Pollock decided that the best way to do this was to drip paint at random on large canvasses to produce complicated patterns. This style became dubbed action painting.

Despite the fact that Pollock's paintings were dismissed by the majority of the public, they won wide critical acclaim. His paintings can now be seen in many museums throughout the world. They have still failed to make much of an impact on the public at large, however.

WHO WAS THE FIRST PRESIDENT OF THE UNITED STATES?

By 1789 the American colonies had won their independence from Britain. They had agreed on a constitution and were ready to take their place as a sovereign nation. All they needed was a president.

Whoever was chosen would have to be a remarkable man. Not only would he need to deal with domestic and foreign affairs, but he would need to cope with all the problems of a new nation.

It was perhaps natural that the Federal Convention should have chosen George Washington. Throughout the fighting with the British, Washington had proved himself to be an able and far-sighted commander. Although he would much rather have stayed on

his plantation at Mount Vernon, Virginia, Washington answered his nation's call. He was installed as President in 1789 and held the office for two terms. He died in 1799.

WHO WAS THE GREATEST ESCAPER OF THEM ALL?

Many people have made a living on the stage by escaping from ropes, chains and locks, but none is as famous as Harry Houdini.

Houdini's real name was Ehrich Weiss. He was born in 1873 at Appleton, Wisconsin, and began a career as a locksmith. Here he learnt the secrets of locks. Combining this with phenomenal physical suppleness and strength, Weiss changed his name and took to the stage as an escape artist.

Not content with escaping from locks on stage, Houdini mounted spectacular escapes to boost his fame. He had himself manacled and thrown into frozen rivers, and hung upside down in a strait-jacket.

This great showman died tragically in 1926. He was unprepared for a heavy punch in the stomach delivered by a stranger trying to prove that the powerful Houdini's claim to be able to withstand such a blow was false.

WHICH WOMAN HELPED MAKE A KING?

In 1899 Gertrude Bell left her comfortable home in Britain and set

A brigand Arab robbed Gertrude Bell and fled

out for Jerusalem. Gertrude Bell was a great traveller, but it was in the Middle East that she fell in love with a land.

Travelling through the deserts for months at a time, Gertrude Bell became enchanted by the solitude and the loneliness. Amid the sands of Arabia, she was alone and at peace. The country through which she travelled was not as peaceful as it might have been. One day a brigand Arab burst into her camp. Threatening to kill her,

the man robbed Gertrude and fled. Despite such rough treatment, Gertrude admired the Arabs. She often joined them in feasts and in their daily life.

During the First World War, Gertrude worked tirelessly to help the Arabs against their Turkish overlords. When peace came, she was instrumental in having the Amir Faisal accepted as King of Iraq. It was for this that she, rather to her own embarrassment, was called the maker of kings.

WHO WAS EDWARD ELGAR?

Edward Elgar was born into a musical family in 1857 at Broadheath, near Worcester. He quickly showed that he was going to follow in the family tradition.

He made a living as a violin teacher, giving occasional performances, until fame came his way at the age of 42. Some time earlier, he had written a series of variations on one tune for his family. When these *Enigma Variations* were performed in public in 1899 they achieved immediate success. Elgar followed the variations with the choral *Dream of Gerontius* before turning to orchestral works.

By this time many of his earlier works were being discovered by the public, together with music he was currently writing. Elgar rapidly became one of the favourite British composers. In 1924 he was created Master of the King's Musick and became a Baronet in 1931. Among his more famous works are the *Pomp and Circumstance* marches, *Falstaff* and the *Cockaigne Overture*. He died in 1934.

WHICH ENGLISH KING IS CALLED "THE GREAT"?

In January 878, a band of pagan Vikings ransacked Chippenham. Looting and killing, the Vikings swept through the town, but they missed the man they were really after. King Alfred of Wessex had escaped.

Wessex was the only English kingdom still independent of Viking rule. After the attack on Chippenham, it seemed that Wessex was also doomed. Alfred was hiding in the marshes of Athelney while the Vikings plundered at will. But Alfred was secretly keeping in touch with his men. In May he called his forces together and fell upon the Vikings at Ethandun. He inflicted such a defeat on them, that the Vikings were forced to become Christians and retreat.

In the years that followed, Alfred reorganised his kingdom. He built dozens of fortresses and set up a national militia. With these Alfred defeated two more Viking invasions and recaptured much of the Midlands. Alfred did not only fight wars; he encouraged learning and religion and made sure that the history of the English was written down. Because he saved English civilisation from the Vikings, Alfred was dubbed "the Great", the only English king to be so honoured.

WHO WAS THE "SUN KING"?

Of all the magnificent monarchs which France has given to history, none can match Louis XIV. He was determined to be known as a great and glorious monarch, an ambition he easily achieved.

Coming to the throne in 1643 at the age of five, Louis had to wait until 1661 before he took control of France. He believed that the only way to halt the civil wars which racked France was to deprive the nobles of their power and influence. He did this by giving them wealth, while concentrating power in his own hands.

Turning to foreign conquests, Louis launched the magnificent French army against a number of foes. Though not always successful, Louis conquered many territories which remain part of France to this day.

The court of Louis XIV was sumptuous and luxurious. He built the huge Palace of Versailles as a masterpiece of Baroque architecture and made it a centre of art and literature. By constantly presenting himself as a splendid monarch, Louis gained the admiration of Europe and the title of the Sun King.

WHO LED RUSSIA DURING WORLD WAR II?

In the early years of this century Joseph Dzhygashvili was an active political agitator in Russia. By 1912 he was so well known to the authorities that he began to use the alias of Stalin.

During the First World War he worked closely with Lenin and helped lead the revolution which brought the Communists to power. After Lenin's death in 1924, Stalin eliminated his rivals for power, and became dictator of Russia. He ordered massive economic upheavals, which created great misery for the people, but Stalin ruthlessly crushed opposition.

During the 1930s he ordered drastic and bloody purges of the army. The result was that when Hitler attacked in 1941 there were no experienced commanders to confront the Germans. Stalin then assumed command of the army himself and organised the defence of Russia. By skilful diplomatic manoeuvring and hard fighting Stalin succeeded beyond his expectations. After the defeat of Germany, Stalin was able to impose pro-Russian governments virtually throughout Eastern Europe. He died in 1953.

WHY IS RAMESES II SO WELL KNOWN?

Rameses II is one of the most famous pharaohs of Egypt. This is not because he was one of the greatest but simply because he was determined to be remembered.

Rameses was a member of the 19th Dynasty and came to the throne about 1300 BC. From the start he was determined to re-establish Egypt as a great power. He launched his armies on a number of campaigns in all directions. Though he did not conquer vast areas, Rameses did establish his frontiers. The rest of his long reign was fairly peaceful.

With no wars to fight, Rameses turned to building. He built massive buildings, such as the Hypostyle Hall at Karnak and the temple of Abu Simbel and many other mighty edifices. Everywhere he built, Rameses erected statues of himself and had his name carved in stone. It is because these monumental works have survived to the present day that Rameses II is so well known.

WHO RALLIED THE FREE FRENCH AFTER THE COLLAPSE OF FRANCE DURING WORLD WAR II?

When France fell to Germany in 1940, many Frenchmen fled to Britain to carry on the struggle. One of these was a general and junior government minister called Charles De Gaulle.

Throughout the difficult war years, De Gaulle organised and led the Frenchmen who were in Britain. His strong personality and inspired leadership took him to the position of leader of France in exile. Those same qualities often grated with his allies and De Gaulle was not popular in Britain.

Following the invasion of Europe in 1944, De Gaulle led his Free French into Paris. He at once became the head of the provisional government. Over the following months, De Gaulle reestablished France as a great power. When peace returned he resigned.

Twelve years later, De Gaulle was brought back as President by popular demand. He was instrumental in pulling French troops out of a hopeless war in Algeria and in granting independence to colonies. He resigned in 1968 and died two years later.

WHAT MUSIC DID COUNT BASIE PLAY?

William Basie was born in 1904 in America. When still a young man he picked up the nickname of "Count" and revealed a talent as a jazz musician.

He began to play the piano to adulating audiences and was soon leading a large jazz band. Playing his own compositions, Count Basie's band soon became one of the most successful in the world. His vibrant jazz music has thrilled fans the world over.

WHO MADE MOVIES POSSIBLE?

The early photographs were made using glass plates covered with light-sensitive chemicals. These glass plates were both heavy and fragile. The American inventor George Eastman decided to try to produce something better.

In 1884, after four years of experimentation, Eastman produced a photosensitive film consisting of paper smeared with a gel. He had solved the major problems of glass plates.

In 1888 he produced what he called the Kodak Camera. This was light and small and made use of a long roll of film so that a number of photographs could be taken without opening the camera. It was an instant success and Eastman rapidly amassed a fortune.

In 1889 the paper was replaced by celluloid. This flexible, transparent substance made possible the next great step in photographic history, the moving picture. By replacing the glass plate, Eastman had made possible Hollywood and all the movies ever made.

WHICH ACTOR WAS CALLED "DUKE"?

Of all the men who have starred in western movies, the greatest was John Wayne. He starred in classic movies and in box office hits from the 1930s to the 1970s.

His real name was Marion

George Eastman produced a photosensitive film

John Wayne

After a lifetime of fine acting John Wayne took an Oscar in 1969 for his role in *True Grit*. Ironically John played a gunfighter dying of cancer in his last movie *The Shootist*, before himself dying of cancer in 1979.

WHY IS HUDSON BAY SO CALLED?

The massive bay which cuts deeply into northern Canada is named Hudson Bay in honour of the man who discovered it and who died there.

Henry Hudson made his first voyage to North America after two previous explorations of the Arctic Ocean north of Europe. In 1609 he sailed to Virginia and then coasted northwards, discovering the Hudson River and a number of other features along the New England coast.

In April 1610 he set out from England again to try to find a passage around the north of America. He passed south of Greenland and Baffin Island before sighting an opening in the coast to the south. Hoping that this was a route to the Pacific, Hudson steered south.

The opening turned out to be the great bay which now bears Hudson's name. The ship was caught in the winter ice. By the following spring the crew had become disenchanted with exploration and Hudson's autocratic behaviour. They mutinied and set him adrift in an open boat. Hudson was never heard of again, but his name lives on through his discoveries.

Michael Morrison so it is probably not surprising that he took to the early nickname of Duke (which he got because of his dog of the same name) with enthusiasm. He took up the name of John Wayne at an early stage in his career. After some years in movies, John Wayne achieved his breakthrough at the age of 32 in the superb film *Stagecoach* which appeared in 1939.

Playing the rugged individualist suited Wayne well, and it suited westerns even better. After *Stagecoach*, Wayne went on to star in such classics as *Fort Apache*, *The Searchers* and *Red River*. John Wayne was not restricted to guntoting cowboy roles. He also made some good war films as well as the good-natured, idealised *The Quiet Man*, set in Ireland.

WHO WAS THE REVOLUTIONARY WHO WAS STABBED IN HIS BATH? .

When the French Revolution broke out in 1789, one of its most ardent supporters was a doctor called Jean Paul Marat.

Marat had been a successful doctor in both Britain and France before devoting himself to revolutionary politics in 1786. Through the newspapers he published, Marat attacked and helped to bring about the downfall of the moderate Girondin party which was then in power. By 1792 he had become a powerful figure in French government and an influential speaker with the people. Marat's extremism and persuasive talking led to the execution of hundreds of aristocrats and others.

Marat contracted a skin disease which could only be relieved by sitting in a bath full of medicated water. He was sitting in this bath on July 13, 1793, when a young woman named Charlotte Corday, who was an ardent Girondin supporter, burst in and stabbed him to death.

WHO WAS THE FIRST LAW-GIVER?

On a large stone slab in the Louvre Museum in Paris are inscribed the laws of a remarkable ruler of ancient Babylon.

When Hammurabi came to the throne of Babylon in about 1950 BC, the surrounding country was divided into a number of small, warring city states. Using his army and diplomatic ability with great skill, Hammurabi conquered these cities one by one. Eventually he had united them all under his own leadership.

In order to rule his new lands, Hammurabi decided to write down the laws so that everybody knew what they were. In part his laws are the traditional rules of Babylonian society and in part his own creation. Covering a wide range of daily life, the law code of Hammurabi remained in use for centuries. It is often regarded as the forerunner of the legislative system of western civilisation.

WHO WAS THE FAMOUS BUCCANEER WHO BECAME LIEUTENANT GOVERNOR OF JAMAICA?

When Henry Morgan left his Glamorganshire home for Jamaica he was only a boy. But in the Indies, Morgan's daring character came into its own.

While still a young man, he became a leader of the buccaneers. These ferocious men sailed throughout the Caribbean attacking Spanish ships and towns for plunder and loot. By 1670 Henry Morgan was the most feared buccaneer in the Caribbean. That year, he gathered together the largest force of buccaneers ever seen. He marched them across the Isthmus of Panama to capture and loot the incredibly rich Spanish city of Panama.

Such an act almost brought war and King Charles II ordered Morgan to return to London to stand trial. Once in England, Henry Morgan charmed so many people, including the king, that he was granted a pardon and knighted. After being appointed Lieutenant Governor of Jamaica, Henry Morgan died in August 1688. A temporary amnesty was proclaimed so that the buccaneers could attend his funeral.

WHO LED A HUNDRED CHILDREN TO SAFETY?

In 1941 the modern and well-equipped Japanese army was invading China. The war had been going for some time before the Japanese reached the town of Yangcheng.

In Yangcheng was the English missionary Gladys Aylward. As well as preaching Christianity, Gladys was in charge of about 100 orphans aged between four and fifteen. She led her children into the hills and hid in a cave. Here Gladys and her charges survived for three weeks, until she learnt that the Japanese had put a price on her head.

Gladys realised that their only hope was to escape to a town called Sian, which was free of Japanese occupation. They set off on foot, over the hills towards the Yellow River. After a week of hard walking, Gladys and the children were exhausted and footsore. One night they ran into a group of Chinese soldiers who gave them food.

Eventually, the missionary and her children reached Sian, only to be refused entry. They had to travel on to a temple orphanage in Fufeng. The long and punishing journey had taken nearly two weeks, but at last they were safe.

WHO SAW THE VISION OF LOURDES?

In 1858, a peasant girl called Bernadette claimed to have seen the Virgin Mary in a small grotto near her home village of Lourdes in southern France.

At first nobody was quite sure whether to believe Bernadette or not. In all, the 14 year old Bernadette claimed to have had 18 visions of the Virgin Mary who appeared in the form of a beautiful lady. Before long, many other people began arriving at Lourdes to see the miraculous grotto. The little town was having trouble coping with the visitors and soon special hotels had to be built.

After a time, the Catholic Church pronounced the visions to have been genuine and the number of pilgrims increased steadily. Today, Lourdes is a major religious centre. A huge church has been built to hold services for the thousands of pilgrims who flock there. Catholics come from all over the world to worship at the shrine of Lourdes.

Bernadette herself entered the Convent of the Sisters of Charity at

Nevers where she lived until her death in 1879.

In 1922 Pope Pius XI canonised her as Saint Bernadette.

WHICH DOCTOR GAVE HIS NAME TO AN INSTRUMENT OF DEATH?

Dr Joseph Ignace Guillotin had spent most of his 50 years healing people when he came up with the idea which made him famous.

In 1789, at the height of the French Revolution, Guillotin suggested using a machine to behead criminals. His idea was based upon the idea that now that privilege had been abandoned, even poor people should have the opportunity to die by beheading. Until the Revolution such a fate had been reserved to the nobility. Guillotin also felt death should be as swift and painless as possible.

His idea was taken up with alacrity by the Revolution. The first execution using a guillotine, as the machine was called, was carried out on April 25, 1792. As the Revolution gained momentum, thousands were sent to their deaths on the guillotine. Though undoubtedly efficient as a killing machine, the guillotine never found much favour outside France.

WHICH EMPEROR WAS CALLED "RED BEARD"?

When Frederick, Duke of Swabia, became Emperor of Germany in 1152 the thing that impressed people who met him was his red beard. In fact he soon became known as Frederick Barbarossa, which means Red Beard.

When Frederick succeeded to the title, Germany was split by civil war and unrest. He commenced his reign by appeasing the nobles and thereby pacifying Germany. He then married the heiress of the Count of Burgundy and subdued the King of Poland. Having secured Germany and both her western and eastern borders, Barbarossa turned south to Italy. He launched his first invasion in 1158 and for the next thirty years was involved in a bitter and seemingly endless war. No sooner did Frederick think he had won, than alliances changed, and he found he was losing.

Eventually peace came to Italy through a compromise agreement. In 1189 Frederick Barbarossa took up the Crusader standard and marched at the head of a magnificent army toward the Holy Land. On the way he drowned while crossing a river.

WHAT WAS THE FIRST COMIC OPERA WRITTEN BY GILBERT AND SULLIVAN?

In 1875 the already successful composer, Arthur Sullivan, teamed up with the humorist and writer William Gilbert to write a comic opera.

It was called *Trial By Jury* and was produced by Richard D'Oyly

Carte. The combination of witty dialogue and lyrics by Gilbert and catchy tunes by Sullivan, made the show an instant success. Two years later they collaborated again to produce The Sorcerer and in 1878 HMS Pinafore appeared. For the next twenty years the two talented men and their producer worked together to create 14 of these comic operas.

In 1897 Gilbert and Sullivan quarrelled and the series came to an end. So perfectly matched are the words, wit and music of their work, that Gilbert and Sullivan operas continue to be performed to this day.

WHICH COMPOSER WAS DEAF?

Ludwig van Beethoven made a living as a pianist until he was 30. Then in 1800, his First Symphony was performed and his fame was assured.

He moved from one success to another and he kept up a truly stupendous output of compositions for the next twelve years. This period of his life was marred by the steady onset of deafness, a terrible blow to a musician. His indefatigable will drove him to try and overcome this tragic misfortune. With the aid of a variety of ear trumpets, and eventually by listening to vibrations, Beethoven managed to continue. composing. Unfortunately, his deafness only brought out the traits of rudeness and bad temper which had always been prominent in his character. Only his undoubted musical genius stopped Beethoven losing his many friends.

Among Beethoven's great works are his fifth piano concerto and the third, sixth and ninth symphonies. It was Beethoven who brought the symphony to its highest artistic expression. In 1827, Beethoven fell ill with dropsy. On March 26, in the middle of a violent thunderstorm, he died.

WHO WAS THE BUDDHA?

Buddhism is a religion which has millions of followers. It is widespread and has its largest following in South East Asia.

The religion is founded on the teachings of a man called Gautama Buddha who lived in India in the 6th century BC. Buddha was born into a wealthy, high-caste family. After seeing the misery of a man with leprosy, Buddha turned his back on the privileged life he led.

He spent time meditating and realised what he considered to be the great truths. He believed that people should strive to escape from the passions of life and to lead a moderate life of health and meditation.

So revolutionary were his ideas that they began to attract publicity and followers. By the time Buddha died, many people were following his ideas. After Ashoka, ruler of the Maurya Empire, was converted to Buddhism, a meeting of the leading Buddhists was held in 250 BC. At this meeting the teachings of Buddha were formalised into a religion and a plan of conversion set out which eventually converted large areas of Asia to the new religion.

WHICH FRENCH PLAYWRIGHT IS FAMOUS THROUGHOUT THE WORLD?

Jean-Baptiste Moliere was probably the greatest French playwright of all time. He wrote brilliant comedies, many of which were savage satires.

His first real success was *Les Precieuses Ridicules* which was first performed in 1659. His sparkling writing won him the admiration of King Louis XIV, who paid him a pension. At the same time his satire created many enemies.

Perhaps his best play, *Tartuffe*, made Moliere his fiercest enemies. The play is about a hypocritical priest who uses his position to exploit other people. It aroused the hatred of the clergy and Moliere was forced radically to revise the play. Moliere died in 1673 while acting in one of his own plays.

WHEN DID BRITAIN GAIN HER FIRST WOMAN PRIME MINISTER?

The 20th century has seen in Britain women being able to vote for the first time. Until then no woman had had the opportunity of being elected Prime Minister.

Late in 1978, the Labour government of James Callaghan was struggling. A winter of bitter industrial dispute followed. When an election was held in 1979, the public turned against the Labour government and elected the Conservative party to office. The Conservatives had a majority in the House of Commons of 43 seats. As the leader of the Conservatives was Mrs Margaret Thatcher, she automatically became Prime Minister. Four years later she won her second General Election.

Then on June 11, 1987, she celebrated a third triumph when her party won the next General Election with a majority of 104 seats. It was the first time this century that a Prime Minister had won three successive elections. It was an amazing victory for Britain's first woman Premier.

WHO FOUNDED THE MING DYNASTY?

The Ming Dynasty is probably the best known Chinese family of Emperors. They ruled for more than 300 years and their period is noted for its magnificent blue and white porcelain and some fine textiles.

The first Ming Emperor came from a very unlikely background. In the 1350s Chu Yuanchang was a Buddhist monk who became increasingly annoyed at the despotic rule of the Mongol Khans. Joining a band of untrained rebels, he quickly showed his skill as a warrior and became their leader. By 1364 he had thrown the Mongols out of the lands north of the Yangtze River. Four years later he stormed into Peking and declared himself Emperor as Hung Wu.

It took another 15 years for Hung Wu to conquer all of China. But at last the Mongol invaders had been thrown out and a Chinese dynasty established on the throne. Hung Wu reigned until 1398. His dynasty lasted until 1644.

WHICH FILMS MADE CLINT EASTWOOD FAMOUS?

Born in San Francisco in 1930, Eastwood served his time in the army and spent his twenties acting bit parts in Hollywood. He then became well known as a character in the TV series *Rawhide*.

From this role he went to Europe in 1964 to star in a low-budget western made by Sergio Leone called *A Fistful of Dollars*. It was an immediate success. Two more Leone films followed in the next two years. Eastwood had created a character who combines cynicism with violence and yet still ends up on the right side.

Following the success of these films, Eastwood returned to America as a film star. He starred in the hugely successful *Dirty Harry* series. He does not only play tough guys; Eastwood also starred in the comedy-musical *Paint Your Wagon* It was as the hard-faced loner, however, that Clint Eastwood achieved stardom.

Clint Eastwood in *Paint Your Wagon*

Around the World

WHY DO THE NAME OF SO MANY CITIES IN ENGLAND END IN "CHESTER", "CASTER" OR "CESTER"?

"Chester", "caster" and "cester" are all corruptions of the Latin word for camp, "castra". Its use as a suffix dates back to the days when Britain was over-run by Roman armies. The inclusion of any of the three suffixes in a city's name indicates that at some time Roman troops camped there. Most likely, they established garrisons.

The city of Chester itself is famous today for the remains of Roman buildings which have been discovered, many in this century.

Other one-time Roman garrison cities are Manchester, Ilchester, Rochester, Colchester, Chichester, Dorchester, Leicester, Cirencester, Alcester, Worcester, Bicester, Lancaster and Doncaster.

WHERE IS THE PANTHEON?

There are in fact two Pantheons, one in Paris and one in Rome.

The Panthéon in Paris is a domed building in the Roman style. It was built in the reign of King Louis XV. Since then it has been used as a church dedicated to St. Genevieve and three times dedicated as a temple of honour to the great men of France.

The Pantheon in Rome is the most perfectly preserved of all the ancient buildings in that city. The Pantheon as it stands today was built by the Emperor Hadrian in the 2nd century AD. It occupies the site of a temple that had been erected just over a hundred years previously. This temple had been destroyed by fire in 80 AD.

On March 6, 609, Pope Boniface IV was given permission by the Emperor Phocas to change the pagan temple into a Christian church. It was dedicated to St. Mary of the Martyrs. The bodies of many martyrs were taken from the Catacombs, just outside Rome and buried here.

The height and diameter of the Pantheon are equal, both being 142 feet (43.3 metres). In the centre of the dome there is an opening 30

The Pantheon in Rome was built by the Emperor Hadrian

feet (9.4 metres) wide so that prayer can freely ascend to the skies.

When the beams of the sun shine through that only opening, it is as if the whole interior of the Pantheon is filled with a golden radiance.

Every year hundreds of thousands of tourists travel from every part of the world to see the magnificent Pantheon in Rome.

WHAT IS A SUB-CONTINENT?

A continent is the name given to a great unbroken land mass of the Earth's surface. In that sense, Europe and Asia form a single continent, but for several reasons, mainly economic, they have become accepted as separate continents.

A sub-continent is a large area of land that forms "part" of a continent. Perhaps the best example of this is India, a sub-continent of Asia.

WHERE WAS "THE ACCURSED PLACE"?

In the 13th century, there stretched from the Hindu Kush to the Persian Gulf and Caspian Sea, the mighty empire of Khwarizm.

In 1221, the ruthless Mongolian conqueror Genghis Khan was leading his armies across Northern Asia in an orgy of pillage and wholesale bloodshed.

The Mongols laid siege to the city of Bamian (in what is known today as Afghanistan). There, more than a thousand monks were living in monasteries. The city defied the Mongol attacks until Genghis Khan himself appeared on the scene and from that moment Bamian was doomed.

Genghis Khan totally destroyed the city to such an extent that it was completely deserted for forty years.

So terrible was the devastation that for many years Bamian was known as "the accursed place".

Some of these ruins can still be seen today.

WHAT IS TIGER'S EYE?

This is only one of the names of a beautifully-marked mineral called Crocidolite.

It is to be found in Griqualand West, a region of the Cape of Good Hope in South Africa.

Another name for it is South African cat's eye. These names are given to it because of its brilliant gleam which is like that seen in the eye of a tiger or a cat.

This mineral contains silky fibres of quartz and the colours are due to the presence of oxide of iron.

FOR WHAT REASON WAS THE PACIFIC OCEAN SO CALLED?

The first European to discover this vast ocean was the Portuguese explorer Ferdinand Magellan.

He first saw it when he sailed westward across the Atlantic

Ocean and through a strait, now known as the Strait of Magellan, near the tip of South America.

It was because the ocean beyond was calm when he first sighted it, that Magellan named it the Pacific, which means peaceful.

WHO IS BELIEVED TO HAVE DRAWN THE FIRST WORLD MAP?

That honour goes to a Greek named Anaximander who lived in the 6th century BC.

From what he had learned, he drew the world as it was known at that time. It was only a very small part of what we know today as Earth, of course. To Anaximander and to everyone else, the world was flat and comprised land and water over which huge balls of glowing fire were continually moving.

A thousand years were to pass before it was realised that the Earth was round and that it revolved around only one ball of fire which we know as the Sun.

WHY IS THE GIANT REDWOOD TREE OF CALIFORNIA CALLED SEQUOIA?

It is named after Sequoya, the world-famous inventor of the Cherokee alphabet. The Cherokee were one of the most powerful tribes in North America when the white man first arrived.

The son of a white man named George Gist or Guest and a Cherokee woman, Sequoya was called Sikwayi by the Cherokees but to his father's people he was known by his father's name, George Gist.

Sequoya's father was an American scout who was taken prisoner by the tribe.

Sequoya was born about 1760 in the Cherokee town of Taskigi, Tennessee. In those days if a Cherokee wanted to read and write it was impossible to do so in his own language for no Cherokee alphabet existed. At the age of 50, Sequoya who was unable to read or write, started to work out a system of writing. He listened to the Cherokees and found they used 85 syllables. He then had to invent 85 signs which he managed with the aid of an English spelling book.

12 years passed before he had completed his weary task.

The head men of the Cherokees approved the alphabet and within a year thousands of Cherokees could read and write in their own language.

As a tribute to his achievement and labours, the American Government awarded him a pension which kept him in comfort for the rest of his life. To honour him even further, his name was given to the giant redwood tree of California. These trees are the oldest living things on the earth. Many of them are 2,000 and 3,000 years old while some of the bigger redwoods are estimated to be up to 5,000 years old.

HOW THICK IS THE EARTH'S CRUST?

The lithosphere which is made up of two layers and forms the earth's crust is 20 miles (32 km) thick.

WHAT ARE THE FENS?

Areas of low, flat marshy lands which sometimes flood and become water-logged.

The fen country is in Lincolnshire and Cambridgeshire.

WHAT IS THE EQUATOR?

An imaginary line which encircles the Earth at its widest and is equidistant from the North and South Poles.

WHERE IS THE LOUVRE?

In Paris. Once a royal palace, it is now a famous museum and among its treasures it houses the world-famous painting, the Mona Lisa, by Leonardo da Vinci.

WHAT IS A DELTA?

When a river branches into two streams at its mouth, the triangle of land between the two branches is known as a delta.

WHICH CONTINENT PROVIDES MOST OF THE WORLD'S OIL?

Asia. In the south west there are the adjoining countries of Oman, Saudi Arabia, Iraq and Iran all of which supply us with oil.

WHAT OCEANS DOES THE PANAMA CANAL LINK TOGETHER?

The Pacific and Atlantic Oceans. The canal, which was begun in 1904, was opened August 5, 1914. Boats using the canal from Liverpool to San Francisco were saved 5,666 miles (9,118.5 km) sea voyage sailing

WHERE IS DRESDEN?

In East Germany. Dresden is famous for the making in china of delicate lace figurines.

WHICH IS THE WORLD'S LARGEST ISLAND?

Greenland. It has 830,000 square miles (215 million hectares) but the ice-free and habitable part is only 132,000 square miles (approx 34.2 million hectares).

HOW MANY CONTINENTS ARE THERE?

There are seven. Africa, Antarctica, Asia, Australia, Europe, North America and South America.

WHO LIVED AT BATEMAN'S?

Rudyard Kipling. Bateman's in Kent is a gothic house of local sandstone and was completed in 1634. Kipling was 36 when he and his wife moved there in 1902. He lived at Bateman's until his death in 1936. When Mrs Kipling died three years later, she left the property to the National Trust as a memorial to her husband.

WHERE IS THE ANTARCTIC?
In the Southern Hemisphere. It is the area surrounding the South Pole.

IN WHICH RANGE OF MOUNTAINS IS THE HIGHEST VOLCANIC PEAK IN THE WORLD?
The Andes, which extend down the South American coast from Panama to Cape Horn. Cotopaxi reaches a height of 19,344 feet (5,896 m).

WHICH MINERALS ARE MINED FOR IN THE ANDES MOUNTAINS?
There are at least 19. Antimony, bismuth, borax, coal, copper, diamods, emeralds, gold, gypsum, iron, lead, manganese, nickel, platinum, salt, silver, sulphur, vanadium, zinc.

WHERE IS HOLYROOD HOUSE?
In Edinburgh. The first Holyrood House was completed in 1504 and it had a north-west tower. In the 17th century, a second tower was added. The events which took place during the 150 years between the building of the two towers, are what made Holyrood famous.

A miner is startled by a troll

IN WHICH COUNTRIES ARE TROLLS WELL-KNOWN?
Norway and Sweden. Trolls are legendary gnomes or ogres who exercise evil power and live in underground caves. They feature in folk stories of these countries.

WHAT IN SOUTH AFRICA IS THE VELD?
The open plateau grassland of South Africa.

WHICH OPERA HOUSE WAS FINANCED BY A LOTTERY?
The opera house in Sydney, Australia. The building was raised primarily from the Opera House Lottery at a cost of £100,000,000. Construction took place from 1959 until 1973 when it was opened in October by Queen Elizabeth II.

WHAT WAS THE FIRST NAME GIVEN TO NEW YORK CITY?

New York City was first founded by the Dutch when they bought Manhattan Island from the native Indians in 1626; the Dutch called it New Amsterdam.

There were a large number of English settlers living in that area at the time and the establishment of a settlement on Manhattan Island roused their anger. They appealed to Britain for help and in 1627 James, Duke of York, sent a fleet which anchored off New Amsterdam. In the face of this threat, the Dutch handed the settlement over to the British and the place was renamed New York in honour of the Duke of York.

In return, the British passed over to the Dutch the colony of Surinam on the north east coast of South America.

WHAT WAS THE SPANISH MAIN?

Hundreds of years ago, when Spain ruled a large part of the Americas, the land bordering the Caribbean Sea was known as the Spanish Main.

Later the Caribbean Sea was often referred to, in a poetic way, as the Spanish Main.

The Caribbean was the main route which Spanish ships took when returning home, laden with silver and gold, from the Americas. It followed that it became "a happy hunting ground" for pirates.

HOW WAS VENICE BUILT?

This wonderful old city in Northern Italy is called the Queen of the Adriatic and stands on a group of mud islands separated by three main waterways and more than 150 narrow canals.

There are about 28 miles (45 km) of canals and the boatmen steer their gondolas and motor launches along them with amazing skill. Thousands of wooden piles were driven into the mud to make foundations strong enough to support the buildings of Venice, some of which are the finest in the world.

The city is linked to the mainland of Italy by a railway viaduct 2.5 miles (4 km) long, and a roadway, the Littorio Bridge, which was built by Mussolini and opened in 1933.

WHERE IS "THE RAILROAD IN THE SKY"?

In Peru. The railroad is so high that the trains carry oxygen equipment for the safety of the passengers. At one point it reaches 3 miles (4.8 km) high, only a little lower than Mont Blanc, the tallest peak in Europe.

This "railroad in the sky," as it is often called, was built between 1870 and 1893. A war between Peru and Chile halted its progress and, when work was resumed, its great American engineer, Henry Meiggs, had died, so a British company finished the task.

The line runs 260 miles (410.7 km) from Callao, the seaport near

Llamas are often used as pack animals

Peru's capital Lima, to Huancayo, and the trip through the towering Andes is one of the supreme tourist attractions on earth.

The railroad is vital to Peru's economy, too, as it links the coast with the high country's rich copper, lead, zinc, silver and gold mines.

More than half the population of Peru live in very high country which is dominated by the Andes Mountains. 50 per cent of the population are Indians and most of the rest are of mixed Spanish and Indian descent.

Because the Indians are used to living at a high altitude they have no difficulty breathing and are, therefore, key figures in the mining industry. They also raise sheep and graze their llamas and alpacas. The llamas are often used by the Indians as pack animals.

Communications are improving every year in Peru, which is necessary in such a geographically contrasted country. As well as the railroads, there are some fine roads, mostly branching off the Pan-American Highway which runs down to the coast.

WHERE IS THE TEMPLE OF HEAVEN?

In Pekin, the capital of China. When Marco Polo, his father and his uncle arrived in Pekin in the year 1275, the ruler there was the Mongol conqueror, Kublai Khan. For some time there had been civil war in China between Kublai Khan and his brother Mangu Khan. Kublai Khan had emerged victorious and he decided to make Pekin his capital.

Two hundred years later the city was walled round. Within those walls was the Imperial City. This, also, was surrounded by wall. A third city had been built inside the Imperial City and this was called the Forbidden City.

Only the Emperor of China and his courtiers were allowed inside the Forbidden City which was beautiful in the extreme. Temples and palaces stood proudly amid elegant gardens, lovely lakes and streams.

Among the wondrous palaces was the Temple of Heaven. It can be seen today with its three splendid circular roofs, an enduring monument to the greatness of China and its Emperors.

DO JAFFA ORANGES COME FROM JAFFA?

Yes and the story of Jaffa is an interesting one. In Biblical times it was known as Joppa. It was a seaside town once visited by St Paul. Later the name of Joppa was changed to Jaffa, the name it still bears.

Jaffa, though, is now a suburb of Tel Aviv, the biggest city in Israel. 80 years ago when the Jews were agitating for a homeland in Palestine, they founded a new suburb to the north of Jaffa. This suburb they called Tel Aviv. During the ensuing 40 years, Tel Aviv grew bigger and bigger and finally became larger than Jaffa.

Today it is a great modern industrial city, noted everywhere for its high standard of education and culture. Jews from all over the world are still emigrating to Tel Aviv to enjoy all the benefits that this splendid city has to offer.

Jaffa, however, is not entirely forgotten. Its name is kept alive by the sweet and juicy oranges that grow there.

WHY ARE THERE NO MEDIAEVAL BUILDINGS FOUND IN OSLO, NORWAY'S CAPITAL?

For hundreds of years Norway has been a big exporter of timber for the country is rich in forests. In the 17th century, Oslo was mainly constructed of wooden buildings. Tragically, in 1624 a great fire broke out and Oslo was destroyed. All its ancient buildings were laid in ruins.

At that time, Norway was part of Denmark and it was King Kristian IV of Denmark who was responsible for laying out the new city that rose from the ashes of the old.

Today Oslo is one of the busiest ports in Scandinavia.

Jacques Cartier lands in Canada in 1534

WHY IS CANADA SO NAMED?

It was the famous French explorer Jacques Cartier who was responsible for the name of Canada.

He was born in St Malo, France, on December 31, 1494. In 1534, he conducted an expedition that crossed the Atlantic to try to find a route to the East. Having reached Newfoundland, he explored the eastern coasts of Canada, but landed on the Gaspé peninsula and took possession in the name of his king.

He recrossed the Atlantic in 1536 and this time was the first to sail up the St Lawrence river. It was he who named the river and he followed it many miles inland until he was stopped by rapids. He scaled a nearby summit which he called Mont Réal,(Mount Royal), a well-known name today, for Montreal is one of Canada's biggest cities.

Cartier also befriended the Huron-Iroquois tribes living there. It was these natives who pointed out various places to Cartier, using the word "kanata" to describe them. In their language, the word meant "village." Cartier applied it to the whole region.

Cartier's first use of the name Kanata, or Canada, was in his description of a meeting he had with natives living in the area which is now known as Quebec.

"On the morrow," wrote Cartier, "the lord of Canada, name Donacona, came to our ship accompanied by many Indians in canoes." Cartier died in St Malo on September 1, 1557.

ON WHAT MEDITERRANEAN IS-LAND IS KIDNAPPING A NOT-UNCOMMON CRIME?

The island of Sardinia has been for many years notorious for the kidnappings that even today are still taking place. Although in the 1970s a British family was kidnapped and held to ransom, tourists are today assured that they have little to fear.

The bandits know very well that the economy of the island depends very considerably on tourism and in no way do they wish to see this source of income decline.

Sardinia is a very interesting and picturesque island. It abounds with ancient ruins of great architectural interest, mementoes of Carthaginian and Roman occupation. There are castles erected by Italian colonialists from Pisa and Genoa. Perhaps the most interesting relics are the Nuraghes. These are great fortresses constructed of huge rocks. They are named after the Nuraghi, an ancient people who built them in 1500 BC. There are about 7,000 of them and are open to all curious visitors who wish to explore them.

Much wine is exported from Sardinia, 200 different types being produced every year.

WHERE IS FRANK WINFIELD WOOLWORTH BURIED?

The chain of Woolworth's stores is world-famous. There are hundreds of stores in Britain and America. F W Woolworth, the American responsible for founding the empire, is buried in Highgate Cemetery in North London.

Woolworth was born near Rodman, New York on April 13, 1852. At the age of 27 he invested his total capital of 240 dollars in a store in Utica devoted to articles retailed at low prices. By 1919 the Woolworth Corporation controlled 800 stores in the U S A and Canada and about 60 in Great Britain. By 1934 the number of stores increased to 1,954 and 600 respectively.

F W Woolworth died on April 7, 1919, leaving a fortune of about 35 million dollars.

WHAT WAS THE POLISH CORRIDOR?

A strip of territory joining inland Poland with the Baltic Sea and separating the main territory of Germany from East Prussia. It was from 20 to 60 miles wide by 120 miles long and was given to Poland by the Treaty Of Versailles after World War 1.

The corridor ensured that Poland would have an outlet to the sea. In the same treaty, the city of Danzig and its surrounding territory at the head of the Corridor was made a free State under the protection of the League of Nations.

For many years Danzig and the Polish Corridor were the reason for a series of arguments and quarrels between Germany and Poland. Finally, Hitler launched his war against Poland in 1939 to seize Danzig and obliterate the Corridor. It was this invasion that started World War II, for Britain and France immediately declared war on Germany.

WHERE IS THE MOUNT OF OLIVES?

It is a low hill near Jerusalem in Israel. It rises above the Vale of Kidron and at its foot is the Garden of Gethsemane where Jesus was arrested. Traditionally, Jesus ascended to Heaven from the top of the Mount of Olives.

WHY IS MIDDLEBURG IN HOLLAND FAMOUS?

Middleburg is the capital of Zeeland, in Holland. It is on the island of Walcheren. It is famous because here, after a siege of 22 months, the Spanish garrison surrendered to Dutch patriots on February 18, 1574. For many years, Spain had occupied Holland and held it under ruthless suppression. The Spanish garrison at Middleburg was the last remaining in the Netherlands.

WHAT IS THE CONNECTION BETWEEN SANTA CLAUS AND THE ASIA MINOR DISTRICT OF LYCIA?

Lycia was once populated with many towns but it is now very bare. Excavations in the early 19th century revealed remains dating back to 1000 BC. Some of the monuments are now in the British Museum.

The Bishop of Lycia in the 4th century was St Nicholas. Nothing is known of his life, but several legends are told of him and he is one of the most popular saints in Christendom. To one legend which records how generous he was, he owes his position as "Santa Claus," that name being a corruption of Saint Nicholas.

WHERE IS THERE AN UNDERGROUND TOWN?

South Australia is very rich in minerals of different kinds. One of the most beautiful of these is the opal. These small stones are very popular in jewellery.

A particularly rich deposit of opals, still mined today, was found in 1911 west of Lake Cadibarrawirracanna.

Although the gems lie close to the surface and are easy to mine, the heat makes mining difficult. When the blazing sun beats down, the temperature often reaches over 50 degrees centigrade (over 120 degrees fahrenheit).

To survive the terrible heat, the miners have built their homes underground. Comfortable houses have been hollowed out of the white and red rock. There is even a church gouged out of the ground. The name of this mining town is Coober Pedy, which in the local Aborigine language means "white man's hole in the ground".

WHAT WAS LENINGRAD FIRST CALLED?

Leningrad, Russia's second largest city, was originally called St Petersburg. It was founded by Czar Peter the Great in 1703. It is built on the banks of the River Neva and on several islands in the rivermouth, in a very marshy area. In its early days, the city was built mainly on piles.

Leningrad has been the scene of many uprisings and rebellions, notably the disorders of the 1905 revolution and the March Revolution of 1917. It was in that year that Russia became a republic and since then Leningrad has become highly industrialised.

From 1914 to 1917, Leningrad was called Petrograd. This was ordered by the Czar, Nicholas II. In 1917 it was re-named Leningrad in honour of the Russian revolutionary leader, Vladimir Ilyich Ulianov Lenin.

On June 22, 1941, Germany under the command of Adolf Hitler, invaded Russia. By September, German armies were at the gates of Leningrad. There followed, for more than three years, a terrifying siege when the people of the city defied three German armies. During this period of stark privation, starvation and bloodshed, nearly half the population of Leningrad were killed by bombs, shells and disease. Thousands died in battle. In the end Leningrad emerged triumphant but at the most dreadful cost. Today, it is a thriving centre of industry.

HOW OLD IS GLAMIS CASTLE?

Glamis Castle is one of the finest palaces in Scotland. The estate of Glamis was granted to the Lyon family in 1372 by King Robert II. To protect themselves and their new lands, the Lyons built a castle.

For three centuries this stark, stout defence was the home of the family. Early in the 17th century, Patrick Lyon, the first member of the family to be Earl of Strathmore and Kinghorne, decided he needed a new home. Incorporating some of the old Glamis Castle, the Earl built himself the magnificent house which can be seen today.

By the 17th century, Scotland was more peaceful than it had been earlier. Patrick Lyon, therefore, built himself a castle which was more devoted to comfort than to defence. The castle is still in the hands of the Earls of Strathmore and Kinghorne and is truly one of the finest in Scotland.

WHERE DOES A CHURCH STEEPLE TWIST IN A SPIRAL?

The vast majority of church steeples are tall, pointed and straight. This is not the case with the famous steeple of the church of St Mary and All Saints · in Chesterfield, Derbyshire.

Not only is it slightly bent, but it is also twisted round upon itself. Nobody is sure whether the builders wanted to create such an unusual landmark or not. The 228 foot tall steeple is 600 years old

Glamis is one of the finest castles in Scotland

and is known to have been twisted for most of that time.

The townsfolk maintain that the steeple was constructed with its twist. However, the wooden framework is clad with lead plates. It is possible that the temperature change between summer sun and winter frost caused the lead and the wood to expand and warp at different rates. This could have created the twist. Whatever the cause, the twisted spire of Chesterfield is a noted local landmark.

WHAT IS THE FREMANTLE DOCTOR?

Perth is the capital and the largest city of Western Australia. Standing at the far southwestern tip of the continent it basks in an almost ideal climate. Sailing and swimming are favourite pastimes in Perth, where the sun shines so often that it can almost be relied on.

Perhaps the most pleasant aspect of the Perth climate goes by the name of the Fremantle Doctor. On sunny summer days, the temperature in Perth can climb extremely high. It is in just these conditions that a cool breeze blows up the Swan River from the port of Fremantle and the sea. As this breeze sweeps up the river and runs through the city streets, it brings a welcome relief from the heat for the citizens of Perth. It is the Fremantle Doctor which stops the city becoming unbearably hot in the summer months.

WHICH IS THE WORLD'S LONGEST RIVER?

The longest river in the world is the River Nile. As one of the largest and most important rivers known to the ancients, many attempts were made to follow the Nile to its source.

The Emperor Nero, for instance, sent an expedition which reached further south than any other Europeans, but even they could not find the river's source. From the stories they had heard, the ancient Greeks and Romans thought that the Nile rose far to the south of Egypt in the Mountains of the Moon.

However, it was not until the end of the last century that anyone could be reasonably certain where the Nile began. The upper reaches of the river were explored by two famous British explorers, Burton and Speke.

It is now accepted that the river rises as a stream which flows into Lake Victoria in the African country of Rwanda. From there the stream flows steadily northwards, picking up several tributaries along the way. After a staggering 4,145 miles (6,671 km) it reaches the Mediterranean.

IS EVEREST THE TALLEST MOUNTAIN IN THE WORLD?

Mount Everest has been known to the Nepalese for centuries. They recognise the peak as a great phenomenon of nature. It was not until an expedition from the Indian government measured the mountain with scientific instruments that people knew its height. They also gave the peak its name, in honour of Sir George Everest, a government official.

It is now generally considered that Mount Everest stands 29,028 feet (8,848 m) above sea level, which makes it the highest point on Earth. However, the title of the largest mountain must go elsewhere. The island of Hawaii is really the peak of a huge, suboceanic mountain. The top of the island is nearly 14,000 feet (4,300 m) above sea level, but when combined with the height of the mountain under sea, the mountain reaches a height of 33,476 feet (10,203 m).

WHY DO PEOPLE VISIT ROTORUA?

The town of Rotorua on the North Island of New Zealand has become increasingly popular with tourists. It is not that the town itself is particularly interesting. Visitors are drawn by the sights around Rotorua.

This is one of the most volcanically active areas of New Zealand. Whakarewarewa is an area of boiling springs and dramatic geysers which shoot columns of scalding water high into the air. The steaming rivers and beautiful calcerite formations cover a seething and violent nature.

In 1886 the mountains ripped themselves apart in a colossal explosion. Many people were killed, several villages were destroyed and the blast heard many miles away. The jagged craters left by the explosion can still be seen at Tarawera. Among the casualties of the eruption were the delicate pink and white terraces which were formed from deposits laid down by the hot springs. They vanished beneath the blast. Rotorua has, perhaps, the most dramatic scenery of New Zealand.

WHERE CAN YOU SEE AN ANCIENT SPORTS STADIUM?

The most important sports games of the ancient world were the Olympic Games. They were held every four years for more than a thousand years in honour of the Greek gods.

These immensely important games were held in a sacred enclosure at Olympia in the western Peloponnese. Though they have suffered from 1,500 years of neglect, the ruins of Olympia can still be seen. They include rooms for athletes and spectators to stay in while the games were in progress. The ruins of large temples, dedicated to Zeus and Hera, stand within the sacred enclosure. The museum at Olympia contains several remarkable statues and other objects, including a statue of Hermes by the famous sculptor Praxiteles.

The most important structure at Olympia was the stadium. Enclosed by grassy banks on which the spectators and judges could sit, the running track where the games were held, lies just as it did hundreds of years ago.

WHERE IS SURFER'S PARADISE?

The aptly named town of Surfer's Paradise lies to the south of Brisbane, in Queensland. It forms part of one of the greatest holiday playgrounds of Australia.

For 20 miles (34 km) an almost unbroken stretch of golden sandy beach runs along the Queensland coast.

As the area has become more and more popular with holidaymakers during the past thirty years, facilities have improved. Every possible beach activity is now on offer, from simple swimming to the more adventurous parascending and surfing.

WHAT DREADFUL SPECTACLES HAPPENED IN THE ROMAN COLOSSEUM?

The Colosseum is a huge amphitheatre which stands in Rome. It was begun on the orders of the Emperor Vespasian in the year AD 72 and from the first was intended to be the scene of slaughter.

It is a sad reflection on the so-called glory and culture of Rome and its civilised people, that a building could have been erected for such a barbaric and cruel purpose. About 50,000 people could be seated at a time in the marbled banks of seats to watch the games.

These games took many forms, most of them extremely bloody. The most famous were the gladiatorial fights. Trained fighters, called gladiators, were made to fight to the death for the amusement of the public. Sometimes the gladiators fought with weapons native to their homelands. Others fought with Roman weapons.

On other occasions wild bears, lions and elephants would be turned loose in the arena to be stalked by skilled hunters. Sometimes condemned prisoners and Christians were thrown into the arena to be torn apart by lions. On one occasion the arena was flooded and ships fought a naval battle for the mob. The games were abolished in AD 404 after Christianity had gained the upper hand in the Empire.

WHAT WAS BELIEVED TO BE HIDDEN ON DEER ISLAND?

On May 23, 1701, Captain William Kidd was hanged as a pirate. Before he died Kidd offered to buy his life with the vast treasure he had captured during his career. The offer was turned down.

For three years Kidd had been plundering ships in the Indian Ocean. Finally he was arrested off the North American coast. By all accounts he had robbed so many ships of so much treasure that his hoard was phenomenal. Kidd himself estimated its value at £100,000 in 1700.

When he died the secret location of his hoard died with him.

Many years later a secret compartment was found in his sea desk. In it was a map of an island with a small X marked on it. Unfortunately, nobody could identify the island. At the end of the 19th century a law suit started in America concerning a large treasure found on Deer Island in Maine. It was claimed to be part of Captain Kidd's treasure. At once hundreds of people rushed to Deer Island, determined to find any other treasure left on the island. Only then was it revealed that the original "find" was a forgery.

WHERE DO PEOPLE RE-ENACT A LEGEND?

The ancient city of Hamelin in Germany has many fine historic buildings, and some are centred around the Market Square. It is here each year, that the citizens of Hamelin stage a drama which relives the city's most famous story.

It is said that many years ago the city was suffering from a plague of rats. Then a piper turned up in a multi-coloured costume and promised to rid the town of the rats, for a fee. By playing his pipe, he made all the rats follow him out of town. The piper then led the rats into the river where they drowned. When he demanded his money, the citizens refused to pay the piper.

People rushed to Deer Island, determined to find hidden treasure

The piper at once started to play a different tune. This time the children of Hamelin were drawn to the music. They followed the piper out of Hamelin and were never seen again. The re-enactment of the story is performed by citizens of Hamelin who dress up as rats in mediaeval costume.

WHAT IS THE WORLD'S TALLEST STRUCTURE?

There are several contenders for the title of the tallest structure in the world. The tallest building in which it is possible to walk around freely is the Sears Tower in Chicago. It stands 1,454 feet (443m) tall and contains 110 storeys. This huge black tower was completed in 1973.

On the other side of the Great Lakes stands an even taller structure, the CN Tower. Begun in the same year that the Sears Tower was completed, the CN Tower stands in Toronto, Canada, and dominates the lakeside city. Its topmost pinnacle reaches 1,822 feet (555m) into the air. There is a revolving restaurant part of the way up the tower and an observation deck. It features in the 1980 film thriller *High Point*.

Both the Sears Building and the CN Tower are self supporting. The Warszawa Radi Mast in Poland is supported by huge steel cables and surpasses all other structures in the world. This radio mast reaches an amazing 2,120 feet (646 m) into the sky.

The tallest building in the world however, is the World Trade Centre in New York which has 110 floors and two separate towers, immortalised in the 1976 film *King Kong*.

WHERE IS THE ATOMIUM?

In 1958 a large and prestigious World Fair was held in Brussels, the capital of Belgium. The main theme of the Fair was atomic physics, then a new science. As the centrepiece of the exhibition was a massive representation of the atomic structure of a molecule. The result was the Atomium.

This structure consists of nine large gleaming spheres supported on huge struts. Stairways run through the struts to connect the various spheres. The lower spheres offer viewing platforms and the highest is a restaurant. The sparkling Atomium is often the first structure that visitors to Brussels see.

WHY ARE THE STAVE CHURCHES WELL KNOWN?

Scattered through southern Norway are several stave churches. These churches date back to the earliest days of Christianity in that area. They are built of wood, but unlike most wooden structures, the planks forming the walls are laid vertically rather than horizontally. It is this which gives the churches their name.

Because many of these churches were built in newly converted areas, there can be little doubt that they were built in the same way as earlier pagan temples. Certainly many of the churches carried carved dragons, interlaced patterns and imaginary monsters of pagan Viking tradition. After the mid-13th century stave churches were no longer built in Norway.

WHY DO PEOPLE GO TO THE GROAGH PATRICK?

The Groagh Patrick is a mountain in County Mayo, Ireland, to which thousands of people flock on the last Sunday of July each year. Passing a large white statue of St Patrick, they climb the hill, pray in the chapel and then walk around the chapel 15 times. The faithful come here because of Saint Patrick and his mission to Ireland.

In 441 AD, while converting the Irish to Christianity, St Patrick prayed and fasted for the 40 days of Lent on the mountain.

Quite apart from its religious significance, the Groagh Patrick is a beautiful spot overlooking green fields, dark mountains and a shimmering stretch of water.

WHICH COUNTRY IS NAMED AFTER ANCIENT RUINS?

When a new name was being sought for the former British colony of Southern Rhodesia, inspiration came from the famous stone ruins which can be found in the bush, unique in Africa.

The ruins date back about a thousand years and consist of huge stone walls and towers. Though archaeologists have examined the ruins in detail, nobody is sure what they were. The local tribesmen knew nothing about them.

Presumably some ordered civilisation had risen in isolation from the rest of the world. When it had fallen the civilisation had been forgotten.

The local name of the towering ruins is Zimbabwe. That is the name now given to the country in which they stand.

WHY IS THE NULLARBOR PLAIN SO CALLED?

The Nullarbor Plain in Southern Australia is one of the most awesome places in the world. It is absolutely flat from horizon to horizon, for hundreds of miles. The land stretches away with hardly a ripple. Scrub bushes and clumps of poor grass dot the landscape but do little to relieve the monotony of the view.

So flat is the Nullarbor that when engineers came to build a railway track across it they could lay it in an absolutely straight line for no less than 297 miles (478 km). This is the longest railway straight track in the world.

The Nullarbor is the top of a massive slab of limestone which was deposited on an ancient seabed and then raised up. The flat-

An exploration party being rescued from an ice floe

ness of the rock has not been changed by erosion because so little rain falls here.

The lack of rainfall is also responsible for the lack of vegetation, and this is what gives the place its name. Nullarbor is a Latin word meaning "no tree", which is a very accurate description of the immense Nullarbor Plain.

HOW THICK IS THE POLAR ICE?

Both the North and South Poles are covered by permanently frozen sheets of ice. They are, however, very different in character. The North Pole is a frozen sea, while the South Pole is situated on a large continent called Antarctica. In turn this affects the type and depth of ice to be found.

The ice in Antarctica is incredibly thick. At the South Pole itself, it is about 9,000 feet (2,743m) thick but in other places the ice is as much as 15,000 feet (4,572m) thick. Much of this ice is permanent, but elsewhere it grinds across the landscape in giant glaciers. When these huge glaciers reach the sea they begin to float. Often they split up to form massive islands of ice. The largest of these ever measured was about 12,000 square miles (19,308km).

The Arctic ice is much thinner. The fact that it floats on the sea stops the ice becoming too thick. Near the edges of the Arctic ice cap the floating ice can be surprisingly thin. When the summer comes, the edges of the ice floes break up and separate. More than one exploration team has found itself stranded on such a free moving floe.

WHICH THEATRE HAS PERFECT ACOUSTICS?

The ancient Greeks believed that medicine should involve bringing rest and relaxation to the mind. The great healing sanctuary of Epidavros, therefore, included a theatre. It was designed by Polycleitos the Younger in the middle of the 4th century BC.

The theatre was cut into the slope of a hill overlooking the rest of the sanctuary dedicated to Asclepios, the god of medicine. Recent excavations and reconstructions have returned this theatre to its former grandeur and plays are now performed there again. The acoustics of the theatre of Epidavros are truly astounding. Everybody in the 14,000 strong audience can hear the smallest sound on stage. Even quiet whispers can be heard in the very back seats.

The perfect acoustics combine with the elegant design and magnificent views to make the theatre at Epidavros one of the finest in the world.

WHICH COUNTRY DOES NOT HAVE A RECTANGULAR FLAG?

Flags have been used as symbols and as rallying points in battle for centuries. The earliest recorded flag was flown in China in about 1,000 BC. Today every nation in the world has a flag.

These flags have their shape in common. They are all square or rectangular. Only one is different. This is the flag of the Himalayan kingdom of Nepal. The Nepalese flag consists of two triangles mounted one above the other. On a red field, within a blue border, are displayed white symbols resembling crescents and spiked wheels.

Wherever the Nepalese flag is flown it stands out from all the others simply because of its shape. The others have to rely on their colours and designs.

WHY WAS THE GREAT WALL OF CHINA BUILT?

For many hundreds of years the farmers of China were raided and pillaged by nomadic barbarians from the north. China was divided into a number of small countries. Each tried to deal with the barbarian problem. Some built up large armies, others built defensive walls along their borders.

In about 221 BC China was united under the Emperor Shih Huang Ti. He decided to try to solve the problem of the barbarians. He co ᴎmanded that all the previous frontier walls should be linked and re-designed to form a single barrier. Thousands of men were forced to work on the wall and many of them died before it was completed.

Eventually, however, China had her wall. Though it did not always keep out the nomads, it stopped many smaller raids. Over the following years the wall has been repaired and changed several times.

Today, the Great Wall of China is about 4,000 miles long (6,436km) including spurs, and stands up to 40 feet (12.2m) tall and 30 feet (9.15m) thick. It is the largest structure built by man and is the only one big enough to be seen from the moon.

WHICH ROYAL PALACE WAS BUILT BY A GRANDFATHER, FATHER AND SON?

In 1697 the Royal Palace of the Kings of Sweden burnt down. It was at once decided to build a magnificent new palace on the site. The famous architect Nicodemus Tessin was sent for and the plans drawn up. The palace was to be a masterpiece of late Renaissance architecture and the design was developed on a grand scale. The palace was designed to form a giant square surrounding a fine courtyard. Work began as soon as the designs were completed.

When Tessin died thirty years later, the palace was still not completed. His son, K S Tessin took over the work. Leaving the exterior as a Renaissance building, he began the interior in the Baroque style which was then in fashion. The decoration of the rooms was finally completed in the Rococo style by Carl Gustav Tessin, grandson of Nicodemus. Much of the palace is now open to the public and is a magnificent example of northern architecture.

WHERE IS THE WORLD'S STRANGEST OBSERVATORY?

When Maharajah Jai Singh II, a powerful ruler in India, wished to study the stars and planets he decided to build an observatory.

In 1728, therefore, he constructed a remarkable series of buildings in Jaipur. A large stairway was built which reached nearly a hundred feet in the air and then stopped. Other ramp-like structures rose for no apparent reason while great curved walls of marble encircled other oddly shaped buildings. These almost grotesque structures all served a very real purpose.

When looked at carefully, they can be seen to be giant replicas of small, hand-held astronomical instruments. With these scaled-up versions, Jai Singh and his scientists could study the movement of the heavenly bodies.

More modern instruments are used by today's scientists and the observatory of Jaipur remains as a tourist attraction.

WHERE DOES THE BULLET TRAIN RUN?

The Bullet Train is the name given to the New Tokaido Service of the Japanese National Railways. The name came about for two reasons. First the blue and white train has a rounded nose which looks rather like a bullet. The second reason for the name was the incredible speed of the train.

The train runs from Osaka to Tokyo, a distance of 100 miles (160.9km) in a regular time of just 58 minutes. This gives the train an amazing average speed of 103 mph (165.7 km/h). It was the first passenger train to average over 100 miles per hour and is one of the finest railway services in the world.

IS THE POMPIDOU CENTRE POPULAR?

When the Georges Pompidou National Centre for Art and Culture was opened in Paris in 1977 many people were not quite sure what to make of it. Many are still confused by the structure.

This extraordinary building was constructed out of glass and concrete. It is supported on the outside by a maze of pipes and girders. Staircases snake outside the building within covered walkways. Bright colours and futuristic design are the main features of this building. Inside art exhibitions and displays are arranged for the public.

The building itself was highly praised by some critics, but others have criticised it harshly. The years which have passed have done little to change people's opinion.

WHERE IS RWANDA?

The small country of Rwanda is situated in central Africa between Uganda, Zaire and Tanzania. It covers only 10,000 square miles and is one of the poorest nations in Africa.

The vast majority of the 4 million people of Rwanda are farmers who only grow enough food to feed themselves and their families. Some farmers grow tea and coffee for sale abroad, and a few are employed in industry. The climate is warm and moist which helps the farming of traditional crops, but the land is poor in natural resources. Rwanda seems certain to remain an agricultural country.

WHAT IS KATHMANDU?

The mountain kingdom of Nepal has its capital in the remarkable city of Kathmandu. It is one of the strangest and most romantic of cities.

Kathmandu is in a valley 4,400 feet (1,341 m) above sea level where farmers cultivate summer rice and winter wheat as their ancestors have done for centuries. The city itself is a strange collection of dull brown houses and colourful temples. The central square is surrounded by magnificent pagoda style temples and beautifully carved statues. Yet it is here that the market is held. Farmers try to sell their produce and woodmen sell firewood as fuel. Kathmandu is a truly magical place.

WHICH IS THE LARGEST LAKE IN THE WORLD?

There are two lakes which are claimed to be the largest in the world. The first is Lake Baikal in Siberia. It is 46 miles (74 km) at its broadest and is 380 miles (611.5 km) long. Deeper than some seas the lake has a depth of 6,300 feet (1,920 m). The claim of this lake rests on the fact that it contains more fresh water than any other lake.

Wilton House was built on the site of a derelict convent

If surface area is taken to be the measure of size for a lake, however, there can be little doubt that Lake Superior, in North America, is the largest.

It covers an estimated 31,800 square miles (82,359 km²) but is far shallower than Lake Baikal. No doubt the controversy about which lake is the larger will continue for some time to come.

WHO BUILT WILTON HOUSE?

Wilton House stands near Salisbury in Wiltshire and is the magnificent home of the Earls of Pembroke. The Earls of Pembroke are amongst the most respected families in Britain, but the man who founded the family's fortunes was far from quiet.

William Herbert came from a good family and could look forward to a secure, if unexciting life. But in 1527 he became involved in a street brawl in which one man was killed. Fearing he would be blamed for the death, William fled to France. Here he joined the army and soon showed himself to be a capable and vicious fighter. When he returned to England, William came with a strong reputation.

He married a lady called Anne Parr. When her sister married Henry VIII, the fortune of William Herbert was made. He quickly made friends with his new brother-in-law, was knighted, granted lands and given a high position at court.

One of the properties he was given was the derelict Convent of Wilton. Sir William planned and erected the magnificent Wilton House on the site. In 1551 he was created Earl of Pembroke. It was on this basis that the future generations of Earls of Pembroke would build so well. The house has changed dramatically since the first Earl built it, but Wilton remains one of the finest houses in the country.

WHICH PORT IS ONLY OPEN FOR A FEW MONTHS EACH YEAR?

The great stretch of water known as Hudson Bay freezes solid every winter. For months at a time no ships can move in Hudson Bay. The only way to move is by sled or by aeroplane.

Despite this, Churchill, in Manitoba, on the west coast of the bay is a large and busy port. The town does all of its business during the few short summer months when ships can steam across Hudson Bay and into the Atlantic.

Churchill is linked by a long railway line with Regina and the great grain belt of the Canadian prairies. When the harvest is gathered in, it is sent to Churchill by rail. Placed in huge grain silos for storage, the grain is eventually shipped out by steamer. When winter closes in, the harbour and all its equipment is simply abandoned. Tugs become trapped in the ice and wharves are blanketed in snow. The busy port becomes the home of polar bears.

WHERE IN ITALY ARE THERE TWO GREEK TEMPLES?

Two and a half thousand years ago, the Greeks were one of the most civilised peoples in the world. They were also among the most adventurous. Not content with their homeland, the Greeks sailed abroad and planted colonies throughout the Mediterranean.

One of the most successful of these colonies was the town of Agrigentum in Sicily. It was founded in the 6th century BC and, for a time, was ruled by the tyrant Phalaris. This man was notorious for his cruelty. He used to keep a bronze bull, inside which he would roast his enemies to death. He was overthrown in a rebellion in about 554 BC.

The town of Agrigentum became one of the most prosperous in Sicily and spectacular public buildings were erected. Of these the temples of Hera and Concordia are by far the best preserved, lacking only their roofs. These two are the most complete Greek temples in Italy.

WHICH AREA HAS MORE WILDFLOWERS THAN ANY OTHER?

Western Australia is famous for its flowers. For most of the time, however, it seems to be remarkably short of flowers.

It is when the rains fall that the landscape bursts forth into a frenzy of colour. In the short time when there is enough moisture for plants to grow, they have to mature and produce seed. The best way to do this is to produce a mass of blooms which carpet the land. These are quickly pollinated, produce seed and die.

The southwestern part of Western Australia has been cut off from the rest of Australia, and the world, for thousands of years by the terrible deserts which make up so much of the continent. In isolation, new types of flower have evolved which are found nowhere else on Earth. At the height of the wildflower season, Western Australia is the most beautiful spot on this planet.

WHICH CITY GREW FROM FOUR TOWNS?

During the 16th century Finland formed part of the Swedish Kingdom. King Gustavus Vasa was keen to break the economic stranglehold held by the Hanseatic League. He therefore set about encouraging trade throughout his kingdom.

As part of these efforts, in 1550, he ordered the entire population of four towns, Porvoo, Tammisaari, Rauma and Ulvila, to start a new city where the Vantaanjoki flows into the Gulf of Finland. He hoped this would serve as a centre for trade. In this way Helsinki, the present capital of Finland, came into being. Eighty years later Queen Christina moved the town to its present site.

WHAT IS A CHINOOK?

A chinook is an unusual type of wind which sometimes strikes the western plains of North America. It happens in winter and has dramatic effects.

The chinook occurs when warm, moist winds move in off the Pacific onto the West Coast of America. As the winds meet the Rocky Mountains they are forced upwards. As the air rises it cools and releases its moisture in the form of heavy rain. When the wind goes over the top of the mountains, it starts to fall. As it falls the air gets warmer. Because it is now dry, the air becomes even warmer than when it left the Pacific. The result is that a hot, dry wind sweeps down from the mountains onto the winter-struck plains.

When the chinook strikes it raises the temperature dramatically and melts the deep snows of winter within hours, causing flash floods. The most dramatic chinook on record swept down across South Dakota on January 22, 1943. The temperature rose from -4 degrees Fahrenheit (-20 degrees Centigrade) to 45 degrees Fahrenheit (7 degrees Centigrade) in the space of just 2 minutes.

WHAT ARE THE CAVES OF AJANTA?

In a narrow gorge at Ajanta in India is a remarkable series of caves. More than two thousand years ago, Buddhist monks settled in this gorge to meditate and lead a life of peace.

It soon became obvious that the natural caves were insufficient to house all the monks who wished to live at Ajanta. The holy men, therefore, began to hollow out artificial caves. The first viharas, or living cells, were simple rooms cut into the rock.

The later temples are very

different. Huge halls have been hacked out of the rock, each one a copy of the interior of a wooden temple of the period. The temples consist of two rows of massive columns supporting an arched ceiling, though of course this is not a building but a hollowed out cave. The interiors are rich with religious sculpture representing the Buddha and a host of other figures. When the caves of Ajanta were revealed to the outside world in the last century they excited as much wonder and excitement as they do today.

WHICH COUNTRY IS NAMED AFTER AN EXPORT?

The Europeans first started exploring the west coast of Africa during the 15th century and they were most impressed by the rich natural resources of the area. In part the explorations were prompted by mere curiosity, but most captains were expected to pay the expenses of the trip through trade with the lands they discovered. In particular the Europeans searched for luxury goods which would make their trips profitable.

One of the most lucrative of these was ivory. Elephants abounded on the inland savannah and were hunted mercilessly to supply ivory. Because of this trade the area became known as the Ivory Coast. The name is still that of one of the countries of West Africa.

Today, of course, ivory is not a major export of the Ivory Coast. Instead, the nation has become one of the world's major producers of coffee and cocoa. The government has even made determined efforts to establish industry as a main trading activity.

Despite all this the Ivory Coast clings to its old name.

WHICH COUNTRY HAS THE GREATEST POPULATION?

Far outstripping all other countries in terms of population is China. It is estimated that the population of China is about 900,000,000. This staggering figure is all the more impressive when it is realised that China is still a basically agricultural country.

The vast majority of China's people live in the highly cultivated areas of eastern China, around the broad rivers which flow down to the sea. Here they farm rice on a vast scale and raise pigs and chickens for meat. Though the majority of the people rely on farming, China has some of the world's largest cities. The biggest of these is Shanghai, which has a population of over 10,000,000 and is one of the most important seaports in the Pacific.

Though the government is doing its best to limit population growth in China to ease economic pressures, it seems that China will continue to be the most populous nation on Earth.

WHY IS PORTLAND BILL SO CALLED?

Anyone cruising up the English Channel, be they in command of a merchant ship or simply out for a day's sailing, will know Portland Bill.

This promontory juts out into the Channel west of the Isle of Wight and is a conspicuous landmark. During the day its surf-fringed cliffs can be seen far out to sea. At night a tall lighthouse flashes its regular beacon to passing ships.

The strategic importance of the headland has long been obvious. The Normans built one of their strong castles here and in 1520 King Henry VIII constructed a massive gun bastion as part of his defences along the south coast. When Napoleon was threatening invasion, troops were stationed here again and Portland saw more military activity in the Second World War.

The origin of Portland Bill's name is probably due to the fact that the actual tip of the headland looks rather like a bird bill. To seamen passing the coast such a resemblance would have suggested the name of Portland Bill.

WHERE DO GAUCHOS USE THE BOLAS?

Stretching in a broad belt across central Argentina, from the Atlantic to the Andes, is the pampas. This is a rolling lands-

Portland Bill is a conspicuous landmark

cape of grassland where the tall, feathery pampas grass waves in the wind.

Throughout much of the past three centuries, the pampas has provided the wealth of Argentina. Vast herds of cattle and sheep roam across the grasslands, grazing on the rich pastures. Looking after the cattle are gauchos who ride horses and herd cattle like the North American cowboys.

The favourite method of the gauchos for catching cattle is to use the bolas. The bolas is simply a number of heavy balls connected by rope. When it is thrown the bolas spreads out so that when it strikes a target the balls wrap the rope around it. A skilled gaucho can throw his bolas from a galloping horse to entangle a cow's legs time after time.

HOW LARGE IS THE GREAT BARRIER REEF?

The Great Barrier Reef is one of the great natural wonders of Australia. It is a massive chain of coral reefs running off much of the eastern coast of Australia.

The tiny, soft-bodied coral polyps which make up the reef live in warm seas where there is plenty of oxygen. In practice this means that the tropical seas off Queensland are ideal. They are warm and the crashing Pacific rollers mix plenty of air into the sea. By surrounding their vulnerable bodies with a limestone tube, the millions of polyps are gradu-

ally able to build up the massive reefs we see today.

The Great Barrier Reef runs for 1,250 miles (2,011.6 km) along the coast of Queensland and varies in width from 14 to 250 miles (22.5 to 402 km). Though there are numerous channels through the reef, these are narrow and shallow. Ships generally steer well clear of the dangerous reef.

WHERE IS THE LARGEST CANYON IN THE WORLD?

By far the largest canyon in the world is the Grand Canyon of Arizona. The measurements of the canyon are overwhelming, but nowhere near as impressive as the sight of the canyon from close range.

In all the Grand Canyon is nearly 220 miles (354 km) long and one mile (1.6 km) deep. At one point it is 13 miles (21 km) wide. At Toroweap a sheer drop of 3,000 feet (914.4 km) lines the canyon. Tourist roads have been constructed along both the north and south rims as well as down the canyon. The beauty and magnificence of the sheer walls, the craggy rock formations and the enormity and splendour of the canyon is breathtaking.

This huge gash in the Earth has been cut, over thousands of years, by the Colorado River. The mighty Colorado thunders along through the narrowest part at the base of the canyon at a frightening speed. ·These waters carry with them large amounts of rock and sand which gouge away at the river bed and are responsible for cutting the Grand Canyon. When in full flood the Colorado may carry as much as 50 million tons of debris a day.

WHICH IS THE LARGEST CAVE IN THE WORLD?

Ever since prehistory men have been exploring caves. Stone Age people sometimes travelled great distances underground to paint caves. Today, potholing is a recognised sport and many people spend great amounts of time underground.

The longest cave system in the world is to be found in North America. Mammoth Cave in Kentucky is a national park, but since it was established potholers have been extending knowledge of the size of the cavern. It is now thought that the passages and caverns extend for more than 180 miles beneath the rock. The Mammoth Cave system is not, however, the deepest. That honour goes to a cave in southern France which plunges more than 4,000 feet below the land surface.

WHAT IS UNUSUAL ABOUT THE CLOCK OF BERNE?

The Swiss have long been famous for their ability to make timepieces. Swiss watches are today recognised as masterpieces of design and accuracy.

During the Middle Ages, the Swiss were no less ingenious. This is shown admirably by the old clock in Berne. Berne is the capital of Switzerland and has as its symbol the bear. A bear appears on the number plates of cars registered there and several bears are kept in pits in the city. Bears also feature on the clock.

When the hour strikes, a mechanical procession begins. Emerging from a door in the clockface a string of figures march around. There are bears dressed as soldiers and as gentlemen. As these bears circle round the clock, a jester nods his head to jangle bells and a large figure hammers out the number of hours on a large bell at the top of the tower. The whole display lasts for some time and is one of the most enjoyable aspects of the city of Berne.

WHICH CAPITAL CITY WAS HACKED OUT OF A JUNGLE?

Rio de Janeiro was established as the capital of Brazil by the Portuguese when the country was their colony. However, independent Brazil increasingly came to feel that it should create its own capital city. In 1956 President Kubitschek de Oliveira was elected to office and he decided to give the country its new capital.

The noted architects Lucio Costa and Oscar Niemeyer were employed to plan and lay out the new city. A site was chosen deep in the interior, in a range of hills called the Serra Geral do Parana and work began.

The jungle was hacked down to make room for city streets, office blocks and housing areas. The name for the new city was declared to be Brasilia. It is probably the best known example of modern town planning, having been started from untouched territory. In some ways it is a wonder of modern architecture, but in others it has failed to become a vibrant, living city as was the old capital.

WHICH COUNTRY IS ENCLOSED BY ANOTHER?

When Chief Moshoeshoe united a large number of refugees in the Drakensberg Mountains in the 1920s he was laying the foundations for a modern African nation.

The refugees had been fleeing the Zulu warriors and were united to form the Basotho by their energetic new chief. In 1966 the Basotho lands became independent of Britain as Lesotho. At once the new nation was faced by many problems. Among these was grinding poverty and poor land. More than three quarters of land in Lesotho is too poor to be farmed and there is little industry to provide employment.

The mountain country is entirely surrounded by the much larger and wealthier South Africa. Large numbers of Lesotho men cross the border to work and send money home. The fact that Lesotho is enclosed by another nation has caused both difficulties and opportunities for what is one of the poorest nations in Africa.

WHICH IS THE COPPER COUNTRY?

Many countries in the world are known for a particular product. For many this is a matter of tradition or of luxury, but for Zambia it is a matter of survival.

More than half of the population of this country live a traditional life, worshipping tribal gods and relying on subsistence farming. The wealth of Zambia, however, is its copper. Running in a broad swathe in the north of Zambia is the Copperbelt, where vast reserves of copper ore are being mined. The industry is government-controlled and produces about nine tenths of all exports from Zambia.

So dependent is Zambia on copper that a fluctuation in the international price of the mineral may mean boom times or depression for the country.

WHO BUILT THE CASTLE OF NEUSCHWANSTEIN?

Standing high on a rocky hill amid the mountains of Bavaria is perhaps the most romantic castle in existence. Neuschwanstein overlooks a beautiful lake and is resplendent with turrets, towers and sheer walls. It contains magnificent Gothic halls and its rooms are packed with paintings of knights and battles. Yet this mediaeval extravaganza was built in the last century.

King Ludwig II of Bavaria was an incurable romantic. His family had ruled Bavaria for seven centuries and could trace their line back to the great days of the Holy Roman Empire. Ludwig looked back to the days of mediaeval glory with longing.

In 1868, inspired by Wagner's operas, Ludwig began to build Neuschwanstein as a mediaeval castle suitable for a King of Bavaria. It took twenty years to build the breath-takingly impressive castle, by which time Ludwig was dead. His castle remains, however, as a stupendous memorial to the man and the past of his family.

WHERE ARE THE NOMADS SETTLING DOWN?

The vast grasslands of central Asia have always been ideal land for pastoralists. On the seemingly endless pastures vast herds of cattle and horses can be tended by nomadic herders. For thousands of years that is exactly what has happened. Often these nomadic peoples have invaded and plundered the settled agricultural regions which line their southern flank.

The most dramatic of such invasions were the conquests of the Mongols under Genghis Khan in the 13th century. The Mongols were nomads who led their livestock across the grasslands in an endless search for fresh pasture.

In recent years that has begun to change. Coal and tungsten are important minerals in Mongolia. The government is encouraging the exploitation of these reserves, together with the advancement of various light industries. More and more, the traditional nomads are being enticed to settle in permanent cities. However, the majority of the population still follow the herds and more than three-quarters of the nation is covered by pasture land.

WHICH CITY WAS THE CAPITAL OF INDIA FOR ONLY THREE YEARS?

Early in the 14th century a force of ferocious Mongol invaders swept down from the northwest onto the plains of northern India. Sultan Mohammed ibn Tughluq was at this time the ruler of Moslem India. Though he pushed the fierce invaders back, he decided to reorganise his country.

One of his first measures was to move his capital from Delhi to Daulatabad, hundreds of miles to the south. At the new city Mohammed built massive fortifications around an already impressive fortress. Strong stone walls and soaring towers surrounded the site of the new capital of India. Mohammed also made the population of Delhi march south to take up residence in the new

Malta is known as the George Cross Island

city of Daulatabad.

Just three years later, Sultan Mohammed decided that he had not really needed to transfer his capital after all. He moved back to Delhi, taking the city's population with him. Daulatabad was left to fall into ruins.

The impressive remains of the city still stand. The massive walls and towers are long abandoned and overgrown, but they remain as a testimony to the ambitious schemes of Sultan Mohammed ibn Tughluq.

WHICH COUNTRY WAS GIVEN A MEDAL?

During the Second World War the islands of Malta were strategically vital for Britain. They formed an important naval base in the Mediterranean and a useful centre from which to launch attacks on German and Italian forces in North Africa.

It soon became just as important for the Germans and Italians that Malta should be neutralised. Vast formations of bombers took off from bases in Italy and North Africa to pound the docks of Malta. The island was subjected to a terrible siege in which supplies ran short and aerial bombardment became a daily occurrence.

The defences of the islands were almost overwhelmed by the attack, but somehow the island held out. The native Maltese showed incredible courage in the face of this attack. In 1942 King George VI of Britain awarded the island the George Cross, a medal for gallantry.

Today, quieter days have

returned to Malta. The traditional high-stemmed craft are rowed across the waters of the port and the wonderful mediaeval buildings are attracting an increasing number of tourists.

IN WHICH COUNTRY ARE 200 LANGUAGES SPOKEN?

Several countries are made up of nationalities which speak different languages. The boundaries of the African countries were decided by European nations more concerned with economic value than national identity. This has led to some surprising results. Perhaps the most unusual of all is the situation in Zaire.

Zaire has a very short coastline but extends for hundreds of miles inland to include much of the drainage basin of the Congo River. Within this huge area are so many different ethnic groupings that it has been estimated that some 200 languages are spoken in Zaire. Among the various groupings are the well known pygmies. These tribes live deep in the dense forests and rarely have contact with the outside world. Like most of the people of Zaire they live on subsistence agriculture.

WHICH MONASTERY IS CUT OFF BY THE TIDE?

Standing on the north coast of France, the Mont St Michel is perhaps the most famous monastery in the country. It stands on a rocky crag and is surrounded by stout walls, once used for defence.

The top of the hill is crowned by the elegant monastery. The Gothic pinnacles and soaring spire of the church seem to reach into the sky. Yet it is not the beautiful church nor the impressive walls which are the most famous feature of Mont St Michel.

The rock on which the monastery is perched stands in the middle of a vast sand flat. At low tide the sand is exposed as a wide sheet stretching out in several directions. When the tide comes in, the waters rush across the flat sand faster than a horse can gallop. Within a short time the Mont St Michel is surrounded by the sea and boats can sail right up to moor there.

IN WHICH COUNTRY ARE THERE MONASTERIES WHICH STAND ON TOP OF ROCKS?

At the northern end of the Plain of Thessaly, in Greece are some remarkable monastries.

In the 14th century, when the Emperors of Byzantium and Trikala were waging war through Thessaly, a number of monks wished to escape the bloodshed around them. They therefore scaled the towering rocks of Meteora and built hermitages for themselves. These rocks are sheer and rise precipitously for hundreds of feet from the plain.

As the centuries passed the

hermitages expanded and the simple buildings became sizeable and beautiful monasteries. The churches of the communities follow the Byzantine style with heavily decorated interiors. The sight of these buildings perched high on inaccessible crags is impressive and unforgettable. Some of them can now be visited by the public, but other monasteries retain their aloofness and independence.

WHICH KINGDOM IS RICH IN OIL?

After its creation in 1932, the Kingdom of Saudi Arabia was regarded as a poor country. Most of its territory was desert and its population almost entirely made up of nomadic tribesmen.

Within a few years, however, the fortunes of the fledgling kingdom were to change dramatically. A few oilfields were discovered and drilled, but it was after the Second World War that the oil boom really began. Vast wealth poured into Saudi Arabia as the oil was sold to an eager world. Under the autocratic rule of its king, the nation has invested this money in diversifying the economy and also in foreign projects.

Of at least equal importance for the position of Saudi Arabia in the Moslem world is the fact that it includes the city of Mecca. It was in this city that Mohammed was born and Islam was created. It is a sacred duty for Moslems to visit Mecca at least once to pray at the holy places. Its wealth and religious importance guarantees Saudi Arabia a leading role in the world.

WHICH CAPITAL CITY WAS FOUNDED BY A PAIR OF PILLARS?

In 874 the first Vikings came to Iceland. They were led by a man called Ingolfur Arnarson who had been forced to flee Norway. They were looking for somewhere to live.

In those days the Vikings were pagans, and Ingolfur was sure that his gods would show him where to settle. When he saw the bulk of Iceland looming up before him he heaved overboard a pair of pillars carved with the images of pagan gods. He swore that he would settle where the pillars were washed ashore.

When Ingolfur and his people waded ashore there was no sign of the pillars. The people decided to build their homes where they were and settled down to farming. It was several months later that Ingolfur found his pagan pillars in a bay some distance away. True to his vow, Ingolfur gathered his people together and ordered them to abandon their new homes for the site selected by the gods carved on the pillars. They loyally followed Ingolfur and settled in the bay called Reykjavik. Their settlement has since become the capital of Iceland.

WHAT DID PADDY HANNAN FIND?

In 1893 Western Australia experienced a truly exciting time which has never been repeated. It began with a rather small Irishman called Paddy Hannan.

Paddy was a gold prospector and in that year he was searching around the town of Coolgardie. One day, Paddy struck it lucky when he found the fabled Mother Lode. He had discovered a reef of gold ore so large and so rich that the area became called the Golden Mile.

Thousands of men flocked in to seek their fortune. On the gold fields a town sprang up called Kalgoorlie which catered to the needs of the miners. Today, the boom times have gone but Kalgoorlie remains. Some 20,000 people still find a living there, some still in the gold mines, and the town is the largest for many miles around. It is a typical outback town with broad streets, covered pavements and the distinctive architecture found in such towns. Paddy Hannan is still remembered in Kalgoorlie. There is a statue of him and a street and a local beer named in his honour.

WHERE IS THE MOST BEAUTIFUL TOMB IN THE WORLD?

In 1630 the empress Mumtaz Mahal, wife of Shah Jahan, died. Shah Jahan was the Moghul Emperor and ruled over a vast area of northern India. Shah Jahan had loved his wife so much, that he devoted himself to immortalising her memory by building the most beautiful tomb in the world. Many people think he succeeded.

Mumtaz Mahal was buried at Agra and the Taj Mahal raised over her body. The famous structure is mounted on a huge pedestal of marble which covers more than two acres (0.8094 hectares). In the corners of the pedestal rise minarets more than 130 ft (39.6 m) tall.

The main building is polygonal, of white marble in exquisite proportions. Deeply recessed walls are topped by delicate spires and a massive dome which rises to 230 feet (70.1 m) and is topped by a golden point. The purity of line and balance of symmetry and grace make the Taj Mahal the most splendid tomb ever built.

WHO FOUNDED SINGAPORE?

Singapore is one of the busiest and most prosperous ports in the Far East. The success of the port is due to one man, Sir Stanford Raffles. In the early 19th century the British and Dutch were competing for the highly profitable trade routes of the Far East. Raffles was employed by the British East India Company.

In the course of his duties, Raffles came to notice a swampy island called Singapore at the tip of the Malaysian Peninsula. Though it was an unattractive place, Raffles noticed that it stood at the crossroads of the very trade

routes for which Britain and Holland were struggling.

In 1819 he founded a British settlement in Singapore and persuaded the East India Company to buy the island from the Sultan of Johore. The wisdom of this move was not at first apparent. When Raffles died in 1826 the company charged his widow for the expenses of the transaction.

Within a few years, however, Singapore had mushroomed into the large and vitally important port which it remains to this day.

WHERE ARE THE LONELIEST SETTLEMENTS ON EARTH?

There are many isolated villages in the world, but none is as lonely as the scientific bases on the Antarctic continent.

Men have been exploring the far south for centuries, but it is only fairly recently that permanent settlements have been established. Several hundred men and women are living on Antarctica. They are all scientists who are investigating various aspects of the far south. They look into the mineral wealth of Antarctica and the effect of its ice on the climate of the world.

The equipment and all supplies for these scientists have to be shipped in at great cost and effort. The homes they have made are surely the loneliest in the world. The sun does not rise for months at a time, the nearest inhabitants are hundreds of miles away and all the time the freezing wind whips around. Snow and ice never melt here. Whenever the scientists venture beyond their heated homes they have to wrap up in furs and insulated clothing. Yet the benefits gained from the research make all this effort worthwhile.

WHERE IS THE RIALTO BRIDGE?

The Rialto Bridge is one of the most graceful and enchanting bridges in the world. Its gleaming white stonework is one of the familiar landmarks of Venice.

The city of Venice is divided in two by the Grand Canal, the widest of the 150 canals. Until the end of the 16th century the only way to cross the Grand Canal was by boat. Then Antonio da Ponte was employed to build a bridge across the canal. He was given a daunting task. Not only did the bridge have to cross the wide stretch of water, it also had to be high enough to allow a war galley to pass underneath. If the Grand Canal were to be closed to galleys, the defence of Venice would be in jeopardy.

In 1592, after four years of designing and building, Antonio finished the Rialto Bridge. Not only was it practical, but beautiful as well.

WHERE IS SAMARQAND?

The Golden Road to Samarqand became an almost legendary journey during the later Middle Ages. The city was the centre of the fabulous empire of Tamerlaine.

On his wars of conquest and vast plundering expeditions, Tamerlaine looted nations as few had done before him. All this wealth was brought back to Samarqand. Not only that, but the trade routes of central Asia were altered so that merchants had to follow the routes through Samarqand which then became one of the richest and most opulent cities in Asia.

Long after the death of Tamerlaine, Samarqand and the surrounding area fell to the expanding Russian Empire. As part of Uzbekistan, Samarqand is still under Russian control. Its splendid palaces and thriving population are things of the past, but the tomb of Tamerlaine still remains. It is an impressive domed building, covered with mosaics and is entered through a huge arch. There is no longer a golden road to Samarqand, but some vestige of the past remains.

HOW WAS BRYCE CANYON FORMED?

Bryce Canyon lies in Utah and is one of the most truly beautiful natural sights in America. Thousands of pinnacles of red rock stand up from the desert floor. Rank upon rank of these knobbly points stand upright. The intricate shapes and soft colour of the rock points make Bryce Canyon unique.

The Canyon is the result of deep layers of sedimentary rock which formed on the floor of huge ancient lakes. Slowly these rocks were uplifted by tremendous geological forces. As the rocks rose up into a dome they cracked and split in a thousand places. Water seeped into the cracks, eroding the rock and making the gaps wider and deeper. After many thousands of years, we see the maze of intricacy which is Bryce Canyon.

The canyon is named after Ebenezer Bryce, a Mormon on whose farm the canyon once lay. His only known remark about the beauty of Bryce Canyon was to say it was "A hell of a place to lose a cow."

WHO RULES THE VATICAN?

The Vatican, or to give it the full title of Stato della Citta del Vaticano, is the smallest independent state in the world. It is ruled autocratically by the Pope, head of the Roman Catholic Church.

At one time the Pope ruled much of central Italy, but the unification of Italy took most of these lands away. In 1929 Pope Pius XI came to an agreement with Italy which set up the Vatican. Covering little more than a hundred acres, the city state is entirely enclosed by the city of Rome. It has its own money, passports and postage stamps. In fact, the Vatican exists mainly as a convenience for the Pope. By living in and ruling his own country he can be seen to be non-nationalistic. The Pope is not an Italian citizen, but the head of the international Catholic Church. For this reason citizenship of the Vatican is restricted to high ranking clergy and officials who are permanently employed within the Vatican.

On the other hand, the Vatican has open borders to allow the public and worshippers to visit such splendid buildings as St Peter's Basilica and the Sistine Chapel. Not only is the state ruled by the Pope the smallest, but also one of the most impressive countries in the world.

WHAT IS AYERS ROCK?

At the heart of the Australian continent lies the massive bulk of Ayers Rock. It stands in the middle of a vast flat plain, rearing up above the surrounding landscape like some sleeping monster.

The rock has the peculiar quality of being able to change and shift its colour as dawn turns to midday and midday to dusk. As the first rays of day light up the plain, Ayers Rock is a black bulk. When the sun beats down on it, the rock is a harsh orange in a hot desert. Sunset brings beauty to the rock as its colour shifts through the range of the richest reds.

The massive monolith is an outcrop of a rock formation, most of which lies buried beneath the desert. The size of Ayers Rock is its most impressive feature. It is more than 1,000ft (341m) high and five miles (8 km) around its base. Ayers Rock is surely the most arresting sight in all Australia.

Notable Events

WHAT HAPPENED WHEN JESUS STOOD BEFORE PILATE?

One of the most momentous meetings in the history of Christianity was that between Jesus and Pontius Pilate, the Roman Governor of Judea.

Because Jesus' teachings angered the Jewish priests, they had arrested him and falsely accused him of blasphemy. The penalty for this was death, but because the priests did not have the authority to execute anyone, they took Jesus to Pilate. They told Pilate that Jesus was a trouble-maker and claimed to be King of the Jews.

If Jesus had claimed to be King, he would be guilty of subverting the authority of Rome.

"Are you the King of the Jews?" Pilate asked Jesus.

"You have said that, not I," replied Jesus. But Pilate repeated the question so Jesus said: "My kingdom is not of this world. If it were, I would have men to fight for me and I would not be in the hands of the Jews."

Pilate was impressed by Jesus.

He realised that Jesus had done nothing wrong, but he had aroused the hatred of the priests. According to the law Pilate could release one prisoner on the feast of Passover, which was then in progress. He therefore told the Jews that he would release Jesus. But the Jews demanded that he release Barabbas, a well-known bandit.

Pilate knew that he could now do nothing to stop the execution of Jesus without breaking the law. He therefore gave the orders for the crucifixion. Pilate then ritually washed his hands of the affair and sadly watched Jesus led away to his death.

WHO CROSSED THE RUBICON?

The Rubicon is a small, insignificant stream in northern Italy. Two thousand years ago, however, it marked the border between the Roman province of Cisalpine Gaul and Italy proper. As such it was a vitally important boundary.

In 49 BC the Roman Republic was in crisis. The Republican gov-

308

Jesus stood before Pontius Pilate, the Roman Governor of Judea

ernment had become corrupt and inefficient. Power rested with successful generals and powerful politicians. One such man was Julius Caesar. He had led a brilliant political career and had conquered many barbarian tribes. In the year 49 BC, Caesar was governor of Cisalpine Gaul.

His success had made many other Romans jealous. Led by Pompey and a group of senators, they decided to destroy Caesar. Their main problem was that as governor of Gaul, Caesar was in command of many troops. It was decided to strip Caesar of his command.

In order to stop them doing this, Caesar decided to march his troops on Rome. For some time he hesitated north of the Rubicon River. Once he took his troops over the river and out of his province there could be no turning back.

On the night of January 10, Caesar led his troops over the Rubicon. In the civil war which followed, Caesar defeated his enemies.

WHEN DID COLUMBUS DISCOVER AMERICA?

In the 15th century nobody in Europe knew that America existed. The hazy Viking sagas which told of land to the west were dismissed as legend.

Many scientists, however, did realise that the Earth was round. It occurred to several seamen that if they could sail westwards far enough, they would reach China. This would enable them to trade with that fabulous country.

One man attracted by the prospects of trade with the East was Christopher Columbus. This Genoese sailor was a magnificent seaman and navigator. He studied winds and geography. This led him to believe he could reach China in only a few weeks if he sailed west.

Columbus persuaded King Ferdinand and Queen Isabella of Spain to give him enough ships and money to make the voyage. He set sail on August 3, 1492. After a few weeks it seemed as though Columbus's calculations were wrong. No land was in sight and the crew began to get restive. They wanted to go home.

Columbus still believed he was right and talked the crew into continuing for a few more days. Finally on October 12, land was sighted. Columbus was thrilled, he thought he had reached China.

The land Columbus had found, however, was not China, but a continent we today call America.

WHEN WAS A KING OF BRITAIN EXECUTED?

Charles I was King of Great Britain during the Civil War of the 17th century. Charles believed that he had a God-given right to rule as he wished. Parliament believed that they should be consulted on all important issues.

Eventually the defiant government of King Charles combined with various religious, social and political issues to bring about civil war. Charles and Parliament both hastily raised armies and tried to force their will on the other.

After three years of fighting, Charles was defeated and imprisoned. Meanwhile, Parliament and its army had fallen out. The army, led by Oliver Cromwell, demanded their pay and a more extreme form of religion and government.

When Charles was discovered to be plotting another Royalist uprising, Cromwell decided that there was only one way to deal with the King. A trial was organised at which Charles was charged with crimes against the realm and people of England. It was a momentous event. For the first time a clear difference was drawn between the sovereign and the state.

Charles refused to recognise the difference and took no part in the trial. He was, nonetheless, found guilty by the packed Court. On January 30, 1649 Charles died on the scaffold. Government by Parliament was to prove unpopular and in 1660 the eldest son of Charles I became king as Charles II.

WHEN DID THE INCA EMPIRE FALL?

The Inca Empire was a magnificent civilisation in South America. In the 15th century the Inca tribe conquered or absorbed all the civilised tribes of the Andes.

They were ruled by a god-emperor called the Inca. Under his government the people lived an ordered agricultural life among the mountains. The gold and silver owned by the empire was almost beyond belief.

Then a terrible new disease, smallpox, arrived from the north which killed the Inca and many of his people. It had been introduced by Europeans into Mexico and had now reached South America. Civil war at once broke out between rival Incas.

When the unscrupulous adventurer Francisco Pizarro arrived in 1532, the civil war had been won by Atahualpa. But the Inca Empire was in turmoil. The Spaniard took advantage of this treacherously to murder Atahualpa and pillage the empire of gold. By 1540 the Inca Empire had been destroyed.

WHEN DID DINOSAURS BECOME EXTINCT?

The giant reptiles known as dinosaurs lived many millions of years ago. and were the largest land animals ever to exist.

We only know of their existence through fossils preserved in the rock. It it difficult, therefore, to be very precise about them. Even scientists disagree with each other about many questions concerning the dinosaurs. It is known that they died out at the end of the Cretaceous period, which began about 136 million years ago and lasted for some 72 million years. We can, therefore, say that dinosaurs became extinct about 64 million years ago.

WHEN DID CAESAR RAID BRITAIN?

After defeating the Celtic tribes of Gaul, Julius Caesar decided to raid Britain. There were several reasons for this. One was that the Celtic warriors of Britain had fought against him in Gaul. Another was that he wanted to gain more glory for himself and his men.

Caesar gathered together an army, and a fleet to transport it, and in 55 BC landed in Britain. A combination of fierce Celtic resistance and bad weather forced the Romans to withdraw.

The next year, 54 BC, Julius Caesar tried again. This time he had 5 legions, 2,000 cavalry and a fleet of 800 ships. Caesar won several victories and imposed a tribute on the tribes of south eastern Britain. Despite this, he was again forced to retreat to the continent. It was nearly a hundred years before the Romans came to Britain again.

WHAT HAPPENED AT THE DUCHESS OF RICHMOND'S BALL?

On the evening of June 15, 1815, the Duchess of Richmond threw a magnificent ball in Brussels. All the important people of the city were invited. The most honoured guest was the Duke of Wellington, commander of the British army.

Officers in British uniforms made up the bulk of the male guests. But as they and their ladies graced the dance floor, terrible news was on its way.

The British army was in Brussels because Napoleon, Emperor of the French, was expected to invade Belgium in July. As the dancers whirled, the Duke of Wellington received a message. It stated that Napoleon had invaded and was at that moment marching on Brussels.

The Duke remained calm. He knew that a sudden end to the ball would cause a panic amongst the civilians. Orders were issued quietly and discreetly. Whispers ran around the ball room. First the officers of one regiment made their excuses and slipped away. Then those of a second regiment departed. Still the ball went on, though there were gradually fewer and fewer dancers.

Soon after midnight the Duke himself slipped off to inspect a map. The officers were marching off with their men to face the French in battle. Three days later many of them would die on the field of Waterloo. Because the Duke of Wellington had not interrupted the Duchess of Richmond's glittering ball, there was no panic and the officers had enjoyed a magnificent send-off.

Whispers ran around
the ballroom

WHAT WAS THE COLD WAR?

The Cold War was a phrase coined to describe the tension and rivalry existing between the communist East and democratic West.

After the defeat of Germany and Japan in 1945 the Allies met to agree on the future. They agreed about practically nothing. Communist governments were imposed on Eastern Europe while the West tried to rebuild shattered economies and hold back the tide of communism.

The rising tension was called the Cold War to distinguish it from a "hot war" when hostilities actually break out. In the years following, many crises and issues brought the Cold War to new heights. At times it seemed as if a "hot war" would start. The tension of the Cold War has lessened in recent years, but the mutal suspicion and hostility between East and West seems never ending.

WHEN DID FARMING BEGIN?

For hundreds of thousands of years early man lived a hunter-gatherer life. This means that he found his food by hunting wild animals and collecting wild plants. The invention of farming changed human life forever.

People who live off the wild have to move around and live in fairly small groups. Farming allows people to stay in one place, enabling them to build houses, develop a technology and organise themselves into societies. In short, farming allowed man to become civilised.

This step was first taken in the Near East. The people in the region slowly began to plant certain plants near their homes. These included grains such as wheat and barley. They also began to herd animals such as goats and sheep as a source of meat. This process took time but it is thought to have been completed by 10,000 BC.

WHAT WAS THE CONGRESS OF VIENNA?

Between 1793 and 1815 the French Revolutionary and Napoleonic wars raged across Europe. Many small duchies and other states were swept away in the tide of war. France imposed new boundaries and governments on many other countries. Eventually France was defeated, but Europe was in confusion.

Many people wanted to return to life as it had been before the wars started. Other people liked the new order of things. Still more wanted to change things again.

The great statesmen and rulers of Europe met at Vienna to decide what to do. They had to consider the interests of various nations, the wishes of the victors in the war and the future of Europe. Over a period of many months such men as Talleyrand, Wellington, and Tsar Alexander I worked out a settlement. The final result may not have been ideal, but it kept Europe at peace for several decades.

WHAT WAS THE BIGGEST KNOWN EXPLOSION?

On the morning of August 27, 1883, a low rumble was heard echoing off the hills in southern Australia. In northern Australia the low rumble was heard as a roar. On the islands further north the terrific noise was followed by a massive wave which swept away 300 villages and killed 36,000 people. The island of Krakatoa had blown up.

Krakatoa was a volcanic island lying between Java and Sumatra. Two thirds of the island disappeared in one explosive moment.

The violent blast set up huge waves which swamped neighbouring islands and travelled halfway round the globe. The air waves set up circled Earth seven times before settling down. The dust thrust into the upper atmosphere affected the weather for months and provided some of the most beautiful sunsets ever seen.

WHEN DID MARCO POLO COME HOME?

In 1295 three strange men arrived in Venice. They were dressed in outlandish Eastern clothes. Astoundingly they claimed to be the Polo family which had vanished twenty four years earlier on a trading journey.

It was only with great difficulty the men persuaded their friends that they were Maffeo, Nicolo and Marco Polo.

They told wonderful stories about their travels and Marco later dictated these to be written down. The 13th century people did not travel much. Europeans had not visited Eastern Asia. The Polos had set out in 1271, when Marco was 15, to visit the court of the Great Khan.

They had travelled through the countries now known as Israel, Lebanon, Turkey, Iran, Afghanistan, Tibet, Russia and Mongolia to reach the Khan's court in China. They stayed there for several years as officials of the Khan. After many years spent in China and surrounding countries, the Polos persuaded the Khan to allow them to go home.

When the people in Europe read Marco Polo's book they were not sure whether to believe him. Nobody had been to China before and Marco Polo told so many strange stories that people thought he was lying. We now know Marco Polo told the truth. His homecoming was a momentous event as it gave Europe its first glimpse of the Far East.

WHO GAVE THE GETTYSBURG ADDRESS?

The Gettysburg Address is probably the most famous speech in American history. It was short — less than five minutes, yet it has become a classic.

It was delivered by the President, Abraham Lincoln, on November 19, 1863, while the country

**Scott and his companions were disappointed
to find Amundsen's flag there**

was fighting a savage civil war. He spoke at the dedication of a national cemetery for those who had died at the Battle of Gettysburg a few months earlier.

In it, Lincoln spoke of the gallant dead and the hopeful future. Though the war was continuing, Lincoln looked forward to the future of the nation and to the determination that "government of the people, by the people, for the people, shall not perish from the earth."

WHO WAS THE FIRST MAN AT THE SOUTH POLE?

At the beginning of this century the South Pole was one of the few unexplored places on Earth.

Two men were determined to be the first to reach it. Roald Amundsen, a Norwegian explorer who had earlier discovered the NorthWest Passage, and Captain R F Scott, the British hero of polar exploration. In 1910 both men set out on scientific expeditions to the Antarctic.

The Norwegian arrived at the Pole first, on December 14. A month later Scott arrived and was bitterly disappointed to find Amundsen's flag there. Heavy-hearted, Scott and his British team began the long trek back to base. The weather closed in on them. Blizzards swept Antarctica and slowed the team down. Despite great heroism, Scott and his team perished on the return journey.

Amundsen, meanwhile, had returned to his base and went on to lead further explorations before his disappearance in the Arctic in 1928.

WHAT HAPPENED AT DUNKIRK IN MAY 1940?
On May 13, 1940, Hitler unleashed a terrific attack in northern France. Tanks and troops swept through the Ardennes. Within a fortnight nearly half a million British and French troops were cut off in northern France.

Dunkirk, their only hope, was the one port still available from which troops could be evacuated by the Royal Navy. It was expected that some 10,000 men could be rescued. The rest would have to surrender.

The indefatigable airmen of the Royal Air Force flew continuously over the port to keep the German air force away from the army — a sitting target for bombers. A combination of low cloud and tenacious fighting by Spitfire and Hurricane pilots kept the Germans away from the beaches of Dunkirk.

On May 27, the evacuation began. Destroyers moved in to collect men from the docks. Thousands of men were waiting on the beaches. The big ships could not move in. Smallboat owners from all over southern England set out for Dunkirk. Pleasure cruisers and fishing smacks appeared off the beaches. Though many were sunk the civilians kept ferrying men from the beaches to the ships under a hail of fire.

Eventually, on June 4, the operation was called off. Instead of 10,000 troops, 340,000 were saved at Dunkirk. Though in effect a defeat, the operation returned to Britain enough trained soldiers to stay in the war.

WHO LED THE MUTINY ON THE BOUNTY?
The *Bounty* was a Royal Navy ship which, in 1787, was sent to collect breadfruit trees from Tahiti for planting in the West Indies.

The ship was commanded by Captain Bligh. Despite his superb skill as a seaman, Bligh was a difficult man. He would fly into terrible rages and morose sulks. After a long and arduous voyage the ship arrived at Tahiti where the crew found peace and plenty. They were reluctant to sail away for the West Indies.

They had not gone far from Tahiti when an officer called Fletcher Christian led a mutiny. Most of the crew, who wanted to return to Tahiti rather than face another tough voyage with Bligh, followed him. Bligh and 18 men were set adrift in an open boat. It is a testimony to Bligh that he navigated the small boat across thousands of miles of sea to reach the Indonesian island, Timor.

Christian later led some mutineers to Pitcairn Island where they lived with their Tahitian women for many years. Their descendants still live there. Other mutineers stayed on Tahiti and were later caught, taken back to England and hanged.

WHO DISCOVERED PENICILLIN?

Penicillin is one of the most important drugs to be discovered this century. It can destroy many different types of infection, without harming the patient. Yet its discovery was almost an accident.

The Scottish scientist Sir Alexander Fleming was experimenting with bacteria in 1928. One day he did not properly clear up an experiment. Next day he noticed a piece of mould growing on the plate. Many other scientists would have washed up and carried on with the experiment. Fleming, however, noticed that the mould had killed the bacteria.

The strange mould was *Penicillium notatum*. It was found that the mould was producing a chemical, now called penicillin, which killed bacteria. After many years a method of extracting the chemical from the mould was found. Penicillin went on to the market and has saved countless lives.

WHAT WAS THE BARBARIAN CONSPIRACY?

The barbarians who lived outside the borders of the Roman Empire often launched raids on Roman territory. These came to nothing but in 367 BC a quite different attack took place.

In the summer of that year the barbarians of the north formed an alliance. The savage Picts launched themselves against Hadrian's Wall. Many forts were overrun and their garrisons put to the sword. The Roman military commander of Britain was surrounded and cut off. At the same time Irish raiders sailed across the Irish sea to plunder the west coast of Britain. Even more serious was the series of attacks launched by the Franks and Saxons in the Channel and North Sea. They eliminated the Roman fleet.

Within a short time, Roman military control in Britain and northern Gaul had been destroyed. The various bands of barbarians could now roam at will through the countryside. They pillaged villages, robbed temples and carried people off as slaves.

It took nearly two years to push the barbarians back and restore peace. The Barbarian Conspiracy of 367 BC was a major blow to the Roman Empire.

WHAT WAS THE CUBAN MISSILE CRISIS?

In 1959 the communist leader Fidel Castro took power in Cuba. He soon became a close ally of Russia, which was awkward for America as Cuba lies just 130 miles from Florida.

In 1962 the Russian leader, Krushchev, began building nuclear missile bases on Cuba. President Kennedy of America imposed a blockade on Cuba in October to stop the Russians delivering the missiles. As Russian ships carrying the missiles continued to head for Cuba it appeared that war between the super powers was inevitable. Right at the last minute, Krushchev ordered the ships to stop. It was the closest Russia and America have ever come to open warfare.

WHEN DID THE HOLY CITY OF JERUSALEM FALL TO THE CHRISTIANS?

During the Middle Ages, devout Christians would journey to Jerusalem to visit the Holy Places. Though the city was held by Moslems, from the 7th century the pilgrims were allowed to travel freely.

In the 11th century a new dynasty of Moslem Turks came to power and everything changed. Christian pilgrims were murdered or seized and sold into slavery. Jerusalem was closed to Christians. In 1095 Pope Urban II preached a crusade. He declared it was the sacred duty of all Christian warriors to win Jerusalem from the Turks so that pilgrims could journey in peace.

Four armies of Christians set out for the Holy Land. Led by nobles trained to fight, the Christians took the Turks by surprise. It had never occurred to them they would have to face an army from Europe.

Throwing themselves forward with religious fervour the Christians fought battle after battle and threw the Turks back. Finally, in 1099, the Christians stood before Jerusalem. After a hard-fought siege the Christians stormed into Jerusalem on July 15. Fired with religious indignation and maddened by the savage fighting, the Christians killed almost the entire Moslem population. Jerusalem was once again temporarily safe for Christian pilgrims.

WHO BURNED PERSEPOLIS?

Persepolis was the capital of the Persian Empire and the richest city in the world. Under rulers who called themselves King of Kings, Persepolis became a magnificent city filled with palaces and temples.

In 334 BC King Alexander of Macedonia invaded the Persian Empire with a small army. King of Kings Darius III set out from Persepolis to crush the invader. At the Battle of Issus, he was heavily defeated. Raising a fresh army which included hundreds of chariots,

Darius attacked again. Again he was defeated and later murdered by his own men.

Alexander swooped on Persepolis. Here he seized the royal treasury of Persia. The gold and jewels he found were almost beyond belief. In the midst of the feasting, Persepolis caught fire. In the blaze, most of the royal palace was destroyed.

Alexander moved on to fresh conquests leaving the ruins of Persepolis, which can still be seen.

WHEN DID MAN EVOLVE?

Finding a date when mankind evolved from more primitive ancestors depends very much on finding fossil evidence. So far our best fossil evidence comes from Africa.

This shows that the species of mankind known as *Homo erectus* evolved something more than a million years ago. Fossil fragments dating from earlier in time may indicate an earlier date, but this is far from certain.

WHAT WAS THE GREAT SCHISM?

For centuries the Pope was the undisputed leader of Christianity in western Europe. All kings, nobles and commoners acknowledged his superiority in spiritual matters, though they occasionally disputed his power in temporal concerns.

In 1378 Pope Gregory XI died and a conclave met to elect the next pope. Under pressure from the Romans, the cardinals chose Urban VI. Urban conducted himself in an obstinate, proud and unreasonable way.

The majority of the cardinals fled Rome and met at Anagni. Here they declared the conclave's choice invalid because it was made under pressure. They held a second conclave and elected Clement VII. Now two men were claiming to be pope. The legal technicalities were complex and Europe was torn between the two.

The dispute was not decided until 1417 when both men were dead. The period of two popes is referred to as the Great Schism, schism meaning a division. It caused harm to the papal institution which at that time lost the respect of many Christians.

WHEN WAS THE RUSSIAN REVOLUTION?

The present Communist government of Russia was brought to power in a violent revolution. The revolution, long fermenting, was caused by the suffering endured in the First World War.

For many years the inefficiency and despotism of the government of the Tsar had been very unpopular. When the war caused thousands of deaths at the front, and shortages and hardships at home, opposition to the Tsar's rule grew.

On July 14, 1789, the mob gathered at the Bastille

In March 1917, the Tsar Nicholas II was forced to abdicate and a liberal government came to power. Many reforms were passed, but not enough for the Communists. In October, the Communists launched their own revolution. They grabbed power, murdered the entire Imperial family and imposed Communism on the country.

WHO STORMED THE BASTILLE?

The Bastille was a royal fortress in Paris. By the end of the 18th century it was used as a prison and arms store. It also symbolised the authority of the king in Paris.

In May 1789, King Louis XVI was forced to call a parliament. The Third Estate, representing the commoners, broke away and declared themselves a National Assembly intent upon reforming the corrupt, inefficient and bankrupt government.

In the excitement which followed, the king began to call his troops towards Paris. The mob in Paris was in an angry mood. They had tasted freedom. On July 14, the mob gathered at the Bastille.

They wanted freedom for the prisoners and large quantities of arms. Governor de Launay refused their demands and opened fire.

Reinforced by rebellious soldiers the mob blasted a hole in the Bastille gates with cannon fire. Surging forward, the mob killed de Launay and took over the Bastille. The symbol of royal authority had been captured by the mob. It was the signal for widespread uprisings everywhere in France. The French Revolution had begun.

WHEN DID GUTENBERG PRINT HIS BIBLE?

Johann Gutenberg is, in the opinion of many people, the most important man in the history of learning. He invented printing with moveable type.

This process enabled vast numbers of books to be printed far more cheaply than they could be copied by hand. At last knowledge could be spread quickly and cheaply to everyone. It seemed only right that the first book Gutenberg should print was The Bible.

In 1454 Gutenberg produced a Bible by printing from wooden blocks. He soon realised that the process of carving wooden blocks was very expensive so tried to find an alternative. His solution was to make letters out of copper. These were cheaper and more durable than wooden blocks. Furthermore, the page could be broken down into its constituent letters and these used to make up the next page. It was a revolution. By the end of the century more than 200 cities had printing presses turning out thousands of books.

WHO WERE THE FIRST MEN ON THE ROOF OF THE WORLD?

When it was discovered that Mount Everest, in the Himalayas, was the tallest mountain on Earth, men have wanted to climb it.

Many expeditions tried, but all had failed until 1953. In that year the two great British organisations, the Alpine Club and the Royal Geographical Society joined forces to organise an expedition to conquer Everest. Equipped with the most up-to-date climbing apparatus, the expedition set out.

On May 29, the New Zealander, Edmund Hillary, and the Sherpa, Tenzing Norgay, reached the summit of Mount Everest. At last men were standing on "the Roof of the World".

WHO CLIMBED THE EIGER IN WINTER?

Men and women have always pitted themselves against tremendous challenges. One of the greatest of these was faced by Anton Mannhardt, Anton Kinshofer, Walter Almberger and Toni Hiebeler in March 1961. They were determined to climb the north face of the Eiger in winter. Nobody had

ever done it before.

For four days they toiled upwards in bitter weather. Each
night they dug holes in the snow
and slept in them. On the fifth day
they scaled the dreaded "White
Spider", a wall of ice. It took all
day to complete the agonisingly
slow and dangerous section. After
what seemed an age, Hiebeler
reached the top and helped his
companions up. Next day they
reached the summit. They went
down by a relatively easy route to
be surrounded by eager admirers.
They had completed a climb many
felt to be impossible.

**For four days the climbers toiled
upwards in bitter weather**

WHO SHOUTED: "EUREKA" AND WHY?

In the middle of the 3rd century BC King Hiero of Syracuse gave a jeweller some gold to make a crown. This the jeweller did, but Hiero suspected the jeweller of cheating him by mixing base metal with the gold. He handed the problem over to the local scientist Archimedes.

The problem centred around finding the density of the crown. If its density was not that of gold, the jeweller had cheated. Archimedes puzzled over the crown. How could he measure its density?

Then one day, he noticed that when getting into his bath the water level rose. In a flash of inspiration he had the answer. Archimedes was so excited that he leapt out of his bath and ran down the street naked shouting "Eureka", which means "I have found it."

Archimedes realised that if the crown was pure gold it would displace the same volume of water as an equal weight of gold. He performed the experiment and found the jeweller had, in fact, cheated.

WHAT WAS THE GUNPOWDER PLOT?

In 1605 a group of fanatics planned to kill the new Scottish King James I of Great Britain. They decided to blow up the Houses of Parliament when James and all the nobles would be there for the opening.

Led by Robert Catesby, the plotters secretly stored a vast amount of gunpowder under the building. Guy Fawkes, another conspirator, was placed in charge of the gunpowder. A third plotter warned his relative Lord Monteagle not to attend Parliament. Monteagle told the authorities and a quick search of Parliament, on November 5, revealed Fawkes and the gunpowder.

The conspirators were arrested and executed. Ever since, the celebration of Guy Fawkes Night with bonfires and fireworks has been an annual festival.

WHO DISCOVERED INOCULATION?

For years the disease smallpox was a killer. Many children died of it in infancy. Among several old wives' tales relating to the disease was one which stated that anyone who caught the relatively harmless cowpox would not catch smallpox.

An English country doctor, Edward Jenner, studied the problem. He soon realised that many people who had cowpox were immune to smallpox. He decided to find out if this was a medical fact.

In a risky and dramatic experiment, Jenner deliberately infected a small boy with cowpox. When the boy had recovered from this mild illness, Jenner infected him with the deadly smallpox. The boy did not catch the disease. He was immune. This process of acquired immunity, known as inoculation, spread rapidly and saved many lives. Today, inoculation can give immunity to many diseases.

WHEN WERE THE PYRAMIDS BUILT?

The pyramids of Egypt are amongst the most impressive monuments of the ancient world. The largest are the three pyramids at Giza. The Great Pyramid of Cheops measures 755 ft (230 m) along each side and stands 481 ft (147 m) high. It has been estimated that it must contain 2,300,000 blocks of stone.

As were other pyramids, the Great Pyramid was built as a tomb for one of the god-kings (Pharaohs) of ancient Egypt. The pyramids were built during the Old Kingdom and date back more than 4,500 years.

WHO WROTE THE DECLARATION OF INDEPENDENCE?

The American Declaration of Independence is one of the most important documents in history. In it the representatives of the 13 original states set out their grievances against Britain. They also state the principle upon which they believe a government should be founded. This great document which begins: "We hold these truths to be self evident, that all men are created equal," was written in the summer of 1776 by Thomas Jefferson.

WHO SANK THE *LUSITANIA*?

Early in the First World War, Germany declared unrestricted U-boat warfare. This meant that if a U-boat, a German submarine, found an enemy ship or a ship supplying the enemy, it would open fire without warning. The British and the French, who were on the receiving end of this policy, protested bitterly but to no effect.

On May 7, 1915, a German U-boat sighted the passenger liner *Lusitania*. The German torpedoed the ship without warning. More than 1,100 people were drowned, 128 of them American. The international outcry which this atrocity raised forced Germany to reconsider her unrestricted U-boat warfare.

WHEN WAS THE IMPRESSIONIST EXHIBITION?

In 1874 a startling new art exhibition of paintings opened in Paris. It was held in the studio of a photographer. Many people ridiculed the paintings. They called the pictures "impressions". The style of art was thereafter called Impressionism.

The Impressionist painters, led by Manet, Monet, Renoir and Degas, emphasised the importance of natural light and soft colours. The style proved to be one of the most dynamic of the 19th century and is now recognised as one of the most charming of all time. Paintings once ridiculed are now worth fortunes.

WHAT WAS THE GLENCOE MASSACRE?

In 1691 the Highland chiefs of the Scottish clans were ordered to take an oath of allegiance to King William and Queen Mary. The chief of the Macdonalds of Glencoe was accidentally late. His enemies used this as an excuse to seek revenge.

The Master of Stair managed to obtain a government order condemning the Macdonalds. He then sent soldiers of the Campbell clan to stay with the Macdonalds. On February 13, the Campbells were ordered to murder their hosts. Ancient clan hatreds came to the fore and the Campbells went about their grim work with a will.

Thirty-eight Macdonalds were killed, but the rest escaped to tell the tale. When it was learnt that the massacre was carried out under government orders there was an outcry which had repercussions throughout government.

WHO DISCOVERED BOTANY BAY?

European ships trading with the Spice Islands in the 18th century, were sometimes blown off course. They reported seeing land far to the south. It was decided to explore this new country.

The greatest of the explorers sent out to map and investigate the Great Southern Land was Captain James Cook. Cook was born in Yorkshire, the son of a Scottish farm worker, but he quickly took to an adventurous sea life.

So good was Cook's navigational ability that in 1768, he was chosen to lead an expedition to the South Seas. In his ship, the *Endeavour*, Cook mapped the coasts of New Zealand so accurately that nobody improved on his charts for generations. He then sailed westward to find the mysterious Great Southern Land.

He made landfall in the far south eastern corner of Australia. Turning northward, Cook found Botany Bay on April 29, 1770. The bay was given this name because of the incredible variety of wildlife found there. After claiming the whole east coast of Australia for Britain, Cook returned home. The British government would later select Botany Bay as the site for its first colony in Australia.

WHEN DID MAN LAND ON THE MOON?

From the moment that the first object was launched into space, there was a desire to land a man on the moon.

At first such an achievement seemed impossible. But the American government recruited the best scientists it could find and poured money into the venture. Finally, a Saturn 5 rocket took off from Cape Kennedy. On board were three astronauts, Neil Armstrong, Edwin (Buzz) Aldrin and Michael Collins.

The lunar landing module separated from the parent craft.

A small boy broke the terrible news to the king

Slowly the module came down to land on the moon. A few hours after landing on the surface of the moon on July 20, 1969, Neil Armstrong stepped from the module declaring the historic words: "That's one small step for man, one giant leap for mankind".

WHAT COULD ONLY A CHILD TELL KING HENRY I OF ENGLAND?

On the evening of November 25, 1120, William, the beloved son of King Henry I of England, and his friends set out in a ship called *The White Ship* from Normandy. They were sailing to disaster.

William, his friends, and the whole crew were roaring drunk when they set sail. Hardly had the ship left port when it struck a rock. The ship quickly began to go down. William escaped in a boat, but when he heard his sister calling for help he turned around. In the resulting confusion, William's boat sank and the heir to the throne of England was drowned.

When the courtiers of King Henry heard the news they were scared. They all knew that the king loved his son and also how dangerous Henry could be when angry. Nobody dared tell him. After a day of indecision, the frightened counsellors compelled a small boy to go to the king and break the terrible news. Henry never recovered from the shock. It is said he never smiled again.

WHEN DID THE FIRST RAILWAY OPEN?

Although the first steam-powered railway had actually run in 1804, it was a private concern hauling industrial loads at an ironworks in Wales. The first railway to open for public use was the Stockton and Darlington Railway in North East England. It carried goods and passengers between the towns of Stockton and Darlington. The railway was opened in 1825 and its trains were pulled by horse for some time before steam engines were introduced.

WHAT WAS THE SEARCH FOR FAWCETT?

In the early 1900s, Percy Fawcett was the most famous explorer of South America. He was an Englishman who first went to South America to survey a disputed boundary between Bolivia and Brazil. His first expedition took place in 1906 and he plunged fearlessly into the rain forest. For months Fawcett hacked his way through the insect-infested territory. Despite the hardship, Percy Fawcett loved it. During the following years, Fawcett led many parties into the forest.

In 1925, Fawcett became intrigued by some ruins in an area called the Mato Grosso. Indians told him that even larger ruins were to be found further into the rainy forest. On April 20, Fawcett set off with his son Jack to find the ruins. Fawcett sent one letter back a month later, but after that nothing was ever heard of him.

The search for Fawcett became a famous cause in Europe. Expeditions were sent out and though they contacted Indians who had seen Fawcett, none knew what had happened to him. The great explorer had vanished.

WHEN WAS THE SAN FRANCISCO EARTHQUAKE?

San Francisco in California lies on the San Andreas Fault. This fault is a massive split in the Earth's crust. The North American Continent is slowly moving in one direction, but the floor of the Pacific Ocean is moving in another.

Often the two grind peacefully past each other. Occasionally, however, the two plates will "jump" a few feet. This sets up massive shock waves in the rocks which cause an earthquake. The greatest earthquake in San Francisco's history occurred on April 18, 1906. Almost the entire city was destroyed and hundreds of people were killed.

The west coast of America has often been rocked by tremors and the possibility of another earthquake as great as the San Francisco tragedy keeps the scientists on constant alert.

WHAT WAS THE BERLIN AIRLIFT?

After the Allies failed to reach agreement following the Second World War, they followed their own policies.

Russia occupied most of Eastern Europe. In the heart of their occupied territory was the German capital, Berlin, part of which was occupied by the Western Allies. Russia ordered the West to leave. When they refused, Russia cut off all road and rail links between Berlin and tried to starve the city into surrender.

The Royal Air Force and the American Air Force at once began to fly supplies into the city. For months the city seemed on the edge of surrender, but the determination of its inhabitants and the massive Berlin Airlift prevailed. In May 1949, the Russians had to accept defeat. West Berlin remained free of Communist control.

WHO WAS THE FIRST FRENCH EMPEROR?

Today France is a republic. This means that it does not have a monarch reigning over it. The head of state is a president who is elected by the people.

This has not always been so. For hundreds of years France was ruled by kings and queens. Then, in 1793, King Louis XVI was executed and France became a republic. Republican government soon proved useless in the circumstances of international warfare and civil disorder in which France found herself. In 1799 power became concentrated in the capable hands of an army general called Napoleon Bonaparte. On December 2, 1804, Napoleon crowned himself Emperor of the French, in the presence of the Pope at Notre Dame Cathedral, Paris.

WHO FOUND A NEW TRADE ROUTE TO INDIA IN 1498?

When the Moslem Turks captured Constantinople in 1453, Europe's trade links with the East were broken. This had been a valuable trade. Another route had to be found.

The Portuguese had, for some time, been exploring the west coast of Africa. In 1497, King Emanuel ordered one of his gentlemen, Vasco da Gama, to command a fleet of four ships. Da Gama was ordered to try to find a route to India round the south of Africa.

He sailed south, rounded the Cape of Good Hope and turned northwards. Da Gama was surprised to find a flourishing Arab trading economy on the east

African coast. He was almost as surprised as the Arabs were to see a European ship. Finally, despite mutinies and fights with the Arabs, Da Gama reached the port of Calicut on the coast of India. His voyage had opened a fresh route to the East.

WHAT IS KNOWN IN AUSTRALIA AS THE FIRST FLEET?

When Captain Cook returned with his reports of the land now called Australia, the British government decided to set up a colony there.

They selected convicts as the best people for populating the colony. So in 1788, Captain Arthur Phillip set sail with a fleet of ships containing convicts and soldiers, to settle in Botany Bay.

When he reached Botany Bay, Phillip decided it was not a good place to found a colony. Instead, he moved his ships a few miles north to an inlet called Port Jackson. Here he built houses and set the men to work farming the land. Soon many more ships arrived with convicts and free settlers and the colony flourished. The fleet commanded by Phillip is still remembered by Australians as the First Fleet and is honoured as the start of their nation.

WHEN DID BEATLEMANIA BEGIN?

The most successful pop group of all time was the Beatles. The four Liverpudlians had been perform-

ing for some time locally before they got together. After topping local charts, the Beatles launched their first record, *Love Me Do*, in October 1962. A second record *Please Please Me* shot to the top of the charts.

The staggering surprise of the Beatles was not their sales, but the effect they had on people. Beatlemania, as it became known, first struck at a concert in London. Police had great trouble controlling the hundreds of screaming fans and had to call for reinforcements.

Country after country fell to the appeal of Beatlemania which heralded the social revolutions of the 60s. Though the heady days of Beatlemania are gone and the Beatles have split up, their songs are still popular.

WHEN WAS THE HEGIRA?

The founder of Islam was an Arab called Mahomet. After a vision, Mahomet formulated the religion which was to carry the Arabs on their career of great conquerors and which endures to this day.

Mahomet was born in the Arabian city of Mecca in AD 570 as the son of a merchant. He turned his back on trading and luxury and took to meditation. Then came Mahomet's vision. Filled with fervour for god, Allah, Mahomet preached in the streets of Mecca.

By 622, the ruling classes of Mecca felt that Mahomet was something of a nuisance and for-

Samuel Pepys was an eye witness to the Great Fire of London

ced him to flee. This flight from the holy city was called the Hegira. The Moslem calendar takes this event as the start of year one. By his death in 632 Mahomet had not only returned to Mecca, but had seen his new religion take over all Arabia.

WHEN WAS THE GREAT FIRE OF LONDON?

The Great Fire of London devastated the city and burned for four days in 1666 before it could be put out. The blaze broke out early on the morning of September 2 in a baker's shop in Pudding Lane, London. In minutes the shop had burnt down and the fire quickly spread to nearby buildings. The houses in London at the time were built of wood, so they caught fire easily. By the end of the day the flames had spread across the city.

Samuel Pepys, an important government official of the day, was keeping a diary. He describes visiting Bankside and seeing "up the hill of the City a most horrid malicious bloody flame" licking around the buildings.

The king, Charles II, assisted in the fight to stem the fire. In desperation, houses were blown up to starve the fire of fresh fuel. Eventually the fire stopped, but it had destroyed thousands of houses and dozens of churches. Almost the entire city had to be rebuilt.

Although the fire must have been frightening for many people, it contained the spread of the plague which had killed thousands of London's citizens earlier in the year.

WHAT WAS THE ST BARTHOLOMEW'S DAY MASSACRE?

In the 16th century, France was bitterly divided between Catholics and Protestants. The two religions struggled for control of the government, and of people's souls. In August 1572, the struggle reached its bloody climax.

In that month many nobles and other dignitaries had gathered in Paris for the wedding of the Protestant King Henry of Navarre to Marguerite de Valois. Catherine de Medici, mother of King Charles IX, a Roman Catholic, persuaded her son to order the death of the Protestants.

On August 24, a mob of Roman Catholics were given the signal to start the killing. On that day 3,000 Protestants were massacred in Paris. The killing spread to the provinces and 50,000 people are thought to have died in all. King Henry of Navarre escaped the massacre and later became King of France.

WHEN DID THE REFORMATION BEGIN?

The Reformation of the 16th century was the great religious movement which split western Christendom into Catholic and Protestant churches. The Roman Catholic church had become rich and corrupt. The Pope, its head, followed selfish policies designed to increase his power. Clergy were slack and did not behave as good Christians. Churchmen even sold forgiveness of sins in exchange for money. This so enraged a German monk called Martin Luther that he decided to do something about it. In 1517, he wrote out 95 criticisms of the Church and nailed them to a church door in Wittenberg. He demanded that the Roman Catholic Church should turn its back on such abuses.

Instead he found that those who wanted to stop such faults left the church entirely. This was not what Luther had wanted and he tried to stop the worst excesses of the Reformation.

WHO FOUNDED THE MOGUL EMPIRE?

In the middle of the 16th century India was made up of a large number of small, independent countries. Within 20 years they would be swept away and replaced by the Mogul Empire.

The Moguls were a ruling class in northern India, descended from the Mongols. One of these, Akbar, was Sultan of Delhi. Though not very powerful, Akbar was determined to rival his ancestors Genghis Khan and Tamerlaine.

In 1556, Akbar started his wars of conquest. Within two decades, Akbar had defeated Afghanistan, Malwa, Gujarat and the Sur Dynasty. Before his death in 1605, Akbar had added much of southern India to his empire. He proved himself to be an able ruler and successfully organised his conquests into an empire which would last long after his death.

WHAT HAPPENED AT THE EUREKA STOCKADE?

In 1851, gold was discovered in Victoria, Australia. Thousands of men poured in to seek their fortune. The colonial government did not welcome this influx of unruly immigrants. They introduced several repressive laws. The most hated of these forced miners to buy expensive licences before they could work.

The miners were not allowed to vote in elections so they stood no chance of having the laws repealed. In anger the miners took to demonstrating and protesting. In 1854 miners burned their licences and refused to obey the government.

The colonial authorities sent in the army to enforce its will. The miners built a fortification called Eureka Stockade and defied the troops. In the fighting that followed some 20 miners were killed and the troops captured Eureka. Though they had lost, the miners eventually gained their demands and a softening of government attitudes.

WHEN DID THE FALKLANDS WAR BEGIN?

For nearly two centuries Argentina claimed that it should own the Falkland Islands. But since 1833, when the islands were colonised by Britain, they have remained in the hands of the British.

Long running negotiations about who should control various aspects of the islands were taking place in the early 1980s. Annoyed at the length of the talks, Argentina launched a large military attack on the Falklands on April 2, 1982. In a short time they overran the islands. Later they also took South Georgia after a stiff fight. By mid-June a task force from Britain had recaptured the Falklands. Both nations still claim the islands.

WHAT WAS D-DAY?

By the summer of 1944 it was clear that the Allies were going to invade Europe from Britain, and that Germany was weakening under the strain of five years of constant war. The build up of forces in southern England had been continuing for months. Thousands of men, hundreds of tanks and vast numbers of planes stood ready for the invasion.

On June 6 the largest invasion fleet in history set sail for the beaches of Normandy. The date was code-named D-Day by the military. The troops stormed ashore and despite stiff resistance from the Germans, secured a beachhead. By the end of the first day of fighting the Allies had succeeded in securing a foothold in Europe. The drive towards Germany could begin.

WHAT WAS THE LEAGUE OF URI?

During the 13th century the people living in the Alps were becoming increasingly unhappy with their government.

The mountain people had their own customs and institutions. These were being interfered with by the rulers of the Holy Roman Empire, of which the Alps formed a part. On August 1, 1291, representatives from the areas of Uri, Schwyz and Nidwalden, met in the Meadow of Rutli. They formed the League of Uri in which they declared themselves to be independent of the Empire. Years of hard fighting lay ahead for the mountain men, but they eventually won their freedom and formed the nation we today call Switzerland.

WHAT WAS THE WRECK OF THE *BIRKENHEAD*?

The *Birkenhead* was an early steamship which sank with great loss of life in the late 19th century. The ship was crowded at the time and there were not enough places in the lifeboats for everybody. Only a few people could be saved. As the ship slowly sank, a body of soldiers drew up on the decks, together with the other men on board. The women and children were loaded into the few undamaged lifeboats and sent off, while the men calmly awaited their deaths. It was from this incident that the custom of rescuing "women and children first" arose.

WHY DID KING JOHN SEAL THE MAGNA CARTA?

When King John agreed to the document known as the Magna Carta in 1215, he guaranteed certain rights to his subjects. More importantly he was admitting that nobody, not even the king, was above the law.

John did not want to agree to such a document, but he had no choice. He had been King of England for 16 years and in all that time had achieved little. He had lost most of the English lands in France, had quarrelled with the Pope and had angered his barons.

Eventually, the chief barons decided to take action. They drew up the Magna Carta with the help of the church. It contained promises that would restrict John's actions.

King John had to
set his seal to
Magna Carta

He had to promise to maintain good government, neither to sell nor forbid justice to anyone, and not to tax anyone unjustly. There were 63 clauses in all.

Satisfied that the promises would improve King John's future behaviour, the barons took up arms. Nobody would support John. Faced with the armed might of the barons, John had to set the royal seal on the Magna Carta. The importance of the document is not so much what it says, but the way it says it. Most of the clauses are now redundant, but they all hold that everyone, even those in government, must obey the law.

WHAT WAS THE BEGINNING OF THE KINGDOM OF SCOTLAND?

In the 9th century Scotland was divided into a number of small kingdoms. In the far north were the wild Picts. In the west were the Scots of Dalriada while in the south were kingdoms of Britons and Angles.

In 834 Dalriada gained a new warrior king, Kenneth MacAlpine. He was immediately faced by Viking raids, but Kenneth defeated the sea raiders so convincingly that they never troubled him again.

In 843 Kenneth claimed the kingship of the Picts. Though the reasons for this remain obscure, it seems that the Picts traced their inheritance through the mother and that Kenneth's mother had been a Pictish princess. With the two peoples united under him, Kenneth was stronger than ever. It was from this beginning that the Kingdom of Scotland grew.

WHAT HAPPENED ON "THE GLORIOUS FIRST OF JUNE"?

In 1794 the long series of wars between Revolutionary France and the rest of Europe were only just beginning.

Early in the summer of that year a French fleet of 26 ships of the line sailed out of Brest to meet, and escort, a fleet of merchant ships. Suddenly, Lord Howe swept down with a British fleet of 25 ships. The battle which followed on June 1, was a victory for Howe, who captured six enemy ships. In England it was hailed as a great victory and dubbed the Glorious First of June.

WHICH WAS THE FIRST SHIP TO SAIL AROUND THE WORLD?

On August 10, 1519, a fleet of five ships set out from Spain. Only one returned.

The fleet was commanded by Ferdinand Magellan, a Portuguese mariner sailing under the command of Spain. His task was to find out whether it was easier to reach the Spice Islands of the Moluccas by sailing east or west.

After coasting down South America, Magellan found what he was looking for. Nobody had ever found a sea route to the Pacific. Nosing gently through the straits between South America and Terra del Fuego, he reached the Pacific in November, 1520. Magellan broke down and cried with joy.

After a storm-tossed voyage, the sailors suffering from hunger and thirst, Magellan eventually reached the Spice Islands. After achieving so much and surviving so many dangers, Magellan was killed when he foolishly intervened in a local war.

By this time only one ship was still seaworthy. Crowding into this ship the *Victoria*, the remaining men set off for Spain, which they reached on September 6, 1522.

WHAT WAS THE INDIAN MUTINY?

In 1857 Indian troops, or sepoys, employed by the East India Company suddenly mutinied and started killing every white person they could find.

The reasons for this rebellion are far from clear. There was growing dissatisfaction with technological innovations brought in by the British and many traditional Indian customs seemed under threat.

The final straw came in the shape of a bullet cartridge. Due to an unbelievable bureaucratic bungle, the cartridges were greased with both pig and cow fat. To Moslem Indians the pig was unclean while Hindus considered the cow sacred.

On March 29, 1857, an angry sepoy, Mungul Pandy, killed a British officer. The mutiny had begun. Within a few months it had spread throughout most of northern India. On the whole it was the army and certain native princes which joined in the rising. The mass of the population remained on the sidelines, awaiting the outcome of the struggle. At first the mutineers had the upper hand. By the end of 1858, however, the British had quelled the violent mutiny.

WHAT WAS THE LEWIS AND CLARK EXPEDITION?

In 1803 the United States of America bought all the land west of the Mississippi from France for $15 million. Unfortunately nobody knew what was there.

President Jefferson therefore commissioned Meriwether Lewis and William Clark to lead an exploratory expedition to the west. In the spring of 1804 they left St Louis with 43 men and headed up the Missouri River. In the two and a half years that they were gone, Lewis and Clark travelled across 10,000 miles of previously unknown territory. They opened up new fur-trading areas and blazed the trail for future settlers. Their expedition was of vital importance to the future of the USA.

WHO FOUND DOCTOR LIVINGSTONE?

Doctor David Livingstone was the most respected African explorer of the 19th century. He spent more than 20 years travelling through the unexplored interior as much to spread religion as to explore.

Starting as a poor missionary in Cape Town in 1841, Livingstone journeyed and preached extensively through southern Africa. By 1856 he had become famous, though this had never been his intention, through his travels. He used this fame to denounce the cruel slave trade carried out by the Arabs in East Africa. Several more trips into the interior followed.

In 1866 he set off again, this time to find the source of the Nile. No messages came from Livingstone to the outside world. By 1870 people were worried and the American Henry Stanley was sent to search for him.

After a journey of many months, Stanley found himself in an obscure African village. In front of him stood a bearded white man. Advancing cautiously, Stanley politely raised his hat and asked: "Dr Livingstone, I presume?" It was, indeed, Livingstone.

WHEN DID TEA REACH EUROPE?

Tea has been known as a drink in the Far East for centuries. According to legend, the Chinese Emperor Shen Nung was boiling a pot of water under a bush when some leaves fell from the bush into the water. The resulting brew tasted so nice that he started planting the bushes throughout his empire. This event was supposed to have taken place about 3,000 BC.

However it began, tea-drinking was a well-established custom when European traders arrived in the Far East. The first to bring tea back to their home country were the Dutch who imported it in 1559. It took another century for tea to reach England. In 1657 the Duke of Buckingham drank a cup. Today, the British are the biggest importers of tea in the world.

WHO OPENED JAPAN UP TO TRADE?

In the middle of the 17th century Japan cut herself off from the rest of the world. Under the rule of the powerful Togukawa family, it was illegal for practically anyone to enter or leave Japan.

Behind its barriers, Japan continued to thrive as a highly traditional society. The disruption brought to societies in other lands by contact with Europeans, was avoided. Life in Japan continued much as always.

European merchants became increasingly frustrated by this attitude. Finally, in 1853 an American fleet arrived at Japan led by Commodore Perry. Despite the protests of the Japanese, Perry came ashore. He forced Japan to open itself up to the rest of the world by signing trade treaties with America, Britain and Russia. It is a tribute to the Japanese that they leapt from a mediaeval society to a modern one in so short a time.

Barkerville was a rough city where fortunes could be won or lost

WHICH GOLD RUSH HAPPENED TWICE?

In 1858 gold was discovered on sandbanks in the Fraser and Thompson Rivers of British Columbia. Thousands of prospectors raced to western Canada.

Within four years the rush was over. All the gold had been removed from the sand and the men were drifting away to return to other work. Only the most determined miners remained.

Then, on August 21, 1862, a man called Billy Barker who was digging a shaft in the hope of finding gold, found what he was looking for. A rich vein of gold stared him in the face. There was more gold than he had ever imagined.

In a matter of weeks the gold rush was on again. A town called Barkerville sprang up on the site. For several years Barkerville remained a rough, bustling city where fortunes could be won or lost. Then the gold ran out for good. Today, Barkerville is more of a museum than a city.

WHEN DID THE *MAYFLOWER* SET SAIL?

In the early years of the 17th century, after getting into trouble with the authorities, a group of Puritans left England for Holland. Puritans were extreme Prostestants who wanted to "purify" the church.

These Puritans soon found they did not get on well in Holland either, so they decided to go to the New World to make a fresh start. On September 6, 1620, they crowded on board an old ship called the *Mayflower* and set sail.

After a month-long voyage, the Puritans arrived off the New World. The men went ashore. The land they found seemed promising for farming so the Puritans settled in the place they called Plymouth, which is now in the state of Massachusetts.

WHAT WAS SAID TO BE THE "GREATEST SCIENCE BOOK IN THE WORLD"?

In 1687 Isaac Newton, the great English scientist, published his book entitled *Principia*. It was the culmination of twenty years of work.

According to an often-told story, Newton began thinking about gravity after an apple fell on his head. Whether this is true or not, Newton did ponder on the problem of gravity. Realising that all masses attract each other, Newton patiently worked out formulae for this attraction. He then used them to prove that it is gravity that keeps the moon in orbit around the Earth and the Earth around the Sun. He published these ideas in *Principia,* a book which has often been described as the greatest science book ever written.

WHICH SHOT BEGAN A WAR?

On June 28, 1914, the Austrian Archduke Ferdinand was visiting the town of Sarajevo. Suddenly a shot rang out and the Archduke slumped forward dead.

The police promptly arrested a young man called Gavrilo Princip for the murder. The Austrian government claimed that Princip had been backed by the government of Serbia, a country which bordered on the Austrian Empire. Austria demanded that Serbia agree to an incredibly humiliating ultimatum. Serbia refused and on July 28 Austria declared war. Russia mobilised to help her ally Serbia. Germany, an ally of Austria, demanded that Russia cease mobilising. When Russia refused, Germany declared war on both Russia and her ally, France. In invading France, German troops passed through Belgium. This disregard for neutrality obliged Britain to declare war on Germany. The First World War had begun.

WHAT WAS THE IRISH POTATO FAMINE?

After the potato was brought back from America by Sir Walter Raleigh it became increasingly popular. Potatoes could be grown on poor soil and produced large crops.

The country in which potatoes were most widely grown was Ireland. On the poor soil of the west, potatoes were planted in large numbers. The population boomed as more and more people could be fed from the same area of land.

Disaster struck in 1846. At first the crop seemed to be growing well. Then, just before harvest, a disease known as potato-rot struck. The potato leaves curled and the potatoes themselves rotted in the soil. With no potatoes to eat, the people began to starve. Though the government tried to help, the disaster was beyond them. Some 200,000 people starved to death and millions more fled abroad. The population of Ireland dropped alarmingly.

WHEN DID THE *TITANIC* GO DOWN?

On April 10, 1912, the most magnificent passenger liner in the world steamed out of Southampton. She was the *Titanic* and she was on her maiden voyage with 2,200 people on board.

At twenty minutes to midnight, four days later, she ran into an iceberg. Though the huge ship hardly shuddered, a massive rip had been torn in her side. Water began to gush in and soon the ship was sinking.

Because the technical improvements were supposed to have made the *Titanic* unsinkable, there were few life-boats on board. Women and children were ordered off first. Though a few passengers panicked, the majority behaved with almost unbelievable calmness. A Major Butt moved around making sure that the women were properly protected with warm clothing. A Colonel Astor carried his bride to a boat, placed her in it and then turned back to make room for another lady.

After the last boats had gone the band continued to play and the men sang. As the *Titanic* sank she took more than 1,500 people with her. The tragedy shocked the world.

WHAT WAS THE BOSTON TEA PARTY?

During the 18th century trade with the British North American colonies was closely supervised and taxed from London. Because of local protests, most of these taxes were lifted, but a tax remained on tea.

In 1773 the British Parliament passed a law which made tea cheaper. Large amounts were shipped to America in the hope of selling them at the new, low price. But a group of radical Americans called "Sons of Liberty" in the port of Boston still objected to the tax. On December 16, 1773, they disguised themselves as Red Indians and boarded a tea ship. In what became known as the Boston Tea

Party, they threw some 300 chests of tea into the harbour. Tea was boycotted throughout the colonies.

In retaliation, Britain closed the port of Boston and put the town under military command. Though the Boston Tea Party was a minor incident in itself, it brought into focus the disputes which led to the American War of Independence.

WHO FOUND TUTANKHAMUN'S TOMB?

Throughout the 19th century interest in ancient Egypt grew steadily. Excavations revealed palaces, temples and tombs of amazing beauty. By the early years of this century it was suspected that the tomb of the Pharaoh Tutankhamun, who died in 1356 BC, was lying undiscovered somewhere near Thebes. A British nobleman, Lord Carnarvon, sponsored the archaeologist Howard Carter to find it.

After years of fruitless searching, Carter decided to dig under a pile of rubble which had been formed when the tomb of Pharaoh Rameses VI was constructed. On November 4, he found a series of steps cut into the rock. They led down to a sealed door. When this was broken open Carter found himself staring at untold treasure.

He had found the tomb of Tutankhamun, and it had not been plundered. Among the fabulous amounts of treasure in the tomb were jewels, furniture, chariots, statues and the body of the pharaoh in a coffin of solid gold. Most of this treasure is now on show in the Cairo Museum.

WHEN DID THE OLYMPIC GAMES BEGIN?

The Olympic Games with which we are familiar date back less than a century, yet they are based upon the ancient Olympic Games of the Greeks.

The original games were first held in 776 BC and consisted of a single race. Over the following years many other athletic events were added. These games were, in fact, a religious festival and the games were held to honour the gods.

While the games were in progress a truce was declared in any conflicts that happened to be taking place between countries such as Macedon and Sparta, so that everyone could participate without being molested.

The games were stopped in AD 394 under pressure from the Christians.

When the Frenchman Baron de Courbetin read about the ancient games in the 19th century he was convinced that such sporting idealism would be welcome in the modern world. After much international lobbying, the first of the revived Olympic Games were held in Athens in 1896. They are held every four years and are still the most prestigious athletics competition in the world.

Both kings stripped to the waist and wrestled together

WHEN DID THE KING OF ENGLAND WRESTLE WITH THE KING OF FRANCE?

In the summer of June 1520 King Henry VIII of England travelled to Picardy to meet King Francis I of France. He brought with him a splendid retinue, for Henry was determined to dazzle Francis with the wealth of England. Francis was similarly determined to outdo Henry.

When the two kings met, the magnificent tents and gorgeous costumes of everyone present earned the meeting the name of the Field of the Cloth of Gold.

Knights jousted with each other during the day and balls were held in the evening.

The two kings were both young and boisterous and they got on well. Suddenly Henry suggested that they wrestle. Both kings stripped to the waist and began. For some time neither had the advantage, then Francis got the better of Henry and threw him off his feet. Laughing and joking the two kings dressed and went off to eat. Though the Field of the Cloth of Gold was a dazzling social success and the two kings got on well, nothing important was agreed.

WHEN WAS A QUEEN OF BRITAIN BANNED FROM A CORONATION?

As Prince of Wales, George IV had married Princess Caroline of Brunswick. However, they soon fell out and started arguing. Caroline left the country. When George became king in 1820, Caroline automatically became queen. She soon returned to take part in their divorce proceedings.

The coronation was fixed for July 19, but because of the arguments, Caroline was not invited. Hardly had the ceremony begun, however, than Caroline arrived. Marching up to the doors of Westminster Abbey, she demanded entrance. Caroline hammered on the doors and began shouting. Soldiers guarding the doors told her she had not been invited and she was not allowed in. Angrily, Caroline turned and stormed off to the cheers of the crowds.

WHAT WAS THE TREACHERY OF SAN JUAN D'ULLOA?

On September 16, 1568, a squadron of six small English ships sailed into the Spanish port of San Juan d'Ulloa in the West Indies. They had been battered by a storm and the commander, John Hawkins, asked permission to put in for repairs.

Hawkins was in a difficult position as he was just finishing a smuggling voyage. The Spanish governor allowed the ships in, however, and repairs went ahead.

Sir Francis Drake

A few days later a Spanish fleet of warships also arrived in port.

For three days the two fleets lay alongside each other. Suddenly, the largest of the Spanish galleons swung round and fired all her cannon at one of the English ships. In seconds every Spanish ship was firing into the English craft. Though Hawkins fought back as best he could, it was soon clear he would have to flee.

Only the two smallest English ships escaped. One was commanded by Hawkins, the other by a man called Francis Drake who would wreak revenge on the Spaniards in future years. All the Englishmen on the other ships were killed or handed over to the Inquisition.

WHEN DID THE EMPEROR OF ROME BECOME CHRISTIAN?

In the early years of Christianity the religion was often persecuted by the Romans. Christians did not worship Roman gods, nor did they sacrifice to the Emperor. Because of this they were regarded as troublemakers and unreliable citizens. Many Christians were killed by being thrown to the lions in the arena, or by simple execution.

Such treatment came to an end in AD 312. When the Emperor Constantius died in York in 306, the legions proclaimed his son Constantine to be Emperor. Six years later Constantine had a vision of a cross. He became con-verted to Christianity and the persecutions ceased. In 325 Constantine summoned bishops from throughout the Empire to Nicea where they discussed various theological issues in one of the most important church councils of all time.

WHAT WAS THE FASHODA INCIDENT?

In the late 19th century European countries were claiming large areas of Africa as part of their empire. Britain helped Egypt defeat the Mahdi of the Sudan and moved south along the Nile. At the same time a French expedition set out from French territory west of the Nile and headed east.

On July 10, 1898, the French hoisted their flag on the banks of the Nile at Fashoda. A large British force then arrived and tactfully asked the French to leave. Feelings ran high in France. For some time it seemed that Britain and France would go to war, but a peaceful settlement was finally reached.

WHICH AMERICAN PRESIDENT WAS MURDERED IN DALLAS?

When John F Kennedy was elected as President of the United States of America he seemed to be ushering in a new era. He was young, charismatic and exciting. People expected much from Kennedy.

On November 22, 1963, President Kennedy was visiting the

city of Dallas in Texas. As his car drove along, gunfire rang out. The President slumped forward. He had been shot in the neck and the head. Though he was rushed to hospital, Kennedy died a short time later. Lee Harvey Oswald was arrested for the murder but was himself gunned down before he could be brought to trial.

WHAT WAS THE MARCH ON ROME?

After the First World War, Italy was an unhappy country. The economic position was bad, there was high unemployment and the country had not gained as much as she had expected from the peace.

It was in these conditions that the braggart politician, Mussolini, came to dominate Milan. Mussolini organised gangs of followers who attacked anybody who opposed him. Through such tactics Mussolini was able to imnpose some form of order in the city.

In 1922 he took advantage of a crisis to order his "Blackshirt" followers to march on Rome. With this impressive display of support, he persuaded the king to place him in charge of government. Mussolini remained dictator of Italy for more than twenty years.

WHEN WAS THE EEC FOUNDED?

During the 1950s several countries in Europe decided that if the continent was to remain economically healthy, the countries should co-operate with each other. Such co-operation was first tried in the sphere of heavy industry. In 1952 the European Coal and Steel Community was formed by six countries, including France, West Germany and Italy.

The idea was so successful that the same countries formed the European Economic Community, or EEC, in 1957. This extended economic co-operation over many areas. In the years since many other European countries have joined the EEC.

WHEN DID COMMUNISM BEGIN?

The Communist system of government now holds sway over vast areas of the world. The giant countries of Russia and China are both Communist as are many smaller nations.

During the French revolution in 1792, the Commune of Paris usurped the city's government. In France in those days, a small territorial division ruled by a mayor and municipal council was called a Commune. The word Commune came to be associated by many people with revolutionary and socialist principles.

The political ideology which Communist countries follow began in the year 1848. In that year the German Jew Karl Marx published a pamphlet called the *Communist Manifesto*. In this he called for the workers in industrial societies to rebel and overthrow their governments.

In later works, including *Das Kapital*, Marx developed his ideas into an organised ideology. The first nation to turn Communist was Russia in 1917. The many Communist states in existence today have adapted Marx's ideas to fit their needs. Often this results in a totalitarian state which represses its own people.

WHO SENT THE FIRST RADIO SIGNAL ACROSS THE ATLANTIC?

The sending of an electrical signal without connecting wires is one of the most popular communication systems in use today. The process was invented by Guglielmo Marconi who was half Italian and half Irish.

He sent his first signal in 1896 across a distance of about a mile. Just five years later, Marconi prepared for his greatest triumph. He announced that he was going to send a message across the Atlantic. If he could achieve this, the whole process of communication would be revolutionised. Crouched over what would today appear primitive equipment, Marconi sent out his signals from Poldhu in Cornwall. Everyone was amazed when he received a reply from Newfoundland.

WHAT WAS THE BLACK DEATH?

The ominously-called Black Death was a terrible disease which swept through Europe and Asia in the 14th century.

It is thought that the disease was a mixture of bubonic and pneumonic plague. The symptoms included huge black, pus-filled buboes (swellings in the groin or armpit), raging thirst and fever. It was almost invariably fatal. The outbreak began in China early in the century. It slowly spread along the caravan routes until it reached the Crimea in Russia in 1347. From there trading ships took the plague to Italy. By the end of 1350 it had swept Europe.

When a city or village was struck by the Black Death the effect was terrible. Within a few weeks more than a third of the population would have died an agonising death. Some villages were simply wiped out. For the living it was a terrible time. Nobody knew if they would be alive the next day. The catastrophe was so great that people could not cope. It seemed that God's anger was on the land.

The whole social fabric of Europe was ripped apart by the Black Death. It contributed to the collapse of the feudal way of life and the introduction of capitalism.

HOW DID CLEOPATRA DIE?

Cleopatra was a ruler of Egypt in the 1st century BC. She inherited the throne jointly with her brother, Ptolemy XII, in 52 BC. With the help of a Roman army, led by Julius Caesar, Cleopatra ousted her brother. After the death of Julius Caesar, Cleopatra involved herself in the civil wars of the Roman Empire. She hoped to gain greater power and influence for herself and Egypt. Instead, she suffered humiliating defeat. In 30 BC, to avoid the terrible fate of being dragged to Rome in chains, Cleopatra died by her own hand. It has been said that she allowed herself to be bitten by a deadly snake, although this is not confirmed.

WHEN DID THE SUEZ CANAL OPEN?

Ever since the sea route to India had been opened up by Vasco da Gama in the 16th century, ships sailing from Europe to Asia had to sail all the way round Africa. Ferdinand de Lesseps, a French engineer, had an idea for a solution in 1854.

He suggested digging a canal which would link the Mediterranean and the Red Sea. He soon won much financial backing and work began in 1859. Ten years later the 103 mile long canal was completed and opened. The value of the canal to international shipping was soon apparent and ships from many nations used it.

In 1956 the canal became the centre of the Suez crisis which culminated when British and French troops invaded the area,

Queen Cleopatra and the snake

only to pull out a few days later. The recent troubled history of the Near East has sometimes closed the canal, but it seems certain to remain a vital link in the world shipping network.

WHAT WAS THE BURKE AND WILLS EXPEDITION?

In the middle of the last century Australia remained very much unexplored. The vastness of the interior was so great that it defied most men.

Then the government offered a large prize for the first man to cross Australia from south to north. In August 1860 a party led by Robert O'Hara Burke and William Wills set out to claim the prize. It was one of the best equipped parties ever to set out for the interior.

At first all went well, and the four-man advance party of Burke, Wills, Charles Gray and John King made quick progress. Then heavy rains slowed them down. The men did not reach the north coast until February 9, 1861. They had barely enough food left to feed them on their long return journey to their supply depot on Cooper's Creek.

During the long trek, Gray died of dysentery. After weeks of hardship, the three remaining men reached Cooper's Creek. To their utter despair the supply depot had given up waiting for them and had left just a few hours before. Exhaustion and lack of food soon took their toll. Burke and Wills died within days. King, the sole survivor, managed to survive with a band of Aborigines until he was rescued a few months later.

WHAT WAS THE TREATY OF VERSAILLES?

After four years of terrible fighting, the First World War came to an end on November 11, 1918. The statesmen of Europe were faced with the daunting task of coming to some sort of an agreement.

The leaders gathered in the French palace of Versailles, near Paris, and spent months discussing the problems. The meeting was dominated by three men; President Wilson of America, Premier Clemenceau of France and Prime Minister Lloyd George of Britain.

In 1919 the 440 articles of the Treaty of Versailles were announced. It completely redrew the map of Europe. The vast, multinational Austrian Empire was divided up into the countries of Austria, Hungary, and Czechoslovakia while part of its territory was given to Italy, Poland, Rumania and Yugoslavia. Germany lost about a tenth of her land to neighbouring countries. Germany was, furthermore, expected to pay large sums of money to the victors and was forbidden to have large armed forces in future. The humiliating treatment given to Germany caused great bitterness and was a contributing cause to Adolf Hitler's rise to power.

Transport

WHEN WAS THE HEYDAY OF THE STAGE COACH?

The great age of coaching was a short one that began at the end of the Napoleonic wars in 1815 and continued until the 1840s when the coming of railways sounded its death knell.

It never was a pleasant or popular form of transport. It was too uncomfortable. Once passengers were aboard and on their way, they had to contend with being jolted as they rattled along badly made roads for hour upon hour, broken only by a hurried meal at an inn. If they were lucky and had not been held up by a highwayman they reached their destination safely, but much the worse for wear. For those people who had been forced to travel outside, the journey had been an even worse experience. They were exposed to the rain, winds and dust, and their ears were frequently assailed by the blast of the coach guard's horn.

Travelling by coach was not cheap by the standards of the day. The fare from Liverpool to London was two guineas, while going to Scotland could cost as much as fourteen pounds, with the cost of staying at coaching inns having to be added to the fare. This could prove very expensive, as even travelling from London to Exeter took more than three days.

No wonder rail travel, faster, much more comfortable and cheaper, proved so popular.

WHO PIONEERED THE PASSENGER DIESEL TRAIN?

In October 1932, Germany surprised the rest of Europe by introducing a new high-speed train. The train was a novelty because it was diesel-driven. It was the first time that this form of power had ever been used for high-speed work. Furthermore, it was streamlined — the first time aircraft technique had been applied to railways. The new train was put into service between Berlin and Hamburg and was soon named the "Flying Hamburger".

The lightweight two-coach

train, seating 102 passengers, was scheduled to cover the 178.1 miles (286 km) in 138 minutes, an average speed of 77.4 mph (125 km/h). This made it the fastest schedule in the world and the first train to be required to run at speeds of over 100 mph (161 km/h) during much of its journey.

The streamlined shape had been based on Zeppelin airship design and had been tested in the Zeppelin "wind canal", the forerunner of the present wind tunnel. The two 410 hp Maybach engines were similar to those that were used in Zeppelin airships.

The success of the train had a great effect on the German State Railways. By 1936, they were running 84 similar trains on services which averaged over 50 mph (80 km/h).

WHY WERE SAN FRANCISCO'S CABLE CARS INVENTED?

Next to the Golden Gate Bridge, the cable car is probably the best known symbol of San Francisco, in California, USA.

This popular mechanical anachronism first appeared in 1873, the brain-child of a cable manufacturer named Andrew Hallidie. He invented the cable car because he felt sorry for the horses which had to pull heavy loads up the steep hills of San Francisco.

The inventor himself was the cable car's first conductor. By 1890 his car was there to stay. There were then eight cable car systems operating in the city.

The cable car runs on rails flush with the road. Below the road are cables which haul the car safely up the steepest hills.

At the end of each route, and at intersections along the roads, are turntables where the car is turned round in order to go in another direction or to go back up a hill. This operation is carried out manually by the conductor and willing passengers.

This form of transport was not confined to San Francisco as it is today. Many cities in the United States had cable car systems.

A San Francisco cable car

WHAT WAS THE FATE OF THE HINDENBURG?

On May 6, 1936, the Zeppelin *Hindenburg* burst into flames just before it landed at Lakehurst, New York. A total of 13 passengers and 22 crew members, including one of the ground crew, perished in the disaster.

It was not the first airship disaster. These had included the R101, which had crashed near Beauvais in France, killing 48 men. It was a British-built airship, and its loss ended British interest in building any further airships.

The fate of the *Hindenburg* had even more far-reaching effects, as its crash virtually put an end to this form of air travel. The main danger was that airships were filled with hydrogen—a very light gas which gave the airship its lift, but is also very easy to set on fire. The only other light gas, helium, was safe from fire but very expensive to manufacture. Nowadays, with the revival of airships, only helium is used as it is now cheaper to manufacture and is non-inflammable.

The cause of the *Hindenburg's* crash was never discovered. Several theories were advanced as to the cause of the fire. One was that an interior staywire had broken and pierced one of the gas cells, simultaneously creating static electricity which ignited the escaping hydrogen. Other theories suggested that the airship had been hit by lightning from a local thunder shower which had surrounded the airship as it neared its landing area. There were even rumours of sabotage, when a Luger pistol was found among the wreckage from which one shot had been fired.

Whatever the reason, it spelt the end of airship travel for nearly 50 years.

WHO INVENTED THE DIRIGIBLE?

The first steerable airship was invented as far back as 1852 by a Frenchman named Henri Giffard. A talented engineer who had already made a small fortune from his various inventions for the improvement of locomotive steam engines, he first became interested in the air after making an ascent in a balloon. The airship he designed weighed only 99 lbs (45 kg) and was tapered at both ends with a sail-like rudder attached to the rear end. A small gondola held the aeronaut and the steam engine.

The airship slowly ascended for the first time in Paris on September 24, 1852. Henri Giffard himself made the first flight wearing a frock-coat and a top hat which he waved at the astonished spectators.

It was the first flight ever of an airship flying under its own power. It ended successfully at Trappe, some 15 miles to the south-west of Paris, after averaging a speed of 5 mph (8 kph).

Although he made several other flights, all of them were made under perfect weather conditions. In an attempt to make a more reliable airship that would be less at the mercy of the winds, Giffard went into partnership with Gabriel Yon, a well-known manufacturer of balloons. The airship they produced together was badly designed and exploded on a trial flight, and Giffard and Yon were lucky to escape with their lives.

Undeterred, Giffard went on to try and design a large airship. But it soon became obvious that the cost of building it would be prohibitive and he abandoned the project, turning his attention instead to making large captive balloons. When the World's Fair was held in Paris 1867, Giffard was there with his latest captive balloon in which 35,000 people received their air baptism.

HOW DID ROLLS-ROYCE CARS COME INTO BEING?

In 1902, a wealthy young man, the Hon Charles Stewart Rolls, formed a company which soon became the leading distributor of cars in Britain. Successful though he was, one thing troubled Rolls. All the cars he handled were Continental models. A perfectionist in all things, he had never found a British car which he considered good enough.

At this time a brilliant engineer named Frederick Henry Royce was living in Manchester. Unlike Rolls, his early life had been a hard one. At the age of fourteen, he was apprenticed at the Great Northern Railway works at Peterborough,

where he discovered he had a special aptitude for mechanics which surprised even himself.

Royce's capacity for hard work and his intolerance of bad workmanship brought him success. He worked for many companies, always learning new things, and by 1900 he owned his own company, making dynamos and cranes.

Then in 1903, he bought his first car — and he was disgusted with it. He decided he could build one far better himself, and to the astonishment of his colleagues, he set about doing so. When he had finished, he had developed a car which many still consider the finest in the world.

It was a man called Henry Edmunds who brought Rolls and Royce together. Edmunds knew both men and tried several times to arrange a meeting between them. At first, neither of them would take time off his work, but then Rolls was finally persuaded to travel to Manchester.

Over the Christmas holidays of 1904, the two men met and forged a partnership which was to make their names and cars world famous.

HOW DID THE BICYCLE DEVELOP?

In 1779, a rather unwieldy four-wheeled carriage appeared in France, and was exhibited at the court of Louis XVI and Marie Antoinette. It was moved along by a footman who pressed down two

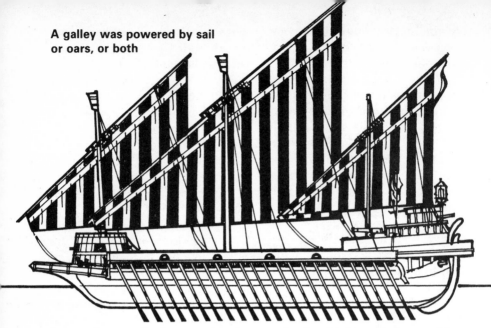

A galley was powered by sail or oars, or both

levers alternately, thus turning the rear wheels. This could be termed the first bicycle ever.

In the early 19th century, a German, Baron von Drais, brought out a machine known as the hobby-horse. This was self-propelled and it was very primitive. The man who first made anything approaching a modern bicycle was a Scotsman, Kirkpatrick MacMillan of Dumfries. He added cranks, pedals and driving rods to the old hobby-horse, and gave the vehicle a comfortable seat.

In 1865 came the "bone shakers". They were given this name because of the enormous vibration which took place when they were ridden over rough roads.

The next step was to provide bicycles with a very large front wheel, which made it possible to pedal at a more leisurely speed. These bicycles became known as "penny farthings".

The last important improvements to the bicycle were the adoption of pneumatic tyres, the introduction of a gear system — which removed the need for a large front wheel — and the invention of the free-wheel device. Before this last advance the pedals revolved at all times.

The result of these improvements was a bicycle in most ways similar to the one we know today.

WHO USED THE FIRST GALLEYS?

The war vessels used by the ancient Greeks and Romans were known as galleys. They were powered by sail or oars, or by both, and had a very low freeboard (that is to say, the height between the deck level and the water level was very small).

To row the galleys was an arduous task. Originally, free men undertook this work and were paid handsomely for it. Later, it became the custom to employ convicted criminals. These "galley slaves" were branded with the letters GAL, and in 1564, Charles IX of France forbade prisoners to be sentenced to the galleys for any period of less than ten years.

The custom of employing criminals became so widespread that the word "galley" became synonymous with "prisoner" and prisoners were called "galleys" long after galleys as such had ceased to exist.

WHEN WAS AN ESCALATOR FIRST USED IN BRITAIN?

Originally an American invention which had first appeared on Coney Island in 1896, the first escalator began operating in Britain at the famous department store of Harrods in Knightsbridge in 1898. It was viewed at first with so much alarm by the shoppers that the management felt it necessary to employ an attendant at the top, ready to dispense brandy and smelling salts to those who professed to be quite overcome with the experience of travelling on it.

The first moving staircase on the London Underground was installed at Earl's Court in 1911. Here again, the public were nervous of using it, so a man with a wooden leg was employed to ride up and down the escalator all day to give confidence to the public.

WHO INVENTED THE FIRST AMBULANCE?

The first ambulance was designed by Baron Dominique Jean Larrey, Napoleon's personal surgeon, and it made its first appearance during the future Emperor's Italian campaign of 1796-97. As the body of the vehicle was mounted on springs, it was a vast improvement on the unsprung carts that had previously carried the wounded from the battle field. The first British ambulance unit was formed in 1854 during the Crimean War.

Motorised ambulances began to appear from 1900, and once again it was the French who were the pioneers in this field. It was an important step forward, but the time when the wounded were to be cared for in the humane and hygienic manner we know today was still a long way off.

WHAT IS A CORACLE?

For centuries men have used this strange river-going craft called a coracle for fishing and travelling from place to place. This unique form of transport is still being used in Wales for fishing and other pursuits. It has remained unchanged in design for 2,000 years. When the Romans came to Britain they saw and described these strange craft which the Britons were using.

In those days they were made from wicker and covered in animal skin, but today they are covered in canvas, and then tarred to make them waterproof.

The coracle is propelled by an oar, a very delicate, skilled operation which, if not carried out correctly, may result in the boat simply revolving in circles.

WHO BUILT BRITAIN'S FIRST FOUR-WHEELED CAR?

Britain's first successful four-wheeled automobile — as against converted carriages or tricycles — was built by Frederick Lanchester. In company with his brother George, Lanchester built two experimental machines. In 1899, the second of these cars won a special gold medal at the Richmond Motor Show after running for 68 miles at an average speed of 26 mph.

But there was a setback during the thousand miles trial in 1900. During this, one of Lanchester's cars split in two, leaving a reporter in the rear seat with the unpowered half!

It was not until 1901 that a production car took to the road, because Lanchester was such a perfectionist. He insisted upon his various models having fully interchangeable parts, something Henry Ford is usually credited with introducing.

During the First World War,

Lanchester was the only British company, besides Rolls-Royce, to build armoured cars, most of which saw service on the Russian front.

After the war, Lanchester continued to build fine cars, but they looked like most other cars of the period. In 1931, Lanchester was taken over by Daimler, which continued to build cars called "Lanchester" but they lacked the character created for them by their original designer.

WHEN DID THE FIRST LONDON TAXIS APPEAR?

On August 19, 1897, the first London taxis appeared on the streets. There were twelve of them, all electric, accumulator driven vehicles with an average speed of 9 mph (14.5 km/h) and with a range of 30 miles (48 km). The taxis were painted yellow and black, and were named "humming birds" by the general public.

For various reasons they did not prove popular. After being in service for two years they were withdrawn and did not reappear until 1904. This time they were a success, with the drivers taking as much as five pounds a day, a large amount of money in those days, especially as petrol was only eight pence a gallon. By 1910, more than five thousand taxis were plying for hire in London, contributing to the slow demise of the horse-drawn cabs which, amazingly, could still be seen until 1947, when the last horse-drawn cab driver retired.

The first petrol-driven taxis appeared in Stuttgart, Germany, in 1896. A few months later a Paris taxi cab service appeared, but went out of business shortly after.

WHO MADE THE FIRST WATER-WAYS?

From the very earliest times, man has used water as a means of transport. At first he used the rivers and the sea, but in the course of time he realised the advantages of constructing his own waterways.

Man-made waterways, or canals, were first constructed in pre-Roman times, but the Romans themselves built many such waterways.

It is not very clear when man was able to build his canals "uphill". Originally, lifts or inclines were made and some are still in use even today. But these can be used only for the transportation of small vessels. For larger vessels, and for greater convenience, man had to invent the lock, and it is not known who, or even which country, was responsible for this. Some say that it was a Dutch invention, others that it was the work of two Italian brothers, who are supposed to have devised a lock in 1481, and still others credit Leonardo da Vinci, but whoever the inventor was, it is certain that locks were in regular use in the 14th or 15th centuries.

One of the earliest canals in Europe was the Languedoc canal, which links the Bay of Biscay to the Mediterranean. This has 119 locks along its total length of 148 miles (238 km) and was designed by Baron Paul Riquet de Bonrepos (1604-80). It was finished in 1681.

WHO WAS SIR HENRY SEGRAVE?

On Friday 13, 1930, Britain's greatest racing driver met his death in his motor boat *Miss England II* on Lake Windermere in the Lake District. This was Henry Segrave, who had devoted most of his adult life to the pursuit of speed. A hero of World War I, who had served both as an infantry officer and a pilot with the Royal Flying Corps until he was invalided out, Segrave took up motor racing after the Armistice. He went on to be the winner of several Grand Prix races before giving up motor racing in 1927, having proved himself the greatest driver of his period by winning 31 out of 49 events.

In the same year he went to Daytona Beach in the United States and there set up a new record of 203.8 mph (327 km/h) in a Sunbeam powered with two giant Matabele aero-engines. Later he returned to Daytona to set new record figures in the most beautiful land-speed record car ever designed, the *Golden Arrow*.

Ten days after breaking the land speed record at 231.36 mph (372 km/h), Segrave won the Fischer Cup race at Biscayne, Miami, in

his speedboat, *Miss England*. Returning home, he was knighted for
his achievement.

He went on to win the German
Water Championship, the European Championship and the Volpi
Cup; he co-designed a new monoplane called the *Segrave Meteor*
and designed the Hillman Segrave
motor car. Sir Henry Segrave was
killed trying to break yet another
record.

WHAT WAS THE *SPIRIT OF ST LOUIS*?

This was the name given by a
young American named Charles
Lindbergh to the Ryan silver
monoplane which he used for his
epic solo flight across the Atlantic
in 1927.

Before setting off, Lindbergh
made all the test flights himself,
calculated the fuel consumption
to the last litre and took full
responsibility for the distribution
of weight in the aircraft. On May
20, 1927, he left Roosevelt Airfield, New York — next stop Paris.

For the first few hundred miles
the visibility was good and Lindbergh flew low over the sea, but his
luck was not to hold out. Storms
broke overhead, heavy rain fell,
ice lay heavily on the wings, and a
blanket of fog closed in. But the
following day, when he saw some
fishing boats he knew land could
not be far away and, to his delight,
he was soon flying over Ireland.

By nightfall he was crossing the
French coast and, just 33.50 hours

after leaving New York, was looking down on the welcome sight of
Le Bourget Airport, where a crowd
of over 120,000 people had gathered to welcome him.

WHO BUILT THE FIRST ELECTRIC CAR?

The first electric car was built by
Professor Ayrton in 1888, and
many others remained on the
roads right up to World War I.

Electric cars were very popular
with the ladies because, compared
with the early petrol engines,
which were both noisy and dirty,
they were quiet, smooth and easy
to start.

The great disadvantage of the
electric cars was, of course, their
short range. Batteries were heavy
and bulky and had to be re-
charged at frequent intervals or
they would run down, and high
speeds could not be maintained
for long periods.

However, because of their rapid
acceleration, electric cars were
ideal for short speed-record
sprints, and the earliest speed records were held by electric cars. In
fact, the first car to travel at more
than 60 mph (96.5 km/h) was Cam-
ille Jenatzy's *La Jamais Contente*.
Jenatzy, a Belgian, astounded the
world with his 100-horsepower
streamlined electric car, which established a world speed record of
65.79 mph (106 km/h) at Acheres
on April 29, 1899.

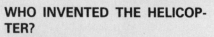

WHO INVENTED THE HELICOPTER?

Surprising as it may seem, the idea of rotary wing flying was first put forward by a Chinese alchemist named Ko Hung in AD 320, when he wrote of the possibility of making a flying vehicle using wood from a jujube tree with ox leather straps fastened to it, on a revolving axis. The idea was later used to make a toy called the Chinese Top.

Ko Hung's idea was carried a stage further by Leonardo da Vinci, who designed a lifting screw. This was the pioneer of helicopter design. No further progress was made until the 18th century when Sir George Cayley, who was to become known as the "Father of Aeronauts", made a

model helicopter top which rose 25 feet.

The coming of the steam engine gave new impetus to helicopter development, but despite the efforts of several inventors no one succeeded in designing a helicopter that worked. In 1923 a Spaniard named Juan la Cierva made and flew a machine which lifted to a height of several metres. Encouraged by this modest success, Cierva developed a number of other models, each one an improvement on the other until, finally in 1928, he developed a rotary-wing aircraft in which he flew across the Channel.

Sadly, he was killed in a flying accident in 1936, and did not see how the helicopter continued to develop.

WHAT IS THE RACE OF 1,000 CORNERS?

When the idea of an annual race through the streets of Monte Carlo was first mooted, everyone believed that a race through the narrow, twisting streets would prove not only very dangerous, but would also fail to provide an exciting spectacle for the onlookers.

However, the racing authorities thought otherwise. The now famous circuit known as the Monaco, and often referred to by drivers as the race of a 1,000 corners, was opened by the Prince of Monaco on April 14, 1929, watched by a huge crowd.

From the start, the cars raced up the incline which led to the well-known Casino. From there, they turned and twisted, plunging downhill past the station to the sea-wall, where they turned sharp right into the famous tunnel, out into the daylight again and down to the harbour wall.

The great feature of this first Monaco Grand Prix was a tremendous duel between the eventual winner, a British driver named Williams, who was resident in France, and Rudolf Carraciola. Williams drove a green Bugatti, while Carraciola handled a great white sports Mercedes Benz. This historic race was won by Williams at an average speed of 50.2 mph (80.78 km/h) and thus the pattern was set for what is now one of the classic races.

The following year, the streets of Monaco echoed and re-echoed to the cheers of the French citizens for it was won by Frenchman Philippe Etanalin.

WHO FIRST HELPED TO MAKE RAILWAY TRAVEL POPULAR?

The introduction of the railway system to Britain was an invaluable contribution to progress. But as is the case with many innovations, it was viewed at first with some suspicion by the public.

Fortunately, on June 14, 1842, most doubts about the safety of the railways were banished. On that day, Queen Victoria became the first reigning monarch to travel by train — and, in so doing, set the seal of acceptance on what was then still a novel form of transport. The journey was made on the "new" Great Western line from Slough, near Windsor, to London. At 12.25 pm the train pulled into Paddington. Hauled by the engine, Phlegethon, it had covered the 21.5 miles (35 km) in 25 minutes — less time than many present-day trains take for a similar distance. As the Queen alighted, accompanied by Prince Albert, she admitted to having been "quite charmed" by the experience, though she expressed some doubts about the speed at which the train had travelled. On her future journeys it was stipulated that the train should not travel at more than 40 mph (64 km/h).

WHAT WAS A BROUGHAM?

In the Victorian age, the most popular form of transport with the middle classes was the brougham. A four-wheeled vehicle, suitable for either town or country, it needed only one horse and a coachman. It was also a popular vehicle for doctors, even though a two-wheeled gig or pony trap might have been more suitable. The brougham, however, was much more of a status symbol, especially as many of the middle class were impressed by the outer trappings of wealth, and were therefore inclined to choose their doctor by his carriage, rather than because of his medical skills.

WHAT WAS CALLED *THE GOLDEN DEVIL?*

King Charles I was a very extravagant king. While on a visit to the royal shipyard at Woolwich, to view his navy's latest ship, Leopard, he commanded the master shipwright, Phineas Pett, to build the largest ship ever seen.

A ship of the line (the Royal Navy), then cost about £6,000 to build but when Sovereign was completed, she had cost £65,586.

The Dutch, in their many engagements with her, called her The Golden Devil because she was gilded from bow to stern.

The carvings portrayed royal monograms, various heraldic beasts, signs of the Zodiac and six beautiful goddesses symbolising Counsel, Care, Industry, Strength, Valour and Victory. The bow had the greyhounds of Henry VII, the Dragon of Cadwallader, the Lion and the Unicorn, and the Roses of England, the Thistle of Scotland, the Fleur-de-lis of France and the Harp of Ireland.

The decoration and carving was done by the royal carver, Gerard Christmas and his sons and assistants, from drawings made by the famous artist, Van Dyck.

One "Sovereign" outlasted another, for King Charles was executed in 1649. In later years, the ship was modified and people hardly recognised the once mighty Sovereign except for her extraordinary size. She took part in many battles and had the proud record of never being defeated.

The paddle steamers were designed to operate in shallow waters

She came to a tragic end in 1696 when an overturned candle caused a fire and she sank in flames.

WHO WERE THE RULERS OF THE MISSISSIPPI?

Among the most beautiful and elegant of all the ships ever built were the paddle steamers. They were designed to operate in shallow waters and, although they are old fashioned and belong to a bygone age, they are still used today in many parts of the world in shallow waterways.

For 60 glorious years they ruled the Mississippi and the other rivers of the American West. They carried passengers and all kinds of goods. Some were floating entertainment palaces, known as showboats.

The kings of the rivers were the ships' captains and the princes were the pilots. They really had to know the rivers. The Mississippi, known as Old Muddy, was called the crookedest river in the world by Mark Twain, who had been a pilot himself. He wrote about it many times.

The first steamer to operate on the Mississippi was the *New Orleans*. This was in 1811, but her power was not sufficient to get the boat back upstream so she went out of service.

The next and most important steamer was the *George Washington*, which was to become the blueprint for more than five thousand steamers which were to chug up and down the Mississippi.

But in the mid-1800s another steam giant—the railway engine—was to take over the transportation business in the United States. Much quicker and cheaper, the "Iron Horse", as people called the railroad, was to mark the end of the golden age of the paddle steamer.

WHO BUILT THE FIRST RAILWAY LINE?

The steam engine itself was not invented by George Stephenson, neither was the steam locomotive. There were locomotives in existence when Stephenson was a youngster. In 1804, a Cornishman, Richard Trevithick, built a road locomotive and ran it along a tramway in South Wales. In 1813, *Puffing Billy* was constructed by Christopher Blackett and William Hedley.

It is for his work in connection with developing steam locomotion that Stephenson is remembered today.

From his youth, Stephenson was associated with collieries, and it was here that he became interested in engines. In 1814 he built his first locomotive. It was capable of pulling a load of 30 tons (30.48 tonnes) at a speed of four miles per hour (6.4 km/h). It did not work well on a gradient, and it was for this reason that it was decided that railroads were necessary. The first line was laid at Hetton Collieries in 1818 and, a little later, the famous line between Stockton and Darlington was laid, and opened in 1825.

In 1829, Stephenson built his most famous locomotive the *Rocket*. (The shell of this engine can still be seen in the Science Museum in London.)

WHAT WAS THE PERMITTED MAXIMUM SPEED FOR THE FIRST BRITISH MOTORIST?

When the first petrol-driven cars took to the roads in Britain, they had to crawl along at the top speed of four miles per hour (6.4 km/h). In addition they had to follow a man carrying a red flag!

This so annoyed the general public and the motorists in particular, that it raised an outcry and forced the government to bring in a new Act setting the speed limit at 14 mph (22.5 km/h). The Act came into being in 1896, and motorists celebrated it by a run from London to Brighton organised by Lawson's Motor Car Club. The winner made the run in 3 hours, 44 minutes and 35 seconds.

WHEN DID THE FIRST BUS APPEAR?

The prototype of the modern bus appeared in the streets of Paris on March 18, 1862, travelling at fixed hours to certain points in the city for a flat fee of five sous. Servants, soldiers and other members of the so-called lower orders were forbidden to use these vehicles which were for the sole convenience of "people of merit".

The first London buses did not appear until July 1829, and were invented by George Shillibeer. The first buses were drawn by three horses abreast and carried 22 passengers, all of them inside. The buses were lightly constructed and therefore fast, but they proved too large for the streets of London and were superseded by others, carrying 12 passengers inside. In 1849, an outside seat along the centre of the roof was added.

WHICH ORGANISATIONS CLAIM TO BE THE MOTORISTS' FRIENDS?

Two associations can claim to be this. The first was the Royal Automobile Club, more commonly known as the RAC. It was formed in 1897 and was responsible for organising Britain's first Motor Show which was held in 1899.

The second was the Automobile Association. It was founded in 1905 by a band of motorists at their own expense. To begin with their main aim was to employ a number of cyclists who were used as scouts to patrol the roads at weekends, looking for speed traps which they then duly reported to their members on the road.

Today, both clubs are still flourishing and provide an invalu-

able service to their members at home and abroad. Among the many services they provide are their patrols who rescue stranded motorists by carrying out on-the-spot repairs to vehicles or arranging to have them towed to a garage or to the member's home, ensuring that the passengers arrive home too.

WHO WERE THE PIONEERS OF MOTOR CAR DESIGN?

The end of the Victorian age and the appearance of the internal combustion engine ushered in the age of motoring.

In the inevitable race to produce cars for the public, France quickly showed that she had every intention of leading the world in car design and power transmission. Companies like Panhard et Levassor, De Dion-Bouton et Cie and Peugeot quickly showed their supremacy, particularly in their production of racing cars, which in turn created a breed of French driver noted for reckless driving.

The first road race took place on July 22, 1894, over a course of 74.5 miles (120 km) from Paris to Rouen. The first three places were taken by Panhard, Peugeot and De Dion-Bouton et Cie, thereby consolidating their already growing reputation in car design.

De Dion, which was the first car to enter Rouen, did the run at an average speed of 11.6 mph (18 kph), after spending six hours and 48 minutes on the road. Although that speed may seem slow today, it was then a considerable achievement.

WHO INVENTED THE FIRST TAXI METER?

The ancient Greeks were the first to introduce a form of taxi meter. This was called a hodometer and was fixed to special horse-drawn chariots which plied the streets of Athens for the sole use of the public. The hodometer was a device connected to the chariot's axle which measured the distance of a journey. Another form of meter turned a dial holding a number of pellets which were dropped into a container at measured distances. At the end of the journey the passenger paid according to the number of pellets that had been dropped into the container.

WHO INVENTED THE STEAM TURBINE-POWERED CRAFT?

The invention of steam-powered ships was a big step forward in the history of seafaring, but at the end of the last century there was a further important advance in the form of the *Turbinia*, an experimental launch powered by a steam-turbine engine. It was designed by a Tyneside inventor named Charles Parsons, who was eager to promote his new invention. The chance came at the annual Naval Review in 1897, which was marking Queen Victoria's Diamond Jubilee.

A magnificent fleet of warships was assembled on the great day when, suddenly, the *Turbinia* rushed out among them. In full view of all assembled, the noisy little ship sped to and fro while the Navy's picket boats could do nothing to stop her. The *Turbinia* was travelling at over 60 kph. Charles Parsons had the publicity he needed and the *Turbinia* was soon famous.

A year after the *Turbinia's* performance at the Naval Review, a small launch was built for an unknown owner. She attracted no publicity and even her name has been forgotten. In its way, this launch was almost as important as that of the *Turbinia*, for it was driven by an internal combustion engine. This unnamed little craft was rescued from a garden compost heap in 1955 and given to the Windermere Steamboat Museum in Cumbria.

WHAT WAS THE FIRST LUXURY LINER?

This was the *Great Britain* built by Isambard Kingdom Brunel and launched from Bristol by Prince Albert on July 19,1843.

The fittings were lavish. There was carpeting throughout the passenger area with 1,000 yards of best-quality Brussels carpet, and fitted mirrors all over the ship, which gave the impression of space, especially in the cabins which were small. In the dining room 12 elegant white and gold columns ran its length. What most delighted the ladies was the beautifully furnished combined sitting room and boudoir created for their exclusive use. Even more importantly, the ship was fitted with 26 water closets — other passenger ships still carried chamber pots.

The *Great Britain* had the latest engineering developments. Many of the ideas had come to Brunel as he worked on the ship.

The famous engineer had intended building a wooden paddle-steamer. Then, in October 1838, Brunel sailed in an iron-hulled paddle-steamer from Bristol to Antwerp and decided that the *Great Britain* would be built of iron.

By 1882 the *Great Britain* had become rather obsolete and, unable to compete with her more modern rivals, she was converted into a sailing ship. After over 40 years' service, and on her 47th voyage, she was wrecked rounding Cape Horn, carrying coal to the American Pacific coast.

Although badly damaged, she limped to the Falkland Islands and put in at Port Stanley. Here she was sold to a company which used her for storing wool. The *Great Britain* remained in Port Stanley until 1968, when a restoration committee was set up in Bristol. A wealthy businessman promised to "see the ship home", and it cost him £150,000. On July 19, 1970, exactly 127 years after she was launched, the *Great Britain* came home to a tremendous welcome. Restoration work was begun on her almost immediately.

WHAT WAS A HANSOM CAB?

This was a popular form of transport which first appeared in 1847 and was named after its inventor, Joseph Aloysius Hansom. His idea was not entirely a new one as cabs had been plying the streets of London since 1825. But unlike the other cabs which had four wheels and were rather slow and cumbersome, Hansom's vehicle was two wheeled, was faster and gave the passenger a more comfortable ride. It held two persons, and the driver stood on a dickey at the back, holding the reins which went across the roof.

Popular though the vehicle was with the general public—there were 7,000 hansom cabs in London towards the end of the century—Hansom made very little out of his invention because he sold it to a company which fell into financial difficulties.

WHICH CLIPPER SHIP STILL SURVIVES?

The *Cutty Sark*, the very last of the great ocean-going clipper ships, is housed in her own dry dock at Greenwich. The *Cutty Sark* was built in 1869 to compete in the cut-throat tea trade from China to England.

On that once-a-year run a single

ship could carry nearly 500 tons (500,000 kg) of tea. If she was the first clipper home, her cargo would earn an additional five-pence per two pounds, two ounces (1 kg). This could mean an extra £30,000, which was an enormous sum of money in those days.

It was the great age of sail, and of all the sailing merchant ships, the clippers that brought back the tea were the most romantic. Sadly, the *Cutty Sark* is the only such ship to survive.

That we can still visit her today is due to another sea captain who, although he had never been the *Cutty Sark's* master, fell in love with her early in his career. By 1922 he had retired, but, while walking around Falmouth's harbour one day, he spotted the old *Cutty Sark* (although her name had by then been changed to *Maria de Amparo* and she sailed under a Portuguese flag).

He decided to buy the ship, even though it cost him twice as much as the *Cutty Sark's* first owners had paid for her. He re-rigged and overhauled her and then sailed the splendid old clipper as a training ship for boys. In 1936 she went to the Thames Nautical Training College, where she remained until 1943.

Britain then almost lost the *Cutty Sark*, but fortunately the London County Council was able to step in and look after her until a Preservation Society, led by the Duke of Edinburgh, had the old ship restored to her original condition. Afterwards, she was berthed at Greenwich.

WHICH GREAT LINER BECAME A HOTEL?

In 1967, the great ocean going liner, *Queen Mary*, passed her sister ship *Queen Elizabeth* on the Atlantic run. The *Queen Mary* was then 31 years old and destined for the scrap heap. However, she was saved by an enterprising American businessman and now rests at Long Beach, California, as a hotel and museum.

The hull of the *Queen Mary* was laid down in 1930 at Clydebank, but work on her was halted for over two years during an economic crisis.

When at last salvation arrived, it was due to government intervention. Facing up to the fact that the two great shipping companies, Cunard and White Star, were both in difficulty, the British government, which wanted to see British prestige on the North Atlantic run rejuvenated, offered them a huge loan. The condition was that the companies should merge.

The offer was accepted, and in April 1934, work was resumed on the *Queen Mary*. Six months later, she was ready for launching.

Despite being bigger and better than her rivals, she rolled. In the years before stabilisers were fitted, passengers wondered how so vast a vessel could smash so much crockery and toss them out of their bunks so easily.

Nevertheless, in 1938, she established a record for making the fastest Atlantic crossing, taking it from the French liner, *Normandie*.

During World War II she continued her honourable career with the *Queen Elizabeth*, running the gauntlet of German submarines in the Atlantic Ocean, clocking up about half a million miles and carrying some 400,000 troops to various ports.

After the war, the two vessels took up a partnership, dominating the Atlantic until well into the 1960s.

HOW WAS CLEOPATRA'S NEEDLE TRANSPORTED TO LONDON?

In the days of Ancient Egypt, two granite obelisks had stood outside a temple on the Nile as a symbol of Egypt's might. Centuries later, Cleopatra had them moved to Alexandria and placed outside the Palace of the Caesars from where they disappeared.

They did not turn up again until the 1860s, when the Earl of Cavan found them lying among the rubble in the slums of Alexandria. The Earl immediately took a fancy to the finest of them, which dates back to 1460 BC. He considered it would be a fitting memorial to the British victories over Napoleon in Egypt.

The job of bringing the needle to England was given to General Sir James Alexander. To advise him, he had an engineer, John Dixon, who suggested putting the needle into an iron hull, like a tube, and rolling it into the sea. If it were given a deck and a rudder, it could be towed to Britain, he said.

The strange craft was manufactured in Britain, and sent in sections to Egypt, where it was reassembled around the needle and named *Cleopatra*.

Pulled by the steamer *Olga* from Liverpool, the *Cleopatra* was towed out into the Mediterranean. The date was August 28, 1877, and fate then played a cruel trick. A sunken rock pierced the iron skin. This had to be mended and meant that the journey to Britain could not begin until September 21.

Had its journey started at the pre-arranged time, the *Cleopatra* would have been clear of the Bay of Biscay before an Atlantic cyclone struck it. As it was, the *Olga* and its strange trailer ran into the worst storm to hit the Bay of Biscay in living memory. *Cleopatra*, which carried rails as ballast, began to list so dangerously that she was in danger of sinking and dragging the *Olga* after her. The tow rope was cast off and *Cleopatra* was left to drift. She carried a small crew, and six men put out from the *Olga* in a small boat to rescue them. But the storm was so severe that the men from the *Olga* were drowned. Disaster followed on disaster when the *Cleopatra* sank. Fortunately, a Glasgow steamer found the iron cocoon containing the obelisk, and eventually it arrived in

London. A home was found for it on the Victoria Embankment, beside the River Thames, where it was erected on September 12, 1878.

WHEN WAS THE *QUEEN ELIZABETH* LAUNCHED?

At Clydebank, on September 27, 1938. The 83,673 ton Royal Mail Ship *Queen Elizabeth* was the world's largest passenger liner, and measured 1,031 feet from bow to stern.

When the Second World War started, the *Queen Elizabeth* was still in the fitting-out basin at Clydebank. She was hurriedly made seaworthy, and on March 2, 1940, she commenced her maiden voyage to New York, where she was converted into a troopship. During her war service, the *Queen Elizabeth* carried 811,325 men and steamed 492,635 miles to Allied ports all over the world. She seldom sailed in convoy but relied for protection on her high speed of 28-30 knots.

After the war, she was used to repatriate American and Canadian troops until March 1946. It was not until October 16, 1946, that she commenced her first civilian passenger voyage from Southampton to New York.

By the 1960s, air transport was taking passengers from the liners, and she began to lose money. In May 1968, the Cunard Company withdrew the *Queen Elizabeth* from service and put her up for sale. It was then announced that a new flagship was to be built for Cunard — the *Queen Elizabeth II*.

The *Queen Elizabeth* was purchased by an American company which tried to turn her into a floating Disneyland, but failed. A wealthy Chinese ship owner then bought her to use as a floating hotel, university and museum, and had her taken to Hong Kong and refitted. Shortly afterwards, she caught fire and was burned out, then rolled over and sank at her moorings. It was a very sad end to a magnificent ship.

WHY WAS BUGATTI'S *BLACK BESS* SPECIAL?

It was the only Bugatti to be built with a chain drive. Known as the *Black Bess*, this 5-litre, 1913 model was bought by the famous French aviation pioneer and First World War flying ace, Roland Gavros.

Ettore Bugatti, the car's designer and builder, was born in Milan, Italy, in 1881, the son of a well-known goldsmith who wanted his two sons to become artists. One of them, Rembrandt Bugatti, was to become well known as a sculptor.

But Ettore loved mechanical things. At the age of 17, he planned and built his own two-engine tricycle. After a year as an apprentice with an engineering company, Bugatti built his first motor vehicle, the forerunner of a line that was to continue for 40 years.

A Bugatti racing car leads in the Monaco Grand Prix

Bugatti established his own factory in 1910 at Molsheim in Alsace. At 28, he was a famed car designer, his talents being used by De Dietrick and Peugeot.

His first production car, Tipo 13, was meant for racing. At about the same time, he produced a road car which was bought by Peugeot and named the Bebe.

Now started a period, ending with the outbreak of the First World War, when Bugatti cars were the leading contenders in over a thousand motor races.

The victories were due to the exceptional stability of the cars and the careful design of the engines. Their famous horse-shoe radiators became the hallmark of success.

Ettore Bugatti died in 1947. The Bugatti car company carried on for some years after his death, but the cars built without the genius of the man who created the line were not true Bugattis.

HOW DID A LIFEBOAT MAKE AN OVERLAND RESCUE?

In 1881, an incredible example of overland transport took place in the Yorkshire coastal town of Whitby. A local trawler had sunk in Robin Hood's Bay, and its crew of eight had taken to the ship's boat. But due to heavy seas they were unable to make it to the shore. All they could hope was that the lifeboat would reach them before they foundered.

Robin Hood's Bay was six miles away, too far away for the lifeboat at Whitby to reach them in the conditions. It was then that the coxswain of the lifeboat made a decision that was to become one of the legends of the sea. They would haul the lifeboat overland to the bay.

Two heavy horses were found and harnessed to the boat's carriage. Slowly, the carriage began to move forward, then to roll back as the horses' shoes slipped and slid on the ice-covered cobbles. Seeing this, the watching townsfolk surged forward and, taking hold of the hauling ropes, they began to heave to the shouted instructions of the coxswain. More help came as the news spread through the district, when farmers began bringing along their draught horses. By the time they were clear of the town there was a line of no fewer than 50 horses as well as scores of people hauling the boat.

Foot by foot, yard by yard, the horses and people of Whitby dragged the boat forward, with the horses often falling in the drifts of snow that lay outside the town. The whole night passed in this manner until at last they reached Robin Hood's Bay, where everyone could see that the eight men were miraculously still afloat.

The carriage was then taken to the water's edge where the lifeboat men clambered aboard and took to the oars. The launchers then waded waist-deep into the boiling waters, rolling the carriage forward until a wave lifted the lifeboat clear.

After fighting the waves, the lifeboat returned with the eight men safely aboard — all of them a living tribute to the bravery of those who had rescued them.

WHICH RAFT MADE A NORWEGIAN FAMOUS?

Until 1947, no one could say with certainty where the brown-skinned people who lived on the tiny islands in the South Pacific were from.

A Norwegian named Thor Heyerdahl believed that they must have crossed the water from Peru in South America, and to prove this theory he decided to build a raft like those used by the Pacific islanders and, making use of the prevailing winds and currents, sail it from Peru. With the assistance of the British, American and Peruvian governments, Heyerdahl was able to put his plan into action.

The raft he had constructed of

balsa wood was named the *Kon-Tiki*. Above the logs, lashed with hemp, was a deck of split bamboo. A cabin of split bamboo and banana leaves was built upon this. To the mangrove-wood masts was fixed a large square sail which had painted on it the face of the Inca god Kon-tiki, after whom the raft was named.

On April 28, 1947, the frail vessel, which was to brave rough seas and danger from whales and sharks, was towed out to sea from the naval dockyard at Callao in West Peru.

After months at sea, Thor Heyerdahl and his five companions finally sighted land more than 4,000 miles from Peru, but their decision to continue sailing westwards almost led to disaster. As they approached the next island, their raft ran hard on to a reef, but was swept safely into a lagoon. At last, on July 21, 1947, they had reached a Pacific island after months of danger with Thor's theory finally proved.

WHO SAILED AROUND THE WORLD IN 1966?

At Gosport, in Hampshire, on March 8, 1966, Francis Chichester's latest yacht was launched. She was the ketch *Gypsy Moth IV*.

Gypsy Moth IV was originally designed for the 1968 Single-handed Transatlantic Race from Plymouth to Newport, Rhode Island, but while she was being constructed, Chichester decided he would like to sail her single-handed round the world, following the route of the old Australian wool clippers. As a result of this decision, her designers, John Illingworth and Associates, made several alterations in the boat's design.

The hull of *Gypsy Moth IV* was of laminated wood, specially moulded to be as light as possible. The yacht, which carried a wide choice of head sails was rigged as a ketch that one man could easily handle.

On August 27, 1966, Chichester set off from Plymouth on the first stage of his 28,500 mile (45,866 km) voyage round the world. After 107 days, during which *Gypsy Moth IV* was buffeted by northeast winds and then becalmed and swept by adverse currents, he arrived in Sydney on the afternoon of December 12.

Before leaving Sydney on the second and final stage of *Gypsy Moth IV's* voyage round the dangerous Cape Horn and up through the Atlantic Ocean to Plymouth, Francis Chichester was appointed a Knight Commander of the British Empire in recognition of his individual achievement and sustained endeavour in the navigation and seamanship of small craft.

WHAT WAS A TRAVOIS?

A carrier drawn by a horse or dog used by American Plains Indians. Two trailing poles served as shafts.

General Knowledge

WHERE WAS KING ARTHUR'S CITY OF CAMELOT?

The exciting tales of King Arthur and his beautiful Queen Guinevere have come to us from legend. Wondrous indeed are the adventures written of Arthur and his gallant Knights of the Round Table; yet the truth is we know very little.

There really lived a British chief named Arthur. He lived in the 6th century. He was the most successful of the British chiefs, though not the king of the Britons. He was the hero of the battle of Badon Hill fought about AD 520 and was the last British leader to withstand the advance of the Saxons.

He was killed, probably in a battle against a rival British chief, at Camlon.

There is no contemporary account of Arthur but he is described in a book *Historia Britonum*, which was written in the 8th century.

Despite all this, the legend of King Arthur and his knights still prevails and many places lay claim to a link with the king, even in counties as far apart as Cornwall in the west of England and Cumberland in the north west. Therefore the site of Camelot, the story-book city in which Arthur held court with his knights, has long been sought.

Camelford in Cornwall, Caerleon in Monmouthshire, Queen Camel and South Cadbury both in Avon, and Winchester in Hampshire — all have been named as the site of the king's city. But there is nothing certain and it seems that Camelot will forever be a city which faded into the mists of time at the passing of a king.

WHY IS THE ALBERT HALL, LONDON, SO-NAMED?

Its very name gives the clue, for the man who dreamed of a great hall where people could come to take part in appreciating the arts and sciences was Prince Albert, the Prince Consort, and the husband of Queen Victoria.

Albert, the son of the Duke of

Artistes come from all over the world to perform at the Albert Hall

Saxe-Coburg-Gotha was born August 26, 1819 at Schloss Rosenau, near Coburg, Germany. He was first cousin to Princess Victoria, the niece of King William IV of England, who did not approve of their marrying.

However, Victoria fell in love with the handsome young prince, and three years after she became Queen, the happy pair were married on February 10, 1840. It proved to be a very happy marriage.

Albert not only loved Victoria. He also loved Britain and always interested himself in the country's welfare. It was he who inspired the Great International Exhibition of 1851 which attracted visitors from all over the world. Then he began to plan for a permanent exhibition hall, in Kensington, West London.

The state opening of the Albert Hall took place on March 29, 1897. It was opened by Queen Victoria, who was then a widow. Sadly, the Prince did not live long enough to see his dream come true. He had died December 14, 1861.

WHAT IS COAL?

It is the fossilised remains of vegetation which grew on the Earth millions of years ago. The vegetation flourished in swampy places like the peat-bogs of the present day. As the vegetation died it fell into the water where, instead of decaying as it would have done in the open air, it underwent certain chemical changes.

First, it was transformed into peat. Later, the surface of the land sank and the peat-bogs became the bottoms of the lakes and seas. Sand and mud was then deposited over the vegetable matter, completely shutting it off from the air. More chemical changes took place, while the weight of the sediment compressed the deposits more compactly.

It was these chemical changes and compression which slowly turned the vegetable matter into coal.

WHY DO WE SHAKE HANDS?
The custom originated when men carried swords. Shaking hands with the right hand indicated that the sword would not be drawn and was a gesture of friendship.

WHAT WAS A TEPEE?
"Tepee" or "tipi" is an American Indian word meaning "the place where one lives." It is from the Dakota Indian language.

The covering of the tepee was constructed of fifteen to eighteen dressed buffalo hides, cut and sewn together in a large semi-circular sheet.

When the tepee had been erected, a fire pit was dug in the centre. There a fire would be built to cook food and warm the tepee.

The Dakotas were the most powerful of the Sioux Indians. They comprised four main tribes, the Eastern Dakota, the Yankton, the Santee and the Teton. The head of a Dakota Indian has appeared on the American penny and nickel.

HOW DID TELEVISION GET ITS NAME?
"Tele" comes from the Greek and means "far." There are several words beginning with "tele." Telegraph, for instance, which means a message sent a long way. Telescope is an instrument through which one can see a long way off. The telephone enables us to speak to someone far away. Telepathy is sending thoughts far away to somebody else. Television, it follows, means seeing a "vision" that is really far away.

WHAT IS BONE CHINA?
It is a very fine chinaware. It is called bone china because the clay from which it is made contains bone ash that is obtained from the grinding up of bones of cattle and other animals.

Josiah Spode invented bone china. He was an English potter born at Stoke-on-Trent, son of a manufacturing potter. He was truly the most successful china manufacturer of the 19th century, popularising and improving the willow pattern and other chinaware. In 1800 he began the manufacture of porcelain of great beauty. His china is highly esteemed by collectors.

WHO WAS YANKEE DOODLE?

There was no one person to whom this term was given. It was certainly a song popular in the United States of America before the War of Independence. It is now regarded as one of American's national tunes.

How the name Yankee Doodle came about is not clear. It is, however, generally believed to have been due to the English surgeon named Richard Shuckburgh. He seems to have introduced the term in 1775 in some verse he wrote that ridiculed soldiers in gaudy uniforms.

WHAT IS A PALINDROME?

It is the name given to a word or sentence which can be read the same backwards as forwards. It is derived from the Greek word *palindromos*, meaning running backwards.

An example of a palindrome is that complaint usually associated with Napoleon: "Able was I ere I saw Elba." Another example is "Madam I'm Adam."

Civic, level, reviver, and noon are all examples of a single word palindrome.

WHY DOES A BAD EGG FLOAT WHILE A GOOD EGG SINKS?

A hen's fresh egg is full of yolk and albumen (the white of the egg). If it is placed in water it will sink because it is heavier than water.

In a bad egg the rotten yolk and the albumen produce gases which make the egg much lighter than when it was fresh. The egg now does not weigh as much as an equal amount of water and when in water, it floats. Likewise a battleship floats for the same reason — it weighs less than the water.

WHY DO CHINESE PEOPLE USE CHOP STICKS?

It is their custom and there are many reasons why. Metal, in olden times, was scarce so the Chinese fashioned chop sticks. Again, Chinese food is not like Western food in its preparation. Meat dishes are cut up beforehand, making knives and forks unnecessary. In any case, chop sticks in experienced hands are as easy to use as our knives and forks. Most chop sticks are made from bamboo, but they are also made from many other materials.

Chop sticks means "quick sticks." In the Chinese language "chop" means quick.

Chinese restaurants are very popular today and are in many countries of the world. They are places, too, where, if you want to, you can learn how to use chop sticks.

WHAT IS THE MOST VALUABLE PAINTING IN THE WORLD?

This is a difficult question to answer truthfully inasmuch as there are many masterpieces which are in famous collections such as the

This is one of Van Gogh's favourite paintings of sunflowers

National Gallery in London, the Louvre in Paris and the Prado in Madrid; but as they are unlikely to come on the market nobody can really state how much they are worth. There are many famous paintings, such as the Mona Lisa by Leonardo da Vinci, which are so valuable that they are considered to be priceless.

It is worth noting, however, that on March 30, 1987, a price of 24.75

million pounds (39.6 million dollars) including the buyer's premium was sold at auction in London for a painting of sunflowers by the Impressionist artist, Vincent Van Gogh. This was a record purchase price for a painting at auction.

WHY ARE SHIPS' PORTHOLES ROUND?

The simple answer to this question is that the portholes are more easily sealed.

In rough weather, the sea might wash up against the side of the vessel and over the portholes. If they were square, there would always be a weakness at the corners. A round aperture can be completely covered by a circular lid or plate.

WHY IS STRONG TEA NOT GOOD FOR YOU?

Tea contains, apart from theine and certain aromatic substances, a substance called tannin. This is an astringent acid which can dry up the digestive juices. Indigestion then follows. Tannin is present in strong tea particularly, and in tea that has been standing for rather a long time.

It is better, therefore, to drink tea that is not strong. It is wise, too, to infuse it for a few minutes only.

After pouring boiling water on the tea leaves or tea bags, three minutes is enough to extract most of the flavour and aromatic substances. That is when the tea should be poured for it will not contain harmful amounts of tannin. The longer the tea infuses, the more tannin will be present.

WHAT IS CAJUN MUSIC?

In 1713 the French colony of Acadia in Canada was ceded to the British who promptly expelled the French settlers who were living there. Most of the Acadians migrated to Louisiana where their descendants now live. The word "Cajun" is a corruption of "Acadian."

The popular form of music which is described today as "Cajun" emanates from South Louisiana. The instrument that the early Cajuns played was the fiddle. Then in the late 19th century they added the diatonic accordion which they obtained from German traders. Washboards and triangles and on occasion second fiddles combined to provide rhythmic accompaniments. Altogether it is a most exhilirating form of modern music and is often sung and played at Country and Western festivals and concerts, in its present-day advanced form.

WHO INVENTED ICE SKATES?

Today's splendid skates have come to us through improvements over the centuries. Perhaps the earliest ice skates were simply the bones of animals which were bound to the feet.

The primitive Norsemen made much use of these bone "runners' and later other people of Northern Europe quickly learned how to travel at speed on icy surfaces.

It is not known when metal skates were introduced. It may have been soon after the people of Northern Europe learned how to work iron into different shapes, as early as the 4th century.

WHAT IS AN OSCAR?

In 1927 the movie magnates decided to do something to honour the best workers in the industry. They founded the Academy of Motion Picture Arts and Sciences. One purpose of this organisation was to present an award each year to the best worker in each field. The trophy took the shape of a man grasping a sword.

The first awards — 15 in all — were given in 1929 for the films of 1928. Four years later, Margaret Herrick, late president director of the Academy, saw one of the awards. "That looks like my Uncle Oscar," she said. The idea of calling the Academy Awards "Oscar" soon caught on and today are seldom referred to in any other way.

WHY DOES NOISE SHATTER A WINDOW?

Noise is an irregular wave in the air. A loud noise outside a house will cause the air to be flung in waves against a building. When they strike a window, the glass is shaken. The noise has only to be so great, the resultant waves in the air have only to be violent enough to shake the glass more than it can stand. Then it breaks.

WHY IS AN ACADEMY SO CALLED?

There was in the days of Ancient Greece a grove or garden near Athens. It was named after Academus, a legendary Greek hero. The park of Academus was known far and wide for its beautiful flowers, its shady avenues of mighty trees and the quietness that reigned everywhere.

It became a favourite haunt for learned scholars such as Plato the famous Greek philosopher and his friends.

Regrettably when the Romans stormed through Greece, they felled the noble trees of Academus and used the wood to build warships. Today no trace remains of the ancient garden but since the days of Plato the word Academy has been given to several places of learning.

Academies were established throughout Italy during the Renaissance and later in France and England.

WHO WAS THE OLDEST MAN WHO EVER LIVED?

We have, of course, the Bible's word that Methuselah, the grandfather of Noah, lived for 969 years. Compared with him, the socalled "Modern Methuselah" was a mere babe. He was a Yorkshire peasant named Henry Jenkins, who was buried in Bolton-on-Swale, England, in 1670 and has a memorial stating that he lived to the "amazing age of 169."

Another very old Englishman was Thomas Parr, known to fame as Old Parr, who claimed to have been born in 1483 and was presented to King Charles I in 1635 as "a piece of antiquity." He died a few weeks after meeting the King and was buried in Westminster Abbey where a memorial states that he had lived to the great age of 152. Positive proof is lacking, though.

There is, however, real proof for the great age of Shigechiyo Izumi, a Japanese who was born June 29, 1865 and died February 21, 1986 at the age of 120.

WHY DOES A MARRIED WOMAN WEAR A WEDDING RING?

It is said that the wedding ring dates back to barbaric times when wives were treated by their husbands as little better than slaves. It was the custom to fasten a chain on a slave as a mark of ownership and often a married woman was forced to wear a chain around her body or a ring around her neck.

Later men realized that a wife was a helpmate in every sense of the word. The custom of treating her like a slave gradually ceased but men still wished to show visible possession of a wife. This took the form of a ring on the finger of the wife's left hand.

WHY WAS A FAMOUS ENGLISH ROYAL FAMILY KNOWN AS PLANTAGENET?

Plantagent was a nickname given to Count Geoffrey of Anjou who married in 1129 Matilda, the daughter of Henry I of England. Geoffrey often wore a sprig of broom, in Latin *planta genesta*, in his cap and his descendants are often referred to as the Plantaganets. In fact the more correct name of the dynasty is the Angevins.

King Henry's only son, Prince William. was drowned when the *White Ship* which was carrying him and his courtiers from France to England foundered in the English Channel. The Princess Matilda's son later became Henry II.

The name of Plantagenet was not used by Henry nor by those who came after him. It was adopted by Richard, Duke of York, the father of Edward IV who ruled England from 1461 to 1483.

WHAT IS A MAHOUT?

The keeper and driver of an elephant in India.

WHO WAS SIXTEEN-STRING JACK?

He was a notorious highwayman, born near the old town of Bath in the West of England midway in the 18th century.

As a boy he was a poor peddler, selling his wares in villages around Bath. He was twelve years old when a lady took him into her service. Some time later he was working in a stable in Brooke's Mews in London.

It is known that in about 1770 he was coachman to a gentleman living near Portman Square, London and was at one time a servant of the Earl of Sandwich. It was while he was working for the Earl that he became known as Sixteen-String Jack because he often wore bunches of gaily-coloured ribbons at the knees of his breeches.

Always fond of expensive clothes and too fond of gambling, he soon found himself in debt. It was then that he took first to pocket-picking and later to highway robbery.

On more than one occasion he was arrested for theft and for this crime in those days, a criminal could be hanged. Somehow or other, Jack Rann managed to be discharged each time, to continue his reckless life of crime.

His end came when he was finally arrested for a robbery on the Uxbridge road. He had held up a Doctor Bell and stolen from him the paltry sum of one shilling and sixpence and a cheap watch. He was condemned and died bravely on the scaffold on November 30, 1774, still clad in fine raiment and bunches of sixteen strings fluttering at his knees.

WHAT DOES THE NAME "ESKIMOS" MEAN?

Eskimos is an American Indian word and is what the Eskimos' Indian neighbours called them. It means "devourers of raw flesh."

The Eskimos call themselves "Innuit" which simply means "people" or "men."

WHY DID SOCRATES KILL HIMSELF?

Socrates was possibly the greatest philosopher of all time. His great belief was that everyone should learn to know themselves. He said that only when a person realises his own limitations and ignorances can he be truly wise.

Socrates was born in about 470 BC in Athens. He loved to sit in the market place of the city and talk to the people who passed. Great though Socrates's contribution was to philosophy, he could not resist ridiculing religion and important people. Eventually the citizens of Athens were tired of Socrates and his sharp tongue. They arrested him on false charges and condemned him to death. Socrates drank deadly hemlock to avoid an execution.

WHY DOES "IN GOD WE TRUST" APPEAR ON AMERICAN COINS?

It was the suggestion of James Pollock, the Governor of Pennsylvania from 1854 to 1857. During the great American Civil War when the armies of the Northern States were battling against the forces of the Southern States, Pollock wrote to the Secretary of the Treasury.

The American House of Representatives in session

He believed that during the violent period, the recognition of God on the national coinage was a bounden duty.

The suggestion was put forward, approved by Congress and a Bill was unanimously passed by the Senate and the House of Representatives.

The words first appeared on U S coins in 1866, the year after the conclusion of the Civil War.

WHO FOLLOWED THE RIVERS OF AUSTRALIA?

In the early 19th century, Australian settlers and explorers had found several large rivers flowing inland from the east coast, but nobody knew where they went. Some people suggested the rivers flowed to some vast inland sea. Others thought they dried up in the terrible desert heat.

In 1829 Charles Sturt, a member of the governor's staff, set out in a 27 foot boat with a few companions to follow one of the rivers. After a while the river changed into a swamp of reeds and narrow channels. Then they reached the junction of a large, smooth river. After several days journey the river they were on joined yet another major stream. It was clear that the rivers all flowed to the same place.

A thousand miles from their starting point the boat and its crew reached a large lake and Sturt and his party could hear the roar of the surf. They had proved that the rivers eventually flowed southwards into the Great Australian Bight and the Southern Ocean.

WHAT IS THE BROCKEN SPECTRE?

Mountaineers climbing the Brocken, a mountain in Germany, have sometimes been startled by a strange apparition. Giant human forms are seen climbing neighbouring peaks. The figures are in fact, shadows of the climbers themselves cast on to mist and cloud. The peculiar shape of the Brocken and the prevalence of low cloud make this phenomenon common. It is sometimes seen on other peaks.

WHY DO WE CALL SOME PEOPLE "NOSEY PARKER"?

When someone is particularly inquisitive about a matter which does not concern them, he or she may be referred to as a "Nosey Parker". This name dates back to Matthew Parker who was Archbishop of Canterbury in the 1560s. Archbishop Parker was a hardworking man who helped with an early translation into English of the Bible and tried to resist extremism in the Church of England. Unfortunately, his activities often seemed prying and full of intrigue to people who disagreed with his ideas.

He became known for his inquisitive nature and because he had such a large nose he was called Nosey Parker.

WHEN WERE THE FIRST BANKNOTES USED?

The earliest money was made of precious metal, such as gold or silver. The design of the coin carried a government's promise that the metal was included in the coin, thus giving it a value.

Paper money is an extension of the design on the coin. Instead of guaranteeing the amount of metal, the note is a promise that a certain amount of real money will be exchanged for the note on demand. Most paper money used today carries such a promise. The first paper money was probably used in China. Marco Polo reported the use of such when he visited China in the 13th century.

The first European banknotes were issued in 1658 by the State Bank of Sweden.

WHERE IS PARMESAN CHEESE MADE?

Parmesan cheese is one of the most famous and delicious cheeses of Italy. It is the same colour as straw, is very hard and has a rich, strong flavour.

In order to maintain the high quality of this cheese, the Italian government has imposed strict rules on the way it is made. If a cheese maker does not follow the rules, he cannot call his cheese Parmesan. Parmesan must be made by hand, with fresh milk from cows grazing near Parma between April 1 and November 11 each year. The cheese is left to mature for at least 18 months before it is sold.

WHAT IS EDAM?

It is a cheese named after a town in Holland. It is a mild cheese in the shape of a ball and coated with a red wax.

WHEN WAS A CHANNEL TUNNEL FIRST BEGUN?

The idea of building a tunnel beneath the English Channel is not new. First mention of it was made during the Napoleonic Wars in the early 19th century. Napoleon, Emperor of the French, considered digging a tunnel in order to transport his army to Britain.

WHICH RECORD IN AMERICAN BASEBALL IS HELD BY BABE RUTH?

When George Herman Ruth, better known as Babe, retired from baseball in 1935 he was acknowledged as the greatest baseball batter in America.

Among the records he held was that of 714 regular season home runs, a season total of 60 and a long hit of 587 feet (179 m). The total number of home runs has now been superseded by Hank Aaron. Babe Ruth's season record has been broken, but only by a player who played in far more games. His record hit, however, has never been bettered in major league baseball.

WHAT ARE FUNERAL BRASSES?

Funeral brasses were popular with knights and the nobility of the Middle Ages. They are large flat plates of brass fixed over the graves of the persons they commemorate and usually an effigy of the deceased is engraved on each plate.

Brasses are of great use to historians as they reveal details of dress and armour.

There are about 4,000 brasses in England, and several more elsewhere in Europe.

WHAT WAS WALT DISNEY'S FIRST FULL-LENGTH ANIMATED CARTOON FILM?

Snow White and the Seven Dwarfs, which was produced in 1937. Without doubt, this was and remains one of Disney's finest productions.

WHO WAS THE GREATEST CRICKET BATSMAN?

Of all the great batsmen in the history of cricket there is one who stands out amongst the others.

Sir Donald Bradman was born

in 1903 and even as a schoolboy had an outstanding batting record. In 1927 he began playing for New South Wales in the interstate matches. Five years later he was in the test team and was writing himself into the record books. His unusual but natural style of wielding a bat was all his own. He had never been trained to be a great batsman, it had just come naturally.

In the 1929 series he scored 452 runs not out against Queensland, a record which was to stand for 29 years.

The records of this extraordinary batsman which still stand are: the highest season average of 115 runs, a career average of 95 runs and a test average of 99.4. It seems unlikely that these amazing figures will ever be bettered.

WHAT IS MOLASSES?

A dark syrup drained from sugar during refining.

WHAT IS A STOCK EXCHANGE "BULL"?

A person who buys securities not for investment but to sell again.

WHICH OF THE NEW TESTAMENT GOSPELS ARE CALLED SYNOPTIC?

Those of the Saints Matthew, Mark and Luke which report facts. The Gospel according to St John is more concerned with the meanings of Jesus Christ's teaching.

HOW DEEP IS THE OCEAN?

The floors of the world's oceans consist of different features. In general, they fall into three.

The first, the continental shelf, is formed by the submerged edges of continents. These waters are usually only a few hundred feet deep. The entire North Sea is part of the continental shelf.

The second is beyond the edge of the continental shelf, where the sea floor drops rapidly to depths of around 14,000 feet (4,267 m). This is the abyssal plain which covers most of the ocean floors. It is marked by hills, mountains, and plains. Some mountains and volcanoes of the abyssal plain rise to the ocean surface to form islands.

Stretching across some areas of abyssal plain is the third feature, the ocean trenches. These narrow cracks in the Earth are extremely deep. The deepest of all the trenches is the Marianas Trench in the Pacific. It has been measured as 36,198 feet (11,033 m) deep.

WHICH OF REMBRANDT'S PAINTINGS WAS DAMAGED BY A VANDAL IN 1975?

The Night Watch which is in Amsterdam's Rijksmuseum.

WHO IN LEGEND WAS THE MESSENGER OF THE GODS?

In Roman legend, Mercury. In Greek legend, Hermes.

The largest tsunami was caused by an earthquake in 1971

WHAT IS A TSUNAMI?

Tsunami is the Japanese word for a phenomenon often called a tidal wave. In fact the two are quite distinct. (*Tsu* means over-flowing and *nami* a wave.)

A tidal wave occurs when the rising tide forces a mass of water along a narrow estuary or strait, causing a rise in water level. The tsunami is very much more destructive. The usual cause of a tsunami is an earthquake or similar event.

The largest tsunami yet measured was 270 feet (85 m) tall and appeared off Ishigaki Island, east of Taiwan in 1971. Far more destructive was the tsunami which swept through Indonesia on August 27, 1883. When the island volcano of Krakatoa exploded that morning it not only blew itself to pieces but created a huge tsunami.

As it swamped the surrounding islands, the wave destroyed 163 villages, killed 36,380 people and carried a warship miles inland. The height of this massive wave is unknown. Fortunately such tsunami waves are rare.

WHAT IN THE DAYS OF THE OLD WEST WAS A ROUGHSTRING RIDER?

A ranch-hand who followed the trade of horse-breaking. The roughstring consisted of the young, old or wild horses that the cowboys could not, or would not ride.

WHAT ARE BROGUE SHOES?

They are heavy shoes with perforations on the toecap and sides. The name derives from the Gaelic brog, meaning shoe and was first applied to raw-hide shoes worn in parts of Ireland and Scotland.

WHAT WAS THE TOMATO FIRST CALLED WHEN IT WAS INTRODUCED INTO EUROPE?

The love apple.

WHEN DID THE ORIENT EXPRESS MAKE ITS FIRST JOURNEY?

At 6pm on October 4, 1883, the Orient Express left Paris on its inaugural journey to Constantinople (now Istanbul).

The guests and paying passengers had been promised a gastronomical feast during the journey, and they were not to be disappointed. After entering the dining saloons lit by huge chandeliers, the diners sat down at tables laid with cutlery of solid silver, glasses made of Baccarat crystal and gold rimmed plates made of the finest porcelain. The meal turned out to be a gargantuan one of ten courses, starting with an hors d'oeuvre which included lobsters, caviar and oysters. The dinner, not surprisingly, lasted for three hours and was served by waiters wearing powdered wigs, tail coats, fine breeches and silk stockings.

When it was over, the gentlemen could retire to a smoking room with comfortable leather chairs, where they could sit and read a book from the library or browse through one of the German, English or Austrian newspapers that were available for their use. The ladies, in their turn could retire to a drawing room containing Louis XV furniture and silk drapes at the windows.

Treated like royalty throughout the journey in a train whose fitments throughout had never been equalled, it was only to be expected that everyone should express themselves as being well satisfied with their journey on the Orient Express. One solitary voice of complaint was heard when a passenger complained that powder from the waiter's wig had fallen into his soup.

HOW ARE DEGREES FAHRENHEIT CONVERTED TO DEGREES CENTIGRADE?

By subtracting 32 from the number of degrees Fahrenheit, multiplying the remainder by 5 and dividing the result by 9.

WHEN, WHERE AND BY WHOM WAS THE FIRST MAN-MADE FIBRE PRODUCED?

It was first produced experimentally by Sir Joseph Swan at Newcastle-upon-Tyne in 1883.

WHAT IS STALEMATE IN CHESS?

A drawn position, when a player is not in check but cannot move without bringing the king into check.

WHAT IS A GLOCKENSPIEL?

A musical instrument consisting of bells played on a keyboard.

BY WHOM WAS THE FIRST FOUR MINUTE MILE RUN?

Roger Bannister, a 25 year old medical student on May 6, 1954. He ran the mile in three minutes 59.4 seconds.

WHY IS A BLACKSMITH SO NAMED?

Because he works in black metals such as iron instead of white metals like tin or silver.

WHY DOES SALT MELT SNOW?

Snow consists of ice crystals and salt melts snow because it has a lower freezing point than snow.

IN CRICKET WHAT IS A WICKET-MAIDEN OVER?

One in which no runs have been scored and in which a wicket has been taken by the bowler.

WHAT IN SAILING IS LEEWAY?

The sideways movement of a vessel while it is travelling forward. When a sailing vessel is sailing with the wind on one side or the other it will move ahead, but at the same time the force of the wind will, to some extent, push the boat sideways through the water.

WHY ARE BRITISH POLICEMEN KNOWN AS "BOBBIES" OR "PEELERS"?

Because Sir Robert Peel introduced the Police Force by his Act of 1829.

WHEN WAS PUNCTUATION, AS WE KNOW IT, FIRST USED?

In Venice about 1500. It was developed by an Italian printer named Manutius, probably from a very early system of signs and dots.

WHAT IS A DIHEDRAL?

It is the angle of tilt of an aircraft's wings.

In 1849 thousands of prospectors were searching for gold in California

WHAT IS A SYNTHETIC MATERIAL?

One that resembles a natural material. Nylon, for example, is a synthetic material resembling silk.

WHAT LANGUAGE DID JESUS SPEAK?

Aramaic.

WHY IS "MATINEE" AN ODD NAME FOR AN AFTERNOON PERFORMANCE IN A THEATRE?

Because it derives from the French word meaning "morning".

WHAT WAS A "FORTY-NINER"?

A prospector who joined the Gold Rush in California in 1849.

WHICH METAL IS LIKE A LIQUID WHEN IT IS COLD?

Mercury.

WHAT ARE "RAPIDS" ON A RIVER?

The beds of rivers sometimes slope more steeply in some places than in others, causing the water to flow more swiftly. These places are called rapids.

HOW HAS THE POPULATION OF THE WORLD GROWN IN THE PAST FEW THOUSAND YEARS?

It is believed that about 12,000 years ago the population of the world was stable at around 4 million human beings. By the time of Jesus, just 2,000 years ago, there were approximately 170 million people on earth. Just 500 years ago there were around 400 million people, and that total had increased to 1,600 million by the year 1900. By 1950 that total had grown to 2,500 million and in the past 37 years it has doubled again to more than 5,000 million people.

WHAT WILL THE POPULATION OF THE WORLD BE ONE HUNDRED YEARS FROM NOW?

Statisticians who study the population of the world are called demographers. After careful scrutiny they believe that the population of the world will grow from its present level of 5,000 million people to about 8,500 million people within the next hundred years; that is, just before the end of the 21st century.

WHAT IS TATTOOING?

This strange skin decoration is usually done by pricking designs with an awl or needle dipped in indelible inks or pigments of different colours.

Primitive tribes once tattooed fierce designs on their faces to present a more frightening aspect to their enemies. Other designs had certain religious meanings while others were signs of deep mourning.

In Japan years ago, it was considered an art, and elaborate colour tattooing took the place of clothing.

Today having a tattoo is less fashionable although it is still popular among soldiers and sailors. Modern tattoo artists use an electric needle for tracing the designs and colouring them.

HOW DID THE EARTH FORM?

In the past there have been many different ideas about how the Earth was formed. Today most scientists agree on one particular theory.

They believe that 5,000 million years ago the solar system was a huge drifting cloud of gas. Gradually gravity began to pull most of the gas into a huge mass at the centre of the cloud. At the same time the cloud of gas began to spin and flatten out into a disc. As a mass of gases collected in the centre, smaller masses of gas came together in the outer reaches of the gas cloud. These continued to spin around the central mass.

After some 400 million years, the mass of gas in the centre began to burn and formed the sun. The lumps of gas orbiting the sun cooled and solidified to form planets. Nearest to the Sun is Mercury, then comes Venus and the third is Earth.

Fire-fighting equipment in the days before fire engines

WHO WAS HARRY HOTSPUR?

One of the most powerful northern English families was that of Percy, the Earls of Northumberland. During the late 14th century the eldest son of the Earl was Sir Henry Percy. who became a hero and earned the name Harry Hotspur.

In 1403 Harry Hotspur raised a rebellion against Henry IV and marched south. The King was too good for him and Harry Hotspur met his death in battle at Shrewsbury, fighting bravely to the last.

WHAT WERE FIRE-HOOKS?

In the days when most houses were roofed with thatch, there was no fire-service to call on for help and a fire was even more dangerous than it is today. Burning straw or sparks blown in the wind could set fire to neighbouring property.

It was important to be able to tackle blazing thatch quickly. Large iron fire-hooks were used to pull down the burning straw. Often these were kept in a well-known, accessible place such as the local church porch. A pair of these fire-hooks can still be seen in Bere Regis Church, Dorset.

WHAT IS THE KOH-I-NOOR?

A famous Indian diamond, now part of the British regalia.

WHAT IS A SIROCCO?

A dry, hot wind which blows north from the Sahara across Libya and the Mediterranean. When it reaches Italy, it is warm and moist.

WHEN WAS THE FIRST AERIAL PHOTOGRAPH TAKEN?
The first aerial picture was taken from a balloon by Gaspard Tournachon over Paris in 1858, using a very simple camera.

WHICH BUILDING IN THE BIBLE WAS DESIGNED SO THAT ITS TOP MIGHT REACH TO HEAVEN?
The Tower of Babel.

WHAT ARE HYPOCHONDRIACS?
People who imagine they are ill.

WHAT METAL IS EXTRACTED FROM SEAWATER?
Magnesium.

WHAT IS A MARIONETTE?
A puppet manipulated by strings.

WHAT ARE THE COLOURS OF THE RAINBOW?
Violet, indigo, blue, green, yellow, orange and red.

WHERE AND WHEN WAS NAPOLEON BONAPARTE BORN?
On the island of Corsica, shortly after it had been taken over by the French in 1769.

IS QUEEN ELIZABETH II THE DUKE OF NORMANDY?
Yes. That is the traditional title of the Queen in the Channel Islands.

WHAT IS A KOPEK?
It is a Russian coin.

A CAPTAIN OF ENGINEERS WROTE WHICH NATIONAL ANTHEM?
The *Marseillaise*. It was composed by Rouget de Lisle. He wrote a lot of other music but nothing so stirring or so famous as the *Marseillaise*.

WHAT IN TENNIS IS THE GRAND SLAM?
It is the holding of the British (Wimbledon), the United States, the Australian and the French Championship titles all at the same time and it can be held for both singles and doubles.

WHEN AND BY WHOM WAS THE BANK OF ENGLAND FOUNDED?
In 1694 by a Scotsman named William Paterson.

WHAT ARE THE TWO CHIEF TYPES OF CARBOHYDRATES?
Sugar and starch.

WHAT IS A GONIOMETER?
An instrument to measure angles.

WHAT ARE BASKERVILLE, MELIOR AND TIMES?
Type-faces used in printing. This book is printed in Melior.

Index